What You're Not Supposed to Know!

Bottom Line Books

www.BottomLineSecrets.com

Contents

2 • SEX

3 • FAMILY SMARTS

7 • PLAY TIME

8 • PLANNING A PARTY?

9 • COLLECTING AND HOBBIES

1

Staying Well

The Only Workout You'll Ever Need

Research shows that moderate-intensity exercise at least three times a week can increase your life span by at least two-and-a-half years.

I've developed a five-day-a-week walking and toning program that takes less than one hour per day to perform. And you don't have to go to a gym to do it.

AEROBIC WALKING

On Monday, Wednesday and Friday, walk two miles in less than 30 minutes—15 minutes per mile.

You may have to work up to this quick pace. Begin with a 20-minute mile, and progress as you feel comfortable.

Be sure to get your doctor's approval before you start this program if you've been sedentary or have a history of heart disease or another medical condition. *Steps to take…*

• **Warm up by walking at a slow pace for one-quarter mile.**

• **Then spend five minutes stretching your hamstrings,** quadriceps and back and arm muscles. This will help to prevent musculoskeletal problems that can occur with any exercise.

• **Walk at your designated,** brisk rate for 30 minutes. Don't worry about checking your heart rate. Instead, keep count of your steps per minute.

To walk two miles in 30 minutes, shoot for a pace of at least 120 steps per minute (60 steps in 30 seconds). To start with a 20-minute mile, walk 90 steps per minute.

Keep your arms next to your body. Bend your elbows, and pump your arms at the same pace you move your legs. The faster you walk and the more you pump your arms, the greater the aerobic benefit.

Kenneth H. Cooper, MD, MPH, president and founder of The Cooper Aerobics Center, 12200 Preston Rd., Dallas 75230. He is an expert in preventive medicine and author of *Controlling Cholesterol the Natural Way*. Bantam.

• **Cool down for five minutes** to prevent lightheadedness or an irregular heartbeat. Sixty-five percent of severe cardiac events occur after a workout because blood has been diverted from the heart and pumped to the exercising muscles.

Walk slowly. After five minutes, take your pulse. If it is still over 120 (and you are under 40 years of age) or over 100 (and you are over 40 years of age), you may be exercising beyond your capacity. The next time you exercise, don't walk as fast or as far.

STRENGTH TRAINING

Developing adequate muscle mass is critical to your health. Otherwise you'll be weak—even if your heart is strong from aerobic walking.

The simplest and most convenient form of toning exercise is calisthenics. They use your body's weight and the force of gravity as resistance to build up muscle strength.

On Tuesday and Thursday, do 20 to 30 minutes of toning exercises. If you prefer to do toning exercises the days you walk, do them after aerobic activity.

Reason: If you perform calisthenics before aerobic activity, you'll build up an excessive oxygen debt in your body that will make it difficult for you to walk fast and may lead to earlier fatigue.

Try to work the main muscle groups—chest, arms, abdomen and thighs—each session. *Essential exercises…*

• **Pelvic tilts** strengthen your stomach and back. Lie flat on your back, and put your hands under your head. Bend your knees with your feet on the floor.

Tilt your pelvis by contracting your stomach muscles and pressing your lower back to the floor. Hold for a count of 10. Release. Repeat three times.

• **Hamstring and gluteal squeezes** strengthen the back of your thighs and buttocks.

Staying in the pelvic tilt position, lift your hips off the floor, but not your upper back. Squeeze your thigh and buttock muscles tightly. Lower and release. Work up to 20 repetitions.

• **Stomach crunches** strengthen your stomach and back. Lie flat on the floor with your knees pulled up to a 90-degree angle. Slowly lift your upper body off the floor using your stomach muscles.

Go only as far as the bottom of your shoulder blades. Lead with your chest and shoulders—not with your head. Work up to 30 repetitions.

Don't place your hands behind your head. You'll be tempted to use them to raise your upper body, and you'll risk straining your neck muscles. Fold them on your chest instead.

• **Quadriceps lifts** strengthen the front of your thighs. Lie on the floor with your arms at your sides.

Keeping the right leg straight and flat, bend the left knee and rest your foot on the floor.

Slowly raise and then lower your right leg, keeping it straight…your ankle flexed…and your toes pointing toward your head.

Progress to 20 repetitions. Then switch legs.

• **Pushups** strengthen your chest, shoulders and backs of the arms.

Lie on the floor, stomach down…hands under shoulders. Push up and rest your weight on your toes and hands. Keep your back, elbows and arms straight.

Lower your body to the floor using only your arms. Then raise your body off the floor using only your arms until your elbows are straight again. Work up to 20 repetitions.

THE BEST TIME TO EXERCISE

Early morning exercisers are the most consistent. Exercising before the evening meal or before the largest meal of the day has the greatest benefit, particularly if weight loss is desired.

Don't exercise until two hours after a heavy meal. Exercising sooner can cause heart problems. Also, don't exercise vigorously less than two hours before bedtime—to avoid affecting your sleep.

Personally, I find that working out for one hour starting any time after 5 pm but no later than 7 pm is optimal.

Most people tend to overeat at this time of day, and exercising keeps the appetite and caloric intake in check.

Also, exercising at this time of day stokes the metabolism for two hours. Your body will burn off calories more efficiently…the stress

2

of the day will be relieved…and endorphins —feel-good chemicals that will put you in a pleasurable state of mind—will be released.

Making a Plan For Wellness

Passing an annual physical exam was once enough to satisfy most people about their health. But today an increasing number strive beyond that—for optimal health or the condition of "wellness," as it is known. Essential to achieving wellness is a plan that is both personal and practical. *How to set one up for yourself…*

•**Try to clarify your most important reasons for living,** and write them down in a clear and concise fashion.

•**With these in mind,** identify the health goals that bolster your chances of living longer and healthier. *Be specific:* Do not plan to lose weight but to lose 20 pounds in six months. *Other possible goals:* Lowering blood pressure by a specific amount, accomplishing a dramatic feat, such as riding the Snake River rapids or completing a marathon.

•**List supportive actions for each goal.** *Example:* Joining a fitness club, training for long-distance running.

•**Also identify the barriers to each goal** and how they can be overcome.

•**List the payoffs for each goal,** whether they are new energy at the office or more fun at the beach.

Virtually no one, however, can hope to stay on a wellness plan without support from friends or a system of benchmarks. Before starting the program, list the network of friends you can rely on for bicycle rides, tennis or other activities in the plan.

Once the plan is under way, set realistic quarterly benchmarks to track your achievements. A log or diary is usually helpful. *Pitfall:* Do not become so involved in the plan that you begin serving it rather than the reverse.

Best Exercise Machine

Jerome Zuckerman, PhD, president of Cardio-Fitness Systems, 345 Park Ave., New York City.

The stationary bicycle is safe, aerobic and noncompetitive. You can ride it rain or shine, and because you work out continually without pauses, you can work off more calories per minute than you would in a stop-and-start sport.

SELECTING A STATIONARY BIKE

•**Durability is an important feature.** The more plastic there is in a bike, the less durable it is.

•**Besides a quality calibration component,** a good bike has a speedometer and an odometer.

•**The seat and handlebars should be adjustable.** *Correct seat height:* When the leg is comfortably extended, with the ball of the foot on the down pedal.

UNDERTAKING THE PROGRAM

•**Start each exercise period with stretching exercises to warm up.**

•**Take an easy workload** for the first three to five weeks.

•**Monitor your pulse rate.** It dictates when to increase the exercise level. *Example:* As you condition yourself to a given workload, your pulse rate will drop. That's the signal to step up the load by adjusting the calibration component.

•**Make up a workout schedule.** Three to five workouts a week is satisfactory.

•**Ignore the handlebars when pedaling the bike.** Sit upright with your arms folded or hanging down. If you have to grasp the handlebars when pedaling, it means you're working too hard. *Bonus:* When working out, you are free to read or watch TV.

•**Elevate your legs on the leg posts of the bike after completion of the exercise period.** *Alternative:* Lie down with legs raised. Or walk around the house for five to ten minutes. *Caution*: Without the cool-down period, you risk dizziness or worse.

Best Exercises for Elderly People

Exercise keeps the joints from becoming stiff and immobile and may even strengthen the bones themselves. *Reason:* The pull of muscles on bones often stimulates the bones to acquire calcium. *Best exercises:* Flexing and stretching. Gently bend, extend or rotate the neck, shoulders, elbows, back, hips, knees and ankles. *Best aerobic exercise:* Walking.

Also beneficial: Swimming, dancing, riding and using an exercise bicycle.

Muscles shrink only from disease or disuse, not from age. Any healthy muscle responds to exercise, no matter what the age of the person. *Point:* Exercise will maintain musculature, and even expand it, after the age of 50.

The Health Letter.

Exercise Payoff

Heart disease risk is significantly reduced with regular exercise. A National Institutes of Health (NIH) panel recommends that adults and children engage in moderate-intensity physical activity for at least 30 minutes on most days—preferably every day.

If you can't set aside a 30-minute period, you'll get similar benefits from three 10-minute sessions of walking, cycling, yard work, etc.

To stick with your regimen: Choose low-cost activities that you enjoy, feel safe doing and can access easily.

Russell Luepker, MD, professor and head of epidemiology, University of Minnesota School of Public Health, Minneapolis. He chaired the NIH Panel of Physical Activity and Cardiovascular Health.

"Space-Age" Exercise Equipment: Facts and Fantasies

The sophisticated machinery that has turned old-fashioned gyms into today's health clubs is designed to offer continual resistance during each of the movement exercises for which you use it. This is a much faster, more efficient way to build muscle strength than using weights, for example.

If you do all the exercises for all the muscle groups on a regular basis, would you be perfectly fit?

No. Strength and fitness are not equivalent. Although muscle strength is a component of fitness, you also need flexibility and heart-lung capacity. Stretching exercises make you flexible, and aerobic exercises such as running and bike riding build up your heart muscle and your lung capacity.

Can working out on these machines help you lose weight?

There is a common myth that strengthening exercises turn fat into muscle. It doesn't work that way. People who are overweight need to follow a calorie-restricted diet and do aerobic exercises, which trigger the body to use up fat. Working out on machines only builds up muscle under the fat layer. However, combining a weight-loss program with strengthening exercises can improve body tone as the weight comes off.

Are these machines safe to use?

You need to learn the proper technique for using each machine, including proper breathing, before you are allowed on the equipment alone. Poor form on the machines can lead to serious injuries. So can using the wrong weight settings.

Good rule of thumb: Use a weight setting that allows you to do eight to 12 repetitions comfortably. If you must struggle to get beyond five, the setting is too heavy. If you complete 10 without feeling any fatigue at all, it is too light. You will have to experiment with each machine to get the right setting. Then, from time to time, you can adjust the weights upward. But be cautious. Pushing yourself too hard not only invites injury but also discourages you from sticking to the program on a regular basis.

Great Exercise Gear

Gregory Florez, president and CEO, First Fitness, Inc., a Salt Lake City company that specializes in sports-and-fitness training and product-information education.

Having the right equipment can motivate you to work out. *Here's some gear to help you make the most of your fitness program…*

• **Weighted jump rope.** Jump ropes provide a terrific aerobic workout. This one has half-pound, removable weights tucked inside its cushioned handles to increase resistance, tone arms and help burn more calories. $15–$20.*

All-Pro weighted jump rope. Available at *www.paragonsports.com.*

• **Weighted padded nylon vest** has pockets to hold up to 40 half-pound weights to increase amount of calories burned while walking… running…hiking…or doing aerobics. $149.95*

Uni-Vest. *www.power-systems.com.* 800-321-6975.

• **Heart rate monitor.** A wireless wrist-watch-style monitor and a chest strap communicate via an infrared beam. Automatically determines heart rate at which your body burns calories most efficiently, so you can stay within that zone when exercising. Doubles as a watch…alarm…daily calendar…and stopwatch. $239.95*

Polar "F55" heart rate monitor. 800-227-1314. *www.polarusa.com.*

• **Body fat monitor/scale.** Uses a low-level electrical current to safely determine percentage of body fat. Step-on scale stores personal data for up to four people. Also measures body weight. $39.99 and up.*

Tanita, 847-640-9241 to find a store near you that sells Tanita products. Available online at *www.tanita.com.*

*Prices are manufacturers' suggested retail.

Walking Mistakes

Gary Yanker, author of many books and audiotapes about walking, including *Walking Medicine: The Lifetime Guide to Preventive and Therapeutic Exercisewalking.* McGraw-Hill.

Although most of us have been walking since we were toddlers, at least 30% of all people still haven't learned how to walk correctly.

Whether you're walking for pleasure, walking for exercise or just walking to get from one place to another, it's important to walk properly.

Mistake: **Not maintaining proper posture.** Poor posture puts extra stress on joints, vertebrae and muscles, causing pain.

Correct: **Tuck your chin into your neck** so your ear, shoulder, hip and ankle form a straight line perpendicular to the ground when you're standing still. Then hold this position as closely as possible when you walk. This avoids undue stress on any one joint or part of your body.

Mistake: **Arching your back.** This causes lower back pain and shortens the length of your steps.

Correct: **Do a pelvic tilt.** Tuck your buttocks under your body and hold in your stomach while you walk. This will take conscious effort at first, but after a while, your stomach and buttocks will stay in automatically. Walking this way strengthens the back and the stomach muscles, which redistributes weight away from the lower vertebrae, eliminating back pain.

Mistake: **Keeping your arms still.** You lose almost half the exercise value of walking—increasing your heart rate and working your shoulder, back and arm muscles—by not moving your arms.

Correct: **Pump your arms.** Bend your elbows slightly for regular walking, and 90° for aerobic walking.

Guide the arms straight forward and back, hands rising as far as the chest—at least to the waist. Let the inside of your arms rub the sides of your body—you should hear your clothing rubbing.

Pumping your arms is an upper-body calisthenic—your shoulders, upper back and chest all get exercised. If you pump your arms during brisk or aerobic walking, it doubles the exercise value.

Mistake: **Walking duck-footed** (with the knees pointed out) or pigeon-toed (with the knees pointed in). This puts stress on the knees and ankles. They are hinge joints—made for forward, not side-to-side, motion. Stress causes knee and ankle pain.

Correct: **Walk with your feet parallel.** And use the heel-toe roll. Land the heel first and turn the ankle out slightly (the width of a finger). Then roll on the outer edge of the foot until you reach the toe. This aligns the lower and upper leg.

Mistake: **Walking with your feet too close together.** This makes it easy to trip and fall.

Correct: **Keep your feet hip-width to shoulder-width apart.**

Mistake: **Taking short steps.** This also reduces the exercise value of walking, and it causes the leg and hip muscles to tighten.

Correct: **By reaching further with each step**—and using arm pumping and the heel-toe roll—most people can lengthen their average step three to eight inches. Longer steps burn more calories, work leg muscles, raise heart rate, increase circulation, make you feel more energetic and increase walking speed.

Walk for Your Heart

Brisk walking keeps your mind sharp. But it also does more. Recently compiled results of a study involving 72,488 women aged 40 to 65 showed that as little as three hours of brisk walking a week reduced the risk of heart disease by as much as 40%. And...five hours of brisk walking cut the risk by 50%.

Important: To obtain this benefit, you must walk at a rate of at least three miles an hour. Casual strolling will not produce the same result.

JoAnn E. Manson, MD, DrPH, chief of preventive medicine, Brigham & Women's Hospital/Harvard Medical School, Boston.

Easy Exercises to Strengthen Your Back

Strengthening the back and stomach muscles is the best protection against a back injury.

•**Flexed-knee sit-ups.** Lie on your back, with knees bent, feet flat on the floor and arms at your side. Sit up slowly by rolling forward, starting with your head.

•**Bent-knee leg lifts.** In the same position as the sit-ups, bring one knee as close as you can to your chest while extending the other leg. Alternate the legs.

•**Knee-chest leg lifts.** Work from the bent-knee sit-up position, but put a small pillow under your head. Use your hands to bring both knees up to your chest, then tighten your stomach muscles and hold that position for a count of 10.

•**Back flattening.** Lie on your back, flex your knees and put your arms above your head. Tighten your stomach and buttock muscles and press your lower back hard against the floor. Hold this position for a count of 10, relax and repeat.

Cautions: Don't overdo the exercises. Soreness is a sign that you should cut back. Never do these exercises with the legs straight. If you have back trouble, consult your doctor before starting this or any exercise program.

American Journal of Nursing, New York City.

Walk for Good Health

Exercise doesn't have to be strenuous or punishing to be effective. Despite its economy of muscle use, walking is considered by most experts to be one of the best exercises. *Benefits…*

• **A preventive and a remedy for respiratory,** heart and circulation disorders.

• **Weight control.** Walking may take off pounds, or keep weight at a desirable level. (Particularly effective in keeping excess pounds from coming back once they have been dieted off.)

• **Aids digestion,** elimination and sleep.

• **Antidote to physical and psychological tensions.**

Walking works as a second heart. Expanding and contracting foot muscles, calves, thighs and buttocks help pump blood back to the heart. This aid is crucial. The heart can propel blood very well on its own, but the body's muscles are essential to the return flow from lower regions (legs, feet, stomach). When the blood transportation system becomes sluggish because of lack of exercise, the heart compensates by doing more work. Heart rate and blood pressure rise. (Elevated pressure can be helped to return to normal by a regimen of walking.)

Best daily routine…

• **Time.** Whenever it can be fitted into daily routine. (A mile takes only 15–20 minutes.) People who do sedentary office work usually average a mile and a half in a normal day. Stretch that by choosing to walk down the hall to a colleague instead of simply picking up the interoffice phone.

• **Place.** Wherever it's pleasant and convenient to your daily tasks. Walk to work at least partway. Or, if you're a daily commuter, walk to the train station. Walk not to the nearest but to the second or third bus or subway stop away from your house. Get off a stop or two earlier than the usual one. Park the car 10 blocks farther away. Walk 10 blocks to and from lunch. Walk after dinner, before sitting down to read a book, watch TV or do work.

• **Clothes.** Comfortable and seasonal, light rather than heavy. Avoid thin-soled shoes when walking city pavements. It may be desirable to use metatarsal pads or cushioned soles. (The impact on concrete weakens metatarsal arches and causes calluses.)

• **Length.** Walk modest distances at first. In the city the number of streets tells you how far you've gone. But in the country you can walk farther than you realize. *Consequences:* Fatigue on the return trip. *Instead:* Use a good pedometer.

• **Pace.** Walking for exercise should feel different from other kinds of walking. *Some suggestions…*

• Set out at a good pace. Use the longest possible stride that's comfortable. Let your arms swing and muscles stretch. Strike a rhythm and keep to it.

• Don't saunter. It's tiring. Walking at a good pace allows the momentum of each stride to carry over into the next.

• Lengthen the customary stride by swinging the foot a little farther ahead than usual. Lengthening the stride speeds the walking pace. It also loosens tense muscles, puts other neglected muscles to work and provides continual momentum that puts less weight on feet.

Most comfortable pace: Three miles per hour. It generally suits the average male and is the US Army pace for long hikes. With the right shoes and unconfining clothes, most women will be comfortable at that pace, too.

Exercise vs. Stroke

Exercise helps prevent stroke…and speeds rehabilitation of people who have already had a stroke.

In one recent study, men who exercised vigorously an hour a day, five days a week, cut their stroke risk in half.

In another study, stroke survivors who exercised regularly regained more of their strength and balance than those survivors who didn't exercise.

Pamela W. Duncan, PhD, director, Brooks Center for Rehabilitation Studies, and professor of health services administration and physical therapy, College of Health Professions, University of Florida, Gainesville.

Exercises for Desk-Bound Workers

Doug MacLennon, The Fitness Institute, Willowdale, Ontario, quoted in *Creative Selling*.

Exercises to do at your desk to stay mentally alert, tone sagging muscles and bring relief to strained muscles…

• **Tummy slimmer.** Sit erect, hands on knees. Exhale, pulling abdominal muscles in as far as possible. Relax. Inhale. Exhale as you draw in stomach again. Repeat 10 to 20 times.

• **Head circles.** Drop head forward, chin on chest, shoulders relaxed. Slowly move head in a semicircle from one side to another, but not all the way around. Reverse direction. Do five to six times on each side.

• **Torso twist.** Raise elbows to shoulder level. Slowly twist around as far right as possible, then reverse. Do 10 to 12 turns each way.

• **Heel and toe lift.** Lean forward, hands on knees. Lift both heels off floor, strongly contracting calf muscles. Lower heels, lift toes high toward shins. Do 10 to 15 complete movements.

Cabbage Leaves for Arthritic Joints

Michael Van Straten, ND, DO, a naturopath and acupuncturist in private practice in London. He is the author of *Home Remedies: A Practical Guide to Common Ailments You Can Safely Treat at Home Using Conventional and Complementary Medicine*. McGraw-Hill.

Cabbage leaves contain powerful anti-inflammatory compounds. Applied to arthritic joints, these compounds are remarkably effective at relieving both pain and swelling.

Arthritis sufferers often rely on over-the-counter anti-inflammatory drugs like ibuprofen (Advil) for relief of their symptoms. But prolonged use of these drugs can cause stomach pain and even bleeding ulcers.

Using cabbage leaves instead helps reduce the amount of medication needed. And cabbage seems to work more effectively than topical creams marketed for arthritis relief.

What to do: Use a rolling pin or knife handle to bruise one or two large, outer, dark-green leaves from a head of a green cabbage.

Warm the leaves in a microwave, steamer or oven, then wrap them around the joint. Cover with a towel. Leave in place for 15 minutes.

The compress should be applied once daily for mild inflammation, two or three times a day for severe inflammation.

Warm cabbage leaves can also be used to curb inflammation resulting from tennis elbow, sprains or other minor injuries. Apply ice and elevate the injured limb to curb the initial swelling. Then apply the cabbage leaf compress two or three times daily until pain and swelling subside.

Odd as it sounds, women with painful breast cysts—as well as nursing mothers with inflamed, cracked nipples—can also get relief from cabbage leaves.

Line the cups of a bra with bruised cabbage leaves. Leave in place for an hour a day. It's not necessary to warm the leaves.

Jogging and Achilles Tendinitis

American Journal of Sports Medicine.

The repetitive impact of running frequently causes inflammation, degeneration and small tears in the heel tendons.

Orthopedists from Boston University Medical School suggest these preventive steps…

- **Decrease weekly mileage.**

- **Cut down on uphill workouts.**

- **Prepare for running by stretching the tendons.** With heels flat and knees straight, lean forward against a wall and hold for 30 seconds.

- **Warm heels and tendons with a heating pad before running.** After running, apply ice for 10 to 12 minutes.

- **Elevate heels by placing small felt pads inside running shoes.** They relieve tension on the Achilles tendon and contiguous structures.

- **Monitor wear on outer sides of shoes.** Tendons tend to become stressed when shoe sides give no support.

- **If these measures fail,** consult a physician about immobilization and anti-inflammatory drugs.

Breathing Your Way To Better Health

Robert Fried, PhD, director of the Stress and Biofeedback Clinic of the Albert Ellis Institute and senior professor of biopsychology at Hunter College, both in New York City. He is the author of several books, including *Breathe Well, Be Well.* John Wiley & Sons.

Everyone knows that taking a deep breath is a great way to cool off when you're getting angry.

And any woman who has used Lamaze breathing during childbirth is aware that the act of focusing on one's breath provides a welcome distraction from severe pain.

But few people realize that how you breathe day in and day out plays a key role in triggering—or preventing—chronic conditions. Among the conditions affected by breathing are high blood pressure…heart disease…migraines…and Raynaud's syndrome, a chronic circulatory disorder marked by uncomfortably cold hands and feet.

THE BREATH–BODY CONNECTION

The world is basically divided into two types of breathers…

- **Belly breathers** take slow, deep breaths, letting their abdomens rise with each inhalation and fall with each exhalation.

This form of breathing is ideal, but relatively few adults breathe this way.

- **Chest breathers** take rapid, shallow breaths. This form of breathing causes the body to expel too much carbon dioxide, adversely affecting how the blood carries oxygen to the organs and tissues.

To find out which kind of breather you are, sit comfortably and place your left hand on your chest, your right hand over your navel. Breathe normally for one minute. Note the movement of each of your hands as you inhale and exhale.

If your left hand is virtually motionless while your right hand moves out when you inhale and in when you exhale, you're a belly breather.

If your left hand rises noticeably—or if both hands move more or less simultaneously in a shallow motion—you're a chest breather.

Being a chest breather does not mean you're going to keel over anytime soon. But eventually, your health will suffer.

Reason: Chest breathing is less effective than belly breathing at introducing fresh, oxygenated air into the lower reaches of the lungs. That's where the tiny air sacs (alveoli) that absorb oxygen are most concentrated.

Less air reaching these alveoli means that less oxygen gets into the bloodstream with each breath. To get enough oxygen to meet all of the body's needs, these people must breathe rapidly.

Rapid breathing upsets the blood's normal acid-base balance (pH), which is measured on a scale that runs from zero to 14.

Ordinarily, blood has a pH of 7.38 (slightly alkaline). When blood pH climbs above that level, arteries constrict, impairing blood flow to all parts of the body.

Result: Increased susceptibility to high blood pressure…insomnia…anxiety…phobias…Raynaud's syndrome…migraines…and, for heart patients, angina.

HOW TO BREATHE RIGHT

No matter how poor your current breathing habits may be, it's reassuring to know that each of us was born knowing how to breathe properly. And—it's surprisingly easy to relearn proper breathing habits. *The keys...*

•**Stop sucking in your gut.** A flat stomach may be attractive, but clenching the abdominal muscles inhibits proper movement of the diaphragm. That's the sheetlike muscle separating the abdomen from the chest cavity.

Since the movement of the diaphragm is what causes the lungs to fill and empty, proper breathing is possible only if it can move freely.

•**Avoid tight clothing.** Like clenching your abdominal muscles, wearing overly tight clothing can restrict movement of the diaphragm.

•**Breathe through your nose.** Doing so makes hyperventilation almost impossible. The only time you should breathe through your mouth is during vigorous exercise.

•**Practice belly breathing.** At least twice a day—for about four minutes each time—sit in a comfortable chair with your left hand on your chest, your right hand on your abdomen.

As you inhale, use your left hand to press lightly against your chest to help keep it from rising. Allow your right hand to move outward as air fills your belly.

With each exhalation, slowly pull your abdomen back in as far as it will go without raising your chest. With practice, your body will find its own natural rhythm.

Good idea: Practice belly breathing when you're stuck sitting in traffic, waiting in line at the store, etc.—whenever and wherever you can. It's a good use for time that would otherwise be wasted. Once you get the hang of it, practice belly breathing without using your hands.

You may want to augment the effects of these practice sessions by combining belly breathing with...

•**Classical music.** Stick with slow compositions, such as Pachelbel's *Canon* or Bach's *Jesu, Joy of Man's Desiring.* As you breathe, imagine that you are inhaling the music...and that it is filling every space in your body.

•**Muscle relaxation.** Imagine that the tension in the muscles in your forehead is flowing out of your body with each exhalation. Do the same thing, breath by breath, with your jaw, neck, shoulders, arms, hands, legs and feet.

•**Imagery.** Close your eyes, and imagine yourself standing on a sunny beach. Feel the warmth of the sun enveloping you. As you inhale, imagine the surf rolling toward your feet. As you exhale, picture the surf rolling back out to sea.

•**Do on-the-spot breathing therapy.** Once you've mastered belly breathing, you're ready to start using breathing as an instant feel-better tool.

A few deep belly breaths can dissipate anxiety...ward off an impending panic attack or migraine...restore circulation to cold, numb fingers and toes...and help ease you to sleep if you're experiencing insomnia.

If you're diligent about practicing belly breathing, there's a good chance it will become second nature. For most people, the change takes about six weeks.

Caution: Breathing exercises are safe for most people. But if you've recently suffered an injury or had surgery, check with a doctor.

Certain disorders, such as kidney disease, lead to rapid breathing to compensate for chemical changes in the body. If you suffer from one of these ailments, slow breathing may be unsafe.

Work Out With the Masters

Liz Neporent, a regular health, fitness and medical correspondent for *The New York Daily News.* She is author of *Fitness Walking for Dummies.* IDG Books.

Get fit in the comfort of your living room. *To begin a home exercise program, try these tapes and DVDs...*

PILATES METHOD

- **Jennifer Kries.** *The Method.* Five videos featuring Kries. They are based on the Pilates Method—a workout that emphasizes controlled movements and concentration to develop posture, abdominal strength and balance. 48 to 150 minutes.

Collage Video, 800-433-6769; *www.collagevideo.com*; DVD only: $14.95.

STEP AEROBICS

- **Petra Kolber.** *PK Step.* Petra Kolber's workout includes leaps, power squats, straddle jumps and a toning section. 56 minutes.

Collage Video, 800-433-6769; *www.collagevideo.com,* DVD only: $14.95.

STRETCHING

- **Karen Voight.** *Pure and Simple Stretch.* Gentle, straightforward stretches for a full-body routine. Voight shows how to modify each move, depending on how limber you are. 38 minutes.

Collage Video, 800-433-6769; *www.collagevideo.com,* DVD only: $14.95.

WALKING

- **Leslie Sansone.** *40 Plus Workout Walk 2.* Walking/marching-in-place, low-impact routine for toning and aerobic workout. Simple moves. Not intimidating. 30 minutes.

Inspired, 800-272-4214; *www.inspiredcorp.com,* DVD only: $12.98.

Stomach Muscles: The Key to Exercise

Pamela Francis, personal consultant and dance teacher, New York City.

The muscles of the mid-torso should be the focal point of any exercise program. Strong midsection or stomach muscles allow you to better control all your movements (to bend without flopping, for example) and increase your stretch. They also improve your posture and take strain off your lower back. *Problem:* Most people are hardly aware of these important muscles and must be taught to use them.

Good first exercise: Lie on your back on the floor. Bend your knees, keeping your feet flat on the floor. Clasp your hands behind your head. Slowly curl up (don't jerk up) from your head forward and see how far you can get. (Don't worry if it's only five or six inches.) Hold the position until you feel strain in the midriff. You have just found the muscles you need to strengthen. Repeat the exercise four times, doing so very slowly.

Note: Traditional sit-ups, with straight legs held down under the couch and arms raised overhead, are dangerous for beginners, who tend to use lower back muscles rather than stomach muscles. Putting hands behind the head keeps the novices from using the momentum of flailing arms to lift themselves.

Second exercise: Lie on your back on the floor. Raise your head and shoulders, put your elbows behind you and rest your upper body on your forearms. Keep your lower back (from just above the waist down) pressed against the floor. With feet together and knees bent, raise your legs four, five or six inches without raising your lower back off the floor. *Variations:* Raise bent legs, stretch them out, return them to bent position and lower them to the floor. Raise both legs and kick vertically, one leg at a time. Raise bent legs together, open and stretch, return to original position, and lower both. Raise bent legs, stretch them out and scissor-kick. Work up to 50 leg movements in four or five minutes.

Standing stomach exercise: This sexy workout uses a combination of leg and stomach muscles to improve lower-back flexibility. Stand with legs apart and slightly bent, and do rhythmic bumps (no grinds). With head and shoulders stationary, alternately arch and curl your back, throwing your pelvis back as you arch and forward as you curl. Use music with a strong beat. Start slowly and work up to double time.

Exercise regimen: Try to work out twice a day. Morning exercises loosen up your muscles and get you going. Later sessions accomplish more in building strength and flexibility because you are already warmed up.

Sauna, Steam Room And Hot Tub Hazards

US Centers for Disease Control and Prevention, Atlanta.

Use a sauna or steam room only about once a week, on a nonexercise day or after the week's final workout. Shower before entering, and go in wet. Your hair should also be wet or covered. Protect your nasal membranes by breathing through a cool, damp cloth. Drape a cool, wet towel over your neck and shoulders to help maintain normal blood temperature. Go in and out of the room frequently, showering between heat sessions to cool yourself down and build heat tolerance slowly. If you feel dizzy when leaving, shower right away with warm (not cold) water, wrap yourself in towels or get dressed, and lie down until you feel better.

Soaking in a communal hot tub contaminates the water with two to three pints of perspiration per hour per person. The salt, ammonia, etc., in perspiration must be neutralized after each use to keep the water clean and clear. *Required:* A sophisticated kit that tests pH, water hardness and chlorine levels.

New Shelter.

Infections from hot tubs are becoming more common because of a bacterium that thrives in the wood of which some are made. The germ causes skin rash and other infections that are painful but treatable. *Prevention:* Put larger-than-normal amounts of chlorine in the water. *Better:* Install a vinyl liner in the tub.

What Your Dreams Mean

Stephen Aizenstat, PhD, founding president of the Pacifica Graduate Institute in Carpenteria, CA. Dr. Aizenstat is a licensed clinical psychologist and marriage and family therapist who teaches courses on "dreamtending."

Dreams provide us with a useful commentary from our inner selves. They put us in touch with an incredibly constructive and intricate source of intelligence that we have very little access to when we're awake.

Dreams don't draw conclusions or make assessments; they locate us, connecting us with our essential position in the world at any given moment. When we're faced with a decision or predicament, dreams can be a helpful resource, often shining a new light on old problems.

Dreams speak to us in the language of images and symbols. The psyche dreams in picture language because pictures tell stories that, if put into narrative form, would fill volumes. *Dreams can be interpreted on three different levels...*

• **The personal unconscious.** Dreams pick up the literal content of your day. We dream about incidents from the past or current problems, usually about incidents that caused some tension. Wish-fulfillment dreams fall into this category.

• **The collective unconscious.** There are patterns of behavior and experience that have been recounted in fairy tales and folklore throughout the ages. These universal patterns of human experience, known as archetypes, can be found in common dream themes that turn up throughout human history.

• **World unconscious.** This level includes a sense of connectedness to everything else in the world.

Recurring dreams signal that the psyche is trying to get a message across. Like someone tugging on a shirtsleeve, a recurring dream tries to get our attention by presenting us with the same theme over and over. If a dream repeats, there's bound to be something of tremendous value in it. *Helpful:* Look back to when you've had repetitive dreams. Did they signal something that was happening at that time?

Dreams speak indirectly in poetic metaphors and symbols. You need to think symbolically to figure out what the images mean. *Reassuring:* No expert knows better than you what your dreams mean. *Caution:* Don't be too literal about the translation. How do you know you've made the right interpretation? You get a tingle, a sense of perfect fit.

• **Losing teeth.** First check out the obvious. Are any of your teeth actually loose or decayed?

At the second level of meaning, losing teeth is connected to the loss of something valuable, often associated with appearance. *Metaphors:* Loss of face, of attractiveness, self-esteem or power. Also, a lost tooth could indicate the loss or death of a loved one.

• **Going back to school.** Usually people have this dream when they're frightened or unprepared. They feel under scrutiny—either at work or in a relationship—or they're being critical of themselves.

Look at where you landed in the dream. Was it in elementary school, high school or college? Explore that. When you were in that school, what were you afraid of? What did being unprepared mean then? How does that relate to what you're going through now?

• **Bathrooms and feces.** Personally, I believe that feces can be one of the most engaging images. Feces are manure, manure means seeds and seeds mean growth. When feces appear in dreams, I get hopeful. Right around the corner there's fertile ground for growth, new possibilities.

• **Nudity.** Usually embarrassment at finding yourself nude in public has to do with feeling vulnerable or exposed. In a second level of interpretation, it's being without a persona, not having your clothes, your mask, that which mediates between you and the world.

This is a very important dream. The vulnerability of it signals openness, availability, willingness to drop defenses and take chances. It usually comes after a time of change in career or relationships. This type of dream may also be compensatory. If you're in a position that requires a rigid persona, such as politics or a conservative law firm, your dreams may be compensating by presenting you as a vulnerable human being.

• **Flying.** The flying motif has something to do with a discovery, a transcendent perspective. *Metaphors:* Flying high, flying off the handle. Sometimes when we're caught in a predicament, flying above it all gives us an overview that allows us to see something we just couldn't see before.

Downside: If we don't have our feet on the ground, we're somehow disconnected. Sometimes flying is a signal of inflation, being too carried away with yourself or flying too high without a lifeline.

• **Falling.** Similar to flying dreams, falling dreams are especially terrifying for children. What catastrophic fear does the fall represent? What's the horrible consequence of falling? *Metaphors:* Falling in esteem, falling down on the job, falling from grace, a fear of dying.

How to deal with falling dreams: Tell yourself each night before going to sleep that when you have the dream you'll continue the fall and allow yourself to land safely. And that when you land you'll find something of value, put it in your dream pocket and take it back to your waking life. That's how primitive tribes worked with this dream.

• **Finding valuables.** Children often dream of finding money. This can be a wish-fulfillment dream or it can compensate for a fear of not having wealth. It can also be a reminder dream, reminding you that you're out of touch with what's valuable in your life. *Ask yourself:* What is there of value in me that I need to treasure even more? What is it I'm out of touch with in myself or am just beginning to value?

• **Sex.** Being sexual in a dream usually has little to do with actual sex. Flying dreams are probably more connected with libido than sex dreams are. Sex dreams can be a form of wish fulfillment—you can have lusty feelings for someone that can't be acted on in real life. The dream allows you to compensate. Like active sexual fantasies, these kinds of dreams are quite healthy.

Useful: What we do in dreams we can often do when we're awake. If you're a timid lover who becomes a magnificent lover in your dreams, you can translate this dream technique into real life.

A dream about intercourse is the most efficient way of suggesting intimate contact. It may have nothing to do with sex—it may be about wanting a relationship. Or if you find yourself having sex with someone you'd never be attracted to in real life, it may have to do with getting in touch with the aspects of yourself that person represents.

Sex is also a metaphor for creativity. There may be an aspect of your personality that's being repressed, causing you to be depressed or sad. Because the creative libido is yearning for expression, the sexual partner represents your hidden creativity.

Sleep Needs Differ

Requiring as much as eight or nine hours of sleep a night can be as normal as needing six or seven. According to one survey, more than 6% of American adults regularly sleep nine to 10 hours, with only about 1% sleeping more than 10 hours. Excessive sleeping can be a symptom of such disorders as narcolepsy, which causes people to become uncontrollably sleepy in the daytime.

Key to healthy sleep: The quality of the wakeful hours. If you're rested and energetic when you wake up, chances are that you needed all that sleep.

Merrill M. Mitler, PhD, one of the founders of the American Sleep Disorders Association (ASDA).

No More Panic Attacks

Elke Zuercher-White, PhD, a psychologist at Kaiser Permanente Medical Group in San Francisco and a psychotherapist in private practice in the San Francisco Bay area. She is the author of *An End to Panic: Breakthrough Techniques for Overcoming Panic Disorder.* MJF Books.

If you've ever suffered a panic attack, you're not alone. Researchers estimate that at least one-third of the population has experienced these frightening episodes, which are marked by intense psychological and physical symptoms.

Examples: Anxiety...a feeling of "unreality" or impending doom...a sense of going crazy or losing control...rapid heartbeat...shortness of breath...dizziness...tingling.

Panic attacks usually strike during times of stress—before giving a speech, for example, or taking a test. But sometimes they strike for no apparent reason.

For some individuals who have had one panic attack, the fear of having another leads to a cycle of further attacks and increased fear. This condition is known as panic disorder.

Left untreated, panic disorder can turn into agoraphobia. This debilitating disorder typically develops over a period of weeks, months or years, as an individual begins avoiding more and more situations in which a panic attack might occur—grocery shopping, riding in elevators, driving, etc.

Good news: Panic attacks can be overcome. *Several antipanic techniques have proven remarkably successful...*

BREATHE SLOWLY AND STEADILY

Diaphragmatic breathing—expanding the belly with each inhalation—stops the rapid breathing that commonly occurs with a panic attack. It also helps curb dizziness, rapid heart rate, light-headedness and tingling.

To learn diaphragmatic breathing: Lie on your back with a pillow or towel on your stomach. Time your breathing so that you're taking eight to 12 breaths a minute. The pillow should move up when you inhale, down when you exhale.

Once you've mastered this technique, put the pillow or towel aside. Place one hand on your belly, just over your navel. Feel your abdomen rise with each inhalation and fall with each exhalation.

Next, practice diaphragmatic breathing while lying down with your hands at your sides. Then try it while slouching on a sofa... then while sitting up straight...and then while standing.

Practice diaphragmatic breathing for five minutes, twice a day, until you master it. That may take one to three weeks.

Focus on your breathing a few times each day. Eventually, you'll be able to do diaphragmatic breathing even in the midst of a panic attack.

CHANGE THE WAY YOU THINK

Panic attack sufferers often worry that a racing heart means they're about to suffer a heart attack...or that irregular or labored breathing means they will suffocate. These catastrophic scenarios do not occur.

Such catastrophic thinking only intensifies the symptoms of panic, making the panic attack more unpleasant than it otherwise might be.

To combat catastrophic thinking, think rationally...

•**Identify the thought that arises automatically each time you panic.** If you fear losing control, ask yourself, "How would someone else be able to tell if I lost control? What exactly am I afraid would happen?"

•**Consider the evidence in support of your automatic thought.** You might think, "I fear I might lose control because I feel disoriented and can't concentrate."

•**Use your rational mind to refute this evidence.** You might say to yourself, "I've felt disoriented before—but I never became crazy or acted out of control." Consider more realistic explanations for your symptoms.

REVISIT THE SITE

People tend to avoid the site where their worst panic attack occurred—even if they don't have agoraphobia. But returning to that spot forces you to confront your fears...and gain confidence in your ability to cope with panic.

You'll probably have to return several times before you feel comfortable at the site. At first, you might ask a trusted friend or family member to accompany you. Keep going back until you can go all by yourself.

BECOME MORE ASSERTIVE

People who suffer from panic disorder often feel they have little control over personal relationships or their emotions. As a result, they direct all their energy into controlling harmless—although uncomfortable—anxiety symptoms.

Assertiveness skills can be learned from books, classes and self-help groups. Try a local bookstore or a nearby hospital.

CHALLENGING AGORAPHOBIA

The key to overcoming agoraphobia is to expose oneself to the dreaded places and/or situations.

These exposures must occur at least three times a week. Each exposure should eventually last from one to two hours.

Helpful: Break exposures into their component parts. If you fear driving, for example, you might start by riding in a car driven by someone you trust...then driving yourself as your friend sits beside you...then having your friend follow you in another car.

If you find that you're having trouble coping with panic on your own, seek professional help. Have a doctor check you for a mitral valve prolapse or another medical condition known to cause panic-like symptoms.

If no medical problem is found, consult a psychotherapist who has used cognitive-behavioral therapy to treat panic disorder.

Antidepressants and antianxiety drugs have been found helpful for panic disorder, but some drugs can lead to dependency. New research suggests they may not be needed.

More information: Contact the Anxiety Disorders Association of America at 240-485-1001, *www.adaa.org*.

Helping Yourself To Sleep Better

Charles P. Pollak, MD, director of the Center for Sleep Medicine at NewYork-Presbyterian Weill Cornell Medical Center.

As the stress of doing business under unsettled conditions continues month after month, the sleeping patterns of executives with top responsibilities become more and more unraveled. Late meetings, travel and racing thoughts that produce late-night or morning insomnia result in irritability, poor work performance and lethargy at times when key decisions must be made.

IMPROVING SLEEP QUALITY

Researchers cannot easily determine how much sleep is optimum for each specific person. But they have determined that, on average, human beings need seven or eight hours of sleep a day.

The evidence is clear, however, that psychological and physical health improves as the quality of sleep is enhanced. *To sleep better, you should…*

•**Determine the right amount of sleep.** *How:* Keep a diary of sleeping patterns for at least 10 to 14 days. If you feel productive and alert, the average sleep time during that period is probably the amount you need.

•**Establish a regular bedtime and wake-up schedule,** then stick to it even on weekends and holidays.

•**Avoid trying to make up for loss of sleep one night by sleeping more the next.** Sleep deprivation of two to four hours does not severely affect performance. Having the normal amount of sleep the next night compensates for the loss without changing the regular sleep pattern. And that has long-term benefits.

•**Relax before bedtime.** *Good ways to unwind:* Take a bath, read, have a snack (milk is ideal for many people), engage in sex. Avoid late-night exercise, work, arguments and activities that cause tension.

FIGHTING INSOMNIA

Knowing the reason for insomnia is the only way to start overcoming it. If the cause is not quickly obvious, see a doctor. Many emotional and physical disorders express themselves as sleep disturbances.

Avoid sleeping pills. On a long-term basis, they are useless and sometimes dangerous. And when taken infrequently, they may produce a drug hangover the next day.

CATNAPS

Avoid naps in the middle of the day to compensate for lack of sleep the previous night. Take them only if you do so regularly and feel refreshed instead of groggy after a nap. *Test:* If you dream during a catnap, it is likely to delay sleep that evening or cause insomnia.

TAMPERING WITH NATURE

Deliberate attempts to reduce the total amount of sleep you need have a dangerous appeal to hard-pressed executives who think they never have enough time to work. *Fact:*

Evidence taken from monitoring subjects in sleep laboratories indicates that these schemes are not only ineffective but unhealthful. *Why:* The daily biological cycle cannot be changed by gradually cutting back sleep over a period of months. It's true that older persons seem to need slightly less sleep, but even here the exact difference is not yet known.

Hard-to-take but essential advice: Do not cut down on sleep in order to meet the clamoring and sometimes conflicting demands of a job, family and friends. You may pay a penalty of spending less time with family and friends or losing the edge at work that compulsive workaholism may provide. But the payoff is better health performance.

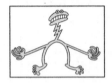

The Best Ways To Beat Stress

Carl Sherman, an award-winning psychology writer. He is author of *Stress Remedies*. Rodale Press.

Stress comes at us from everywhere—the overbearing bureaucrat…the traffic that stops dead when we've got to get somewhere fast…the big bill we forget until the second notice arrives…and so on.

And—there are life-disrupting events, such as retirement, moving, divorce or the death of a loved one or friend, that are always ready to bombard us.

But actually, the feeling of stress doesn't come from the outside. It happens inside of us.

When we feel under pressure, our body releases chemicals, such as adrenaline, that ready us for action. We breathe faster, our pulse and blood pressure rise, our muscles tighten.

These physical symptoms comprise what is commonly known as the "fight-or-flight" response—a leftover from the days when most crises could be either fought or fled.

Today, however, we usually have to endure them. This endurance causes stress, which takes its toll on physical and mental health.

Some stress is unavoidable. But too much stress leads to troubles that range from upset stomachs to anxiety attacks to heart attacks.

Fact: As many as 90% of doctor visits are for stress-related symptoms.

What can you do to combat stress? There's a whole arsenal of stress remedies to help you change a difficult situation—or the way you interpret it—to reduce your body's response to stress and restore a calmer state.

The more you understand your stress, the better you can choose defenses that work for you. *Most effective...*

MEDITATION

Taking time every day to disengage from the demands of the world can ease your mind and your body into a deeply relaxed state—the opposite of the stress response.

Meditation fosters your ability to step back from life and observe the passing scene—and your own thoughts—in a detached way. Studies have linked the regular practice of meditation to reductions in anxiety, work-related stress...and blood pressure, too.

There are many meditation techniques, but I know of one that is simple—and the best that I have found...

• **Sit quietly and comfortably** in a place where you will not be disturbed.

• **Focus your attention on your breathing.** Feel the breath as it comes into your nose... and when it goes out.

• **Other thoughts will enter your mind.** Just observe them and let them go. Return your attention to your breath.

Start by practicing meditation for five to 10 minutes a day, gradually increasing it to 20 to 30 minutes.

Keep a clock nearby so you can keep track of the time. *Caution:* A clock alarm or kitchen timer is too jarring. Some people, though, set their wristwatch alarms.

EXERCISE

Physical activity neutralizes the fight-or-flight response, easing tension and anxiety and leaving you invigorated. Regular moderate exercise reverses much of the damage caused by stress, and it can also improve immune function, lower blood pressure and improve your mood.

Intense aerobic exercise—running or aerobics classes at a gym—is an effective stress-buster, but so is more relaxed walking.

Do what you want to do—any exercise that you find enjoyable—and do it for at least 20 minutes every day. More, though, isn't always better.

Trap: If you think of exercise as a burden, it will add to your stress.

BIOPHILIA

Human beings have an inborn affinity for nature. Scientists call it "biophilia." Contact with scenes of nature and living things has been shown to reverse the effects of stress. *Examples...*

• **Employees whose windows look out on trees and grass** report less work stress than those with views of parking lots.

• **An aquarium** in a dentist's waiting room lowers anxiety.

• **By eating lunch on a park bench,** your body will relax.

• **Spending a half hour in your garden** will make your work worries recede into the distance.

• **If you live in a city,** consider a back-to-nature vacation—a week in the mountains will recharge your batteries more deeply than a short stroll in the park.

• **Let a little piece of nature into your daily life**—get a pet. Persian cat or parakeet, goldfish, beagle or mouse—it doesn't really matter. Pet owners are healthier and respond better to stress than other folks.

HUMOR

The ability to take yourself—and your life—less seriously is the stress antidote *par excellence.* How tense can you be when you're laughing at yourself?

Try to look for the lighter side of every situation. Indulge your taste for entertaining books and movies.

Does a newspaper cartoon tickle your funny bone? Tape it to your bathroom mirror as a reminder to lighten up.

The next time your spouse acts up, ask yourself, *What would Groucho Marx have to say about this?*

Have funny props around. Keep a clown nose in your glove compartment to transform a traffic jam into circus time. Why should kids have all the fun?

FRIENDSHIP

Close ties to others make you feel warm inside...and they also temper your body's reaction to stress. The world feels safer when you know that other people are on your side. Expressing your worries and troubles to a sympathetic ear often makes them easier to bear.

The mere presence of a friend blunts the pulse and blood pressure rise that accompany stressful tasks. People with many friends have lower cholesterol and stronger immune systems. They live longer than loners, too.

Eat Right—and Live Longer

Brian Morgan, MD, PhD, associate clinical instructor at the University of California, San Francisco, Fresno, School of Medicine.

It's not too late to change the eating habits of a lifetime when you reach middle age. As a matter of fact, it's probably a necessity because of the changes the body undergoes at that time. *Most obvious change:* Slowing of the metabolic rate. Individuals who don't reduce their caloric intake after age 45 commonly gain 10 pounds a year regardless of the amount of exercise they get. It takes 12 hours of tennis to burn off 3,500 calories, which is roughly equivalent to one pound.

Unfortunately, a fine steak is often associated with success and reward. Steak, however, is highly caloric, and its fat content has been linked to coronary disease and colon cancer, two potentially fatal disorders that plague older people. Chicken and fish are more healthful alternative sources of protein.

Bones begin to grow progressively brittle after age 30. To counteract the condition, the body needs more calcium. But this important mineral can be absorbed effectively only by reducing the intake of protein (from meats) and phosphorous (from carbonated soft drinks). To prevent the brittle-bone problem, a calcium supplement of 1,000 to 1,500 milligrams per day is recommended by the National Institutes of Health.

Older people are vulnerable to anemia, one form of which is iron deficiency. The best source of iron is found in meat, especially liver. But to avoid eating too much meat, you should turn to iron-fortified foods, especially cereals. Absorption of iron is helped by intake of vitamin C, which is abundant in citrus fruits, broccoli, kale, red peppers and brussels sprouts. For some older people, taking an iron supplement may be necessary. If you have an iron deficiency, consult your doctor to be sure you don't have hidden causes of iron loss, such as undiagnosed intestinal bleeding.

Because many older people secrete less hydrochloric acid, they also have trouble absorbing vitamin B-12. A B-12 deficiency can lead to pernicious anemia, which can cause severe neurological problems. Strict vegetarians may be particularly at risk unless they take supplemental B-12 because the vitamin is found exclusively in animal products (especially liver) and shellfish. Multivitamin supplements may be needed to ensure that you get the right amount of each vitamin.

Caution: Although all the evidence is not yet in, most nutritionists advise against taking vitamin megadoses, which contain several hundred times the Recommended Daily Allowance. In the case of vitamins A and D, megadoses are highly dangerous.

Exception: Vitamin E, large doses of which may help to combat several disorders, including colon cancer and the painful blood vessel spasms in the legs that older people often experience. Even with this vitamin, however, you should consult a physician before considering taking megadoses.

Digestive problems associated with aging make fiber especially important to persons over 45. *Sources:* Whole grains, fruits, vegetables.

Older people generally use more drugs than others, but their doctors often overlook the interaction of medication and nutrition.

Some chronic aspirin users can suffer microscopic bleeding of the gastrointestinal tract, a condition that also causes loss of iron. Aspirin can also increase requirements for vitamin C and folic acid. Laxatives may deplete vitamin D, and antacids can lead to a phosphate deficiency. The diuretics prescribed for hypertension can promote the loss of potassium. In all these cases, vitamin and mineral supplements may be the solution.

Aging Bodies Need More Water

An aging body needs at least six glasses of water every day. *Reason:* A young adult's body is 60% water, but this amount decreases with age. *Result:* Skin dries out, and the kidneys do not flush wastes as well. Drinking more water means the skin has less chance of becoming dry. And the water dilutes the salts and minerals that pass through the kidneys, helping to prevent the formation of kidney stones. *Suggestion:* Have a glass of water with every meal and another before going to bed. Take the other two glasses during breaktime. Substitute water for that second and third cup of coffee.

Stay Healthy with Spices

Some common spices help to prevent food poisoning. Food microbiologists studied the effect of 23 different spices frequently used in cooking on food infected with *E. coli* bacteria, the most common villain in food poisoning. They found that five of the spices—garlic, cloves, cinnamon, oregano and sage—were particularly effective at killing bacteria in any food. While the experiment used very large amounts of the different spices, researchers report that the moderate amounts typically used are helpful in giving protection to home cooking—but do not kill all bacteria.

Daniel Y.C. Fung, PhD, professor of animal sciences and industry, and food science, Kansas State University, Manhattan.

Salt and High Blood Pressure

For about 30% of people who suffer from hypertension, cutting down on salt is a therapeutic necessity. For other victims of high blood pressure and for the general population, salt reduction may be an unnecessary hardship with possible risks. New research suggests that many factors other than salt are linked to hypertension. Obesity is one. Calcium deficiency is another. *Problem:* Reducing sodium in the diet may adversely affect the body's ability to absorb and use other necessary nutrients.

John Laragh, MD, director of the cardiovascular center, NewYork Presbyterian Hospital–Weill Cornell Medical Center, and David A. McCarron, MD, president of Academic Network LLC and visiting professor at the department of nutrition at University of California, Davis.

Beware the "Salt-Free" Label

Absence of the word "salt" on a list of ingredients does not necessarily guarantee that the product is salt-free. Other "salty" substances commonly used in food preparations include brine, disodium phosphate, sodium glutamate, baking powder and baking soda.

Almonds Cut Cholesterol

In one study, 45 people with high cholesterol levels were placed on a diet rich in almonds, olive oil or dairy products.

Result: After four weeks, the almond group had LDL (bad) cholesterol levels an average of 16 points lower than the olive oil group...and 33 points lower than the dairy group.

Almonds are rich sources of monounsaturated fats, fiber and the amino acid arginine. Each of these contributes to the cholesterol-lowering effect. Even if you are currently taking cholesterol-lowering medication, consider including almonds in your diet...along with lots of fruits, vegetables, beans, soy foods, whole grains and garlic.

Gene Spiller, PhD, director, Health Research and Studies Center, Los Altos, CA.

How Much Caffeine Is Too Much?

American Council on Science and Health, New York City.

Americans are suddenly adding caffeine to their growing list of health worries. Decaffeinated colas now join decaffeinated coffees in luring the public away from the caffeine habit. *Some facts about caffeine...*

• **Low doses can increase alertness and motor ability,** reduce drowsiness and lessen fatigue. Small to moderate amounts of caffeine pose no health danger, according to the Clinical Nutrition Section of Boston's University Hospital. Heavy doses produce ill effects —nervousness, anxiety, irritability, headache, muscle twitch and insomnia.

• **Tolerance of caffeine varies widely from one person to another.** Two cups of caffeine-rich coffee make some people nervous. Others cannot survive the day without several cups. *Most sensitive to caffeine's effects:* Children and the elderly.

• **How much is too much:** Four cups of coffee a day (500 milligrams of caffeine) is a heavy dose for most people. *Note:* The caffeine quantity in coffee depends on how it is brewed. The drip method produces a higher caffeine content than does the percolator technique. Instant coffee contains much less caffeine than brewed coffee. Tea contains half as much caffeine as coffee, and cola drinks have even less.

Irony: Most of the caffeine taken from coffee in the decaffeinization process is bought by the soft-drink industry and added to soda.

While cola drinks have far less caffeine than coffee, they are still the best-selling drink among Americans. Americans consume an average of 54 gallons of soft drinks yearly. *Comparison:* 22 gallons of coffee.

Caffeine has been linked to many health problems, but there are questions about its adverse effects. *Examples...*

• **There is no evidence that caffeine is a causal factor** in either arteriosclerosis or heart attacks.

• **It does not increase the blood pressure** of regular users.

• **Caffeine does not seem to be a cancer hazard,** but other compounds (found in negligible amounts) in beverage coffee are known carcinogens in animals.

• **Caffeine is a much less important factor than cigarette smoking** in heart disease, hypertension, bladder cancer, peptic ulcers and cystic breast disease.

• **It does stimulate the central nervous system** and can help reduce boredom from repetitive tasks, increase the body's muscle strength and relieve certain types of headaches by dilating blood vessels and reducing muscle tension.

What Vitamin Manufacturers Don't Tell You

You should be careful when taking *any* supplement, but there are some specific dangers in taking vitamins. *Be aware of the following...*

• **Vitamin poisoning.** Certain high-dose B-6 tablets sold in health stores can be dangerous. The body needs only one or two milligrams of B-6 a day. Overdoses may lead to loss of sensory and motor control.

New England Journal of Medicine.

• **Vitamin E should be used with restraint.** High doses can cause blood clots, phlebitis, hypertension, severe fatigue, breast tumors and disturbances in the reproductive system. How much is too much? Dr. H. J. Roberts, MD, of Florida's Palm Beach Institute for Medical Research suggests that daily intake of more than 100 to 300 units of "active tocopherol" is excessive.

Journal of the American Medical Association.

• **Too much vitamin A and D.** Unlike some vitamins (the Bs and C) that are passed out of the body through the kidneys when taken in excess, vitamins A and D are stored in fat and the liver, where they can do damage. *Problems from overdoses:* Cirrhosis of the liver. Dry, itchy skin. Fatigue. Painful muscles. Loss of body hair. *Note:* A deficiency of vitamin A is believed to be related to the onset of cancer. But there is no evidence that increased amounts help prevent this disease. *Best:* Eat a balanced diet. Limit supplementary intake to the recommended daily dietary allowances.

The Health Letter.

• **Niacin is not a tranquilizer,** despite the stories about its calming effects. Taking niacin tablets in search of tranquility can cause niacin toxicity. *Symptoms:* Flushed face and blotchy skin on arms.

Other good phenol sources: Cranberry juice...apples...red grapes or red grape juice ...red wine.

Eric Gershwin, MD, distinguished professor of medicine and chief, division of rheumatology, allergy and clinical immunology, University of California at Davis.

Raisins and Cancer

Raisins may help prevent cancer. They contain a compound that helps the colon get rid of waste more efficiently...and this keeps the colon healthy. The compound—tartaric acid—is found mainly in raisins and grapes. Raisins are also high in potassium and protective antioxidants.

Gene Spiller, PhD, director, Health Research and Studies Center, Los Altos, CA.

Microwave Oven Trap

Cooking chicken in microwave ovens won't kill harmful salmonella and other bacteria. *Reason:* Microwave ovens heat food through molecular friction, leaving surface temperatures too uneven to kill the contaminants.

Solution: Cook chicken in conventional ovens at 350°F until the meat thermometer registers 185°F in both the breast and thigh areas or until the juices run clear.

Ruth E. Lindsay, nutritionist, Georgia Southern College.

Cholesterol Fighter

Apple juice may be the best source of cholesterol-fighting phenols. Phenols are plant compounds that protect the arteries from the adverse effects of "bad" LDL cholesterol. A recent study showed that drinking apple juice daily may reduce LDL cholesterol damage by 34%.

Minerals for Better Health

For the best absorption of iron supplements, take them with orange juice or with a meal containing meat or poultry...and avoid tea or coffee when taking iron. For the best absorption of calcium, take half in the morning and half

21

in the evening. Take iron and calcium supplements at different times of the day—calcium can block the absorption of iron.

Not necessary: Chelated minerals, which are sold in health-food stores. Chelation describes a type of chemical bond. It's no better for the body than standard mineral supplements.

James C. Fleet, PhD, professor, department of foods and nutrition, Purdue University, West Lafayette, IN.

or arsenic. Never use filters that fit over the faucet. The water runs through too quickly to be properly filtered. *Note:* Filtered water is not necessary for such functions as dishwashing. The filter should have a bypass valve.

Visit the Environmental Protection Agency's Web site for water reports, *www.epa.gov/safe water/faq/faq.html.*

Cleaning Up Your Drinking Water

Although public health systems must publish results of water safety tests, pure drinking water piped into the home must not be taken for granted.

Problems: Toxic chemicals such as nitrates, asbestos, arsenic, lead, trihalomethanes (THM). *Also:* High sodium levels are dangerous for people on sodium-restricted diets.

Statistic: Approximately 55% of the American population lives in areas with inadequate water-treatment plants.

Signs of possible contamination: Water has an odd taste, color or smell. *Possible problems:* Heavy construction or sewer installation in the area, a change in pesticide use, antiquated water-treatment facilities.

What to do: Get the most recent results of your town's water test as required by law. If you suspect the problem is with your home's pipes, consider testing the water yourself. Consult the *Yellow Pages* under "Laboratories—Testing" for a lab that handles water samples. *Cost:* From $15 to $200.

How to get cleaner drinking water...

• **Bottled water.** *Hitch:* There are no standards for purity. Some may contain traces of harmful substances. Of course, labels do not indicate this.

• **Water filters.** The only effective ones contain granules of activated carbon (GAC). *Useful:* They are effective only against THM, not lead

Fight Asthma with Better Breathing

Although it is unconventional, this non-drug asthma treatment teaches patients to breathe differently in an attempt to lower their medication needs.

Key: Take in small breaths through the nose to fill the lungs, hold for an extended period, and breathe out gently through a wide-open mouth. Repeat as needed. Advocates say it can significantly reduce dependence on medicines. But before modifying medication, check with your physician.

Andrew L. Rubman, ND, director, Southbury Clinic for Traditional Medicines, Southbury, CT.

Diet Tips to Combat Stress

For short-term periods of stress, follow a high-carbohydrate, low-protein diet. The carbohydrates deliver energy to the body. *For longer stressful periods:* Reverse the diet—that is, consume more protein and fewer carbohydrates.

Example: Lean meats, eggs, fish, skinless poultry, low-fat milk and soy foods.

Other foods that fight stress: Those rich in vitamins C and A. Try raw carrots, peppers and broccoli. *Bonus:* Chewing crunchy foods helps dissipate the tension.

Sound Therapy Relieves Pain and More

Sound therapy is used to treat pain, Alzheimer's disease, attention deficit disorder, alcoholism, anxiety and some forms of depression.

To use sound: Listen carefully to various types of music and feel how each affects your mind and body. Then choose pieces to listen to on the basis of how you want to feel.

Examples: Bach's Goldberg Variations were commissioned to treat insomnia and are still effective in combating sleeplessness. Mozart's music lowers stress and increases concentration. New Age music can aid relaxation. Upbeat popular music can boost energy.

Kerri Bodmer, coauthor of The Giant Book of Women's Health Secrets. *Soundview.*

Be Savvy About Herbal Supplements

Be careful when taking herbal supplements. Scientists are not certain of how and why most herbs affect the body, and they sometimes cause serious side effects or even death.

Purity standards have been published for some popular herbs, but many supplements are complex mixtures of different herbs with poor quality control. Because they are classified as supplements rather than drugs, they are not strictly supervised by the US Food and Drug Administration (FDA).

Bottom line: Be as cautious in using supplements as you would be in taking prescription or over-the-counter drugs.

Norman R. Farnsworth, PhD, research professor of pharmacognosy—the study of the medicinal properties of plants—at the University of Illinois in Chicago.

New Approach to Chronic Disease

Writing has been shown to fight chronic disease. Patients who write about traumatic life experiences sometimes gain relief from such diseases as chronic asthma or rheumatoid arthritis.

Patients who wrote about the most stressful event in their lives for 20 minutes a day, three days in a row, were in better health four months later than those who didn't. Writing may help them make sense of bad experiences.

Study of 107 patients with chronic illnesses led by Joshua M. Smyth, PhD, Syracuse University, published in The Journal of the American Medical Association.

Oils That Improve Health

Eucalyptus is an antibacterial that soothes acne and relieves sinus congestion.

Geranium soaks up facial oiliness and also can tighten skin temporarily.

Lavender soothes tension headaches and migraines.

Rose hydrates and soothes sensitive, dry, itchy or inflamed skin.

Tea tree fights athlete's foot, dandruff, insect bites, cold sores and acne.

Caution: Except for lavender and tea tree, don't apply full-strength oils directly to skin. Dilute in a vegetable carrier oil such as almond oil or grape seed oil.

Victoria Edwards, founder, Aromatherapy Institute & Research, Fair Oaks, CA, quoted in Self, *4 Times Square, New York City 10036.*

The Secrets of Herbal Remedies

Ethan Russo, MD, clinical associate professor of medicine at the University of Washington School of Medicine in Seattle. He is author of *Handbook of Psychotropic Herbs.* Haworth Press.

People often assume that because herbs are "natural," they pose little risk. Not true. Some herbs are too toxic for medicinal use. Even some that are generally safe can cause liver or kidney damage. And like drugs, herbal remedies can react dangerously with certain drugs or foods.

How can you use herbal remedies for maximum safety and effectiveness? *It's important to follow these guidelines...*

•**Avoid herbs known to be dangerous.** Given their inherent dangers, it's best to avoid chaparral, comfrey, life root, germander, coltsfoot, sassafras and ephedra (ma huang).

•**Don't be misled by wild claims.** Federal law forbids herbal remedy manufacturers from saying their products offer outright cures.

But manufacturers often tout their products as providing relief from a ludicrously wide range of ailments.

Take manufacturers' claims with a grain of salt. The best manufacturers often make no health claims for their products.

•**Seek reliable information.** The average doctor knows little about herbs. The same is true for the average druggist.

Health-food store clerks may sound knowledgeable, but their information often comes from herbal remedy manufacturers—hardly a source of unbiased information.

The most reliable source of information on herbs is *The Complete German Commission E Monographs: Therapeutic Guide to Herbal Medicines,* published by the American Botanical Council.*

•**Work with a knowledgeable practitioner.** For referral to an herb-savvy medical

*Your library may have this book. If not, it can be ordered from the American Botanical Council, *www. herbalgram.org*...or via an on-line bookseller.

doctor in your area, contact the American Botanical Council at 512-926-4900...or see its Web site at *www.herbalgram.org.*

Alternative: See a naturopathic physician. In addition to basic medical training, naturopaths have extensive instruction in the safe use of herbs.

For referral to a naturopath in your area, contact the American Association of Naturopathic Physicians at *www.naturopathic.org.*

•**Buy only standardized formulations.** Standardized herbal extracts have been formulated to provide the active ingredient or ingredients at a specific concentration. This increases the odds that the product is both potent and safe to use.

Look for the word "standardized" or the words "German standards" on the label.

•**Follow label directions carefully.** Like drugs, herbs work best at specific dosages. Take only the recommended dosage, and be sure to take the herb with or without meals, water, etc.—as indicated.

•**Don't mix herbs and drugs.** Herbs can boost the potency of certain medications. If you're taking a prescription drug, don't begin taking any herbal extract until you've checked with a physician or naturopath.

If a doctor has prescribed a drug for you, let the doctor know about any herbal remedies you're already taking. He or she may need to adjust the dosage.

Common herb–drug interactions include...

•**St. John's-wort and fluoxetine** (Prozac). The combination can raise brain levels of the neurotransmitter serotonin. "Serotonin syndrome" can cause delirium and other symptoms.

•**Ginkgo biloba and anticoagulants.** Like aspirin, *warfarin* (Coumadin) and other anticoagulants, ginkgo thins the blood. Taken along with an anticoagulant, ginkgo can cause internal bleeding.

•**Watch out for allergic reactions.** Introduce herbs one at a time. Don't add a second herb until you've taken the first for an entire week without experiencing any symptoms of an allergic reaction—rash, upset stomach, dizziness or headache.

If you experience any of these symptoms, stop taking the herb at once. Try taking it again one week later. If symptoms return, stop taking the herb for good.

Caution: If you become short of breath after taking an herb, you should call for an ambulance at once.

• **Don't take herbs during pregnancy.** Ginger, garlic and other herbs that are popular as foods are generally okay. But other herbs can cause serious problems for pregnant women.

It's also best to check with a doctor before giving any herbal remedy to a child under age 12.

Assertiveness Power Alleviates Stress

Sharon Anthony Bower, president of Confidence Training, Inc., an assertiveness and public speaking training company in Stanford, CA. She is coauthor of *Asserting Yourself*, which details her DESC method. Da Capo Press.

We all know that psychological stress takes its toll on us physically as well as emotionally.

Stress has been linked to high blood pressure, increased susceptibility to colds and greater sensitivity to pain.

Stress also contributes to headache, backache, peptic ulcers, digestive problems and insomnia.

Meditation and other relaxation strategies help curb stress. So does regular aerobic exercise. But it's much better to prevent stress in the first place. One highly effective—and often overlooked—way to do this is simply to be more assertive.

WRITE YOUR OWN SCRIPT

Many intelligent people avoid speaking up for themselves because they fear they'll get flustered and be forced to back down.

It's helpful to have a "script" to follow. Committing your thoughts to paper forces you to clarify the stressful situation…figure out what you want…and then come up with the best way to get it.

You needn't memorize your script word for word. But by practicing your main points, you'll develop the confidence to stand up for yourself.

Helpful: As you rehearse your script, breathe slowly and deeply. Say to yourself, "I can meet this challenge." Visualize yourself speaking with confidence and power.

THE DESC METHOD

To write an effective script, use the "DESC" method…

• **Describe the behavior that bothers you.** Do not waste time trying to identify the other person's motives. Instead, focus on the specific behavior or behaviors that bother you.

Example: "Several times during the past few weeks, you asked me to baby-sit at the very last minute."

• **Express your feelings about the troublesome behavior.** Be calm but firm. Use "I messages" to avoid putting the other person on the defensive.

Example: "I'm inconvenienced when you ask me to baby-sit on short notice. I'm also frustrated because I then act tense with the kids."

• **Specify what you want the other person to do.** Make sure your request is reasonable.

Example: "I'd like you to give me at least two days' advance notice when you ask me to baby-sit. Will you do that?"

• **Consequences.** List all the benefits the person will reap if he or she agrees to your conditions.

Example: "Given two days' notice, I'll be happy to watch the kids two or even three times a month. Since I'll feel relaxed, the kids and I will be better able to enjoy our time together."

In some cases, you'll have to specify negative consequences that will come to pass if the other person doesn't cooperate. Negatives should be used only if the positive approach fails.

Example: "If you fail to give me advance notice, I'll say no next time you ask me to baby-sit."

Not every situation calls for a detailed four-step script. Often, you can get your point across in a single sentence, such as, "This radio has a defective speaker" or, "The line starts back there."

If you're caught off guard by someone's behavior and find it hard to be assertive right then and there, simply say, "Let me think about that. I'll get back to you in an hour." Use the time to write an assertiveness script.

Good news: Once you write a few DESC scripts, you'll find it easier to assert yourself on the spur of the moment.

DEALING WITH DETOURS

What if the other person keeps you from sticking to your script...or tries to "detour" the conversation? Imagine his reactions and objections—in advance—and prepare a detailed response.

Good ways to respond...

•**Persist.** Repeat your main point—the "specify" part of DESC—as many times as necessary.

•**Agree...but.** Acknowledge that the other person has a right to his feelings...but disagree with the notion that you must feel the same way.

•**Disagree.** Say something like, "I hold a different view" or "I see it another way."

•**Emphasize your feelings.** Give more details about your feelings or thoughts...or state them more firmly. *Common detours...*

Put-off detour: "Let's not go into that now"...or, "I'm too busy right now." *Reply:* "It's important to me that this be settled. If this isn't a good time, please name a time today when we can talk."

Reinterpreting detour: "I only meant that remark as a joke." *Reply:* "Perhaps so, but I didn't think it was appropriate. I felt hurt."

Blaming detour: "You're going through a tough stage now. You'll see things differently in a few weeks." *Reply:* "This is no stage. The problem isn't me, but the way you've been treating me."

HOW TO GET STARTED

Each day for the next few weeks, try one of the following exercises. *Each time you try*

one, pay attention to what happens—and how you feel...

•**Ask for clarification.** If someone criticizes you—or seems to be criticizing you—ask for more details.

Example: "I'm not sure what you mean when you say I've been defensive. In what ways have I been defensive?"

•**Ask for help.** When you feel overwhelmed, get help. Don't feel that you must be a superperson all the time.

Example: "I want to do a good job on this project, but I'm feeling overwhelmed. Could we hire an assistant?"

•**Fight the urge to justify yourself.** You have every right to your feelings. Devise simple statements that show you won't be drawn into an argument.

Example: "That's how I feel about the issue, and I don't have to supply you with more reasons. Let's get back to the issue at hand."

•**Use assertive body language.** Make eye contact, but shift your gaze every few seconds. Staring makes you seem aggressive.

Eliminate distracting gestures—covering your mouth, touching your hair, clearing your throat, shifting your weight back and forth, etc.

Practice your DESC message with a friend or in front of a mirror—or record yourself and play it back—until you can use it comfortably.

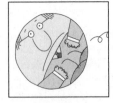

Control High Blood Pressure Without Medication

Sheldon G. Sheps, MD, emeritus professor of medicine at Mayo Medical School, Rochester, MN. He was editor in chief of *Mayo Clinic on High Blood Pressure*. Mayo Foundation.

High blood pressure is a time bomb—but it's one that ticks very quietly. This "silent killer" causes no symptoms, but elevated pressure in the arteries eventually causes severe damage to several organs.*

This damage sets the stage for stroke, heart attack, kidney failure…and premature death.

Fifteen million Americans are unaware that they have high blood pressure (hypertension). Of the 35 million who know they have it, only two out of five are getting adequate treatment.

A generation ago, doctors tended to think of blood pressure as being "normal" or "high." Now the National Heart, Lung and Blood Institute (NHLBI) recognizes different levels of blood pressure. *Each succeeding level is associated with a higher degree of risk…*

- **Normal**…below 120/80.

- **Prehypertension**…120/80 to 139/89.

- **Stage 1 hypertension**…140/90 to 159/99.

- **Stage 2 hypertension**…160/100 and above.

Cardiovascular disease risk doubles with each increment of 20/10.

If your pressure is elevated, here's how to get it down…

- **Follow the DASH diet.** In 1997, the Dietary Approaches to Stop Hypertension (DASH) study concluded that high-normal people and stage 1 hypertensives could achieve significant reductions in blood pressure simply by switching to a diet that stresses fruits, vegetables, grains and dairy products.

On average, study participants who followed the DASH diet lowered their blood pressure by 11 points systolic…and 5.5 points diastolic.

That was virtually the same level of reduction that is typically achieved with pressure-lowering medication—without the side effects associated with medication.

The daily DASH meal plan consists of…

- Seven or eight servings of grains, bread, cereal or pasta—preferably whole-grain varieties.

*Blood pressure readings are expressed as fractions —130/80, for example. The numerator (top number) represents *systolic* pressure—that existing in the arteries when the heart's main pumping chamber (left ventricle) contracts. The denominator (bottom number) represents *diastolic* pressure—that which exists between beats.

- Four to five servings of fruits and vegetables.

- Two or three servings of nonfat/low-fat dairy products.

- Two or fewer servings of meat, poultry or fish.

The DASH diet also calls for four or five servings per week of beans, peas, nuts or seeds.

- **Eat less salt.** Only about 40% of people with high blood pressure are salt-sensitive, but it's hard to know who falls into this category. *For this reason, everyone should limit sodium intake to 2,400 milligrams a day…*

- Read food labels and tally the sodium content of the foods you eat in a typical day.

- Cut out offending foods—such as fast food, cheese, bacon, pickles—as required.

- Avoid salt at the dining table…and in food preparation. Flavor foods instead with red pepper, cumin, onion, dill, lemon, etc.

It can take up to six weeks for your taste buds to adapt to less salt—so be patient. Once your taste buds adapt, you'll find you no longer crave salt.

- **Cut back on caffeine—**and nicotine. The caffeine that is in coffee, tea and soft drinks causes blood vessels to narrow for several hours. This then causes a transient rise in blood pressure. People who have hypertension should limit their daily caffeine intake to two cups of coffee, four cups of tea or four cans of caffeinated soda.

Like caffeine, nicotine causes a transient rise in blood pressure. Smoking just two cigarettes boosts systolic and diastolic pressure by up to 10 points. This increase persists for up to 90 minutes. Smoking can also interfere with the action of blood pressure medications.

- **Limit your drinking.** Excessive drinking—more than two drinks a day for men or one for women—is clearly a major contributor to hypertension.

If your drinking exceeds these levels, cut back. Do so gradually, over a few weeks. Going "cold turkey" can cause a rapid and potentially dangerous rise in blood pressure.

• **Lose weight.** The heavier you are, the larger the network of blood vessels your body must maintain. The larger this network, the more forcefully your heart must pump. This means higher blood pressure.

If you're overweight, losing as few as 10 pounds is often enough to lower your blood pressure significantly.

• **Alleviate psychological stress.** Stress causes the body to produce hormones that constrict blood vessels, thereby raising your blood pressure.

What to do: Get organized…make lists of tasks…set priorities…clean out clutter…say "no" to additional responsibilities…delegate work…and try meditation and other relaxation techniques.

• **Get more physical activity.** Walking, cycling, running and other forms of aerobic exercise boost your heart's pumping efficiency. The more efficient your heart, the wider the arteries open and the less forcefully the heart must contract.

Bonus: Regular exercise helps alleviate stress and promotes weight loss—thereby augmenting its pressure-lowering effect.

Aim for five to seven 30-minute workout sessions each week.

WHEN MEDICATION IS NECESSARY

If these lifestyle strategies are not enough to bring blood pressure to a healthy level, they may at least enable you to use a lower dosage of pressure-lowering medication. That's important, given the side effects associated with drug therapy.

How to Read Nutrition Labels

Men's Confidential.

Your local supermarket aisle now contains a lot more useful information than it used to. The Food and Drug Administration has decreed that all packaged food must have new, easier-to-understand labels.

"This is a step that could change the way America eats forever," declares the FDA's Edward Scarbrough, PhD. *Using a label from a bag of tortilla chips, we'll show you exactly what the new labels can do for you…*

• **The tip-off.** A "Nutrition Facts" label has replaced the old title "Nutrition Information per Serving."

• **Realistic serving size.** An old trick was to list calories and fat for an impossibly small serving size. No more playing the one chip game. The new serving size is more realistic and the same for all foods of a given type. A serving of tortilla chips, for example, is listed as one ounce, about 10 to 12 chips.

• **A simplified fat finder.** Calories derived from fat are listed so you can easily compare this number with the total calories. If it looks like the product gets half its calories from fat, beware. Fat should only comprise 30% of your total daily diet.

• **A way to keep track of the bad stuff.** Grams in each serving is pretty self-evident, but what's this "% Daily Value"? It has a confusing name, but a simple meaning. Just remember—for items that are potentially damaging to your health, you're aiming to stay below 100 percent each day for each of the items listed in this section of the label.

Let's take as an example one of the worst offenders—saturated fat. Percent daily value is listed here as 5 percent. That means you're spending five cents of your daily saturated fat dollar on this handful of tortilla chips. You've got 95 cents left for the rest of the day.

Zero in on what you're most worried about. If you're battling heart disease, try to spend less than your daily dollar on cholesterol, saturated fats and sodium.

For sugars and protein, there's a gram value listed, but no percentage. If you're diabetic or on a special high- or low-protein diet, check with your doctor about what daily totals are best for you.

AND THE GOOD STUFF

Your approach here is just like that to the undesirables, except here you'll want to celebrate if your percent daily values add up to 100 each day.

With dietary fiber, the key component in keeping you regular, you want to spend at least a dollar. These chips only used four cents —not too fiber-intensive. You'll need to spend 96 more during the course of the day.

All new labels also feature the big four nutrients…

• **Calcium.** Strengthens bones…may decrease risk of colon cancer and high blood pressure.

• **Vitamins A & C.** Antioxidants, possible cancer fighters, antiagers.

• **Iron.** Essential mineral, but men should stay below 100 percent.

Listing other information such as polyunsaturated and monounsaturated fat, potassium, other carbohydrates, vitamins and minerals is optional unless health claims are made, such as "rich in niacin."

• **Safety net.** If you don't like the percent daily values system, or if you tend to eat 2,500 calories a day instead of 2,000, then add up all the grams you've eaten on a given day of saturated fat, total fat or cholesterol and make sure they stay below the maximum value.

• **Proving an important point.** One gram of fat has more than twice the calories as a gram of carbohydrates or protein. The FDA thinks this is so important that they're including this reminder right on the label. Keep close tabs on your intake of fats.

NEW TRUTH IN ADVERTISING

The FDA is also cracking down on health claims made on food labels. In the past, some manufacturers have glibly used terms like "low fat" and "light" without a firm scientific basis. Now if they talk the talk, they've got to walk the walk.

• **"Free"**…means that a product has little or none of a particular nutrient.

Calorie-free = less than 5 calories

Fat-free = less than 0.5 grams (g)

Saturated fat-free = less than 0.5 g

Cholesterol-free = less than 2 milligrams (mg)

Sodium-free = less than 5 mg

Sugar-free = less than 0.5 g

• **"Lean"** and "extra lean," used to describe meats, poultry and seafood, has strict criteria to live up to. Here are some definitions for the most popular "eye-catchers."

Lean = Less than 10 g of fat, 4.5 g of saturated fat and 95 mg of cholesterol.

Extra lean = Less than 5 g of fat, 2 g of saturated fat and 95 mg of cholesterol.

• **"High"**…is now defined as an "excellent source of" by the FDA and will be used for products with 20% or more of the Daily Value.

• **"Light" or "lite"** products must contain at least one-third fewer calories, or no more than half the fat, of their reference food. Light cream cheese, for example, would need to be 5 g of fat or less than 67 calories per serving compared with regular cream cheese (100 calories, 10 g of fat per serving). Light can also apply to sodium if the product has at least 50% less sodium than a comparable food.

• **"Percent fat-free"** refers to the actual amount of a food that is fat-free. A product could be 95% fat-free, but if it has a lot of calories, that 5% could pack a fatty punch. The new regulations limit the use of this phrase to products that are low calorie to begin with.

• **"More"** reveals that a food has at least 10 percent more of a nutrient's Daily Value, again compared with the standard product.

• **"Reduced,"** used for nutritionally altered foods, lets you know that a product has at least 25% less of a nutrient compared with the regular product. For example, reduced-cholesterol mayonnaise must contain less than 75% of the cholesterol of regular mayonnaise.

• **"Low"** can only be associated with foods that can be eaten frequently without exceeding dietary guidelines.

Low-calorie = less than 40 calories

Low-fat = less than 3 g

Low-saturated fat = less than 1 g

Low-cholesterol = less than 20 mg

Low-sodium = less than 140 mg

Very-low-sodium = less than 35 mg

• **"Good source,"** as in "a good source of protein, vitamin C, etc.," can only be used if a product has 10% to 19% of the Daily Value of a particular nutrient.

The FDA is also requiring that manufacturers back up claims that their products prevent health problems such as cancer, high blood pressure or heart disease. Take, for example, the link between dietary fat and certain forms of cancer. For a product to make a health claim, it has to meet the requirements of a low-fat food (3 g or less per serving) and restructure its claim ("a diet low in total fat may reduce the risk of some cancers").

These little labels are having big impact. According to a recent study in the *American Journal of Public Health,* these labels are expected to save more than 300,000 lives over the next two decades. Coronary heart disease and colon and prostate cancer are just a few health problems the FDA hopes to reduce. Taking advantage of this information will change the way you look at food forever, and it could just save your life.

The Value of Fiber

High-fiber diets fight heart disease. In a recent 10-year study, the risk of developing heart disease was twice as great among women who had the lowest intake of dietary fiber as among those who had the highest.

When researchers compared the types of fiber the women ate—from cereal, vegetables or fruit—they found that only fiber from cereal guarded against heart disease.

This finding presumably applies to men as well as to women.

Alicja Wolk, DMSc, professor of nutrition epidemiology, Karolinska Institute, Stockholm. Her study of 68,782 women 37 to 64 years of age was published in *The Journal of the American Medical Association,* 515 N. State St., Chicago 60610.

Dangerous Condiment

Wasabi, the green and fiery-hot horseradish condiment that is typically served with sushi, should be eaten only a dab at a time—especially if you're not used to it. One man who gulped a large amount began sweating heavily, became confused and required a full day to recover. This reaction could be fatal in someone who has a heart condition or a tendency toward strokes.

Daniel Spitzer, MD, cited in *East West,* 838 Grant Ave., San Francisco 94108.

Milk Tip

Supermarket milk retains its nutrition better in fiberboard cartons than in clear plastic containers.

Reason: When exposed to fluorescent lights, low-fat or skim milk loses 90% of its vitamin A in 24 hours.

Research at Cornell University, Ithaca, NY.

Removing Pesticides From Produce

Pesticides cling to fruits and vegetables even after a water washing.

Best: Scrub the produce with a vegetable brush under running water. To be extra sure, use a mild detergent. Soak apples and pears in water containing one-fourth cup of vinegar before scrubbing.

The Practical Gourmet, Middle Island, NY.

Calcium vs. Memory

Memory impairment may be caused by too much calcium. Calcium is involved in the transmission of messages along brain neurons in the portion of the brain thought to direct memory functions. Studies have shown that as rats age, calcium flow into nerve cells increases, impairing the flow of messages.

Implications: If similar results occur in humans, calcium-blocking drugs might be used to prevent memory loss. Similarly, calcium supplements theoretically may contribute to memory loss though there is no evidence for this yet.

Philip Landfield, MD, professor and chair, molecular and biomedical pharmacology, University of Kentucky College of Medicine, Lexington.

Five Healing Foods for Your Regular Diet

Jamison Starbuck, ND, a naturopathic physician in family practice and a lecturer at the University of Montana, both in Missoula. She is past president of the American Association of Naturopathic Physicians and a contributing editor of *The Alternative Advisor: The Complete Guide to Natural Therapies & Alternative Treatments*. Time-Life.

Of all the questions I get from my patients, none is more common than, "Doctor, what foods should I eat?" Here are my favorite foods. They're tasty, easy to prepare and available in grocery or health-food stores. And unlike white flour products, luncheon meats, soft drinks and the other foods that many of us subsist on, these foods can help prevent—and even treat—certain illnesses.

• **Beets.** Both the red root—the part we ordinarily eat—and the green tops—the part we throw away—are full of magnesium and iron. These minerals are essential to good health.

But watch out. Like spinach, beet tops are rich in oxalic acid. This compound has been linked with formation of kidney stones. Beet tops are off-limits for anyone with stones or a history of stones. The red part is safe.

Beet tops can be torn like lettuce and added to salads. They can also be steamed and then added to soup—or served as you would serve spinach.

You can also eat beet roots raw. Grate directly into salad...or onto a sandwich made with lettuce, onion, tuna or fresh turkey and whole grain bread.

• **Kale.** I eat this dark, leafy green veggie at least twice a week during winter and early spring. At this time of year, the body's need for vitamins and minerals rises—the result of reduced exposure to sunlight and consumption of fresh food.

Kale is a fabulous source of calcium, iron, vitamins C and A, folic acid and chlorophyll. Unlike corn, beans and tomatoes, kale can be found fresh all year long.

Kale improves circulation and helps ward off colds. The compounds that give kale its bitter flavor help improve digestion and decrease the production of mucus.

Lightly steamed kale is delicious. It tastes a bit like spinach, though more flavorful. I eat the whole leaf, but you may want to avoid the stems. They can be tough.

• **Nuts.** Brazil nuts, almonds, filberts and walnuts are packed with minerals, folic acid, vitamins B and E and beneficial oils.

I recommend buying unshelled nuts—for two reasons. First, the shell keeps nut oil from going rancid. Second, the effort required to crack each nut by hand helps ensure that you won't eat too many of these nutritious—but calorie-dense—treats.

• **Parsley.** Though best known as a garnish, parsley has much more to offer. It improves digestion, freshens the breath and curbs breast tenderness associated with premenstrual syndrome. It's also a tonic for the adrenal glands, which can become "exhausted" as a result of hard work or stress.

I like to add abundant amounts of chopped raw parsley to salads or pasta, or simply eat sprigs as a snack. Ounce for ounce, parsley contains three times as much vitamin C as an orange.

Women who are pregnant or nursing should have no more than a sprig of parsley per day. More than that, and it can cause breast milk to dry up. It can even cause premature labor.

• **Sweet potatoes.** This starchy vegetable is rich in vitamin A and other carotenoids, which are necessary for healthy eyes, skin and lungs.

Bake them or combine with onions, garlic, tomatoes and chickpeas to make a hearty stew.

Perils of Crash Diets

Crash diets actually make people fatter in the long run. *Reason:* When dieters consume fewer than 1,200 calories a day, they lose muscle tissue as well as fat. If they go far enough below that level, their percentage of body fat will increase even though their weight may go down.

Berkeley Wellness Letter, Berkeley, CA.

• **Repeated crash dieting can increase the chance of heart disease.** The faster weight is lost from the body, the faster it tends to go back on. It is this rapid accumulation of weight that results in higher levels of blood cholesterol. Quick weight gain also accelerates the rate at which cholesterol is deposited in the blood vessels.

The 100% Natural, Purely Organic, Cholesterol-Free Megavitamin, Low-Carbohydrate Nutrition Hoax by Elizabeth Whalen. Simon & Schuster.

• **Crash diets impair the immune system response** and make dieters more vulnerable to infection. *Special danger:* Surgery patients with poor nutrition have a much higher rate of contracting postoperative infections.

The late Peter Lindner, MD, director of continuing medical education, American Society of Bariatric Physicians, quoted in *Prevention,* Emmaus, PA.

The "Don't Think" Diet

Robban Sica-Cohen, MD, a holistic doctor in Orange, CT. She specializes in environmental and nutritional medicine.

People do lose weight on trendy diets. But most of them gain back the pounds —and then some. Successful weight loss occurs only when you make a permanent commitment to replacing refined, calorie-dense foods with foods that are natural and unrefined. It's not that difficult.

Typical American dinner: A big piece of steak, a heap of fries and a tiny pile of vegetables. You can slash fat and calories simply by shifting the proportions. Eat one-half or one-third the portion of meat (or substitute fish) plus two big piles of veggies—and brown rice or another whole grain. You'll still feel satisfied.

To cut fat even more, replace the meat with lentils or beans. *Caution:* If you don't feel well on a vegetarian diet, do not force yourself. I'd estimate that one-third of the population has trouble metabolizing grains, fruits, vegetables and other carbohydrates. For these people, a carbohydrate-intensive diet can cause big trouble—including heart disease or a cholesterol or blood sugar problem.

The mineral chromium is a great weight-loss aid. It burns fat, builds muscle and helps reduce cravings for sweets. And chromium may lower levels of LDL (bad) cholesterol and raise levels of HDL (good) cholesterol.

It's hard to get enough chromium from food. Vegetables are poor sources—most are grown in chromium-depleted soil. Organ meats and dairy products contain chromium—but they're too fatty. Whole grains are chromium-rich, too, but they contain phytates, compounds that block the body's absorption of chromium and other trace elements.

Solution: Supplements of chromium picolinate. I recommend 200 micrograms (mcg)—three times a day, with meals—for any overweight adult, especially those who crave sweets or who have a blood sugar or cholesterol/triglyceride problem. *Caution:* Chromium can cause glucose levels to drop in diabetics, requiring a reduction in dosage of insulin. Even if you don't have diabetes, talk to your doctor before taking chromium.

To further boost your fat-burning power, team chromium with the amino acid L-carnitine. *Recommended:* 250 milligrams (mg) three times a day, with meals.

Garlic and Your Health

John Milner, PhD, chief, nutritional science research group, division of cancer prevention, National Cancer Institute, Bethesda, MD. Dr. Milner chaired a major conference on the health benefits of garlic.

Recent studies conducted in the US, Europe and China suggest that garlic can lower cholesterol levels…fight bacterial and viral infections…prevent cancer…and boost memory.

How strong is the evidence? Could you benefit by adding more garlic to your diet…or by taking garlic pills?

GARLIC VERSUS CHOLESTEROL

As proponents of garlic are quick to point out, numerous studies suggest that regular consumption of garlic—one clove a day or the equivalent in supplement form—cuts serum cholesterol by 7% to 15%. Garlic seems to be especially helpful at reducing LDL (bad) cholesterol.

Other studies suggest that garlic has little or no effect on cholesterol levels.

Example: A study conducted at the University of Bonn and published in *The Journal of the American Medical Association* showed that cholesterol levels remained unchanged even when garlic oil equivalent to four to five cloves of garlic was consumed on a daily basis for 12 weeks.

What explains the inconsistency of the studies? It may be that only some people respond to garlic. It's also possible that garlic interacts with the other foods in one's diet.

Another possible explanation for the inconsistency may be the fact that the studies have used various garlic preparations. Some have used unprocessed garlic. Others have used a garlic extract—which might or might not have the same biological activity as whole garlic.

GARLIC VERSUS CANCER

Research suggests that garlic can help prevent a variety of malignancies…

• **Stomach cancer.** In a 1984 study conducted in China, people who ate garlic regularly had an unusually low rate of this potentially deadly cancer.

• **Colon cancer.** A 1994 study of women in Iowa found that the incidence of colon cancer was 50% lower among those who consumed the most garlic.

• **Prostate cancer.** A 1997 study conducted in Oxford, England, found that men who consumed garlic two or more times per week were one-third less likely than other men to develop prostate cancer.

If garlic does protect against cancer, the explanation may lie in the sulfur compounds it contains.

Some laboratory studies have demonstrated that these compounds block the synthesis of carcinogens known as nitrosamines. In the absence of sulfur, the digestive process leads to the formation of nitrosamines each time nitrates and nitrites are consumed.

Nitrates and nitrites are both found in preservatives and also in beets, spinach and certain other foods.

Garlic also stimulates the body to synthesize glutathione. In addition to deactivating certain carcinogens, this natural antioxidant protects cell membranes against damage caused by renegade molecules known as free radicals.

Recent studies suggest that it might be possible to derive cancer chemotherapy drugs from garlic.

In one study, a garlic derivative called S-allylmercaptocysteine inhibited the growth of human prostate tumors that had been transplanted to mice.

In another study, a garlic extract called diallyldisulfide inhibited the growth of human breast cancer cells.

HOW TO EAT GARLIC

There is no proof that garlic can reduce cholesterol, lower cancer risk or do anything else to protect your health. But given the evidence in garlic's favor—plus the fact that the only downside to garlic consumption is bad breath—it makes sense to include some in your diet.

One to three grams of garlic per day—the equivalent of one clove—should be enough.

If you want to cook with garlic, be careful to preserve the potentially beneficial sulfur compounds. To do this, peel garlic, chop or crush it and then let it stand for 15 to 30 minutes before cooking. This "waiting period" facilitates chemical reactions that yield the biologically active compounds.

If you don't like the taste or smell of garlic, deodorized supplements are available. These products contain compounds similar to those found in raw garlic.

Foods That Fight Prostate Cancer

D. Duane Baldwin, MD, former chief resident urologist, Loma Linda University Health Care, Loma Linda, CA.

It's now clear that a low-fat diet helps prevent prostate cancer. *In addition, certain foods are beneficial...*

•**Allicin.** This garlic compound has potent anticancer properties. Add minced garlic to pasta sauces and stir-frys...toss a peeled clove into the juicer when making fruit juice.

•**Citrus fruits.** Oranges, lemons, etc., are loaded with pectin, a fiber that fights cancer. Since most pectin is found in the peels of citrus fruits, try zesting small slices into salads and stir-frys.

•**Gluten.** In a recent study, men who ate gluten-based meat substitutes were two-thirds less likely to have an elevated level of PSA (prostate-specific antigen), a marker for prostate cancer. Try the meat substitute seitan. It's sold in health-food stores.

•**Omega-3 fatty acids.** In recent studies, men who ate little omega-3 acids and lots of saturated fat were three times more likely to develop prostate cancer than other men. Omega-3 fatty acids are found in salmon, mackerel and other cold-water fish.

•**Selenium.** In a recent study, men who took selenium supplements had a lower risk for prostate cancer. *Good source of selenium:* Brazil nuts.

•**Soy.** Tofu, tempeh, miso and other soy foods contain genistein and other isoflavones, which are compounds that retard the growth of cancer cells. Eat two to three ounces of soy foods a day.

•**Tomatoes.** They're rich in lycopene, a pigment that develops anticancer properties once it's been cooked. Make homemade tomato sauce or grill fresh tomatoes.

Eat Tomatoes— Fight Cancer

Eating tomatoes cuts risk not only of prostate cancer, but also of cancers of the lung, stomach and cervix. Preliminary evidence suggests that eating tomatoes also helps prevent cancers of the pancreas, colon, rectum, esophagus, mouth and breast. In 57 of 72 studies, tomatoes and tomato-based products, such as pasta sauce, were found to have anticancer properties.

Theory: An antioxidant called lycopene in tomatoes protects cells from oxidants that have been linked to cancer.

Edward Giovannucci, MD, ScD, professor of medicine, Harvard Medical School, and epidemiologist, department of medicine, Brigham and Women's Hospital, both in Boston. His review of 72 studies of tomatoes and cancer was published in the *Journal of the National Cancer Institute,* Bethesda, MD.

Stroke-Reducing Nutrients

Eating bananas and other foods rich in potassium and/or magnesium can reduce the risk for stroke among people with high blood pressure.

Recent finding: Men with high potassium intake faced a stroke risk 36% lower than that of men with low potassium intake. Stroke risk was also lower among men using potassium supplements—but not magnesium supplements.

Fruits and vegetables—particularly oranges, cantaloupe and tomatoes—are good sources of potassium. Foods rich in magnesium include green vegetables, whole grains and beans and peas.

Alberto Ascherio, MD, MPH, DPH, associate professor of nutrition and epidemiology and researcher, department of nutrition, Harvard School of Public Health, Boston.

Lower Cholesterol With Peanuts

Peanuts may be heart-healthy after all. Health-conscious individuals have long shunned the nuts because of their high fat content. *New finding:* Levels of LDL (bad) cholesterol and triglycerides were lower among healthy men and women who regularly ate peanuts, peanut butter or peanut oil than among people who ate a low-fat diet but didn't eat peanut products.

Theory: Like olive oil, peanuts are a good source of heart-healthy monounsaturated fat.

Penny Kris-Etherton, PhD, RD, distinguished professor of nutrition, department of nutritional sciences, Pennsylvania State University, University Park. Her study of 22 men and women 21 to 54 years of age was presented at the Experimental Biology conference in San Francisco.

Spa Cuisine Every Day

Get recipes for high-nutrition, low-fat dishes made by spa chefs by visiting the Web site of *SpaFinder* magazine, *www.spafinder.com.* The recipes show many creative ways of serving fruit, vegetables and whole grains.

What's Good for You Can Be Bad for You

Fruit juice can be hazardous to health. Six ounces of apple juice contain the equivalent of more than five teaspoonfuls of sugar—40% more sugar than a chocolate bar and more sugar per ounce than cola. Blood-sugar-sensitive types who experience a temporary lift from sugar followed by fatigue should be cautious about fruit juice intake. *Recommended:* Eat a whole apple or orange instead of drinking juice. The fiber dilutes the sugar impact. *Alternative:* Eat cheese, nuts or other protein with juice.

• **Nondairy cream substitutes,** often used by those on low-fat diets, usually contain coconut oil and have a higher fat content than the dairy product for which they're being substituted.

• **Decaffeinated coffee** leads to significant stomach-acid secretion, causing heartburn and indigestion in many people. Caffeine was assumed to be the culprit, but a new study shows that decaffeinated coffee is even worse. The effect is seen in doses as small as a half cup of decaffeinated coffee. People experiencing ulcer symptoms, heartburn and dyspepsia should avoid decaffeinated as well as regular coffee.

Journal of the American Medical Association, Chicago.

• **Most commercial products billed as alternatives to salt** are based on potassium chloride. *Problem:* Although potassium chloride does enhance flavor, it leaves a slightly bitter or metallic taste. And excessive potassium may be even worse for your health than too much salt. *Alternatives to the alternatives:* Mrs. Dash, a commercial blend of 14 herbs and spices…Lite Salt, a half-sodium, half-potassium blend…or try adding parsley, a delightful herb that enhances flavor all by itself.

• **One of the few proven substances** that can bring on flare-ups of acne is iodine. Excessive, long-term intake of iodine (a natural ingredient of many foods) can bring on acne in anyone, but for people who are already prone to the condition, iodine is especially damaging. Once iodine hits the bloodstream, any excess is excreted through the oil glands of the skin. This process irritates the pores and causes eruptions and inflammation. *Major sources of iodine in the diet:* Iodized table salt, kelp, beef liver, asparagus, turkey and vitamin and mineral supplements. For chronic acne sufferers, cutting down on these high-iodine foods and looking for vitamins without iodine may bring relief.

• **Chronic diarrhea, gas and other stomach complaints** are often linked to lactose intolerance, the inability to digest milk. One of every four adults suffers from this problem. *Reason:* Their bodies don't make enough lactase, the enzyme that breaks down milk sugar in the intestinal tract. *Among the offending foods:* Milk, ice cream, chocolate, soft cheese, some yogurts and sherbet. Lactose is also used as a filler in gum, candies and many canned goods.

• **People on low-sodium diets** should check out tap water as a source of salt intake. Some local water systems have eight times the amount of sodium (20 milligrams per quart) than people with heart problems or hypertension should use.

The Sodium Content of Your Food, Federal Citizen Information Center, Pueblo, CO.

• **Health-food candy** is really no better for you than traditional chocolates. *Comparison:* Health-food candy contains about the same number of calories. The fat content is as high or higher. Bars made of carob are caffeine-free, but the amount of caffeine in chocolate is negligible. And the natural sugars in health bars have no nutritional advantage over refined sugars.

What's Bad for You Can Be Good for You

Chocolate lovers will be pleased to know that chocolate is not as dangerous to teeth as other candies. Antidecay factors in cocoa counter the damaging action of the sugar. Cocoa tannins seem to inhibit plaque formation, and the fat in cocoa may protect teeth by forming an antibacterial coating.

National Institute for Dental Research.

• **Treat a cold with booze fumes.** Take a thick mug and fill it with boiling water. After about two minutes, throw the water away. Put in two ounces of brandy or bourbon,

and then fill the mug almost to the top with boiling water. Cup your hands over the top of the mug to make a nose cone. Place your mouth and nose inside the cone. Blow on the surface and inhale the fumes for 15 minutes. You should feel the vapor penetrating your sinuses. Drink the mixture if you want to. Take a cold pill to keep your sinuses open overnight, and repeat the treatment in the morning. If you start this at the first signs of a cold (before nasal passages are blocked), your cold should vanish in 24 hours.

What Doctors and Hospitals Don't Tell You

Medical Economics.

Always count the pills in the bottle you get, and check the total against the prescription. Discrepancies between the number of pills the doctor prescribes and the number the pharmacist gives you are quite common.

• **Physicians routinely neglect to inform their patients about the possible side effects of the drugs they prescribe.** About three-quarters of patients do not receive these briefings, according to the Food and Drug Administration. And 35% of all patients get no information at all about prescribed drugs. *Protection:* Question your doctor until you know all about the drug you are to take.

• **Diagnostic error.** Poor bite is often misdiagnosed as a migraine or pinched nerve. People with faulty bite often unconsciously grind their teeth to align them better. *Result:* Headaches, earaches and pains in the jaw, neck and shoulders. *Treatments:* Spot grinding by a dentist to even the bite. Exercises to relax the jaw muscles. A plastic device that fits over the upper and lower teeth to protect them from grinding, help readjust the bite and ease pressure on jaw muscles.

• **Doctors who operate frequently have better safety records because they maintain their skills.** *Guideline:* The doctor should have a minimum of 40 to 50 operations a year, even more for heart surgery. Aim for a hospital that does many similar operations. *Best bets:* Teaching and specialty hospitals. A good one substantially improves the chances of avoiding serious complications or death.

• **Postoperative delirium is a short-lived but frightening phenomenon** common to patients who have undergone serious surgery. Some become disoriented or lose touch. Others suffer hallucinations. Patients who are warned about this possibility before an operation are much less likely to experience it. If they do, the effects are much less severe.

Nursing Research.

• **Keep your medical records private.** Never sign a blanket medical release form. The only medical release forms you sign should specifically identify the following: Information to be released, who is releasing the information and who is to receive it. Releases are not self-limiting as to time. A form you signed 10 years ago can still be used to obtain information, but a period of one year is suggested.

• **Many hospital procedures can be managed at home**—effectively and efficiently—which will spare the patient's pocketbook. A home chemotherapy program run by M.D. Anderson Cancer Center in Houston saved an average of $1,500 per patient. Home recipients of intravenous feedings through a Cleveland clinic reduced their bills by an estimated $100 a day. In Nashua, New Hampshire, patients who took intravenous antibiotic therapy at home instead of in the hospital saved $286 a day. *Bottom line:* Check with your doctor about local home-care programs the next time a loved one is hospitalized. Keep in mind that insurance companies may not pay for some home-care services.

• **Wrong pills in hospitals.** Since 1962, when a study of hospital medication practices uncovered an error in every six doses given to patients by nurses, the handling of drugs in US hospitals has upgraded appreciably. A majority now have central pharmacies that make up unit doses that are to be dispensed by nurses and/or technicians in most of their departments. Where unit dose systems are in place, errors average only three per 100. However, that 3% can be fatal, and the number of errors in departments and hospitals not served by the central pharmacy is still very high (8% to 20%). *The problem:* Overworked nurses, confusing and similar drug names and packaging and illegibly written prescriptions. *How to protect yourself:* Be sure you know exactly which drugs and what dosages your doctor has ordered for you. Never accept medication without knowing what it is and what it is for.

• **Blood pressure readings taken in a doctor's office may not be accurate** because of the anxiety of being there. *Better:* Using portable devices, patients can measure their own pressures during the day while continuing their normal activities. These measurements are particularly helpful in deciding whether to start medication in patients who have borderline hypertension. Be sure to check the accuracy of your device by bringing it with you to the doctor's office.

Journal of the American Medical Association.

• **Doctors' handwriting.** When doctors write the names of drugs on prescription slips, a misreading by the pharmacist can be disastrous. A drug for arthritis, Tolectin, has been mistaken for Tolinase, which lowers blood sugar in diabetics. Coumadin, a drug that thins blood in heart-disease patients, was confused with Kemadrin, which is for Parkinson's disease. *Useful:* Tell the pharmacist the disease for which the medicine is being prescribed. The pharmacist can then check it.

2

Sex?

Dating for Mature and Successful Singles

Some 20 years ago, Abby Hirsch started a dating service, The Godmothers (no longer in business), for achievers whose lives are full of options, the kind you would think have no problems meeting all the right people. Not so. Singles now settle into comfortable friendships with a peer group and have no way of getting out of it. Everyone is afraid of dating people from the office. Women are working and don't have time to give the dinner parties that used to introduce people.

The 500 or so Godmothers clients in each city (New York, Washington, Philadelphia) range in age from 18 to 67. Most women are in their 20s and early 30s, and most men are in their 30s and 40s. *Second largest group:* Men in their 50s and women in their early 40s. They have a wide spectrum of working credentials and interests. For a fee, each gets three different introductions.

SELECTION PROCESS

Prospects send in autobiographical, professional and personal data, information on what worked and what did not work in their most recent relationships and what kind of person they would like to meet now. From this material the staff determines those who have a chance of being successfully matched. The preliminary screening is followed by a 45-minute interview.

Who is rejected? People who ask for much more than they have to offer. Those who are too rigid and make requests the service cannot fill. People who are extremely overweight (no one will go out with them). Anyone whose only goal is marriage risks disappointment and is not encouraged. *Acceptable:* Those who would like to find a mate eventually but are aware that there can and should be many pleasurable experiences on the road to permanence. *What's hot, what's not...*

- **Highest priority.** Nonsmokers.

Abby Hirsch, founder of The Godmothers (no longer in business), New York.

38

• **Second highest priority in Washington.** Someone not connected with politics (no one wants to talk about politics at night).

Women: Most are making reasonable amounts of money. You don't hear, "Find me a man who is going to be able to support me" but rather, "Find me a man who's going to be loving and sharing and wants to spend time with me."

Men: It's not the prettiest girl on the block that they want. The demand is for a woman who really likes her work but has time for a man in her life.

The staff tries to redirect unrealistic requests. *Example:* If you're interested in someone who plays tennis but you play only one hour a week, maybe there are other issues that are more important. There is often a wide difference between what people ask for and what they respond to. *Example:* A woman whose last relationship had been with a photojournalist who was almost always away on assignment asked for a solid Brooks Brothers type. She liked the stockbroker she was introduced to but soon became bored. What she really wanted was someone dependable but more adventurous. They found her an attorney whose hobby is ballooning. They're planning to marry.

DATING TIPS

• **Avoid talking too much about a former spouse.**

• **Reexamine your priorities,** and try to be more flexible.

• **Don't judge another person in the first 10 minutes of a date.** Stay open.

• **Keep a sense of humor**.

• **Listen to what the other person is saying.** Be interested, not only interesting.

Those who have the toughest time finding acceptable dates: (1) Very beautiful women. Men are afraid to approach them. When they do, it's usually not for the right reasons. (2) Very successful men. Women stay away from them because they feel such men have so many other choices, creating too much competition.

Availability: Whether or not you will date successfully depends a great deal on whether you are really available for a relationship.

Advice to those who want to become more available: Think through why you are asking for particular qualities in another person and why you are responding as you are. Reexamine your priorities.

Winning at the Personal-Ads Game

Judy Kuriansky, PhD, professor of clinical psychology, Columbia University Teachers College, fellow of the American Psychological Association and New York *Daily News* Sex & Romance columnist. She is author of several books on relationships, including *The Complete Idiot's Guide to a Healthy Relationship*. Alpha Books.

What are the best places to run a personal ad? Focus first on personal ads in publications that you read regularly. If a magazine or newspaper attracts you, it will probably attract people like you and people whom you will like.

The personal ads on the Internet are also useful. Search for sites by typing in the word "dating" or "personals." From there you'll find a subset of people looking for others who share their interests.

What are the ingredients of an ad that attracts a good match?

Many people have trouble writing personal ads because they try too hard. The result is often stiff and formal.

Before placing an ad you've written, read it into a tape recorder. Play it back and listen. It should sound fast, snappy, honest and sincere. You want your ad to get noticed, but you don't want to attract those who are attracted to the wrong version of you—or somebody you've invented.

Run your ad by your friends. Ask them if it truly reflects your best qualities—without going overboard. Look at past ads. Find some ads you like…and change words so that they fit you.

What's the best way to answer an ad that requests a phoned-in response?

Many ads today ask you to call a number and leave a telephone message on a voice-mail system. Speak honestly and freely, as if to a good friend. But if you're at all nervous about leaving a message, prepare your script first. Then rehearse so you can read it naturally into the phone when the time comes.

Be confident. Push past shyness. Focus on what you're looking for and why you're an ideal person to meet. Avoid saying "Uhhh"... or putting yourself down.

How do you do a background check on people who answer the ad?

Ask for the person's work number. Call to find out if it is really a business and if the person actually works there. Keep in mind that some people may ask their friends to pose as phony employers.

Also, if the person mentions that he/she loves certain activities, such as yoga or going to the gym, you can find out where he goes and see if the locations really exist.

What about asking for a photograph before you meet?

This is a must. Ask for a full-body shot and not just a head shot.

Reason: Not only do you want to see what the person looks like, but you also want to see if the photo looks dated or doctored.

What's the best strategy when you speak directly to someone who responded to the ad?

Just be yourself, but prepare in advance to talk about things that interest you most. Speaking passionately will inspire your response.

Ask questions that can't be answered by a simple yes or no.

Example: Don't ask, "Do you like seeing movies?" Ask, "What's the last movie you saw that you really liked and why?"

The idea is to get the person talking so you can learn more about him.

When is the right time to meet in person?

Probably after two or three telephone conversations.

When you finally agree to meet face to face, meet during the day, in daylight, in a public place—restaurants work well...for lunch...or a coffee shop. Consider bringing a friend for safety and feedback.

Define a limited meeting time for a painless parting in case it doesn't go well.

Always end with appreciation. Never give false promises to call if you have no intention of doing so. Simply say you are busy for weeks ahead.

Love in Middle Age And Beyond

Johnette Duff, Esq., 323 Webster St., Ste. 1237, Houston, TX 77002. Ms. Duff is a certified family mediator and author of Love After 50: The Complete Legal and Financial Guide. *Legalines.*

Becoming involved in a serious relationship in middle age is more complicated legally and financially than it is for younger people...

• **There may be family members to care for**—*the children from prior marriages, ex-spouses, parents...*

• **The couple may have heavy financial obligations**—*alimony payments, child support...*

• **They may have piled up assets in which others have a stake.**

Examples: Pensions (one spouse has a legal interest in the other's pension)...business interests.

To avoid pitfalls that could undermine the relationship—the legal and financial issues the parties face must be thought through.

Should we marry...

Marriage has positive and negative financial consequences. A positive one is that marriage may entitle a nonworking spouse to employer-paid health coverage. *Other considerations...*

• **Responsibility for the support of the new spouse.** Obviously, those in a relationship help to support each other. But when you marry, this becomes a legal obligation that can create serious burdens for older people should one spouse need long-term nursing care.

- **Being responsible for the debts of your spouse.** Mature adults may have significant debt on credit cards, business loans or back taxes. Premarriage debts may become the responsibility of a new spouse.

- **Losing alimony payments from a previous marriage.** These payments often cease upon remarriage.

- **Losing Social Security benefits based on the earnings of a former spouse**…as long as you're married to your new spouse.

- **Being able to file a joint tax return.** For some couples, this may result in tax savings, while others may face a "marriage penalty" (paying more taxes than they would as singles living together).

…Or just live together?

State, as well as federal, law may affect the rights and obligations of an unmarried couple. *State law may…*

- **Make it illegal to live together**…even though this law is seldom enforced.

- **Recognize palimony rights**…should you decide to split up (although most states have enacted laws against this).

- **Recognize contracts**…including oral agreements made between the parties concerning property divisions, support or other financial arrangements.

While state law may not provide unmarried couples with the protections afforded married couples, people who decide to live together can create these protections through agreements or contracts.

Example: State law generally doesn't impose any support obligation on an unmarried person, but a couple can provide in a contract for continued support even if they decide to split up.

KEEPING EVERYONE HAPPY

For older individuals, there are usually more people to consider, as I mentioned earlier. There are former spouses, children from prior marriages and even grandchildren.

Often, concerns center on estate planning issues, such as who's going to get what.

Planning to keep everyone satisfied isn't easy, but it can be done. *Some approaches to consider…*

- **Don't rely on state law to determine who inherits what if you die without a will.** Under state law, someone you wanted to benefit may well receive nothing.

Example: State law does not provide any inheritance at all for a significant other who's not a legal spouse.

Protection: Make out a will spelling out who should get what when you die.

- **Use trusts to provide for more than one person.**

Example: Instead of giving the house to your companion, use a trust to give that person a lifetime interest in the house. When he or she dies, your children (or anyone else named in the trust) can inherit the home. *Impact:* Your mate has protection for life. The children are the ultimate beneficiaries of the house.

- **Review all beneficiary designations.** Retirement plans and IRAs allow individuals to name one or more beneficiaries. Well-considered designations can ensure that all parties get the protection you intended.

Example: A new spouse can be named as the beneficiary of a company pension plan, while children can be beneficiaries of various IRA accounts.

- **Use prenuptial agreements to spell out all your intentions.**

Example: Older spouses may each have sufficient assets so that they are willing to waive any legal claims they have to one another's estates.

KNOW WHERE YOU STAND

In making your decision about a long-term commitment and whether to do so under the umbrella of marriage, *be sure to…*

- **Get all the legal facts.** Be sure you understand the legal and financial ramifications of your decision.

- **Negotiate the terms of any arrangements you make.** Unless both parties are satisfied with the deal, it may not hold up later on.

- **Review your decisions with professionals.** Talk to an attorney about wills and other documents you may need in order to cement the arrangements you want. Talk to an accountant who can assess the tax impact of your decisions.

Sexual Habits of American Women

Think you know your partner? *Results from professional surveys might surprise you...*

• **Extramarital affairs.** In a *Cosmopolitan* poll, 54% said they fooled around, 21% in a poll conducted by *Ladies' Home Journal,* 34% in *Playboy,* and 43% in a survey by the Institute for Advanced Study of Human Sexuality. *Playboy's* poll also showed that almost 65% of wives have had affairs by age 50.

• **Skill.** A majority of women think they are good at sex. *Playboy* found 80% who claimed they were skilled. Some 65% of those polled in the *Journal* rated themselves good to excellent. And 64% in the Institute poll admitted they were "great."

• **Frequency.** Most polls say that married women make love two or three times a week.

• **Orgasms.** Roughly half the women questioned said they had orgasms regularly.

• **Oral sex is practiced by more than 85% of the women questioned by *Cosmopolitan* and 95% of those by *Playboy.*** About one-half of married women incorporate it into their lovemaking.

• **Sex in public places is indulged in by about one-third of those polled by *Playboy.***

• *Family Circle* **found that 85% of wives are satisfied with their sex lives.**

• **One-third of the women polled by the Institute have had venereal disease or herpes.** About 91% use sex lotions or gadgets.

• *Playboy* **discovered that among young married couples,** wives play around more than husbands do.

Common Sexual Concerns

Judy Kuriansky, PhD, professor of clinical psychology, Columbia University Teachers College, fellow of the American Psychological Association and New York *Daily News* Sex & Romance columnist. She is author of several books on relationships, including *The Complete Idiot's Guide to a Healthy Relationship.* Alpha Books.

The act of sex should be the most natural thing in the world. But for some people, sex causes anxiety and concern. *There are several issues that are very common...*

AMONG MEN

• **Premature ejaculation.** The answer to this problem lies in learning to control the timing of ejaculation. This is easier than you think. You have to find the point at which you can no longer stop yourself from ejaculating. During masturbation, practice ways in which you can decrease or increase feelings of arousal. Discover which fantasies or behavior triggers your excitement and what diminishes it, and learn how to focus on the latter in order to postpone ejaculation. It's not a good idea to use the old-fashioned trick of thinking about baseball scores or work. Thinking about such totally nonsensual experiences is destructive to sexuality. Instead, focus attention on any sensation in your body, or minimal sensual thoughts—which at least keeps you in the realm of being sensual (but not at the peak of being excited).

• **Sexual deviations and fetishes.** Men are very much concerned with what they consider to be unnatural desires, such as the wish to be spanked by women. It arises from the need to be punished for feeling sexual, and also they need to be forced into sexuality as a way of avoiding responsibility for engaging in it. ("The devil made me do it.") Cross-dressing is the desire to put on women's clothes. Husbands and lovers who do this may keep the practice hidden or may be indulged by their partners until it becomes disturbing. A desire to put on women's clothes usually reflects sexual problems related to a desire, left over from childhood, to be "close to Mommy." (Mommy may not be near forever, but her clothes can be.) It may also be a sign of difficulty in integrating the passive "feminine" side of a man's nature with the active "masculine" side. *Example:* A man who has trouble expressing his passive side, as evidenced in the inability to cry, may find it easier to do so by putting on women's clothes.

• **A desire for more sexual aggressiveness from female partners.** A great many men wish that their wives or lovers would take the sexual initiative and behave less passively. *Theory:* If women could act out the more masculine side of themselves and thus come across to men in a more familiar way, physically and emotionally, far fewer men would have difficulties relating to women sexually. (This is borne out by homosexuals, who explain that what they get from relationships with men is missing from relationships with women.)

• **Erection problems** (failure to get or maintain erections). This is much more complex than premature ejaculation and more difficult to deal with. It is often complicated by emotional problems, such as insecurity or hostility to the partner, so psychological treatment, rather than special physical exercises, is usually required.

• **Penis size.** A very common concern, disguised with such euphemisms as "I have a handicap." (*Translation:* "I think my penis is too small.") The solution is to understand that physiologically the small penis is not a deterrent to sexual pleasure. It is important to find out what penis size means to you or your partner and the ways it affects your desire and pleasure.

AMONG WOMEN

• **Not having orgasms.** The first part of the solution is to learn not to focus on the missing orgasm—if it is missing. Studies show that at least half the women who think they don't have orgasms in fact do have them. *The dynamics:* They're looking for some ideal of an orgasm that they've heard about. *For the genuinely nonorgasmic:* This is relatively easy to overcome, often within a brief period of treatment that involves learning to achieve orgasm by yourself via masturbation. *Goal:* To learn to accept that sexual pleasure is for you, too, not just for men, as so many women have

been brought up to think. After acquiring the capacity to accept the sexual pleasure she has learned to give herself, a woman can usually go on to the next step, the pleasure of orgasm with a male partner.

• **Conflict over the way they're treated in relationships with men.** Men are much more concerned with sexual performance and physical fears than are women. Women care far more about the psychological and emotional aspects of relationships than do men. *Most common conflict:* The still very common tendency among women to settle for "half a loaf" in a relationship, usually out of the mistaken belief that "That's all you can hope to get, so make do." The first step out of this trap is to refuse to accept such reasoning and to reject the false security of relationships that offer so little satisfaction.

• **Problems integrating the role of parent and lover.** It isn't only men who suffer from the madonna-prostitute complex (separating women into categories such as the "pure madonna" and the "sexy enticer"). Women can also suffer from this syndrome. *Example:* The woman who has a child and thus comes to feel that she isn't sexy and shouldn't feel sexy because she is now a mother. *Usual symptoms of the problem:* She avoids sex on the grounds of fatigue, a problem with the baby or concern over money.

Frequently asked by both sexes: Is it healthy to get involved in a sexual relationship with someone much older or much younger? *Answer:* There usually isn't a great deal wrong with these relationships. These couplings are often a holdover from incestuous childhood desires. When such desires are acted out by two adults, it can be taken as psychological information, but nothing else.

Sex in Long-Lasting Marriages

Clifford J. Sager, MD, psychiatrist and psychologist in private practice in New York City.

The importance of physical intimacy in long-term marriages depends on each couple. Sex is great and enjoyable, but in this country it's been overrated.

Many people like holding, cuddling and sleeping together but not intercourse. However, sex can be a matter of substantial importance if one partner (or both) doesn't find pleasure in sexual activity with a mate.

Some women want intercourse only to have children. And some men have sex with their wives only for children and go elsewhere for pleasure.

Many women used to feel that their sex lives ended with menopause. And an astounding number of men used to give up sex after 60. Today we know it doesn't have to be that way. Men may need more stimulation and more time before having another erection or ejaculation. But sexual pleasure for both men and women can go on and on.

It's not unusual for married couples in their late 50s or early 60s who haven't had sex together for several years to say, "We're happy, we enjoy and love each other, but maybe we're missing something."

If they have a desire for more sexual expression, physical causes for lack of sexual desire should be checked, followed by psychological causes.

Many men and women are turned on by other lovers but not by a spouse. Familiarity is one cause. Outside partners always have an advantage because they don't have to deal with day-to-day problems. Sex is important to someone who has affairs, but is it important in the marriage? If it is, the big problem is how to redirect it to the marriage. This isn't always possible.

Example: A man of 73 with a wife of 65 couldn't get an erection with his wife even though he wanted to. But with a woman friend two years older than his wife he had excellent sex a couple of times a week on a regular basis.

After a number of unsuccessful therapy sessions, the problem was discovered. His abrasive, cold wife wanted sex only because she thought her husband was neglecting her. The other woman, who was warm and had a zest for life, really enjoyed sex.

WHAT TO DO

More and more people in long-term marriages want to do something about the lack of sexual desire in their marriage. Those who've been married for 20 years or more may not know how to cope with changes and may be drifting apart, but they don't want to run out on the relationship.

It is important to determine whether the cause or causes of reduced sexual interest are interactional (routinizing of sex, depression or other emotional problems) or organic in nature (arteriosclerosis of the arteries to the penis, postmenopausal problems in women, low levels of testosterone in men). A small number of partners are aware of the fact that over time their sexual desire has shifted from heterosexual to homosexual. Outside relationships also preempt the interest of one or both partners.

There is a moralistic attitude toward extramarital affairs in this country, and until recently, it was a major cause of divorce. We can learn from other countries, where married people have a love relationship with somebody else but still maintain the family structure without bitterness whether or not there is sex between husband and wife.

Example: A French patient and her husband both had lovers they talked about openly. The married couple had problems between themselves, and seeing other people was part of their annoyance with each other. They wanted to improve their own relationship. They did get closer, but they had no intention of giving up the other partners.

Very often people with sexual problems also have problems being open about other feelings. Increasing openness about sex helps. *Suggestion:* Talk about your fantasies and try to incorporate them into your sex life.

Executives in high-powered jobs want to come home to a loving, relaxing place. They are impatient if their needs aren't understood, making them turn off sexually. So they look for sex outside (where they can find it quickly and easily on a short-term basis) instead of working out the problem at home.

Sex After 50

Saul H. Rosenthal, MD, author of *Sex Over Forty*. Tarcher.

Middle age can be an opportunity to make sex better and more satisfying than ever before. *Basic reasons:* People of mature years have had more experience in lovemaking. (Research shows that many women don't experience a climax until they are in their 30s, though this is beginning to change as men learn more about orgasm.) The pressures of career building are less frantic, leaving couples with more time to share.

The children have grown up and left home, giving adults more privacy and fewer demands on their time. And as men age, they lose the pressure to get right to intercourse and a quick climax. They can concentrate on a fuller sensual and sexual experience in lovemaking.

Most common mistakes about age and sex…

• **Believing that your sex life is essentially over by the time you're in your 50s.** Society tends to reinforce this notion with its emphasis on youth—the absence of advertisements showing older people as objects of sexual interest, for example. People behave according to the expectations that the culture sets for them and begin to give up on their sexual lives when they reach middle age. This is in many ways the equivalent of giving up on life itself.

• **Failing to understand that the physiological changes affecting sexual function are normal** and can be adapted to without the loss of a sex life. Middle-aged men suppose that these changes are signals that sex is (and is supposed to be) over for them. They become fearful that they can no longer function. Once this fear sets in, sexual function really is seriously

affected. *Example:* Many men ages 55 to 60 or older worry when they don't get a spontaneous erection when seeing their partner undress as they did when they were 20 or 30.

But this does not mean sexual function is over for them. It only means that they now require more direct stimulation. Many men put off having intercourse until they get a spontaneous erection for fear their wives will think they have some sexual problem. Sex in these circumstances becomes less and less frequent, and this is what causes wives to be fearful that their husbands are no longer interested in them.

• **Believing that sex requires a climax every time.** As men get older, they need longer and longer periods between ejaculations. A man in his 60s may require a full day or even several days between ejaculations. This does not mean that he cannot enjoy intercourse and lovemaking in between. Sex partners get into serious trouble when they think climaxes are essential and that the male, particularly, must have one. (The man feels he must because his partner expects it. The woman feels that if he doesn't, he no longer cares for her.) You can enjoy all the sensations of sexual arousal without climax. Remember how pleasurable it was just to neck in the back of a car in your younger days, when mores were less permissive?

Lack of lubrication, the problem for aging women: Oral estrogen therapy can alleviate this condition. However, this should be discussed with your doctor as recent evidence has suggested that it increases the risk for breast cancer and other maladies.

The problem of impotence: Many factors can cause impotence. Contrary to the opinion that has prevailed since Masters and Johnson did their research, not all impotence is caused by psychological problems. New research shows that a variety of physical problems can cause impotence and that these are treatable. (Included are hormonal problems and vascular and neurological conditions.)

Impotence may be caused by medical or organic factors (rather than psychological ones) if…

• **Medications are being taken to lower blood pressure,** or antidepressants, tranquilizers, antihistamines or decongestants are being used.

• **Alcohol is being overused.** Alcohol has very strong negative effects on sexual functions, including possible long-term problems such as reduced production of the male hormone, decreased sperm production and reduced sex drive.

• **A major illness, especially diabetes,** thyroid disease or arteriosclerosis is experienced. Illness isn't necessarily the cause of erection problems but should be considered one possibility.

• **The man has lost his sexual desire** (as well as capacity).

Impotence is probably caused by psychological factors if…

• **There are firm erections under some circumstances** (waking at night or in the morning, during masturbation, etc.). This indicates that the physical mechanism is in good working order and that emotional factors are the more likely cause of impotence.

• **Firm erections are lost just before or after entry.** The odds here greatly favor an emotional cause.

• **The problem started suddenly,** over a period of a month or less. This is more likely to be an emotionally caused impotence, since physical problems affect sexual function more gradually. *Caution:* There are exceptions. Emotional causes are not always sudden in their effect. And medical causes can be sudden in their effect, especially if a new drug is prescribed.

• **The problem started after a very stressful emotional experience** (the death of a spouse, the loss of a job, a divorce, rejection by a partner).

Jump-Start Your Sex Life…Naturally

Chris D. Meletis, ND, executive director, the Institute for Healthy Aging (*www.theiha.org*). He is author of several books, including *Better Sex Naturally* (HarperResource), *Complete Guide to Safe Herbs* (DK Publishing) and *Instant Guide to Drug–Herb Interactions* (DK Publishing).

Well before erectile-dysfunction drugs, people relied on aphrodisiacs to increase sexual desire…boost stamina …improve performance…and increase pleasure. Many of these compounds owe their reputation to folklore, but several herbs and dietary supplements have proven sex-enhancing effects.

Good news: Products that improve sex naturally may be less likely to cause serious side effects than prescription drugs. Many strengthen the cardiovascular system and help regulate hormone production. That's as important for good sex as having an erection or being sufficiently lubricated.

Unlike sildenafil, sex-enhancing herbs and supplements aren't taken just an hour or so before sex. They're taken daily until there's a noticeable improvement in sexual performance.

At that point, some people take a pause to see if the herbs and supplements are no longer necessary. Others continue taking the preparations indefinitely.

Important: Use herbs and supplements only under medical supervision. That way you'll be sure to get the product and dosage that's right for you.

Caution: Fresh or dried herbs differ greatly in potency from batch to batch. Use capsules or tinctures, instead. They've been standardized to contain the proper amounts of active ingredients.

For better sex, try one of the following natural enhancers. Select the one that best suits your needs. Give each preparation a few months to work. If you see no effect, try another.

GINKGO BILOBA

Ginkgo contains a variety of compounds that relax blood vessels and increase circulation to the brain and pelvic area.

For women, increased blood flow improves vaginal lubrication and sexual responsiveness.

For men, adequate blood flow is essential to achieve and sustain erections.

Typical dosage: *Capsules:* 40 mg to 60 mg of 24% standardized powdered extract three to four times daily. *Tincture:* 30 drops three to four times daily.

Side effects: Ginkgo may cause dizziness, headache or heart palpitations.

Caution: Ginkgo is a blood thinner and can increase the blood-thinning effects of aspirin and warfarin (Coumadin). Check with your physician before using ginkgo if you're taking either medication.

MUIRA PUAMA

Also known as "potency wood," this herb contains sterols and other compounds that boost levels of testosterone, a hormone that plays a critical role in sexual desire in women as well as men.

Muira puama also contains volatile oils, including camphor and beta-carophyllene. They're thought to restore sex drive by stimulating nerves in the brain's pleasure center.

Typical dosage: 250 mg three times daily in capsule form.

Side effect: Muira puama may lower blood pressure by as much as 10%. Check with your doctor before using this herb if you have low blood pressure (hypotension).

GINSENG

This herb is an "adaptogen," meaning it helps the body compensate for extended periods of stress. Stress can cause sexual desire and performance to plummet.

These compounds also improve blood flow to the penis, help tissues use oxygen more efficiently and boost production of testosterone in men and progesterone in women.

Typical dosage: *Capsules:* 10 mg to 50 mg one to three times daily. *Tincture:* 30 to 60 drops daily.

Side effect: Ginseng may cause diarrhea …high blood pressure…sleeplessness.

ASHWAGANDA

A member of the pepper family, this herb contains withanolides, substances that increase the activity of testosterone and progesterone. Ashwaganda also relieves stress and anxiety.

Typical dosage: *Capsules:* 1,000 mg once or twice daily. *Tincture:* 60 to 90 drops two or three times daily.

Side effects: Because ashwaganda has antianxiety properties, it should not be used by anyone taking medications to treat anxiety and/or depression. The herb could intensify the drugs' actions as well as their side effects. Ashwaganda may also trigger miscarriages.

ARGININE

Taken in supplement form, this amino acid has been shown to relax smooth muscle contractions. This boosts arterial dilation, bringing more blood to the pelvic area.

The body uses arginine to produce nitric oxide, a chemical needed to achieve erections. (Sildenafil works in part by making nitric oxide more readily available in the body.)

Typical dosage: 1,000 mg to 2,000 mg twice daily in capsule form. Take capsules between meals, since many foods contain lysine, an amino acid that counteracts arginine's effects.

Side effect: Don't take this herb if you get cold sores caused by the herpes simplex virus. Arginine stimulates viral replication.

FOR MEN ONLY

The herb *yohimbe* is approved by the FDA for treating impotence and low sex drive.

Yohimbe contains a compound called *yohimbine,* which helps dilate blood vessels in the penis. Most men who take yohimbe experience an increase in sexual desire within an hour.

Typical dosage: 15 mg to 25 mg daily in capsule form. Divide into several doses throughout the day to minimize side effects. Take smaller amounts at first—for example, 5 mg or 10 mg a day—then gradually increase the amount over several weeks.

Side effects: Elevated blood pressure, nausea, racing heart and anxiety. Use yohimbe only under medical supervision.

FOR WOMEN ONLY

The herb *dong quai* contains plant sterols that help correct estrogen deficiencies.

Studies suggest that dong quai can increase sexual desire as well as the intensity of orgasms.

Typical dosage: *Capsules:* 1,000 mg three to four times daily. *Tincture:* 45 to 60 drops two or three times daily.

Caution: Pregnant and lactating women should not use dong quai. The herb also increases sensitivity to sunlight.

Sex Therapy

Shirley Zussman, EdD, coeditor of the *Sex Over 40* newsletter and director of the Association for Male Sexual Dysfunction, New York City.

It isn't easy for couples who have sexual problems to seek out professional help. They're embarrassed. They believe that therapy takes years, costs more than they can afford and might not work. Sex therapy isn't cheap. But if you do have sexual difficulties with a loving partner, there's a good chance new techniques can help in a matter of a few months.

The most common problems: Lack of interest. Trouble with erections and orgasms. Pain, real or imaginary.

WHEN TO CONSIDER THERAPY

When the problem becomes so great that it jeopardizes the relationship and preoccupation with the problem becomes so overwhelming that work suffers and enjoyment of life wanes.

One spouse often knows instinctively when a problem reaches a critical point. When you say to yourself, "I can't go on like this anymore," you're usually telling the truth. *Especially dangerous to a relationship:* Trying to avoid the problem by drinking, abstaining from sex or turning to extramarital partners.

Another self-deception: Believing that only one partner has a problem. It may originate with the man or woman, but once one has a problem, both have a problem.

FINDING A THERAPIST

Since sex therapists are not licensed, anyone can claim the title. Occasionally unethical persons do. To find a reputable therapist, ask your physician or county medical society for a recommendation. The American Association of Sex Educators, Counselors, and Therapists (AASECT) publishes a directory of its members, for whom it sets education and training standards.

Most qualified therapists have degrees in a behavioral science (psychology, psychiatry) as well as training in sex therapy. Although sex therapy focuses primarily on sexual problems, a knowledge of psychology is essential because sexuality is so inextricably connected with total personality and life events.

Important first step: Get a medical examination to find out whether the problem is a physical one. Often it is, especially when the problem is pain during intercourse or difficulties during erection. If a sex therapist doesn't ask during the first visit whether you've had a medical exam or refer you for one, find another therapist.

FACTS AND MYTHS

In some states therapists often use a surrogate partner (a paid partner) during treatment. Someone experiencing sexual difficulties is taught how to overcome them during supervised foreplay and other sexual activities with the surrogate. But many therapists consider the use of a surrogate to be inappropriate.

If you're married, it's more effective to undergo therapy as a couple. *Reasons:* Since successful therapy may mean a change in sexual practices, your spouse will inevitably be involved. Moreover, many sexual difficulties, such as lack of interest and failure to be aroused, are often the result of a breakdown in communication between partners.

A typical session lasts one hour, and therapists usually recommend one session per week. Most difficulties can be successfully treated in three to six months.

Some people are helped significantly in a single session because they only think they have a problem. *Example:* A woman who fails to have an orgasm during sexual intercourse. Or a man who feels guilty when his partner fails to have an orgasm during intercourse. *The fact:* Most women do not have orgasms during intercourse.

EMOTIONAL REASONS FOR PROBLEMS

Lack of sexual interest, the most common problem, takes longer to treat. Therapists now recognize that although some declining interest is normal during a relationship, it's often aggravated by depression, stress or emotions that build up at home.

The new technique of sex therapists is to deal with these outside causes, with the specific goal of increasing sexual interest. The therapist may also recommend that a couple experiment at home with activities designed to heighten sexual interest. *Examples:* Different kinds of foreplay, verbal excitement, different positions during intercourse. Lack of interest often develops because a couple haven't been communicating their preferences in sexual activity to each other.

The most common mistake couples make is assuming that sex must always be spontaneous. Few things in life really are. Most couples don't think twice about making reservations at a restaurant, but they wince at the idea of scheduling sex. It works, say the therapists. And it's one of the simplest and most effective ways out of the problem.

Does Running Affect Sex?

Running can improve a man's sex life if he doesn't take it too seriously, according to recent surveys of runners. Those who clocked less than 35 miles a week reported increased sexual desire, more frequent sexual activity and greater sexual satisfaction. However, more than half the runners training for marathons and covering more than 35 miles a week admitted to sometimes feeling too tired for sex.

The Runner.

Heart Attacks Don't End Your Sex Life

Older heart attack and stroke victims can usually resume sexual activity in three to four months without risk. Doing so may actually reduce the chance of another attack.

Sexuality in Later Life.

Sensual Stimulation Misconception

A woman's breasts may not be erogenous. Alfred C. Kinsey found in his early sex studies that nearly half the women he interviewed were not sexually stimulated by having their breasts stroked. More recent studies have confirmed that women vary widely in the parts of their bodies that give them the greatest sexual satisfaction.

Michael Carrera, EdD, adjunct professor of community medicine, Mount Sinai Medical Center, New York City.

Delayed Desire

A minority of women feel their greatest sexual drive right before menstruation rather than midcycle. Doctors suggest both physical and psychological reasons. Physically, estrogen/progesterone stimulation may excite them. Psychologically, relief from worry about conception and an emotional need for affection may make them more open to sex.

Ewa Radwanska, MD, PhD, reproductive endocrinologist, writing in *Medical Aspects of Human Sexuality.*

Not Necessarily Dull

The missionary position for intercourse (woman on her back, man on top) doesn't deserve its reputation for being boring and staid. Some men and women can't reach orgasm any other way. It rarely causes anxiety, since most people are very used to it. It permits a lot of face-to-face, torso-to-torso contact. It gives many men an intense orgasm.

Sleeping After Sex

Sleep following sex comes much more quickly to men than to women. A woman's body takes longer than a man's to return to a nonaroused state (10 to 15 minutes). If a woman has had no orgasm, the problem of getting to sleep can be even worse. Studies show a strong correlation between sexual frustration and insomnia. *Solution:* Patience, communication and trust between sexual partners.

Samuel Dunkell, MD, director of the Insomnia Medical Services, New York City.

Orgasms Don't Mean Better Sleep

It's commonly believed that satisfactory sex with orgasm leads to better sleep for both partners. But a recent experiment did not prove this. The sleep of volunteers who deprived themselves of sex with their wives for one week was compared with the sleep of those same volunteers following sexual satiation. *Result:* No difference in the quality of sleep, nor in how rested each person felt on awakening. *Upshot:* There are widespread individual differences in responses to orgasm. Some people even feel more energetic after sex.

Charles Fisher, MD, writing in *Medical Aspects of Human Sexuality.*

Drugs Ease Painful Orgasms

Pelvic pain that radiates to the inner thigh, bladder or rectum in the period preceding and during orgasm is experienced by many older men. Their ejaculatory intensity diminishes, and the time required until the next orgasm increases (in some cases up to several days). Small doses of testosterone (via prescription pills or shots) are often effective.

Medical Aspects of Human Sexuality.

Headaches During Sex Can Be Treated

Orgasmic headaches are caused by sudden reduced blood flow to the brain during intercourse. They may be related to sudden sexual excitement or to outside factors such as extreme heat, drugs or alcohol. A history of migraine attacks frequently contributes.

Not related: Age or gender.

Pattern: Headaches usually don't occur often. Pain, which may be severe, lasts only a short time.

Preventive measures: Avoid alcohol and hot showers before intercourse. Take an aspirin an hour before sexual activity. Change sexual positions, or try an activity that produces less physical stress.

Important: See your doctor if orgasmic headaches occur often.

George W. Paulson, MD, professor emeritus of neurology and codirector of the Parkinson's Center of Excellence, Ohio State University College of Medicine & Public Health, Columbus.

Improve Sex During Menopause

Soy can be sexy for women going through menopause. Soy foods are full of natural plant estrogens. Eating three to four ounces of tofu daily—or drinking one cup of soy milk—can provide an estrogen boost that makes sex more pleasurable.

Julian Whitaker, MD, founder, Whitaker Wellness Institute, Newport Beach, CA, and author of *Shed Ten Years in Ten Weeks.* Diane Publishing Company.

Condoms Lessen VD Risk

Men who are exposed just once to a woman who has gonorrhea have a 22% to 40% chance of contracting the disease. But some men won't catch it even after repeated exposure.

Why: They have antigonococci organisms in their urethras or residual immunity from previous infections.

To decrease risk: Use a condom.

When Condoms Prevent Disease and When They Don't

Condoms offer protection against some venereal diseases (gonorrhea, nongonococcal urethritis and yeast infections). They are less effective against herpes, venereal warts and chlamydia, which are small enough to pass through the pores of the condom. Condoms do not offer 100% protection against HIV, but they greatly lower the risk of transmission. If either partner has an active urethral infection or genital lesion, the only safe course is sexual abstinence.

Michael Carrera, EdD, adjunct professor of community medicine, Mount Sinai Medical Center, New York City.

Contraceptive Update

New intrauterine devices (IUDs) are small. Some are impregnated with minute amounts of copper and progesterone to enhance efficiency. But they can still cause side effects, some serious.

Examples: Cramping, pelvic infection and painful intercourse.

Women who want children later in life are discouraged from using IUDs because in some cases they can lead to sterility.

International Fertility Research Program, Research Triangle Park, NC 27709, and the National Center for Health Statistics, Hyattsville, MD 20782.

Antibiotics That Defeat Birth-Control Pills

Women who use oral contraceptives should be aware that their effectiveness is lessened by some antibiotics. Contraceptive failure has been linked with tetracycline (Achromycin, Panmycin, Sumycin), ampicillin (Amcill, Omnipen, Pensyn), chloramphenicol (Chloromycetin), sulfamethoxypyridazine (Midicel) and rifampin (Rifamate, Rifadin, Rimactane).

Particularly susceptible: Low-dose estrogen contraceptives.

RN, 123 Tice Blvd., Woodcliff Lake, NJ 07677.

Best Ways to Boost Your Sexual Fitness

Robert N. Butler, MD, president, International Longevity Center (*www.ilcusa.org*), former chairman, department of geriatrics and adult development, Mount Sinai Medical Center, New York City. He is coauthor of *The New Love and Sex After 60.* Ballantine.

Everyone knows that some medical conditions, including diabetes and hormone deficiency, can cause sexual difficulties ranging from impotence to lack of desire. It's also well known that many drugs, including antidepressants and blood pressure drugs, often produce unwanted sexual side effects.

What few people realize is that a significant number of sexual difficulties are not linked to a medical condition or medication.* *For these cases, keeping your body fit—with proper diet, exercise and rest—is the best solution…*

EAT SMART

Excessive dietary fat and cholesterol produce artery-clogging plaque that not only increases your risk for heart attack and stroke but also restricts blood flow to the genitalia. This can hinder a man's ability to achieve or

*If you experience sexual difficulties, see your doctor for a thorough evaluation to rule out a treatable medical condition.

maintain an erection and may also possibly reduce vaginal and clitoral sensitivity in women.

Self-defense: Consume no more than 30% of your daily calories as fat. Avoid saturated fat and trans-fats (abundant in fried foods and commercially baked goods). Choose unsaturated fats, which can be found in olive and flaxseed oils, nuts and fish.

Warning: Overindulging in alcohol can dampen sexual appetite and diminish sexual performance. Although alcohol lowers inhibitions, it's known to depress physical arousal.

Eating until you're uncomfortably full can leave you feeling too bloated and sluggish for sex. To avoid unnecessarily straining the heart, it's advisable to postpone sex for a few hours following a heavy meal.

Heart attacks during sex are extremely uncommon. According to a study conducted at Harvard University, the risk for heart attack during sex among people who have coronary disease is 20 in one million.

GET MORE EXERCISE...

For the stamina and flexibility required to enjoy sex, you need to exercise. Brisk walking usually provides the best overall workout for people age 60 or older. Aim for 10,000 steps daily, five to six days a week (2,000 steps equals roughly one mile).

If that sounds daunting, consider that even relatively inactive adults average 3,500 steps a day. Simple changes—taking the stairs instead of the elevator or walking rather than driving to a store, for example—can add to that number substantially. That means a two- or three-mile walk may be all that's required to reach your overall goal.

...AND MORE SLEEP

At least half of all adults over age 50 suffer from sleep disturbances. Insomnia, illness, pain or frequent nighttime trips to the bathroom can interfere with sleep cycles, depriving you of sufficient rapid eye movement (REM) sleep—the kind associated with dreaming. Chronic sleep deprivation can leave you too exhausted for sex and may also lead to a deficiency of important hormones, including human growth hormone, which helps keep your body lean, fit and energized.

Important: After age 60, it's common to experience a sleep pattern that occurs when you fall asleep at dusk and awaken before dawn. This can disrupt your sex life, particularly if your partner maintains a traditional sleep schedule.

Fortunately, the problem can usually be reversed with regular sun exposure in the late-afternoon. Aim to get approximately 30 minutes of sun *without sunscreen* between 4 pm and 6 pm. This will not only correct sleep patterns, but also help prevent osteoporosis by triggering production of vitamin D in your skin.

Warning: Avoid unprotected sun exposure between 10 am and 2 pm, when harmful ultraviolet rays are most intense.

ADDITIONAL STRATEGIES

Improved nutrition, exercise and rest typically lead to more satisfying sex within a matter of weeks. *For more immediate results...*

• **Use visual, tactile stimulation.** Men, especially, are aroused by sexual images and touch. Turn down the lights and watch a steamy movie. Women may want to wear sexy lingerie. Share a gentle massage or engage in mutual stimulation.

• **Fantasize.** Imagining sexy scenarios can heighten arousal for both partners. Interestingly, however, one study showed that men's ability to fantasize may diminish with age. This may explain why men tend to rely on sexy pictures, videos and other visual aids.

• **Use lubricants.** Postmenopausal women, especially, may find their enjoyment of sex hampered by vaginal dryness. Water-based lubricants, such as Astroglide, can help. Oil-based lubricants may lead to vaginal infections.

• **Plan around arthritis pain.** A hot shower before sex can help reduce joint pain and stiffness. So can taking your pain medication 30 minutes before sex. If you suffer from osteoarthritis, try sex in the morning, before joints have a chance to stiffen or become inflamed. If you have rheumatoid arthritis, sex in the late afternoon or evening may be preferable, since symptoms often subside with activity.

• **Vary times and positions.** Don't get stuck in the rut of always having sex at night, in the missionary position. If you or your partner are too tired for sex at night, plan a morning or afternoon sex date. If one of you has a heart condition, hip or back pain, let that person take the bottom position, which requires less vigorous movement.

•**Practice seduction.** Good sex starts in the brain, which means it should begin hours before you actually arrive in the bedroom. Throughout the day, give your partner caresses, kisses and other outward signs of affection. Genuine intimacy is the best aphrodisiac.

Jockey Shorts Lower Sperm Counts

Athletic briefs may lower the sperm counts of men who wear them. The form-fitting underwear increases scrotal temperatures, which often leads to a reduction of sperm production. Men with impaired fertility sometimes try to avoid things that raise scrotal temperatures, such as hot baths.

Note: Even if the shorts lower sperm counts slightly, there is no evidence that they affect male fertility.

Stanley A. Brosman, MD, writing in *Medical Aspects of Human Sexuality.*

Sperm count is reduced by poor health but not by aging. A recent study showed that healthy men between 60 and 88 had higher counts, with comparable fertilizing capacity, than a group aged 24 to 37.

Journal of Clinical Endocrinology and Metabolism.

Women's Infertility Can Be Predicted

Infertility in women can now be predicted with 95% certainty by chemical analysis, tests and a physical exam.

Point: A woman need not have a baby just to see if she can. When the tests determine her childbearing status, she and her husband are then free to delay having children if they decide to do so.

Stanley T. West, MD, chief, division of reproductive endocrinology and infertility, St. Vincent's Hospital and Medical Center, New York City.

Surprising Cause of Infertility

Infertility in men is often caused by varicocele, an enlarged vein in the testicles.

Corrective procedure: A varicocelectomy. Done with local anesthetic, sometimes on an outpatient basis, the operation ties off the enlarged vein to reroute the blood flow.

Result: About 70% recovery rate (men able to impregnate their wives).

No one knows why this vein causes infertility. But it can affect the fertility of men in their 30s and 40s who were fertile in their 20s.

Everything You Could Want to Know About Sperm Banks

Sperm banks store human semen in deep freeze for future use in artificial insemination. Today sperm banks create possibilities for family planning unimagined 20 years ago.

One in seven married couples in the United States is infertile. These couples, as well as single women who want to have children, can turn to a sperm bank for semen from an anonymous donor. The world's largest sperm bank pays its donors (often medical students) $25 for each specimen deposited. It charges its clients $200 to $425 plus packing and shipping for each specimen ordered. A woman may need to be inseminated several times before a pregnancy results.

For those considering artificial insemination, the first step is selecting a doctor they really trust. The doctor then coordinates with the sperm bank and performs the artificial insemination. Some sperm banks are not subject to federal regulation, and state laws vary widely. Since many physicians are unaware of the disparity between various facilities, it is important to know what to look for in a sperm bank.

Does the bank have a full-time medical director, and is he a pathologist?

Is there an affiliation with a university or hospital?

Is the bank a member of the American Association of Tissue Banks? Does it follow the recommendations of the association's Reproductive Council?

How are the donors screened? A complete physical description, personal and genetic histories, medical evaluation and laboratory analysis of the semen should be standard. The donor should be tested for such things as genetic disorders, damage resulting from environmental conditions, diseases such as AIDS and hepatitis, and sperm count and motility (ability to move). Some sperm banks subject a donor's semen to more than 40 different tests, far more than the average blood donor would undergo.

Will you or your doctor receive a detailed description of the donor, including general information about his education, background and interests? Some banks supply only limited information that is of questionable accuracy.

Although donor anonymity should be scrupulously maintained, is there a coding system that allows you to see whether sperm from the same donor will be available if you decide to have a second child?

What is the bank's minimum acceptable sperm count? The average American sperm count is just over 50 million motile sperm per milliliter. Banks vary in their criteria, and donor sperm may contain from 65 million to more than 100 million sperm per milliliter.

Some men arrange for long-term storage of semen before a vasectomy, chemotherapy, exposure to hazardous waste or numerous other situations. Essentially, they are purchasing fertility insurance, putting aside a deposit of sperm on the chance that they may want to father a child at a time when they are no longer fertile. Pregnancies have resulted from sperm that was stored for more than 20 years.

A complete deposit of three to five cubic centimeters of semen may take two to three days of abstinence to accumulate.

Abortion Is Safer Than Childbirth

Legal abortion is safer for women than childbirth, according to new studies. Death rates after elective abortion have fallen to .8 per 100,000, while maternal death rates run 7.5 per 100,000 live births. Abortions are safest for women 19 or younger and most risky for those over 35.

Journal of the American Medical Association.

Vaginal Delivery Is Possible After A Caesarean

Caesarean deliveries need not necessarily be repeated for subsequent births. New guidelines adopted by the American College of Obstetricians and Gynecologists give conditions for allowing women to choose vaginal delivery after an earlier Caesarean. *Among them:* A low transverse type of incision in the earlier operation. A single fetus with head-first presentation, weighing less than eight pounds. A delivery room with equipment to monitor fetal heart rate and the uterus. Nonrepeating reasons for the earlier surgical delivery. However, in case of difficulties, the mother may have to have another Caesarean.

Choosing the Sex of Your Child

When nature takes its course, slightly more than half of all newborns are male. Now, parents have new ways to tip the odds in favor of one sex or the other. The new methods, however, have still not received the full support of the medical establishment chiefly because it is not known how effective they are and due to ethical concerns.

For couples who want to increase the chances of having a boy, Dr. Ronald Ericsson, a former Western Michigan University professor of reproductive physiology, has developed a means of separating sperm bearing the Y, or male, chromosome, and then using artificial insemination.

IMPROVING THE ODDS

According to Ericsson, the odds of having a boy are improved to about 75% to 80%. Recent tests by licensed sperm centers have confirmed these odds. Ericsson's company, Gametrics Ltd., has licensed approximately 50 centers in the US and worldwide to use the procedure.

Dr. Ervin Nichols of the American College of Obstetricians and Gynecologists says that controlled studies have not yet been performed in sufficiently large numbers to make certain the procedure is really effective.

Ericsson's organization is currently conducting clinical trials on a method that seems to put the odds of having a girl at about 73% to 75%. *How it works:* The procedure is the same as the artificial-insemination process for boys, except that the mother takes Clomid (clomiphene citrate), a drug used for many years to enhance fertility.

Less certain method: For some reason, women who are artificially inseminated with isolated sperm after taking Clomid have a disproportionate number of girls.

Home methods that rely on the timing of intercourse and changing the chemical environment of the vagina to increase odds for either a boy or a girl are rejected by the medical community as ineffective.

Example: Planning intercourse at the time of ovulation and douching with an alkaline solution to increase the chances of conceiving a boy.

COUPLES WHO USE SEX SELECTION

- **Women in their early 30s.**
- **Those who have more than two children.**
- **Those who have children all of one sex** and want one of the opposite sex.
- **Those who use sex selection to complete their family**—not to start a family.

Is Exercise an Aphrodisiac?

Researchers and common sense have long held that exercise enhances health and makes people feel better about themselves and their bodies. This in turn makes them more sexually attractive and responsive. Now studies are suggesting that exercise is a potent stimulus to hormone production in both men and women. It may, in fact, chemically increase basic libido by stepping up the levels of such hormones as testosterone.

Whole Body Healing by Carl Lowe and Jim Nechas. Rodale Press.

Men and Women Are Jealous for Different Reasons

Women are more threatened by the physical attractiveness of other women... men, by the possibility that another man is a better lover. Women focus more on the emotional involvement of a spouse with someone else...men, on sexual involvement.

Surviving Infidelity, coauthored by Rona Subotnik, licensed marriage/family counselor, San Diego. Adams Media Corp.

3

Family Smarts

How to Make Better Friends and Be More Influential

 Many people complain that it's harder than ever to make friends. And they're right. *Reason:* There are fewer opportunities for people to meet and interact.

Many of us spend our days involved with machines rather than people. We work with computers and go home and sit in front of the television.

Result: The time we spend with people is diminished and so are the opportunities to practice relating to others.

Also, our society has become more fast-paced. This means people have less time to get to know one another.

Example: In Nebraska where I grew up, people who first met would spend some time "rolling the cob." The term describes the way Nebraska farmers would sit around rolling a corncob under their feet and just talking about unimportant things. It was a way to slowly get to know the other person and develop a friendship.

People no longer have time for such a slow, easygoing process.

Sign of the times: At one time people handled disagreements by getting together and talking things out. Today they are more apt to hire lawyers to settle disputes, creating a litigious society that is costing us a fortune. In addition to all the *new* reasons that make it tough to make friends, the *old* reasons still apply.

Many people have trouble making friends because they're shy and think they shouldn't impose themselves on others. They feel standoffish, reluctant to push themselves forward to meet and get to know people.

Trap: We all have a *comfort zone*—an area in which it's relatively easy for us to relate to other people. This area is made up of people we

J. Oliver Crom, former president, Dale Carnegie & Associates, Inc., 290 Motor Parkway, Hauppauge, NY 11788. The company was founded by Dale Carnegie, pioneer of the self-development movement and author of *How to Win Friends and Influence People.* Simon & Schuster.

already know—our families, colleagues in business, old friends. Anything that forces us to move beyond that area causes discomfort and fear.

Example: At a meeting or party, most people immediately look around for someone they know to chat with rather than walk up to someone new and introduce themselves.

Although making friends and maintaining friendships involve a variety of skills, there are a few basics that anyone can follow...

•**Overcome shyness.** A big part of shyness is a lack of self-confidence. Before you can accept new friends, you have to learn to accept yourself. This calls for self-awareness—knowing both your strengths and your weaknesses and accepting them all.

Once you realize that you're a whole person—and that other people also feel awkward and unsure of themselves—it will be easier for you to make the first move. Inside everyone there's a confident, friendly person who wants to get out.

•**Banish fear.** Millions of people are more afraid of speaking to a group than they are of dying. *Reason:* They're sure they will only embarrass themselves or appear foolish.

But most people discover that once they stand up to address a group—or approach someone new to start a conversation—it isn't horrible or embarrassing at all.

What we really fear is the unknown. The way to overcome that fear is by doing the thing that scares you and keep doing it.

•**Broaden your thinking.** We all have a tendency toward pigeonhole thinking—applying what we know to just one part of our lives. But most of our skills can be used in different aspects of our lives.

Example: Many people take courses in order to enhance their public speaking skills. They're surprised to discover that what they learn also helps them to get along better with people.

The following tips on how to make friends come from Dale Carnegie's book, *How to Win Friends and Influence People*...

•**Don't criticize, condemn or complain.**

•**Give honest, sincere appreciation.**

•**Arouse in the other person an eager want.**

•**Become genuinely interested in other people.**

•**Smile.**

•**Remember that a person's name is to that person the sweetest and most important sound in any language.**

•**Be a good listener.** Encourage others to talk about themselves.

•**Talk in terms of the other person's interests.**

•**Make the other person feel important**—and do it *sincerely.*

June Marriages

June is still the favorite month of 12.3% of brides marrying for the first time. Among women remarrying, 10.2% choose July and another 10.2% choose December. *Most popular day:* Saturday (53%). *Least popular day:* Wednesday (4.2%). Religious ceremonies are chosen by 80% of first-time brides but by only 60% of women who are remarrying.

Put a Little Fun Into Your Marriage

Life is difficult—marriage even more so. To have a successful marriage, make sure you keep some fun in your marriage. Here are some ideas for you. But the possibilities are, of course, endless, and they are limited only by your loving imagination.

•**Start a scrapbook.** It helps you to relive the happy moments of your life together.

•**Buy a bulletin board.** Keep it in the kitchen or another room so you can leave funny and/or meaningful messages each day.

•**Serve each other breakfast in bed.** On odd Sundays, it's your turn...even Sundays, your mate's.

- **Buy a treat a day, large or small,** but with a light touch. *Examples:* Kiwi, a little American caviar, a red rose, some champagne, a trinket, a funny sign.

- **Make your home beautiful.** It should be a place that is fun to return to each night and to be in together away from the harsh world.

- **Buy something special for your house** that you can both enjoy. *Examples:* A piano, a video recorder.

- **Use satin sheets.** They are a treat for special occasions.

- **Make yourself look as good as possible.** Stay slim, trim and well-groomed.

- **Read aloud to each other.**

- **Buy subscriptions to your local theater group.** Go together or with close friends.

- **Enjoy sports together.**

- **Do things for each other.** *Examples:* Cut each other's hair, give each other massages, take care of each other's needs.

- **Start a hobby together,** such as collecting stamps or autographs.

- **Go to dancing school.** Learn special, fun dance steps that you can practice together.

- **Throw a big party** for your friends for absolutely no reason at all.

- **Plan a really special trip** in the coming year. Have fun planning it together.

- **Enjoy television together.** Subscribe to cable TV and see games and movies together.

- **Plan a treat a week.** One week, it's your treat…the other week, your mate's.

- **Buy a hot tub.**

- **Say nice things to each other.** See who can give the best and most compliments.

- **Make a ritual of dinner.** Replace paper napkins with linen napkins. Use sterling silver, fine china and candles. Drink good wine.

- **Become involved in community affairs together.**

- **Join a health club together** and work out daily.

- **Take a shower together.** It has great potential.

- **Allow plenty of time** for each partner to "do his or her own thing" alone.

Strategies for Feisty Couples

James L. Creighton, PhD, a psychologist in Los Gatos, CA, who specializes in conflict resolution. He is author of *How Loving Couples Fight* (Aslan Publishing) and coauthor of *Getting Well Again* (Bantam).

It is a myth that happy couples never fight. In fact, many happy couples regularly disagree with each other.

What sets loving couples apart is that they disagree in loving ways. They don't let disagreements turn into nasty battles. And their "fights" strengthen, rather than hurt, their relationships.

Handling conflict in a healthy way is a skill that can be learned.

ACCEPT CONFLICT AS NORMAL

Trying to ignore disagreements or bury resentments doesn't get rid of them. It only allows them to grow below the surface. When we face conflict and deal with it openly, it's easier to let it go and move on. *Steps to take…*

- **Express what you *feel,* not what you think.** Couples who fight lovingly start by talking about how they feel, not about what they think is "wrong" with their partner.

They frame arguments by saying, "I'm hurt/angry/frustrated" rather than, "You're rude/sloppy/a jerk."

When one spouse does something that bothers the other, he or she says so *immediately.* But he describes the specific behavior —not his interpretation.

Example: "I was upset when you didn't return my call" expresses how the person feels. "I'm mad because you're inconsiderate" expresses what the person thinks.

It's tempting to blame your negative feelings on the other person's inadequacies. Resist this urge.

Attacking or accusing may make you feel temporarily powerful. But it erodes trust, creating emotional fallout that is very difficult to clean up.

- **Listen—rather than talk**—your way out of conflict. When someone is upset, the natural reaction is to try to talk him out of it. We do this by making excuses for the person…or trying to come up with solutions to the problem…or pointing out all the reasons why there's no need to be upset. But this response implies that the other person doesn't have a right to his feelings. So talking often makes matters worse.

In reality, all it takes to stop the person from being angry is to acknowledge how he feels.

Key to effective listening: After your partner has finished speaking, summarize the feelings and ideas that were just expressed. Don't evaluate whether those words are right or wrong…and don't try to "fix" anything. Just repeat what you've heard.

When you're first learning this technique, it can feel artificial or even patronizing—but it works very effectively.

Many of the couples I work with get around this by using the *five-minute rule*. Either partner can invoke this rule at any time.

How it works: One person has five minutes to speak without interruption. Then the other person has five minutes. If you can't decide who should start, flip a coin. Sometimes you both may need *another* turn to speak.

By the end of the second round, both people have usually gotten most of their frustration out of the way and can start discussing the problem more constructively.

FIGHT FAIRLY

Happy couples follow several unspoken rules that keep their small arguments from escalating into big ones…

•**Stick to the issue.** If he's mad because she's not ready to leave at the agreed-upon time, that's the subject the loving couple talks about.

They don't get sidetracked by accusations, such as, "You don't care how I feel" or, "One of us has to live in the real world."

They also don't keep bringing up past grievances. If an issue keeps coming up over and over, they'll talk about it—but not as a way of punishing each other when they're arguing about something else.

•**Don't hit below the belt.** Loving couples don't try to hurt each other by attacking sensitive areas, such as weight, job status, etc.

•**Don't drag other people into it.** Don't say things such as, "I'm not the only person who feels this way. Your sister and brother do, too."

Trying to bolster your side of the argument by bringing up someone else not only escalates the fight but also poisons your partner's relationship with that person.

Some couples find it helpful to make these rules explicit—and remind each other gently if one of them breaks a rule.

Don't turn these reminders into occasions to gloat. A simple reminder, such as, "Remember, we agreed not to do that" usually is enough.

Important: The best time to agree on rules is right after a fight, when you've cooled down enough to talk reasonably. The memory of the fight you just had—and how unpleasant it was not to be following the rules—will motivate you to do things differently.

HUDDLE TO SOLVE PROBLEMS

Sometimes just hearing each other out helps partners understand one another's point of view—and resolves the conflict. When that's not enough, happy couples work together to find a better way of dealing with the issue. *Problem-solving steps…*

•**Agree on what the problem is.**

•**Brainstorm alternative solutions.**

•**Agree on a solution that best meets your needs and those of your partner.**

•**Agree on a way to put the solution into practice.**

•**Evaluate how well the solution is working.**

If Your Spouse Returns to School

A spouse's return to school tests a marriage. The student develops new friendships or starts to regard the partner as an intellectual inferior. To make the process easier, enlist your mate's support before enrolling. Agree in advance to share household chores. Don't let all conversations center around school. Develop new activities with your partner to establish a fresh common ground. To keep your sex life healthy, set aside unbreakable dates for time alone together.

Internet "Affairs" and Your Marriage

Internet "affairs" can wreck a marriage—even if the people communicating over the Internet never actually meet. Internet relationships often begin in chat rooms or as E-mail on topics of professional or personal interest.

Trap: People you have not met face to face can be anything you want them to be. It's easy for those fantasies projected on them to seem better than reality—and they can wreak havoc on a marriage.

Danger signs: If you start to have romantic feelings about the person—or begin thinking that the person understands you better than anyone else.

Helpful: Consider counseling to help you understand the needs the cyber-relationship has been filling.

Betsy S. Stone, PhD, psychologist in private practice, Stamford, CT.

How to Avoid Divorce

Clifford J. Sager, MD, psychiatrist and psychologist in private practice in New York City.

If one or both partners have definitely decided to get a divorce, there's usually no stopping them. If they are ambivalent, they should spend at least as much time considering the question of divorce as they did that of marriage. (If the courtship took a year, they should spend a year trying to stay together.) It's wise to get counseling or therapy if help is needed.

Two households can't be supported on the same amount of money and in the same style as one household.

Children may have problems at the beginning, but if the situation is handled well, the impact that divorce has on children can be minimized. *Important:* Parents should not denigrate each other or use their children as go-betweens. Both must give them time, attention and emotional support.

SYMPTOMS OF A TROUBLED MARRIAGE

Poor communication: Possibly due to lack of intimacy, of a sense of closeness, of being able to talk, of really being heard when you do talk, loss of sexual desire and a sense of not being understood.

Sexual infidelity: This is no longer a common cause of divorce, but often it is a sign that something is wrong with the relationship. Today people are more likely to accept some degree of infidelity. But it is always a sign of trouble in a previously monogamous relationship.

Children: Increasing use of children in struggles between adults.

Some people fail to make the shift from short- to long-term bonding. Short-term bonding is the initial period of being intensely in love. The partner isn't seen realistically. There is a strong sexual attraction and a desire to be with the loved one as much as possible. In long-term bonding, love is no longer a "sickness" but a more quietly satisfying feeling of caring and wanting to build together. The other person is seen more realistically and deficiencies are accepted. Some of the passion wears off, but it can be reawakened from time to time.

Motivation: You have to want to progress to long-term bonding and to accept the other person despite some shortcomings. It takes a lot of work to solve the problems of communication. For instance, you must want to communicate.

Example: A couple with an infidelity problem has to realize where they are in the short-term/long-term cycle. People who have to be intensely in love all the time go from one short-term relationship to another to get their "fix." Do they want to change? Although anger is a common cause of outside affairs, there are people who need them. They may say, "I'm not taking anything away from you. This is the way I am." If the spouse can truly accept it, fine. But if the infidelity is sadly tolerated, the prospects for the marriage are poor.

First step in finding a solution: Once you know why things aren't working out, ask yourself whether you are contributing to the problem. It's easy to see what your spouse is doing wrong, but what are you doing that you should consider changing?

MOST LIKELY TO SUCCEED

Maturity: The best candidates for staying together (or for getting divorced) are the most mature. They know their own minds and are realistic in their expectations.

Good complementariness: The partners meet each other's emotional needs and dove-tail well.

Mutual respect: The ability to compromise on both practical and emotional levels is necessary. *Example:* "I don't mind your being dependent on me at times because it's not that onerous. And when we're at a party, you always make sure I'm having a good time and not standing by myself." Some couples berate each other about personality traits they don't like. But not being able to lovingly accept such characteristics spells trouble.

Stay Friendly with In-Laws After the Divorce

To remain friendly with in-laws after the divorce, allow a cooling-off period before making contact. Then don't hesitate to make the first move. Get the approval of the family member who carries the most weight. Call a family meeting to bring resentments out into the open. Don't force your in-laws to take sides. Behave with them as you always have. Be patient—time is on your side. *Important:* Remember that your in-laws are your children's grandparents. Children need to be reassured that they won't lose other family members in the wake of a divorce.

How to Avoid the Alimony Trap

Lenard Marlow, JD, a divorce mediator practicing in New York, and founder of Divorce Mediation Professionals, one of the oldest divorce-mediation facilities in the US. He is the author of *The Two Roads to Divorce.* Xlibris Corp.

When a married couple finally decides to call it quits, both spouses usually feel a profound sense of failure and loss. Then the divorce proceedings begin, often bringing with them increasing levels of stress and anger that only make an already emotionally difficult situation worse.

But not every divorce has to be expensive or painful. In fact, a divorce can be mediated for less than what a divorce attorney charges.

AVOID HIRING SEPARATE LAWYERS

Divorce is not a legal problem. It is a personal problem with certain legal implications. The purpose of the divorce proceedings is to get it done, not to seek revenge.

The problem with hiring separate attorneys is that our legal system, by its very nature, is adversarial. Once put into motion, divorce proceedings take on a life of their own, usually at great financial and emotional cost to both parties.

How it works: Each attorney tries to get as much as possible for his/her client. A couple may believe they have hired two lawyers to negotiate a settlement, but negotiations do not begin for several months, to allow for "discovery" of financial conditions, often entailing "his and her" accountants, appraisers and auditors.

Trap: During this period, attorneys file orders of support and various motions that usually cause additional hurt and anger between the divorcing couple.

Inevitably, couples are swept into scenarios of distrust, pettiness, resentment and greed that are no longer within their control. Because both spouses usually have unrealistic expectations, the result is usually a settlement neither party feels is fair.

THE BENEFITS OF A MEDIATOR

Most divorcing couples can't communicate productively on their own. But given proper help, most divorcing couples are capable of deciding how to distribute their property and support their children, just as they did during marriage.

A professional mediator meets with both parties together. One spouse is never pitted against the other. The effort is to negotiate a fair settlement. *Benefits...*

• **Speed.** A mediator generally meets with a couple weekly. After about five to seven meetings, the parties reach the point at which an agreement can be drafted. Most divorce lawyers, on the other hand, don't even have their first meeting with each other in the first two months, while they are collecting information.

• **Cost.** Cost is a function of speed and complexity. The combined fee for a mediated agreement is usually less than the retainer that one spouse would have to pay just to initiate an adversarial proceeding, which is usually a fraction of the final fee.

All of a mediator's time is spent working out an agreement, while divorce lawyers spend much of their time filing and responding to pleas and motions.

• **Professionalism.** A mediator will inform the divorcing couple of all financial and child-custody issues and possible outcomes. These must be reviewed openly and provided for in the agreement. The mediator will also help the couple overcome impasses in their negotiations without needlessly pressuring either party.

Divorce lawyers, meanwhile, tend to overlook issues they believe may be detrimental to their own client.

• **Fairness.** The world of divorce is not different from the world of marriage—not everything is "fair." But two people who have worked to reach an agreement that both parties can live with feel far more satisfied with its fairness than a couple told by a judge how to conduct their affairs.

• **Closure.** *Divorce attorneys have a saying:* "Divorce never ends." That's because a drawn-out, acrimonious divorce can create painful repercussions far into the future—and take unresolved issues into subsequent marriages.

Mediators can help allow divorcing spouses to put the past behind them. A mediated divorce offers people a better chance to start anew.

How to find a mediator: Contact the Association for Conflict Resolution at 202-464-9700, 5151 Wisconsin Ave. NW, Washington, DC 20016, *www.acrnet.org*. You can also find a referral to mediators on the Web site, *www.mediate.com*. Or check your local *Yellow Pages* under "Mediation Services."

About half of all divorce mediators are therapists with expertise in matrimonial law and child custody. This is important only insofar as it applies to your particular needs.

Examples: If you have a complicated estate to distribute, you may prefer an attorney. If your primary struggle is over the kids, you may prefer a child-custody expert.

Note for couples beginning or in the midst of divorce proceedings: Couples may consult a mediator at any time during the divorce process, even if one or both spouses has already retained an attorney. But a mediated divorce is likely to be more complicated and time-consuming if lawyers are involved.

Single Parenting

Girls raised by their mothers without a father are stronger and more independent than those who are brought up in two-parent households. *Key:* Most children act the way their parents expect them to act. If a mother wants her daughter to be strong and independent, the daughter will develop these traits. *Insight:* Fathers often encourage their daughters to exhibit so-called feminine behavior. Daughters learn to act that way to please fathers rather than to emulate feminine mothers. *Role in society of a woman raised by a mother:* She is at no greater disadvantage in her relationships with men as any other woman.

Single parenting produces boys who are just as masculine and girls who are just as feminine as those in two-parent families. *Scholastic levels:* In the long run, both sexes do well after initial difficulties when parents separate.

Kathryn Black, PhD, professor emeritus of psychology, Purdue University.

How to Be a Good Stepparent

Barbara C. Freedman, CSW, director of the Divorce and Remarriage Counseling Center, New York.

Both partners in a remarriage usually have unrealistic expectations about their roles in the new marriage. As parents they are not prepared for the problems they will have to face when they get their collective children together through various custody and visitation arrangements. The children, of course, are not prepared for difficulties either.

Some people sail through the transition period, but for most there are many fantasies that can cause trouble. *Examples...*

• **Children expect the new parent to replace a deceased parent** or to provide something their custodial parent doesn't.

• **A stepparent who has never had children anticipates becoming an ideal mother** or father with an instant family.

• **Parents who have failed with their own children think they have a second chance.** But they may not really understand what the failure was about in the first place, and they often end up making similar mistakes.

It is not easy to adapt to new roles in the stepfamily. *Here are some of the problems that can arise...*

• **Children vie for seniority.** A girl who has been the oldest in one family finds that she is now number two or three. *Result:* Rivalry, jealousy, hurt feelings. The role of the new stepfather becomes difficult, too. He is sought after by all the children, which causes conflict between his loyalty to his own children and the need to relate to the stepchild.

• **Blood ties versus nonblood ties.** It is always more difficult to love, or even to get along with, someone else's children. A parent tolerates more inconvenience and conflict from a natural child than from a stepchild and suffers from feelings of guilt and hostility.

• **Differences in parenting style.** Watching one's spouse cope with a child in a way that you do not approve of can exacerbate an already tender situation. *Example:* A man who had long-standing problems with his adolescent son married a woman he thought would take care of these problems. She didn't consider it her role to be the disciplinarian. As she watched her husband tolerate abuse from his son, she began to lose respect for him.

Marriage and parenting are skills that one learns from parents. You blunder along, imitating or rejecting their behavior. But most people never had any role models for stepparenting. *Useful guidelines...*

• **New rules.** Families have different rules of conduct. Some rules have to be negotiated between the parents. It is helpful to establish times for the family to get together to work on decisions in which the children can be included.

• **Love is not instant.** While it is important for members of the family to be considerate and to allow one another space for self-expression, the pressure to love a new family can cause guilt and hurt feelings. Someday you may learn to love stepchildren, and they may learn to love you—but not necessarily.

• **Respect old ties.** A new stepfamily has many complicated connections with relatives. A natural parent and child have a unique relationship that may never be duplicated by stepparent and stepchild. People should not feel that a new family has to do everything as a group. Allow children time to be alone with natural parents, grandparents or other relatives.

• **Coparenting.** The basis for any successful remarriage is for ex-spouses to be as considerate of the children as possible. Conflicts between parents should be dealt with by them. Children should not feel they are included in these problems.

• **Divided loyalties.** Even the best stepparent can feel hostility from a stepchild for reasons that have nothing to do with the stepparent. It may arise from the child's feeling that the natural parent won't approve if he/she likes the new stepparent.

• **Children can love more than two adults as parents.** It's an enriching experience for a child to have more than two parents, two sets of grandparents, etc. The natural family should understand that it may be better for the child to develop a close relationship with someone in the stepfamily. Both sides should stand back and let children choose whom they want to love.

• **The couple relationship is primary.** This is the core of the new family unit despite the fact that each partner comes in with strong loyalties to their family of origin. Children have to know that the new couple is an unshakable combination and cannot be broken up (which they often try to do in order to get their own parents back together again). Seeing that the partners love and respect each other is an important role model.

• **Discipline.** You cannot discipline even your natural children unless you have a good relationship. It may take a year or two before this happens with stepchildren. In the meantime, the natural parent should be the disciplinarian for natural children. The authority of an absent natural parent should be vested in the stepparent. This must be made clear to the children.

• **Ironing out discipline policy.** Parents should discuss priorities and compromises. If they can't work out their differences, they should look into getting professional help.

To keep things in proper perspective, observe before acting. Then step in and do what you can. But don't expect too much. The romantic ideal of the nuclear family was never true, despite some ideal moments. It is the same with a stepfamily. There will be some wonderful times, but you should be prepared for the pain as well.

Skillful Parenting Pays Off

John Gottman, PhD, professor emeritus of psychology at the University of Washington and cofounder of the Gottman Institute, both in Seattle. He is author of *The Heart of Parenting: Raising an Emotionally Intelligent Child.* Simon & Schuster.

Many parents think of their children's intelligence in terms of academic achievement. While grades are important, so is a child's emotional intelligence —the ability to understand feelings and express those feelings appropriately.

Your child's emotional intelligence is critical because his/her ability to navigate the world of emotions determines success in all relationships with family, classmates and teachers—and later in adult life.

After conducting two 10-year studies of more than 120 families, I've concluded that there are five significant steps that parents can use to coach children to be more emotionally intelligent…

• **Recognize your child's emotions.** Many parents are keen observers of their children's behavior, but they don't always detect the emotions that are behind the behavior.

Example: If a child is scribbling on the walls or grabbing toys from another child, it's natural to focus on curbing the misbehavior.

But look as closely at the *why* as the *what.* Why is the child upset? Why is he angry?

Even when no misbehavior is involved, it's important to notice low-intensity emotions— such as sadness when a toy breaks—before they escalate into problems.

Helpful: To become more attuned to a child's feelings, parents need to be more aware of their own emotions first.

Think about how you handle worry…sadness…anger…and fear.

Are you temperamentally intense—or more easygoing? As you think about, and become more aware of, your emotional reactions, you'll be better able to decode your child's feelings and behavior.

• **See your child's emotions as opportunities for intimacy and teaching.** View a child's negative emotions as a chance to bond and teach, and you can turn negative situations into positive interactions.

By viewing behavior differently, children's anger, sadness and fear become more than just a reflection on you and your parenting style.

Helpful: When children are upset, comfort them and listen…and talk about how they feel rather than immediately moving to discipline them. This type of reaction lets children know they are understood, loved and valued.

Like coaching an athletic skill, our concern gives children a chance to practice how to express emotions and solve problems each time an occasion arises.

• **Listen carefully.** Listening means more than passively collecting information through your ears. It means tuning in to the child's current emotions by paying attention to his body language and facial expressions as well as to his words.

Then you're ready to see the situation from his perspective, and you can reflect his emotions back to him in soothing, noncritical words.

Example: At first, your responses may be a brief "Ummm,"…"Okay"…or "I see." But as you draw out your children, you can better assess their emotional situations.

You can also acknowledge their feelings by giving those feelings their proper names— "Sounds like you're anxious about…" or "You seem to be a little timid. Why?"

This part of emotional coaching shows your children that it is acceptable to feel the way they do…that you're interested enough to listen patiently…and that you believe they are able to cope.

By listening carefully, you also have refrained from jumping in with a ready-made solution. You haven't minimized or contradicted your children's genuine feelings by saying, "Don't feel bad. It will be all right if you…"

Instead, you have given your children a chance to express their emotions and, in the process, search for their own solutions to the problems at hand.

• **Help your children find words to name their emotions.** Words have power. When you help your children label their feelings, you give them some control of those feelings.

Naming emotions helps a child transform a scary or vague feeling into something real that can be defined and is normal.

Example: To a young child, jealousy may be an indistinct, unpleasant feeling. The child knows he doesn't like the fact that other children are being called on in school. But he hasn't yet reached the developmental milestone of abstract thinking, so he cannot identify his uncomfortable feeling.

If we use the term *jealousy* to name it, he learns that the amorphous feeling he has whenever other children are given special attention in class is acceptable. The feeling has a name. Other people know about it, and it's fine to feel that way.

Simply naming emotions will have a calming effect on children when they're upset.

By knowing and using the names of their feelings, they can learn to soothe themselves. Kids who learn this early in life are more likely to concentrate better, achieve more in school, enjoy good health and have better relationships with their peers.

Remember that children, like adults, experience mixed emotions. Children, however, don't know that unless we teach them.

Example: A child who is about to go off to camp may feel both proud of his independence and fearful that he'll be homesick. Parents can guide him by exploring his range of emotions and reassuring him that it's normal to feel two or more emotions at the same time.

• **Set limits on behavior** as you explore strategies to solve problems. If the emotion-of-the-moment is anger and the behavior is bopping a sibling on the head with a ball, you need to let the angry child know that hitting is absolutely unacceptable but feeling angry is acceptable.

Strategy: You might say, "Hitting isn't allowed," as you take the child away from the sibling. "I see you're pretty angry at Johnny, but you cannot hit people. Can you tell me why you're so mad at him? Maybe you would like to draw an angry picture to show me how you feel?"

Help your child try to find his own method of expressing emotions in acceptable ways.

Strict vs. Lenient Parenting

In a follow-up look at a group of adults whose mothers had been interviewed on parenting practices when the children were five years old, two patterns emerged.

The children who had been subjected to the strictest feeding schedules and toilet training had the highest need to achieve as adults.

The youngsters whose mothers were most permissive about sex and aggression (allowing masturbation and fighting with siblings, for example) showed the highest need for power as adults.

Practices the researchers expected to relate to adult characteristics did not show clear correlation in the study. How warm the mother was with the infant or how long the child was breast-fed, long assumed to be important to a child's well-being, did not match up directly with specific adult traits.

Study by psychologist David McClelland, Harvard University, reported in *Journal of Personality and Social Psychology*.

Encourage Expressiveness In Children

Fear of public speaking begins early. Parents may unwittingly make children feel foolish when they speak.

Helpful: Ask for children's opinions even when they are very young. Let them express negative as well as positive opinions. Avoid correcting or enlarging on everything they say. Encourage discussions at dinner. Tape-record children, and offer suggestions as they mature.

Clarissa Whitney, speech instructor, Santa Ana College, CA, quoted in *The Toastmaster*.

Temper Tantrums

A child's temper tantrum is best handled by simply walking away. This usually stops the display, as the child grows bored without the attention. Realize that tantrums are part of the process by which toddlers declare their individuality. Tantrums usually occur when the child is tired. Don't rush to the child and try to soothe him/her. This may make you feel better in front of onlookers, but it doesn't help. Don't automatically accept blame for the problem. Don't berate the youngster.

Best: Let the storm pass. Allow the child to have a nap, and don't mention the incident later.

Dennis Allendorf, MD, pediatrician, Columbia University Medical Center, and assistant clinical professor, New York-Presbyterian Hospital, both in New York City.

When a Child Needs a Therapist

Pearl-Ellen Gordon, PhD, child psychologist, New York City.

Children don't come to parents and say they need a therapist. They don't perceive the focus of the problem as themselves. They'll blame it on parents or school. Treatment revolves around helping children to see how they contribute to their problems.

Most children begin therapy because a teacher or school psychologist suggests it to a parent. Parents often do not recognize deviant behavior until the child goes to school. But many problems can be corrected if they are caught early.

Major tip-off: A child is arrested in development and is not doing what one would expect of a child in his/her age group.

Signs of poor emotional development...

• **A four-year-old in nursery school** cries and misses his/her mother.

• **An eight-year-old with no friends** comes home after school and watches television.

•**Rigid rituals.** The child's bedroom has to be a certain way. Particular foods must be served on certain nights.

•**Major sleep disturbances.** Frequent nightmares, waking in the middle of the night.

•**Lack of learning progress.** The child is not performing at grade level in school.

•**Psychosomatic illnesses.** Whatever the root cause, ailments are exacerbated by stress (ulcerative colitis, asthma, etc.).

When in doubt, ask the school psychologist or pediatrician to recommend a therapist. Don't bring the child in for the first visit. Request a consultation. In some cases there may not be anything wrong with the child. The parents may be the ones who need help.

Parents should use psychologists and psychiatrists more freely to help assess problems with children. *One answer:* More parenting centers where parents can go to ask questions and get guidelines about developmental progress.

Early Signs of Adolescent Drug Addiction

Boys who were both shy and aggressive in first grade are most likely to become abusers of drugs, alcohol and tobacco later in life, a study shows. These children were usually loners who did not participate in classroom activities and were hostile to their classmates and to school regulations. When these boys became adolescents, 45% smoked marijuana, 60% were heavy cigarette smokers, 18% drank hard liquor and 60% drank beer or wine. *Next most likely:* Boys who were aggressive without also being shy. *The least likely:* Those who were merely shy had the lowest percentages. Only 10% smoked marijuana as adolescents, 5% were heavy cigarette smokers, 20% drank wine or beer and none tried hard liquor.

A study of 1,200 youngsters by Sheppard G. Kellam, MD, senior research scientist and director of the Center for Integrating Education and Prevention Research in Schools at the American Institutes for Research, Washington, DC.

Great Gifts for Kids— On-line

With a little quick searching, it's easy to find fun stuff on the Internet for all the kids in your life. *For example...*

Custom jigsaw puzzles: Puzzles are made from your favorite photos...can have pieces in animal shapes or other unusual forms. *www.jigsawpuzzle.com.*

Kids' products: Independent reviews of award-winning, age-appropriate books, videos, software, toys, etc. Includes toll-free numbers for ordering. *www.toyportfolio.com.*

Better Family-ing

When parents disagree *politely,* adolescents and young adults benefit mentally as well as emotionally. Effective communication among parents and offspring as well as between husbands and wives without the offspring present was associated with young adult adjustment. When parents criticize each other harshly, children are more likely to develop social and psychological problems such as anxiety, nervousness and substance abuse.

Clifford Notarius, PhD, professor of psychology, Catholic University, Washington, DC, and author of a three-year study of 54 families.

•**Better work at home—with a child around.** Near your work area, set up your child's workplace. Include a craft desk with toilet-paper rolls, stickers, crayons, paper, glue, tape and similar items. *Schedule:* Set a timer for work time. While the timer runs, focus on work and have your child do the same. When the timer goes off, reset it for play time—and focus totally on your child. When the timer goes off again, return to work and reset it for the next play break. Decide how long to set the timer based on your child's age.

•**Teach kids to use the phone in case of emergencies.** Children should learn their phone numbers—including the area code—as soon as they become verbal. They should know it is all right to dial 0 or 911 in an emergency, even before calling home. Teach them how to dial from various phones—home, cell, pay, hotel and business. Tell them to dial 911 and leave the phone off the hook if they are in danger—since emergency operators can trace the call rapidly.

Jan Wagner, founder, SAFE-T-CHILD, Austin, TX, and coauthor of *Raising Kids in an Unsafe World.* Avon Books.

• **More fun reading with young kids.** Just talk about the pictures in a book. Skip over plots and the books' real text if children are not ready for them.

You don't have to read the whole book. Let your child's interest level guide you.

Read things you enjoy yourself. If you are not having fun, neither will your child.

Try adding movement or touching. *Example:* Bounce your child on your knee when the book says a pony trots.

Keep favorite books with you in a diaper bag, purse or glove compartment—to read when waiting at a restaurant or a doctor's office.

Nancy Hall, contributing editor, *Parents,* 375 Lexington Ave., New York City 10017.

The Internet and Your Child

To block Internet sites that you do not want children to see, make sure they have plenty of good ones to visit. Try sites recommended by the American Library Association, *www.ala.org,* and Yahoo! Kids, *www.kids.yahoo.com.* Preview sites without your children. Bookmark favorites.

Filtering options: Some Internet services, such as America Online, offer optional control systems. Or try Cyber Patrol, *www.cyberpatrol.com,* or Net Nanny, *www.netnanny.com.* But remember that filters block some sites that are fine for most kids, such as Barenaked Ladies, a musical group popular with preteens.

John Edwards, high-tech consultant, Gilbert, AZ.

Stay in Touch with Your Children When You Travel

The late Lee Salk, PhD, former clinical professor of psychology in psychiatry, New York Weill Cornell Medical Center.

The same principles of child rearing apply to parents who travel on business as to those who do not. These elements contribute to a child's emotional health and give him/her the skills to cope with life's problems later on.

FUNDAMENTALS

• **Options.** Children need to feel that they have choices. If other people make all their decisions for them, children lose their motivation, become depressed or angry and feel helpless. Being offered appropriate choices —which book to read at bedtime, for instance—gives children more motivation to learn. It helps them to make responsible decisions later on and to be less vulnerable to peer pressure.

• **Acceptance.** All children need to feel that they are accepted regardless of their strengths or weaknesses. Parents who are high achievers frequently put too much pressure on children. Rather than demand perfection, it is far more important for a parent to make sure a child feels successful at a realistic level.

• **Approval.** Children need someone to say, "That was a nice job." They also need to be aware of disapproval. Communicate when you are unhappy about something, too. Being a responsive parent doesn't mean you mustn't say no. Disapproval is a response, too.

If you're a responsive parent and feel comfortable giving your children choices, you have laid the groundwork for being able to meet your obligations even while you travel. Not being there to respond can be detrimental to your child, but parents can respond from wherever they are.

Here are some of the ways to stay in touch with your children...

• **Minimize time away.** Even if you travel a great deal, make it a rule not to be away from home for more than one week at a time.

• **Call children twice a day.** When you are away, bracket the day with one telephone call in the morning and another at night. Your presence is there even if you're not.

• **Plan children's time during your absence.** Before going on a business trip, try to set up the options your children will have while you're gone—a guest for dinner, an overnight visit at a friend's house. This allows you to participate in their lives even though you're not there. While you're away, you're not supervising or controlling but simply looking in to see what's going on.

• **Gifts should be special.** Parents shouldn't be expected to bring back gifts. If you find something special, then it's a surprise that says, "I was thinking of you." But bringing gifts every time you make a trip becomes a ritual. Kids who grow to expect a gift because they have always received a gift can become ambivalent about their parents' traveling. *The unfortunate lesson:* Materialistic values are more important than human values.

• **Take children along.** When possible, take your children with you. Missing a day or two of school is well worth it for the benefits of family closeness and the educational experience of travel. For longer trips, arrangements can be made with the school to bring lessons along and to do special projects. (In fact, the trip itself may provide the basis for a personalized school report.)

• **Communicate your feelings about separation.** Let your children know how much you miss them and that staying in hotels is a lonely business. When you telephone, say to your children, "I wish I were home with you."

• **When you return, let the children know how happy you are to be home.** It's nice if they can look forward to something special, like dinner out, to celebrate.

How to Talk With Your Child About Sex

The late Mary Steichen Calderone, MD, former medical director of the Planned Parenthood Federation of America and cofounder and president of SIECUS (Sex Information and Education Council of the US).

Parents who want to give their children mastery of the facts about sexuality have to start early in the child's life. That's when you should also begin to build the attitudes your children will need to enjoy themselves as sexual beings and respect the sexuality of others.

A child is born sexual, just as he or she is born with the capacity to walk and talk. Parents joyfully help children to develop their ability to walk and talk but rarely treat sexual pleasure the same way. Once you understand and accept your children's sexuality as normal and beautiful—the same as their other human endowments—you will be free to help them in their sexual socialization.

The process of socialization starts in infancy. You socialize your children in other natural functions such as eating. You praise them for using a spoon instead of plunging their hands into the cereal bowl and for other appropriate eating behavior.

A child also needs the guidance and support of parents in developing appropriate sexual behavior that fits in with the parents' own cultural norm and value system. *The beginning...*

• **Establish a sense of intimacy and trust** with a newborn by touching and holding. The cuddling, kissing and hugging should continue—do not stop when the child reaches three, when some parents feel awkward with physical demonstrations of affection, especially with boys.

• **When you start the game of naming parts of the body, include the sexual organs.** Avoidance of the area between the waist and the knees causes confusion and lays the groundwork for problems in adult life.

• **Don't interfere with a child's natural discovery and enjoyment of self-pleasuring.** Genital play is normal. At six or eight months, a child learns to put his/her hand where it feels good. Don't slap on a diaper, pull the hand away or look upset or disapproving. Leave the child alone. As the child gets older, teach what you consider to be appropriate behavior. You don't want your child masturbating in the supermarket or living room even at 15 to 18 months, so you pick up the child and, smiling, carry him/her to the bedroom. Explain that the place to pleasure yourself is in your own room with the door closed—that sex is good but should be private.

• **Parents need privacy, too.** *Tell children:* "When our door is closed, you don't come in without knocking and being invited. When we see your door closed, we'll do the same for you. Everyone likes privacy during sex games." This is when you can introduce the idea that sex games are something people who love and respect each other can play together.

• **Sex play between children is normal.** If parents banish the play, it will only drive the child underground. It's better to keep the lines of communication open and reinforce socially appropriate sexual play. *Inappropriate:* Sex play with someone older. Child molestation is more commonly practiced by someone who is in the family or known to a child than by a stranger. *The message:* You don't have to let anyone touch your body against your will. You are in charge, and you can say *no.*

Few parents are aware of how much sex education is transmitted before nursery school by attitudes and body language—how parents react to scenes on TV, the tone of voice or facial expression in sexual conversations or situations, significant silences.

Children delight in affection openly expressed between their parents. Withholding such demonstrations can indicate sexual hang-ups.

Don't avoid opportunities to discuss sex or to answer questions. Always speak only the truth. You may wish to withhold some of the details until later. Explain appropriate behavior outside the home. "In our family, we are open with each other about sex. But most other families don't talk about it the way we do. So we keep what we do private. It's a good thing to respect what other people believe."

A child who doesn't ask questions by the age of four or five has gotten the idea that the parent is either uncomfortable about sex or that sex is not an open topic. Or perhaps the child knows that he/she is not being given straight answers. Parents should be the ones to give children sexual information. Initiate a discussion. *One idea:* Tell your child about your own questions when you were the same age. If there is no response, try again another day to prove you're available.

Choose a time when you (or both parents) are alone with the child and have plenty of time. Be encouraging about behavior that is appropriate or shows maturation. Give recognition to a good line of thought. Respond positively even if you are criticized.

COMMON MISTAKES

The most damaging mistake is to associate sexual parts of the body with dirt, ugliness or sin. Guilt and shame transmitted about such a wonderful part of our human birthright will never be erased.

Parents should never lie, although they may find it necessary to tailor the truth to the level of the child. *Example:* To a three-year-old who asks, "Do you have to be married to have a baby?" the correct answer is, "No, you don't, but..." Then you go into your own value system about why marriage is important—on a level that a three-year-old can understand.

Talking with children about sex should be a shared responsibility. A harmonious front is important. Both parents should be clear on attitudes toward standards and rules and on what they agree and disagree on. If there are differences of opinion, call them that. Undermining the other parent shakes the child's confidence in the parent who's doing the undermining. Children trust parents who are for each other.

If you have laid the groundwork between birth and six or seven, you can take advantage of the major learning years until 12. Before puberty is when to pour in reliable information about sexually transmittable diseases, reproduction, etc. Keep the lines of communication open. Give opinions when they're asked for. Avoid judgments—they tend to close off discussions. Express your own values frankly and give sound reasons. Young people will respect them even if they don't share them.

How to Explain Death To a Child

Explaining death to a child of three or four years of age is best done with simple, direct sentences. *Example:* Explain that death is when a person is broken and no one can fix him/her—not a doctor, nurse or anyone. Young children know that badly broken toys cannot be repaired, so they can relate to this. Save more complex explanations for when the child is older.

Salk Letter.

Finding the Right Books For Your Children

Teach children how to find books at their reading level. *Technique:* Tell the child to open the book near the middle and read from the top of any full page. If there are five words the child doesn't know before getting to the end of the page, the book is too hard.

Is Your Child Gifted? by Eliza Graue and David Graue, Oak Tree Publications.

Choosing a New Pet... Wisely

Susan Chernak McElroy, located in Jackson, WY, who has worked as a veterinarian's assistant, Humane Society educator, dog trainer, wildlife rehabilitator and zookeeper. She is author of *All My Relations: Living with Animals as Teachers and Healers.* New World Library.

Pick a pet with the same care you would use if adopting a child or getting married. Are you committed to taking care of it in sickness and in health?

FISH AND OTHER

Aquariums are mesmerizing. You can stare at the antics of fish all day.

Or you can put frogs or newts in an aquatic, aquarium-like setting.

Gophers are big enough to sit on your lap and play with you.

White rats are easy to care for—and deserve to be more popular. For affectionate companionship, they can't be beat. Rats know and adore their owners, answer to their own names and love to snuggle.

DOGS AND CATS

Find the best cats and dogs at your local animal shelter. Mixed-breed animals are usually far hardier and less costly than purebreds. Giving an animal a new lease on life provides a heartfelt sense of joy. *Factors to consider...*

•**Cats.** Although they love their independence, many cats will curl up near or on you. When you're sick, cats keep you company day and night. Unlike dogs, they don't have to be brushed, washed or walked.

•**Dogs.** A new puppy is fun, but it is usually high-strung and untrained. Older animals are mature and calm, often with good house manners. Which would suit you better?

Also consider size. For a pooch that can cuddle with you on the sofa or in bed, go small. Also, smaller dogs tend to live longer. If you want a dog to deter strangers, go big. The bigger the animal, though, the bigger the grocery bill.

BIRDS

Caged birds are great, especially in apartments and in nursing homes that ban dogs and cats.

Pound for pound, parakeets offer more features than other pets. They have a lovely song, can learn tricks and their names and live eight to 12 years. You can have their wings clipped and open the cage door. In a very short time you'll find them sitting on the edge of your plate and sharing your salad.

Parrots are extremely sociable and smart—some have the mental abilities of a five-year-old child.

When you've decided you want a parrot, find one that wasn't imported illegally. Find a veterinarian who practices avian medicine, and ask him/her what types of parrots to consider and for reputable sources.

LOOKING TO THE FUTURE

Older singles often write to me asking if they dare get a pet that would outlive them. I say yes, but do some advance planning. *Options...*

• **Find a family member to take the pet.** Shop together for an animal that pleases both of you.

• **Identify a neighbor or extended family member** who would assume responsibility.

• **Adopt an older pet from a humane society.** Grow old together.

The right way to give: Never give a pet you picked out as a present. *Acceptable:* A gift certificate to a pet shop with a note saying, "I want you to have an animal in your life. You choose."

Sex Education and Promiscuity

Sex education in school does not lead to promiscuity among teenagers. And young women who have had sex education are less likely to become pregnant than those who have not. These are the findings of surveys of teenagers. *Overwhelming conclusion:* There is no connection between sex education and sexual activity.

Family Planning Perspectives.

Safety On-line

Student Safety on the Internet provides information about keeping your kids safe when they meet people on-line. *web4j1.lane. edu/safety.* Always supervise children's computer use.

When You Are Invading Your Child's Privacy

Howard M. Halpern, PhD, author of *Cutting Loose: An Adult's Guide to Coming to Terms with Your Parents.* Simon & Schuster.

How much should parents know about their children's lives? The answer really depends more on how much the children are on their own than on age. Their lives become more and more their own business as they move away from parental supervision. Having an increasingly greater private life and knowing that you don't have to tell your parents everything is an essential part of growing up.

During the years when children are under your roof, the key to keeping track is dialogue. If communications are good, then you've developed a relationship in which children will want to share information with you that you should be aware of. If the relationship is sound and there are matters they don't want to share, they may have a good reason, and you should respect their privacy.

How to elicit information: When you are concerned about a serious issue, questions can work. *Better:* It's more of an invitation to open up if parents talk more about their feelings on what's going on in their own lives—being worried about this or embarrassed about that—or about feelings concerning something the child is experiencing. This helps create an atmosphere in which the child can talk about his/her feelings, too. *Particularly inviting:* A nonjudgmental parent.

Setting the stage: When you have something difficult to discuss with your children, do it in the car. No one can get up and walk out. You don't have to look at each other if that is a problem. Pick a trip that will last at least half an hour. Try not to ask questions.

Sometimes it is enough to give your opinion on a subject even if you elicit no information. *Example:* A divorced father with custody of his 16-year-old daughter had a conversation about her relationship with a boyfriend... "You and David are getting very close, and I think that's fine. I don't know how active a sex life you're having, but I hope you will delay a full sex life. I think you're too young for that. But whether in six weeks or six years you do go all the way, the one experience I don't want you to have is getting pregnant. I want you to feel free to come to me to ask for the name of a doctor."

Her response: "We're not doing anything like that now." A month or two later, she said she was having problems with menstrual bleeding and asked for the name of a gynecologist. The father had expressed what he wanted to say and had opened the door. The child didn't invite him in, but she certainly received the message.

How serious is the issue? Whether invasion of privacy is justified depends on the stakes. It is indefensible for parents to read a child's diary simply because they're curious about his/her sex life. If the problem is something that would be damaging to a child living under your roof, even if the child is 18, 19 or 20, you should intervene. *Example:* A parent who suspects that a child is getting involved with drugs should search the child's room thoroughly.

Less serious problems: If the communication is good, the child might tell you about them. But a child who is on drugs may have a change in personality, and this will probably adversely affect a previously healthy relationship.

When and how you intervene depends on the severity of the issue and how it will affect a child's life. It also depends on what you can effectively do. *Examples...*

• **Movies.** Some parents might be concerned about sexuality or violence in films. They wouldn't want a 12- or 14-year-old to see a frightening or perverted horror film. They might, though, be more lenient about sex that isn't X-rated. *For this age group:* Strongly advise against an unsuitable film. Refuse to pay for it. If necessary, prohibit seeing it.

• **Friends.** If you're going to press a negative opinion, have a good reason. *Check yourself:* Do I object because this is not my preference for a friend? Do I think no one's good enough for my child? Am I afraid of competition? If the association is dangerous, you can refuse to allow the friend into your house, but it is impossible to police whom your child sees outside the house.

How much can a parent control a child? You can exercise more control of what goes on in the house than of what takes place outside. If you don't know that your child is getting drunk at parties, there's not much you can do. If your 15-year-old comes home drunk, you can say, "You're grounded. This has got to stop." If you pass a prohibition ("You're not to get high anyplace at any time"), obviously you'll have no way of enforcing it.

In general, keep the lines of communication open by expressing your own feelings and values. It may not always yield information, but at least it creates a receptive climate for exploring important issues.

School Sports Cautions

Pushing young athletes can result in "overuse" injuries such as stress fractures, tendonitis of the shoulder, bursitis of the hip and tennis elbow. These injuries in children were unheard of before the advent of organized sports programs after World War II. Even now, doctors rarely see these problems in youngsters who play sports among themselves without special coaching. (Children do not push themselves too hard.)

Most frequent cause of injury: Inappropriate or excessive training. Children are particularly susceptible to injury when they are tired or in pain.

Remedy: Make sure the coaches or trainers who work with your children are sensitive to this issue and that they have a proper perspective on what a sports program is really about.

Lyle Micheli, MD, director of sports medicine, Children's Hospital Medical Center, Boston, quoted in *The Ladies' Home Journal.*

Aspirin Can Be Dangerous

Aspirin given to children who have chicken pox or flu increases the risk of Reye's syndrome, a mysterious illness that sometimes follows viral ailments. *Symptoms:* Vomiting, fever leading to convulsions, coma and even death in about one-quarter of the cases.

US Department of Health and Human Services and the Centers for Disease Control and Prevention.

If Your Child Is Hospitalized

Parents of hospitalized children are now usually permitted (and often encouraged) to stay, even overnight, with the child in the hospital. This is a sharp departure from previous practice, when parents could visit only during visiting hours. *Why the change:* Parents provide continuity between the home and hospital. It is important that acutely ill children, especially the very young, don't see the hospital as a place of abandonment.

Why You Shouldn't Feed Honey to a Baby

Hold the honey for babies under one year of age. *Reason:* Even "pure" or "filtered" honey contains tiny amounts of bacteria. Although harmless to older children and adults, these can lead to infections and even botulism in an infant. *Symptoms:* Constipation, lethargy and feeding problems.

Vegetarian Times.

Prevent Children's Ear Infections

Andrew Rubman, ND, director, Southbury Clinic for Traditional Medicines, Southbury, CT.

Most children's ear problems result from inflammation, not bacterial infection, so antibiotics will not help.

Danger: Use of antibiotics can increase the risk of infection by decreasing immune activity against common, normal oral bacteria.

Better for older children: Stir a teaspoon of salt into a half-cup of very warm water. Have the child sniff the vapor into his/her nostrils. Repeat until the ear pressure is relieved—often within a few minutes.

For young children: Place a very warm, wet cloth from the ear down along the side of the neck for five minutes, three times per day.

Consult your health-care provider if: Fluid is visible in the ear, or a greenish nasal discharge accompanies the earache, *or* the ear feels hot or appears very red, or the child has a fever.

To prevent ear problems: Stop giving children milk. Milk is the most allergy-provoking substance in the human diet and can aggravate ear problems. Cheese and yogurt are better tolerated, although still allergy-provoking.

Medicines Not to Give Your Child

Alcohol-based medicines can make children nauseous, confused or sluggish. If taken intensively for an extended period, they can even lead to heart and respiratory problems.

Trap: Alcohol is an unlabeled ingredient in many liquid antihistamines, cough syrups and anticolic medicines.

Advice: Ask your pediatrician to prescribe a nonalcohol-based alternative.

Jean Lockhart, MD, former director of the American Academy of Pediatrics, quoted in *Body & Soul.*

How to Deal with a Defiant Teenager

Clifford J. Sager, MD, psychiatrist and psychologist in private practice in New York City.

The problem of the teenager who defies parental authority is rooted in changes in the outside world as well as in the relationships in the home. In recent years we have seen a breakdown in discipline and a disruption of family authority. Family structures are not as strong as they were, nor are roles as well defined. Often there is conflict between parents. Increasingly, peer involvement has usurped family involvement.

In this society, with its breakdown of law and order, children are apt to see parents cheating on income taxes or using drugs. They know of illegal acts committed by people in the highest positions in the country. The attacks on September 11, 2001, and the proliferation of the nuclear bomb encourage children to ask, "What's the sense of it all?" They say to parents, "Who are you to tell us what to do? Look at how you're living your life and how you messed up the world."

Even with these changes, adolescence is a period when children must separate from the family. At the same time, they still need guidance. Parents still need to know how to exercise the right proportions of flexibility and supervision. How parents set limits will influence their success in maintaining them. *Some suggestions...*

• **Parents should have their own standards,** but it's a good idea to check with other parents, and perhaps the school, about the prevailing views on curfews, use of alcohol and allowances. You can't always trust children to give you an accurate report of regulations observed in other families.

• **Both parents should agree on a course of action** and support each other. Kids will use every opportunity to take advantage of differences between parents.

• **Discuss the rules with children.** Explain your position calmly, and be prepared to back up your ideas. *Remember:* Things have changed a great deal since you were your child's age. Listen to your children carefully, particularly the oldest one, who usually has the toughest time because he/she is a trailblazer for those who follow.

• **Rules must be geared to the ability of the child to handle responsibility.** Development during adolescence is uneven not only physically but also emotionally. One child of 16 may be able to manage a flexible curfew, but another may not be mature enough.

If rules are being flouted, parents must first examine their own roles, expectations and motivations. Are they contributing to the problem? Are their demands arbitrary and unreasonable? *Examples...*

• **Bad language.** What kind of language do the parents use?

• **Rushing away from the dinner table**—not participating in family discussions. What is the dinner table ambiance? Is it one a child would want to get away from?

• **School grades.** Are parental expectations realistic?

Next, avoid hostile confrontation and open warfare. Create an atmosphere in which attitudes can be expressed and there is a positive feeling about learning, the intellectual spirit and the arts. The child should feel that home is a comfortable place and that his/her friends are welcome.

When stress periods come, and calls from the outside begin to run counter to family standards, the child has something to fall back on, a basis on which to make choices and parents to turn to.

Praise the child for what he is doing right before you tell him what he is doing wrong.

If a child is told he is bad, he begins to live up to that reputation and is more likely to get into trouble.

Defiant behavior is generally used to get attention or test limits.

Always deal with your child with understanding. Children react best to fairness. But it's all right to be angry if your anger is motivated by your concern for his safety. It is your job to protect him.

Don't impose restrictions you can't enforce.

Always give a warning.

Important: Don't deliver threats for punishment you're not able or willing to carry out.

Effective punishment requires the cooperation of both parents. What kind of punishment? Withholding part of the allowance or a planned trip or other treat is better than corporal punishment.

The punishment should fit the crime. Lesser matters (untidy rooms) may not call for the same approach as more urgent ones (drugs, alcohol).

Important: Do not discipline your child in front of other people, including siblings— and especially not in front of his friends.

Lethargy Can Be Caused by Allergies

Slothful teenagers may be allergic to common foods, not to work. In some youngsters, reactions to such staples as sugar, milk, corn, wheat or eggs can interfere directly with brain function, causing an inability to concentrate or think clearly. *Some signs beyond lethargy:* Nasal congestion, headaches, abdominal pains, pallor and dark circles under the eyes. *Test:* A special diet that eliminates certain foods, such as dairy, wheat or corn, from the child's meals. If dramatic improvement in health lasts more than 48 hours, an allergy seems likely. By reintroducing the youngster's regular foods one at a time, the source of the problem can be identified.

William G. Crook, MD, pediatrician, writing in *Medical Tribune.*

How to Get Better Test Scores

Dr. Harold T. Fox, former professor at Ball State University, Muncie, IN, and George A. Ball, business consultant.

There are several ways students can give their best effort when taking tests. *A few ideas...*

• **Keep current.** Prepare for tests as if they occurred without prior notice. Instead of memorizing the subject matter, paraphrase it and integrate it into your total store of knowledge. Most people do better on tests if they do not cram.

• **Be prepared.** Bring several pens and pencils to the test. Arrive a few minutes early. A little excitement may improve your performance, but do not let anxiety interfere with clear thinking. *Important:* Self-control.

• **Quickly scan the entire test at the start.** Ask the instructor immediately about any unclear phrasing. Be sure to follow all instructions exactly and to understand the criteria. *Example:* If a list is requested, do not compose an essay. Ask if wrong answers will be penalized. If not, guessing may improve your score slightly.

• **Mentally schedule your answers and set priorities.** For example, if the test lasts two hours, answer at the rate of 1% each minute. This pace gives you a little reserve time for the more difficult questions and for a complete review.

• **Study each question carefully and plan your answer.** Conserve time by avoiding repetitions. *Examples:* Label (do not write out) each question. Give as much detail as is requested but no more. Omit side issues, especially if they encroach on other questions. Do not write out the same answer to more than one question. Cross out wrong answers (instead of taking time to erase them). *Exception:* Computer-scored tests require complete erasures of mistakes.

• **Avoid dogmatic presentations.** In an essay on a controversial issue, give all sides before justifying your view. In an objective test, choices are usually wrong if they contain such words as *always* or *never.* A statement is false if any part of it is wrong.

• **Don't belabor the obvious.** For example, don't write that a company should set goals. *Instead:* Specify what goals are appropriate. Try to cover all bases, but do so briefly. Most teachers disdain padding.

• **Use clear expressions.** Define technical terms so that someone who is not familiar with them would understand. *Example:* Saying a computer's byte equals eight bits conveys nothing at all.

• **Allow time for review.**

• **Use the test as a springboard for further learning.** Don't blame the teacher or text if the grade you received is less than expected. Pinpoint and remedy the weakness.

• **Achievement test scores, not Scholastic Aptitude Test (SAT) ratings,** give the best indication of freshman-year college performance. Many top schools are now relying less on the SATs than on achievement tests in specific subjects and also recommendations from high schools.

Driver Education in School Is Not Enough

Driver-education programs in schools place teenagers behind the wheel for only 20 to 40 hours. Follow up by having one parent supervise the new driver for another 500 miles in light to medium traffic. Practice defensive maneuvers for 10 to 20 hours more in heavy traffic.

North American Professional Driver Education Association, Chicago.

Summer Jobs for Kids

Friends and relatives are the best source of help in finding summer jobs. Ask them for contacts or ideas.

Summer camps hire students for all sorts of jobs. *Usual requirements:* Camp experience, age 19 or older, and at least one year of college. Find out about job opportunities through the American Camp Association, 5000 State Road 67 North, Martinsville, IN 46151, on the Web at *www.acacamps.org.*

The National Park Service of the Department of the Interior provides summer jobs (and many winter jobs) annually. Applicants must be 18, provide a college transcript and be US citizens.

One useful approach: Advertise your services on local store and community-center bulletin boards. Two brothers kept busy painting houses (a very profitable enterprise) after putting up a note in a supermarket advertising their availability.

Many countries allow foreign students to work in temporary, seasonal jobs. The pay is usually low, but jobs can be interesting. *Example:* Working on the French grape harvest.

Here's How To Choose a Summer Camp

Laurie Edelman, former executive director, American Camp Association, New York section.

The best time to choose a camp for your child is the summer before. This enables you to visit a few prospective camps and see them in action. However, if this is not possible, begin your selection process in the fall for best results.

To learn about camps: Talk to friends, attend camp fairs, read advertisements and make use of the American Camp Association (ACA) guidance service, 800-777-CAMP. The guidance service will help you narrow your choices to three or four camps that are specifically appropriate to your child and your family's needs.

QUESTIONS TO ASK YOURSELF

•**Is my child ready for camp?** If he/she cries or behaves poorly when separated from you, or states firmly that he won't go, he's probably not ready for camp.

Helpful hint: Find out why the child doesn't want to go. Does he have false, preconceived ideas about going away to camp? If so, you may be able to change his mind, especially through a visit to camp during the summer.

•**What does your child want in a camp?** Consider his personality and take stock of his interests and the kinds of things he wants to learn and accomplish at camp. Then find a camp that will satisfy his interests, as well as what you want for him.

Example: If he likes to "hang out" and you want him to be active, seek a camp with structure and supervision but a variety of activities.

•**What is wanted in a camp?** Determine your child's needs, what he will tolerate and what he would be willing to give up.

Example: If your child won't swim in a lake, pick a camp with a pool. If your child enjoys a lake and wants to learn to water-ski or sail, look for a program that includes these activities.

•**How long will your child stay?** Pick the longest time period you can afford. *Reason:* A child adjusts better and learns and grows more the longer he is in the camp environment.

•**Should your child go to camp with friends or alone?** If you are considering sending your child with a friend, make sure both of them have the same interests—and that you and the other child's parents have the same criteria. Otherwise, one child will be unhappy. If your child wants to go alone, let him. One of the wonderful experiences camp provides is the chance to make new friends.

WHAT TO ASK PROSPECTIVE CAMPS' DIRECTORS

It's important to talk to camp directors before picking a camp to be sure it's a good match for your child. Eliminate a camp if any answers don't make sense or you are uncomfortable with the responses of the director.

•**What kinds of programs are available?** Parents who want their kids to have a fun, relaxing summer may prefer a recreational program. Those who want their children to learn something they can't during the winter may prefer an instructional program.

Example: On the tennis court at an instructional camp, campers are drilled on strokes and the emphasis is on proper form. At a recreational program, the emphasis is more on play than on drills.

•**What is a typical day like?** Have someone talk you through the program, including evening events. *Find out:* How much instruction is private and how much is in groups, which activities are required and which are elective, if your child can get as much as he likes of any one activity, who makes sure he gets to each activity and what types of trips might he take?

•**How many counselors and children are in each group?** How do you recruit new counselors? What are your selection criteria? How old are the counselors?

Helping Children Gain Independence

Clifford J. Sager, MD, psychiatrist and psychologist in private practice in New York City.

Having the family all together for the holiday season may be cheerful, but togetherness can pall if it is overdone. And low starting salaries, high rents and a scarcity of apartments are keeping many young people at home and economically dependent on their parents well beyond graduation from college.

While some families welcome a return to lifestyles in which adult children, as well as grandparents, live together, the trend is potentially dangerous. Among other hazards, children fail to develop independence quickly enough when they live at home as adults. And the household and life-cycle rhythms are off.

Financial dependence on parents through the schooling period is directly proportionate to the slower maturing of young people today.

To help encourage independence, parents should...

• **Supplement their children's income at the outset** so that they can live in their own quarters. There is no substitute for the experience of having to manage a household.

• **Charge for room and board** if children must live at home. Some parents put this money aside as a stake for the child's marriage or business.

• **Put a time limit on living at home**—six months, a year or until the first salary raise. Whatever the arrangement, make it clear that independence is the goal.

Grown children's social lives often present problems to parents who matured in a different type of society. *But parents should not be afraid to set standards...*

• **If they are not comfortable when their children bring sex partners home,** they should say so. Making their feelings clear before a guest arrives avoids unpleasantness later.

• **Parents should not be afraid to ask grown children under their roof to help with chores** and with family obligations such as visiting relatives.

• **After children mature, some parents want to simplify their lives** by moving into a smaller house or apartment or closer to work. Do not be deterred by sentimental arguments the children pose. Independent parents foster independent children.

How to Improve Scores on Standardized Tests

Stanley H. Kaplan, founder of Kaplan Inc., 888 Seventh Ave., New York City 10106. *www.kaplan.com.*

No matter how smart you are, no matter how well prepared, there are strategies you can use to improve your scores on any standardized test, including the SAT, GRE and MCAT.

WHAT TO DO

• **Get to know the test beforehand.** Every standardized test is different. *Important:* Read the test booklet provided by the testing firm to find out what subjects will be covered, the precise form questions will take and the directions. If you have to spend two minutes reading the directions when the test is in progress, you'll lose two minutes of valuable test-taking time.

• **Review the subjects that will be covered.** If the test you're planning to take has a mathematical section, bone up on math beforehand. Likewise with logical reasoning, science and so on. Start reviewing basic skills three or four months in advance.

• **Take practice tests.** Sample exams prepared and distributed by the testing organizations themselves are best. They will familiarize you with the material and give a fair indication of your actual exam score. If you are unhappy with your projected score, delay taking the exam until you have improved and are satisfied that you can do well.

• **Arrive an hour in advance.** If you're unfamiliar with the test site, make a trial run a few days beforehand.

• **Come prepared.** Bring your admission ticket, personal identification and six No. 2 pencils with dull points—they allow you to fill in the circles faster than sharp points and don't break as easily. If you're prone to headaches, bring an aspirin or your favorite analgesic.

•**Keep anxiety in check.** Cramming the night before the exam encourages anxiety. If you become anxious while you are taking the exam, breathe slowly and deeply. Get up and walk around during the break.

•**Use strategies.** Answer the short or easy questions first. Save the long reading passages for last.

If you have trouble with one question, put a mark by it in the test book and go on to the next question. Then go back if you have time.

In reading comprehension sections, some find it easier to scan the questions before reading the passage. This will clue you in on what to look for as you read.

If you finish the test early, go back over your answers.

•**Mark answers carefully.** Make sure the circle you're marking corresponds to the question you intend to answer. Many students mark column after column of circles only to discover they're ahead or behind where they should be.

Self-check: Every five questions, stop to make sure that the question and answer numbers correspond.

•**Know when—and when not—to guess.** A few tests penalize you for wrong answers (the SAT, for instance), others don't. Find out beforehand whether your test does.

On tests where there is no penalty for wrong answers, fill in every blank—no matter how unsure of the answer you are. On tests where there is a penalty, guess only if you can rule out at least one of the possible choices.

In some exams (the SAT for instance) questions at the beginning of each section are usually easier than those toward the end. As a result, if you arrive at a quick, easy answer on an early question, and that answer is listed among the multiple choices, chances are you have the right answer. But if you come up with a quick, easy answer on a question deep into the exam and that answer is among the multiple choices, watch out. There are no easy answers at the end of the test.

•**Don't let difficult questions rattle you.** If one section seems harder or less clear than most of the others, it could be an experimental section being used to try out new questions

and will not count toward your score. Just do your best.

•**Don't panic!** If you think you bombed the test, notify the testing organization immediately (use overnight mail). For most tests you have a few days following the exam to ask that your test not be scored. You can take it again without penalty, although your record will show that you canceled a previous test.

If your test is scored and your performance falls shy of what you had hoped for, you can always take the test again. Most schools look only at the higher score. *Exception:* Most law schools average your scores.

College Applications

Florence Janovic, writer and marketing consultant.

The pressures and anxieties of first finding the right colleges and then filling out all the forms make a child's senior year in high school a difficult time for the entire family. Parents can offer support and assistance without adding to the turmoil if they are discreet.

•**Learn from your friends.** People who have recently gone through the application process have practical, first-hand information that is valuable. Find out which books they found most helpful (for example, *Fiske Guide to Colleges 2009* by former *New York Times* education reporter Edward B. Fiske, or *Peterson's Four-Year Colleges 2009*) and provide them for your child. Don't worry about your friends' personal biases about particular schools. Just pass on factual information about the housing crunch for freshmen at an urban college or the attitudes toward women at a formerly all-male campus.

•**Encourage an early deadline for finishing applications.** Thanksgiving is a good target date. Then the child can concentrate on his or her schoolwork before the end of the semester and keep his grades up. First-term senior-year grades are important to the colleges that will be considering them.

• **Make copies of all the finished applications** and correspondence. Most colleges acknowledge the receipt of completed papers with a postcard so you will know if anything is missing. If too much time passes without such an acknowledgment, you can call and check. Having a copy on hand will save time and trauma.

• **Consider early-action applications** or at least one or two schools with rolling admissions to get early decisions. Neither admissions policy commits the student to that particular campus, but knowing before April 15 that at least one school wants him can alleviate the pressure.

• **Talk to the high-school guidance counselor.** Be sure your child is applying to schools where he has a better than average chance of being accepted. One or two long shots are reasonable, but young egos are badly damaged by a series of rejections. Make sure there is at least one or two "safety" schools on your list, preferably with rolling admissions.

• **Budget for campus visits to potential colleges.** If time and money are a consideration, save the visits for after the acceptances come in and real choices have to be made. Be sure your youngster sees the college while it is in session. Admissions offices will arrange for dormitory stays and opportunities for going to class if your child doesn't know anyone at the school.

• **Don't be arbitrary.** A youngster's first choice may not work out, or it may prove to be a mistake. Let your child know now that he can transfer from one college to another with no loss of face. In fact, some colleges are easier to get into as a transfer student than as a freshman.

How to Visit Colleges

High school seniors who are touring colleges should make sure that their visits pay off. *Here's how...*

• **Find out as much as you can about the colleges before you go.** Check out their Web sites and explore them thoroughly. You can also see if your high-school guidance office has information.

• **Contact the colleges to request a view book,** a freshman class profile and other descriptive material.

• **Look for what the college doesn't, as well as what it does, tell you.** The college literature is promotional material designed to "sell" the institution. In this period of declining enrollments, many colleges are as image-conscious as Madison Avenue.

• **Seniors.** Talk with graduates of your high school who are attending the colleges you're interested in, and call neighboring high schools for the names of graduates attending these colleges. After you have written to a college for materials, a local representative of the college may call—usually an alumnus. Many representatives remain close to their alma mater and can be very helpful. Applicants should watch out for the occasional alumnus whose main source of information is a romantic memory of his/her own undergraduate years.

• **High school students.** If possible, visit colleges during the summer after your junior year. It will help you to cut down your list. The admissions director will have more time to talk then than he/she will in the fall or winter, and visitors will find out how they react to the physical environment.

The two or three colleges at the top of your list should be visited in the fall or winter, preferably on a weekday so that you can attend a few classes. The admissions office will arrange overnight stays in an undergraduate's room, as well as a complete tour of the campus with a student guide.

At the interview, applicants should be open and candid. Don't try to impress the interviewer with a long list of questions that you should already have answered for yourself ("Is this a coed school?"). Concentrate on crucial questions to which you have no way of knowing the answers…"Are freshmen classes much larger than classes for upperclassmen?" "What happens on weekends—do most students stay or leave?" "Is the library crowded?"

If you know the field in which you want to major, go to that department and talk with the professors. They can give you a sure sense of what will be expected.

Most important: Spend an hour or more sitting in the student union building or some other gathering place where you can talk to students and ask them what they like best about the school—and what they think is wrong with it. This way, you can find out about social mores as well as courses and professors.

Financial Aid Wisdom

Dianne Van Riper, former assistant inspector general in the Office of Inspector General at the US Department of Education, Washington, DC. 800-872-5327, *www.ed.gov*.

S tretching the truth to maximize financial assistance is riskier than most parents or students realize.

The penalty includes paying back up to three times the amount of aid you received and fines as high as $10,000 per lie. Cheats also may be arrested and charged with a felony.

Here are the most common ways that parents and students get into trouble on financial aid applications…

Trap: Using a dishonest college consultant. College consultants may charge several hundred dollars to help parents negotiate the student aid application maze. While most consultants are honest, a sizable minority are willing to bend or break the rules for clients.

When you sign the financial aid application that a consultant has prepared, you are legally certifying that you have reviewed the information, and it is accurate.

When choosing a consultant: Beware of those who "guarantee" to win your child student aid. There are so many variables involved in deciding which students are—and are not—awarded aid that guarantees are impossible.

Read and review the application instructions with the consultant. They're surprisingly clear and easy to understand. If you don't understand some of the instructions, call the college financial aid officer.

Trap: Underreporting household income. By law, colleges are required to verify the incomes that are claimed by 30% of the students who applied for financial aid. They usually do this by requesting copies of the families' tax returns.

But now, the US Department of Education has the authority to check all applications by matching them against the original tax data you provided to the IRS.

Trap: Claiming your child isn't your dependent. An independent child's student aid is based on his/her income, which can be meager.

There are very explicit requirements for a student to be declared independent. Applicants can access these rules from college financial aid offices…or at the US Department of Education Web site, *www.ed.gov*.

There are also rules for orphan or ward-of-the-state status.

Trap: Claiming more dependents than you actually have. Many cheats say they have more children than they actually do, to increase the amount of aid they receive. This information, too, will soon be checked against actual tax returns.

Trap: Falsely claiming that the child lives with the lower-earning parent, if you and your spouse are divorced.

Trap: A married college student who claims to be single or divorced so that his spouse's income isn't figured into the student aid calculation.

Trap: Falsely claiming that there are more members of the household in postsecondary education than are actively enrolled.

Interviewing for College

An unfavorable interview may work against a prospective college applicant. *Alternative:* Group-information sessions. These are usually best for the student who does not have specific, detailed questions about the college. *Reminder:* The student should have a personal interview if one is "recommended" but not required. Group-information sessions should be considered only when the personal interview is optional.

Excellent Educations for Much, Much Less

Edward Custard, former college admissions officer and president of CollegeMasters/Carpe Diem ETC, an education consulting firm, Box 183, Sugar Loaf, NY 10981.

The average cost of a college education is at an all-time high—and is expected to rise at about 5% annually. *Here are top colleges whose annual tuitions and fees are below the average...*

CALIFORNIA

University of California/Berkeley. The intellectual flagship of California's formidable public system, Berkeley is highly competitive. More than 95% of its freshmen were in the top 10% of their high school classes. Though it is a huge state school, more than half the classes have fewer than 24 students. *Tuition:* In-state/$8,932...out-of-state/$20,608. 510-642-6000, *www.berkeley.edu.*

GEORGIA

Georgia Institute of Technology/Atlanta. Top-notch engineering school—without the mega-competitive admissions profile of MIT or Cal Tech. Most people don't realize this is a public school. *Tuition:* In-state/$6,040...out-of-state/$25,182. 404-894-2000, *www.gatech.edu.*

ILLINOIS

University of Illinois/Urbana-Champaign. Highly rated engineering school that also has a first-rate computer science program. It was the training ground of Marc Andreessen, cofounder of Netscape. The school also gets high marks for its biology and business programs. *Tuition and fees:* In-state/$11,416...out-of-state/$25,200. 217-333-1000, *www.uiuc.edu.*

MARYLAND

University of Maryland/Baltimore. This up-and-coming branch of the state university system has about 5,400 students. The school offers several different degree programs (including dental, nursing and pharmacy), which are available at different tuition requirements. 410-706-3100. *www.umaryland.edu.*

MISSOURI

Truman State University/Kirksville. This school of approximately 6,500 students has one of the nation's most thorough liberal arts core programs. Among the top programs are business, biology and English. The average class size is 22 students. *Tuition:* In-state/$6,458...out-of-state/$11,309. 660-785-4114 or 660-785-4000, *www.truman.edu.*

NEW JERSEY

Rutgers University/New Brunswick. This State University of New Jersey excels in psychology, nursing and English and has a highly rated performing arts school. *Tuition:* In-state commuter/$9,268...out-of-state/$19,482. 732-932-INFO, *www.rutgers.edu.*

NEW YORK

State University of New York/Geneseo. This less-famous branch of the SUNY system is cloistered away in this small town 30 miles south of Rochester. *Tuition:* In-state/$4,350...out-of-state/$10,615. 585-245-5211 or 866-245-5211, *www.geneseo.edu.*

NORTH CAROLINA

University of North Carolina/Chapel Hill. Known for its athletic program, this college also is an academic powerhouse that is set in a bucolic college town. *Tuition:* In-state/$3,705...out-of-state/$20,603. 919-962-2211, *www.unc.edu.*

TEXAS

University of Texas/Austin. This campus with 50,000 students is located in a beautiful town known for music and nightlife. Excels in liberal arts, business and communications.

Tuition costs vary depending on what course you take. *Tuition:* In-state/from $8,090 to $9,354 …out-of-state/from $26,672 to $30,770. 512-475-7348, *www.utexas.edu*.

WASHINGTON STATE

University of Washington/Seattle. This urban campus with a view of Mt. Rainier has a population of 39,000 students. Business, biology and psychology are the most popular majors, but there are 13 undergraduate colleges overseen by a 3,360-member faculty. *Tuition:* In-state/$6,802…out-of-state/$23,219. 206-543-9686, *www.washington.edu*.

How to Sell Yourself Off The College Wait List

Frank Leana, PhD, former educational director, Howard Greene & Associates, educational consulting firm, 39A E. 72nd St., New York City 10021.

Instead of simply sending back the card telling the school admissions office that you want to remain on the wait list, include a letter restating your interest in the school and how you plan to make use of the facilities.

Example: A student planning to study journalism might mention his/her work on his high school's award-winning newspaper.

If possible, guarantee that you will attend the school if you're chosen. Schools hate it when wait-listed students turn them down. *Also tell the college…*

•**If you've been accepted by any other equally prestigious schools.**

•**About any new accomplishments since your initial application,** such as exemplary senior-year grades or additional recommendations.

Helpful: A follow-up call, one to two weeks later, to show your continued interest in attending.

Bottom line: By separating yourself from the rest of the wait-list crowd, you improve your odds of being moved nearer to the front of the line.

Better College Aid Strategy

Certain unsecured debts, such as consumer loans, credit card balances and personal loans, do not count when colleges determine how much aid to award. By paying off credit card and other debts, you reduce your net assets and automatically become eligible for more aid.

Example: If you have $20,000 in a money market fund but owe $5,000 on credit cards, colleges will value your assets at $20,000—not $15,000.

Homeowners: When calculating your assets, colleges are increasingly allowing you to exclude some equity in your home. But at many schools, paying off your mortgage to reduce available funds will not get you more aid.

Kalman Chany, president, Campus Consultants, Inc., an organization that assists families in maximizing financial aid, 1202 Lexington Ave., New York City 10028. *www.campusconsultants.com.*

Eight Essential Skills to Improve Your Relationships

Redford Williams, MD, director of the Behavioral Medicine Research Center at Duke University, and Virginia Williams, PhD, cofounders of Williams LifeSkills Inc. *www.williamslifeskills.com.*

Strong, positive relationships with friends and family certainly make life more pleasant.

But study after study has shown that good relationships also keep us healthy. Unfortunately, today's fast-paced lifestyles work against good relationships.

To the rescue: After years of research, scientists have identified eight distinct skills that are necessary to create and maintain strong relationships…

DECIPHERING THOUGHTS

If you fail to understand what you're thinking and feeling, you are likely to behave in ways that hurt others. You're not likely to get what you want, either.

Essential: Learn to pay attention to your inner life. Carry a small notebook for a few days, and use it to keep a log of daily events—and your reactions to them. Jot down bodily sensations…your emotions…and any words that run through your mind.

EVALUATING NEGATIVE THOUGHTS

Too often, we respond automatically to annoyances by shouting, withdrawing, etc. *To learn more effective ways of responding, practice asking yourself four fundamental questions…*

• **Is this situation important?** In many instances, merely asking yourself this question enables you to "let go" of anger.

• **Are my thoughts and feelings appropriate?** You have a right to your reaction, but it may not be in your interest to act on it.

• **Can this situation be changed?** Life is filled with negative circumstances we're powerless to change. Of course, some circumstances do lie within our control. It's crucial to be able to distinguish one from the other.

• **Would taking action really be worthwhile?** Standing up to a nasty boss might make you feel better. But are you willing to risk losing your job?

ACHIEVING ACCEPTANCE

If the answer to any of the above questions is "no," look for ways to live with the status quo. *Three strategies are especially helpful…*

• **Reason with yourself.** If you're upset by the actions of another person, don't assume that you know why he behaved that way. Instead, come up with alternative theories that might explain his behavior.

• **Distract yourself.** Read a magazine article. Hum your favorite song. Rearrange the living room furniture.

• **Meditate.** Calm yourself by focusing on your breathing. Silently repeat a soothing sound such as "peace" as you do.

SOLVING PROBLEMS

If you answer "yes" to all four of the fundamental questions, it's time to take action. *Use this problem-solving flow chart…*

• **Define the problem.** Consider the facts as objectively as possible. Decide which aspects of the situation you'd like to change.

• **Brainstorm ways to react.** Think of three or four realistic alternatives.

• **Make a decision.** Consider the positive and negative consequences of each action. Then choose the one that's likely to have the biggest payoff.

If the action you try fails to produce the desired outcome, repeat the chart…and try again.

BEING ASSERTIVE

Strong relationships involve a balance of giving and getting. If someone with whom you have a relationship does something that bothers you, you must be willing to speak up. *Here's how to proceed…*

• **Describe the bothersome behavior.** Be objective, not judgmental. "The first thing you did when you came home was to criticize me for being messy."

• **Explain how you feel.** "Right now I'm feeling hurt, angry and upset."

• **State your request.** "When you come home, I'd like your first comment to be affectionate—not critical."

Another part of assertiveness is learning to say "no." While it's fine to add "I'm sorry" or "I know how important this is to you," avoid complicated excuses.

IMPROVING COMMUNICATION

Real listening is rare. Most of us *think* we're listening when we're really just waiting for the other person to finish talking.

Using these simple techniques, most people can dramatically transform their conversations—and their relationships…

• **Don't interrupt.** Say nothing until the other person has finished speaking. Most people who try this for just one day are amazed to discover just how often they interrupt others.

• **Look interested.** Use attentive body language. Uncross your arms, lean forward and make eye contact.

• **Reflect back what you heard.** Restate the points or emotions that the speaker just expressed.

•**Be willing to be changed by what you hear.** Be open-minded. Don't pass judgment until you know all the facts.

How you speak is as important as how you listen. Saying "I like," "I feel," etc., is less likely to cause offense than telling the way things "are" or what's "wrong" with the other person.

BEING EMPATHETIC

To hone your empathy skills, think of an annoying habit of someone you're close to. Imagine you are that person, and describe his position using "I statements."

EMPHASIZING THE POSITIVE

Being positive doesn't necessarily mean being Pollyanna-ish. Having a good outlook can save relationships.

Recently, University of Washington psychologist John Gottman, PhD, taped interactions between newlyweds.

His findings: Marriages with at least five positive interactions for every one negative contact were most likely to last.

In addition to strengthening your relationships, this skill can boost your happiness. The happiest people aren't those who feel the most *intense* joy or excitement…but those who have mostly positive feelings all day long.

50th Anniversary Greetings

White House greetings for anniversaries of couples married at least 50 years or for birthdays of people at least 80 years old can be arranged. Send name, address and date of event six weeks in advance to The White House, Attn: Greetings Office, Washington, DC 20502-0039. Or fax to 202-395-1232 (preferred method). Free. *www.whitehouse.gov/greeting.*

How to Select a Nursing Home

Placing a relative in a nursing home is a heart-wrenching ordeal. To ease the way, know when a nursing home is the only answer. *Deciding factors:* A loss of control of body functions, a loss of memory or an inability to perform the basic activities of daily life such as shopping, cleaning and dressing. People do not age physically and emotionally at the same rate.

Never coerce a person into a nursing home. Instead, open the decision for discussion. When possible, have the person accompany you when you shop for the proper home.

The nursing homes with the best reputations, highest staff-to-patient ratios and longest waiting lists are nonprofit. That is, they are run by churches, fraternal orders and charities. *Hitch:* Only about 25% of all homes are nonprofit. The majority of nursing homes are for profit, or proprietary. *Other differences among homes…*

•**Health-related facilities emphasize personal,** not medical, care. These are generally nonprofit homes.

•**Skilled nursing facilities are for patients with serious mental and physical disabilities.** Most of these places are proprietary.

Nonprofit homes usually charge a flat, high monthly fee with no extras for added services. Proprietary homes ask a lower monthly fee with extra payments for services. Always be certain that you understand the rates and service charges.

Many proprietary homes don't take Medicaid patients. The amounts paid by the state and federal health plans aren't always enough to cover the costs. Patients who have no money should be placed in a nonprofit home.

To select a home, start by asking the patient's physician, relatives and friends who have gone through a similar experience for information. Also, get information from the state departments of health and social services.

Begin the search to find a nursing home long before it becomes necessary. *Caution:*

Many emotional problems among the elderly occur during the waiting period because of the stress of being in limbo.

Since this is an emotional experience, take a close friend with you when you inspect nursing homes. The person will look for things that you might forget.

WHAT TO SEEK IN A HOME

•**Good location.** The right home is close enough for convenient visits. Avoid places in run-down or dangerous neighborhoods. *Best:* A residential area with gardens and benches.

•**Well-lit, cheery environment.** Also, doors to the room shouldn't have windows. This is a home, not a hospital.

•**The home's affiliations with hospitals and associations.** Find out how many patients are on Medicaid. If the number exceeds 50%, the home is not likely to provide adequate care.

•**A professional staff.** There should be a full-time or regularly visiting doctor with specialized knowledge in geriatrics. The total number of registered nurses, licensed practical nurses and nurses' aides should be at least 40% of the number of beds.

•**The residents.** Nothing speaks better for a nursing home than active, vital patients. Observe the staff to see if they treat residents with respect. Talk to the residents and ask for their complaints. *Bad signs:* If more than 3% of the residents are indoors at one time. If patients are still in bed or in bedclothes at 11 am. If many residents are catheterized to avoid linen changing. Ask what happens when a patient is hospitalized. Is the nursing home bed still available to him/her afterward?

•**Handrails in hallways and bathrooms.**

•**Smoke alarms in public areas and each room.** Ask to see the latest fire inspection report and note the date.

•**The dining room should be clean, bright and inviting,** with no dirty trays around. Are special diets adhered to?

•**The residents' rooms should be comfortable and attractively furnished.** Be sure the room can be personalized with pictures, plants, knickknacks. Drawers should be lockable.

•**Happy patients are those who are plugged into the outside world.** Newspapers and large-print books should be readily available. The home should show movies, bring in entertainers and provide outside trips. *Other necessary activities:* Gardening, workshops, education courses, lecture series and discussion groups. Find out about religious services and provisions for voting.

•**Special services should include visits by a licensed physical therapist** and workable therapy equipment that the patients can use. *Visits by other specialists:* Speech therapists for stroke victims, audiologists, dentists, psychiatrists, optometrists and podiatrists.

WHAT TO WATCH OUT FOR

•**Patients who are sedated** in order to keep them quiet.

•**The home asks for a large sum of money up front.**

•**Doctors who hold gang visits** (they see 40 to 50 patients during each call).

•**You are denied visiting rights** to the kitchen, laundry and/or library.

•**The Patient's Bill of Rights** isn't displayed.

Home Care Know-How

Peter J. Strauss, Esq., senior counsel in the law firm Epstein Becker & Green, PC, 250 Park Ave., New York City 10177. He is a fellow of the National Academy of Elder Law Attorneys and coauthor of *The Elder Law Handbook—A Legal and Financial Survival Guide for Caregivers and Seniors.* Facts on File.

Only the very rich can afford not to be concerned about the likelihood that some day they will need home care or nursing home care.

But the rest of us do have to worry about becoming incapacitated. And most of us would prefer to be cared for at home. *Questions we all have...*

•**How much does home care cost?**

•**Will Medicare pay for some of it?**

• **What quality of care can one expect** from the government?

• **Do I need a Medigap policy?**

• **What about a long-term-care insurance policy?**

MEDICARE

Medicare generally covers a very limited portion of the cost of care provided in the home. Although home care typically follows a hospital stay, Medicare does not make hospitalization a prerequisite for coverage.

As long as the care is necessary for treatment of an illness or injury, Medicare coverage applies. This coverage, however, includes only the items defined as "home health care benefits." *These include…*

• **Medical social services.**

• **Nursing care** (part-time or intermittent).

• **Medical supplies/equipment.**

• **Physical therapy.**

• **Occupational therapy.**

• **Speech therapy.**

• **Home health aides** (part-time or intermittent), but only if a skilled service—such as therapy—is provided also.

The benefits *must* be prescribed by a doctor and provided by a home-care agency that has been certified by Medicare.

• **Medicare does not cover everything.** For instance, Medicare limits coverage for part-time or intermittent home care—fewer than five days a week on an infrequent basis—to 28 hours per week. If continuing care is needed —care for a period of up to 21 days—then coverage can be for up to seven days a week, but only for up to 56 hours a week.

If a home health aide and nursing services are needed, the amount billed must be kept under 28 hours a week to be considered intermittent.

• **Medicare does not cover the cost of long-term care** or personal assistance care. Both of these are considered custodial-type care rather than medical care. This kind of care applies to those with chronic conditions, such as Alzheimer's disease, Parkinson's disease, etc., who need assistance with daily living activities (eating, bathing, getting in and out of bed, going to the bathroom, etc.).

• **Medicare does not cover the cost of housekeeping.** This is often needed by a person with a chronic condition.

MEDIGAP COVERAGE

Supplemental Medicare insurance—Medigap insurance—picks up only the amounts of Medicare-covered expenses that Medicare does not pay for, such as copayments and deductibles.

Medigap *does not* cover the cost of long-term care, since Medicare doesn't provide this coverage.

MEDICAID

Medicaid is a state/federal partnership program intended to serve the nation's most needy and vulnerable populations. Income limits for Medicaid eligibility are set separately by each state and the federal government pays a share of each state's Medicaid costs.

Some home care services, such as personal care services that help with the basic activities of daily living (ADLs), may be provided by the Medicaid program through what are called "Home and Community Based Services (HCBS) Waivers" as an alternative to institutional care.

Every state has at least one HCBS waiver. There is great variation in the scope and nature of services provided under the many different waivers, with some offering as many as 30 different services and some as few as one or two.

States have a great deal of leeway in administering their programs. For instance, they must review any transfer of personal assets a person may have made for less-than-fair-market value to other parties if they are trying to get Medicaid to help pay for care in an institution. This so-called "look-back" at asset transfers is not mandatory for those seeking home care, but many states are considering instituting such reviews in light of extreme fiscal difficulties and the increasing costs of Medicaid programs.

LONG-TERM-CARE INSURANCE

A growing number of older people are buying private insurance policies—long-term-care insurance—to cover the cost of nursing care. The policy should cover both care in a nursing home *and* care in their *own* home.

You can also buy policies that cover only in-home care or only nursing home care, but this is usually not wise.

Caution: Make sure a policy labeled a "nursing home policy" also includes coverage for at-home care.

These policies are expensive: They get more expensive the older you are when you buy them. *Best:* Buy them by the time you are in your 60s. Make sure you take an inflation rider!

CONSIDERATIONS

•**What is the extent of insurance coverage?** Some policies pay for home care only a fraction of what they pay for nursing home care.

•**What is the "triggering event"** for payment of expenses under the policy? Some policies pay much more quickly than others. Find out what the lag time is in policies you're considering.

Bottom line: Make sure that the level of coverage and the event that triggers payment are clearly spelled out in the policy.

TAX INCENTIVES

The tax law now provides breaks that defray some custodial care costs. A person needing home care can take an itemized deduction for "qualified medical expenses" to the extent that total expenses exceed 7.5% of adjusted gross income (AGI). *Deductible medical expenses include...*

•**Out-of-pocket medical costs,** including out-of-pocket payments to home health aides.

•**Medicare copayments** and deductibles.

•**Long-term-care insurance premiums** up to a dollar limit (depending on age).

•**"Long-term-care services"**—up to any amount—provided to a person who is chronically ill. The meaning of "long-term-care services" is liberally interpreted to include rehabilitative services and personal care services. This is so even though personal care service probably would not qualify as a deductible medical expense were it not a long-term-care service.

Taxes: Some part of the benefits provided under a long-term-care policy may be taxable.

Senior Aid

Now more than ever, seniors have helpful resources they can rely on. *For example...*

•**Weatherization Assistance Program.** Available at no charge to seniors who meet specific guidelines. The grant goes to the state, which allocates dollars to nonprofit agencies for purchasing and installing energy-related repairs. *Average value of weatherization services:* Over $2,500 per year.

Weatherization Assistance Program Branch, EE44, US Department of Energy, 1000 Independence Ave. SW, Washington, DC 20585. 800-342-5363.

•**The Eldercare Locator.** Provides access to an extensive network of organizations serving older people at state and local community levels. Services cover home-delivered meals, transportation, legal assistance, housing options, recreation and social activities, senior center programs and more.

Eldercare Locator, 800-677-1116 (Monday through Friday 9 am to 8 pm ET). *www.eldercare.gov.*

Your Home

Save Money (Even Make Money) On Housing for Your College Student

If you're sending a child to college away from home, be prepared to pay big—and not just for tuition. For the 2007–2008 academic year, the average cost for room and board at public universities is more than $7,400, the College Board reports, up 5.3% from a year earlier. At private colleges, the average cost is nearly $8,600, up 5% from 2006–2007.

Bottom line: You can expect to spend $30,000 or more for room and board for each child who goes away to college for four years.

Strategy: *Buy* your child a place to live near the campus. In today's buyer's market for housing, you might find a very good deal.

If you sell the property a few years from now, you may get a better price. Even if you just break even on the real estate, you'll save by not paying for college housing.

REAL TAX BREAKS

In a simple example, you might buy an apartment where your daughter can live while she goes to school.

Tax benefits: If you itemize, and as long as you're not subject to the alternative minimum tax, you will be able to deduct the property tax you pay. If you use a mortgage to help finance the purchase, the interest you pay will be tax deductible, too. In essence, the apartment would be taxed as if you were using it as a second home.

Final accounting: When you sell the apartment, assuming that you've owned it for more than a year, any gain will be taxed at only 15%, as a long-term capital gain.

Trap: A loss on your sale won't be treated as a capital loss because you can't take a capital loss on the sale of a residence, so you would get no tax benefit.

Greg Weyandt, CPA, MPA, director of operations, Welch Group, 3940 Montclair Rd., Birmingham, AL 35213. A partner in a wealth-management firm, Mr. Weyandt profited from an investment in near-campus housing when two of his children went to Auburn University.

Strategy: Rather than take a loss, you may prefer to rent the apartment, perhaps to a different student, after your daughter moves on. You can receive rental income while you wait for your apartment's value to recover.

ALL IN THE FAMILY

A more ambitious venture is to buy a larger apartment than your child needs or a house near the campus.

Next step: Let your own child live in this residence *and* rent space in it to one or more other students. Because they'll pay rent to you, the residence will become income-producing property.

Tax treatment: Operating costs will become tax deductible. That could include everything from utility bills to insurance.

You also will be able to take depreciation deductions for the real estate, furnishings, fixtures, etc.

Management fees: Name your child as property manager. Your child's responsibilities could include screening tenants, getting leases signed, collecting rents, arranging for property maintenance, and so on.

For those services, you could pay your child a management fee. Approximately 10% to 12% of the rental income received from tenants might be reasonable, depending on other property management fees in the area.

Loophole: Such management fees will be deductible for you, the property owner. They can reduce taxable income from rents or contribute to a loss for tax purposes.

At the same time, income from these management fees probably will be tax free to your child. In 2008, because of the standard deduction, single taxpayers may have up to $5,450 in earned income and owe no tax.

Therefore, this arrangement can be a tax-efficient way to give your collegian spending money.

Travel smart: What's more, your trips to visit the college town may be deductible if your primary purpose is to check up on your investment property. *Note:* Be sure to document that you checked on the house's condition, spoke with the property manager (your child) about maintenance, met with student-tenants to see if they have concerns, researched nearby rents, etc.

LOSS LEADER

Deductions for management fees, depreciation, travel, and other expenses may generate a taxable loss from the property each year. This might be the case even if you have positive cash flow from rental income.

Tax treatment: Such a loss would be considered a *passive loss*. As long as your adjusted gross income (AGI) is less than $100,000, up to $25,000 worth of passive losses can be deducted each year.

As your AGI goes from $100,000 to $150,000, your maximum passive loss phases out, from $25,000 to zero.

End of the deal: When you ultimately sell the property, you can use any passive losses not previously deducted. Those losses can decrease a taxable gain or increase a capital loss from rental property.

PROCEED WITH CAUTION

Tax benefits will help a near-campus investment, but there is risk in any real estate venture. Some basic precautions can increase your chance of success.

Location: This is always crucial for real estate investing. Look for a place not far from the school in a neighborhood that's safe and doesn't seem intimidating in any way. A good location will help make student-tenants and their parents feel comfortable. Moreover, it will make it easier to eventually sell the property.

Tenant tactics: Be cautious about selecting tenants. Get references from employers to see if the students have been reliable. Have the students' parents sign 12-month leases and provide guarantees that they'll be responsible for the rent.

Documenting The Deed

Your house deed will be recorded among the land records in the jurisdiction where your house is located, so don't worry if you find you have lost it when it comes time to sell the house. The title attorney handling the sale of the house will be able to prepare a new deed from these records. *Alternative:* The attorney or title company that conducted your settlement. Either of these two parties might have the original recorded deed in their company files.

Important house documents to keep (in addition to the deed to the house): The settlement sheet (for future tax purposes), the deed of trust and the promissory note that you sign with your lender.

Evaluating a Condo... A Checklist

When you evaluate a condominium, consider first the physical appearance of the grounds and the units for sale. *Ask yourself these questions...*

• **Are the building exteriors and the common areas well-maintained?**

• **Does the development offer the amenities that you enjoy?**

• **Are there recreational facilities that you will not use but will pay for?**

• **Are the living units well-constructed,** with good-quality materials and fixtures? Is there adequate soundproofing?

• **Does the floor plan suit your lifestyle?**

• **Is the location of the unit within the development a desirable one?**

• **Is the development itself well-situated,** with easy access to shops and community facilities?

• **Does it offer a safe, secure living environment?**

• **Will you and your family have sufficient privacy?**

• **Would you enjoy having the other residents as neighbors?**

H.L. Kibbey, author of a series of books for home buyers and sellers, including *The Growing Older Guide to Real Estate.* Panoply Press.

Self-Defense for Tenants

Tenants are rapidly becoming a beleaguered species as rents skyrocket and vacancies in desirable urban areas plummet. Confronted with a booming seller's market, landlords often become greedy and take advantage of tenants' desperation. Most states with major populated areas now have some form of protection for tenants, however. Tenant remedies vary according to state or local laws. But there is one power that a tenant anywhere has and should use when circumstances warrant it—the power to withhold the rent. If you understand the basic concepts of tenant law, you will know when and how to use your ultimate weapon.

Your apartment must be suitable for habitation by a human being. If it's not, the law in most states requires the landlord to do whatever is necessary to make it habitable. *The following must be provided...*

• **Heat,** hot and cold water.

• **Electricity or a facility for it** if it's metered through a public utility.

• **Air-conditioning** if it's in your lease.

• **Absence of roaches and vermin.**

• **Clean public areas (lobbies, halls)** in the building.

• **No dangerous health conditions** in the apartment. *Examples:* Falling plaster, peeling lead-based paint.

The warranty of habitability deals mainly with health, not with cosmetics. If your bathtub is cracked, it isn't a violation of the warranty unless water is leaking. The crack might be a violation of the local tenant-protection act, however, which varies from state to state.

The question of unfair leases came up because landlords were taking advantage of the scarce housing situation to force tenants into signing leases with unconscionable provisions. *Examples:* Clauses saying the landlord doesn't have to provide heat and hot water; clauses waiving a tenant's right to trial by jury in a landlord/tenant conflict; clauses giving the landlord the right to change a tenant's locks if the tenant doesn't pay the rent—all without going through the court system.

Recommended: Sign whatever lease the landlord offers. Then take him to court if some of the provisions prove unconscionable.

The best way to find out the law in your area is to call your local congressperson. Many local legislators have a hotline or an open evening for community residents to air their problems. At the very least, a local legislator can point you in the right direction—to a community group or a tenants' organization in your area.

Don't run to a lawyer immediately. Try a community group first. If you do decide to hire a lawyer, make sure he's a specialist in landlord/tenant law. This is a very specialized and volatile area. Laws change frequently, and an amateur can do you more harm than good.

The most effective method of confronting the landlord is through a tenants' organization. If you are having problems with your landlord, the same is probably true of the other tenants in your building. If you approach the problem as a group, your chances of success improve immeasurably.

HOW TO GO ABOUT IT

- **Talk to the other tenants in your building and distribute flyers calling an organizational meeting.** At the meeting, elect a committee of tenants to lead the group.

- **Pass out questionnaires to all tenants,** asking them to list needed repairs in their apartments.

- **When the questionnaires have been collected,** a member of the committee should call the landlord and suggest a meeting with him to negotiate complaints. Many landlords will comply with this request, since the spectre of all their tenants withholding rent can be a frightening prospect. Negotiation is always preferable to litigation. It is a very effective tool. *Also:* Negotiation can be desirable for a landlord who is not getting his rent on time. Tenants can emphasize that they are willing to improve the landlord's cash-flow problems by paying on the first of the month if he is willing to make repairs.

- **If negotiation fails,** organize a rent strike. That's a procedure whereby tenants withhold rent collectively, depositing the money each month in an escrow fund or with the court until

repairs are made. If your tenant organization is forced to go this route, you will need a good lawyer. Be prepared for a long court battle.

If the other tenants won't cooperate, you can withhold your rent as an individual. *Reasonable grounds:* Lack of services (heat, hot water, garbage collection, elevator). Don't withhold rent unless you have a good reason. If you lose, you'll be liable for the landlord's attorney's fees plus court costs. *Advantage of withholding:* You'll get your day in court and the opportunity to explain to a judge what the problem is. Even if you lose, you will be allowed to pay rent up to date and not be evicted. The harassment value of forcing your landlord to take you to court will probably make him more compliant in the future. Get a lawyer to represent you if the problem is severe.

Tenant versus tenant. *If a tenant in your building is involved in crime or drugs or is excessively noisy, a number of possibilities are available to you...*

- **Take out a summons,** claiming harassment or assault. *Probable result:* The court will admonish the tenant to stop causing a disturbance (which may or may not have any effect).

- **Sue for damages in civil court.** You may win (although collecting the judgment is another story).

- **Try to persuade your landlord to evict the undesirable tenant.** *Best way:* Put pressure on him through your tenants' organization. A landlord can't be forced to evict anyone. He has the right to rent to whomever he chooses. But if your association has a decent relationship with the landlord, he might comply, especially if the tenant is causing a dangerous condition or destroying property.

- **You do have the right to break your lease** if you're being harassed by another tenant, but this may not be much comfort if apartments in your area are scarce.

Moving Fragile Objects

When moving valuables, consider carriers other than household movers. Special handling is important for irreplaceable and fragile objects as well as for jewelry, collections and currency. *Options:* Air freight, UPS, armored service, registered US mail, yourself.

Moving Does Not Have to Be Traumatic

Cathy Goodwin, PhD, author of *Making the Big Move: How to Transform Relocation into a Creative Life Transition.* New Harbinger Publications. She has moved more than 12 times in her life. Dr. Goodwin is a former professor of marketing at Nova Southeastern University in Fort Lauderdale, FL.

Whether you are moving to a smaller space in the same city...to a retirement community in another state... or to an apartment across the country, there are steps you can take to minimize the disruption that relocation invariably causes.

First, make sure moving is something you want to do. People who feel forced to move often experience anger and resentment on top of all the normal relocation-induced feelings of loneliness, anxiety, excitement and expectation.

PSYCHOLOGICAL ISSUES

If moving is something you've decided is right for you, make it easier on yourself by working through some of the psychological issues ahead of time.

• **List the activities you most enjoy doing.** Think of the roles you play in life that define you. Ask yourself what it is about your home environment that energizes you.

It's often the seemingly trivial routines and comforts—like a morning cup of cappuccino at the local coffee shop—that we miss most in a new location. If you make careful note of these comforts, you'll be able to duplicate them in your new home.

• **Prepare for moving by deciding who you are.** Decide what you need around you in order to fully express your identity.

Exercise 1: Who are you? As quickly as you can, complete the sentence, "I am a _____" 10 times.

Examples: I am a mother, I am an artist, I am a gardener, etc.

Review what you've written and think about what it reveals about you. What, if anything, will change if you move to a new location?

Exercise 2: Which routines are most important to you? You will gain a better understanding of the importance of your daily routines by writing them down. *As thoroughly as possible, write down...*

• **What you do on weekday mornings.**

Example: Wake up without an alarm clock ...walk the dogs...drive to the local newsstand for the paper...stop at the corner coffee shop.

• **What you do to relax in the evening.**

• **How you spend Saturday mornings.** When you've completed this exercise, ask yourself how you'd feel about interrupting these routines.

Though the details you record may seem trivial, it's often these little changes and losses that increase the psychological trauma of moving.

PRESERVING COMFORTS AND ROUTINES

By understanding which routines and comforts are important to you, you'll more easily develop replacements in your new community. *Do some homework before the move...*

• **Learn all you can about your prospective community.** Use the Internet to research the community and learn about its character/ culture.

By typing in the city and state you're considering, you can learn about museums and theater programs...local businesses and restaurants...opportunities for continuing education ...medical services...transportation, etc.

Use the library to research the archives of the local newspaper.

Better: Make a premove visit to the area you're considering and talk to people of all ages about what it's like to live in the area.

• **Visualize how you'll spend a day in the new location.** Begin by visualizing your new home for 15 to 20 minutes. Relax, close your eyes and get comfortable.

Ask yourself: What is my ideal home? Where does the sun rise and set? Are there skylight windows? Lamps? Overhead lighting? What is the shape of each room, and what kind of furniture do I see in each? Who or what do I see in the home with me (spouse, dog, cat)?

After you've pictured your new home in your mind, visualize a day in your new community. See yourself waking up. What will you do next? What familiar roles might be useful in your new location? What new roles or activities might you engage in? What problems might you encounter (e.g., no coffee shop!) and how will you deal with these problems?

When you've completed this exercise, write down any insights you've gained, then compare your notes with your real life in the new location after you've moved.

FOR RENTERS

If you choose to rent, place a "Rental Wanted" classified ad in the local paper. I've done this twice. As a result, I've learned about really fine properties that are typically only rented by word-of-mouth.

And, contrary to what many people think, I didn't get any crank phone calls.

Sample ad: Model tenant with steady income seeks single-level, three-bedroom apartment. References provided.

PLANNING A NO-TEARS MOVE

• **Use the checklists provided by moving companies** as well as lists found in books. *For example…*

> • *Smooth Moves* by Ellen Carlisle (Teacup Press).

> • *Steiner's Complete How-to-Move Handbook* by Clyde L. Steiner and Shari Steiner (IIP Consumer).

• **Put together an emotional first-aid kit.** Your kit can include coping statements such as, "I will just let go and relax"…"I can deal with this"…or "I've survived this before—and I can do it again."

Add to the kit meditation and visualization books and tapes. Also include the phone numbers of old friends—at least one to laugh with, one to listen to you and one who moved recently and can give good advice. Pick up a journal in which you can record your thoughts, concerns and feelings.

Making the Most of Your House

Charles Jacob, Irving & Jacob Architects, Norwalk, CT.

Many homeowners are taking a new look at their houses with an eye toward either extending and upgrading through additions and renovations or constricting living space for greater efficiency.

Procedure for additions or renovations: The architect compiles a set of preliminary drawings to obtain a rough idea of costs from contractors. Next, a complete set of drawings makes closer estimates possible. For small jobs, rely on the cost estimate of a reputable local contractor. For more complex work, get estimates from two or three contractors. No estimate is reliable unless it is based on a complete set of drawings.

Costs: Per square foot, a new bathroom is the most costly room in the house. *Next most expensive:* The kitchen. *Least expensive:* A bedroom.

Planning: Try to have all the outside work done during the fair-weather months and save the interior finishing for winter.

Problem: Kitchen renovation. No matter what time of the year this work is done, you end up with sawdust in the scrambled eggs. *Best:* Take a vacation while the kitchen is being rebuilt. *More realistically:* See that as much work as possible is done outside the kitchen. Then have the actual installation of items such as cabinets, counters and appliances concentrated in one burst of activity. This might take as little as one week.

In the search for more living space, many owners convert an attached garage into a family room. A new, level floor should be installed over the existing concrete slab, which is often pitched. *Important:* Insulate the space under this new floor. Slip new windows and doors into the old openings. *Convenience:* A new bathroom for this area. If the plumbing is prepared properly, a kitchenette can be added later. Thus the family room can be quickly converted into a rental apartment for added income when the kids have grown up and moved out, assuming local zoning allows for accessory apartments in residential neighborhoods.

Parents whose children no longer live at home often adopt a country-kitchen style of living. The couple centers its activities around the kitchen, even sleeping in a nearby room. *Aim:* To conserve heat by warming only the core of the house in winter.

New source of heat and comfort: An old-fashioned wood-burning stove. *Warning:* Charming as these stoves are, they can cause fires if they are not installed properly.

Other things to know...

• **Zoning and building permits are required** before the construction of most additions. *Key word:* Setbacks. These are the hypothetical lines on your property beyond which you are not allowed to build without a variance.

• **No addition may encroach on an existing water well,** septic tank or septic field. Find where these are located and plan accordingly.

• **Know the capacity of your present electrical service.** An older house may receive only 60 to 100 amps. You may have to push service to 200 amps to meet the demands of the newly finished space.

Choosing a Building Contractor

Before you hire a contractor, do some homework so you know what to expect. *For example...*

• **Get bids from three contractors** whom you have selected by looking at their work or through friends' recommendations.

• **Make sure your job specifications are the same** for each contractor so that all the bids will be for exactly the same requirements.

• **Watch out for low bids.** They may presage shoddy workmanship or inferior materials.

• **Run a thorough check on the contractor** you decide to use (credit, bonding references, insurance, etc.).

• **Be specific about every detail of the job,** leaving nothing in doubt when you draw up the final agreement.

• **Pay one-third up front,** one-third when the job is almost done and the balance at the conclusion of the job, if you are satisfied.

• **If you make changes during construction that are not in the contract,** get all the costs in writing before the alterations are made.

Getting Your Money's Worth from a Home-Improvement Contractor

Plunging ahead with major improvements or additions to your home without a carefully thought-out contract is asking for trouble. What to get in writing?

• **Material specifications,** including brand names and a work-completion schedule.

• **All details of the contractor's guarantees,** including the expiration dates. *Also:* Procedures to be followed if materials or workmanship should prove defective. *Trap:* Do not confuse manufacturers' guarantees with the contractor's guarantees of proper installation.

• **An automatic arbitration clause.** This provides that an impartial board will mediate if problems of excessive cost overruns arise.

• **A clause holding the contractor responsible** for negligence on the part of subcontractors. Check with your lawyer for specifics.

• **A cleanup provision** specifying that all debris be removed.

DOS AND DON'TS OF A CONTRACT JOB

• **Do consult a lawyer** before signing a complex contract.

• **Don't sign a contract with any blank spaces.** Write "void" across them.

• **Don't sign a work-completion certificate** without proof that the contractor has paid all subcontractors and suppliers of materials.

• **Don't pay in full until you are completely satisfied.**

• **Don't pay cash.**

Beware of Certain Home Improvements

Edith Lank, a real-estate broker who writes a nationally syndicated column about real estate. She is also the author of *The Home Seller's Kit, Fourth Edition* (Real Estate Primer Publishers) and *The Homebuyer's Kit* (Dearborn Trade Publishing).

A big problem for some home owners—the house you bought for $50,000 in the 1960s is now worth $500,000...and you'd like to put some of the profit into your pocket. There are effective steps you can take now to enhance the value of your house whether you decide to sell or to get cash from it by renting or mortgaging.

Most people are now aware that when they sell a house, they never recoup the value of swimming pools, finished basements and most other major improvements.

But what many people don't know is that these additions can actually decrease the value of the home.

Reason: Some prospective buyers don't like swimming pools, and others have their own ideas about finishing the basement. By making these improvements yourself, you simply lose these prospects.

Even if you are lucky enough to find a would-be buyer who wants a pool, you won't get your money back because the price of your house is largely determined by the average home price in your neighborhood. Prospective buyers looking for a more expensive house will look in a neighborhood that has many houses in that price range.

Exceptions: Good bathrooms and kitchens do help to sell a house. If yours are in bad shape, fix them up. It pays to consult an agent if you're in doubt about fixing up a room. Tell the agent you're selling in a year, making it in the agent's interest to give you free advice.

Ironically, the improvements that really help sell a house are basically cosmetic and inexpensive. In today's market, however, they can be very important. *Some of the easy and inexpensive improvements you can make...*

- **Trim the lawns and shrubs.**
- **Paint the front entrance,** and put a couple of pots of geraniums by the door.
- **Make sure the porch light and the bell** are in working order.
- **Clean the house thoroughly,** and keep the windows clean. If this isn't your forte, hire a cleaning service.
- **If rooms are even the slightest bit cluttered,** move out some of the furniture.
- **No matter what you have in your closets,** take at least half of it out. Remove at least half of what you have on your kitchen counter.
- **Tighten any loose knobs or faucets.**

And, before the agent shows the house, be sure you...

- **Close the garage door.**
- **Park the kids and the pets with a neighbor.**
- **Put away the kids' toys.**
- **Remove all conspicuous personal items** such as awards, souvenirs and religious items. (They might make you more interesting, but not the house.)
- **Turn on all the lights and open all the curtains.** *Exception:* Leave the curtains drawn if the window looks out on a used-car lot.
- **If there's a smoker in the house,** remove ashtrays and all other evidence of tobacco.
- **Use an air freshener if the house doesn't smell fresh.** But don't bother if there's a nice cooking aroma coming from the kitchen.
- **Turn off appliances.** It's okay, however, to have very soft music playing in the background.

How to Have a Successful Garage Sale

Monica Rix-Paxson, coauthor of *The Fabulous Money Making Garage Sale Kit.* Sourcebooks, Inc.

The most profitable garage sales are the ones with the most merchandise. Tables should be laden with goods. Lots of clothes should be hanging on racks. Boxes to rummage through should be everywhere.

Suggestion: Get your friends and neighbors to join in the fun and be cosellers—and coworkers. Tell them to bring over any and all of their recyclable household goods and turn the garage sale into a big event—so everyone makes money …and has a good time, too.

Once you've interested your friends and neighbors, the next step is to start planning and organizing. A garage sale requires preparation and creativity, but your efforts will pay big dividends.

Start by setting up a schedule of activities that begins at least two weeks before the first bargain hunter arrives—and preferably four weeks before—and ends the day after you make your final sale.

TWO TO FOUR WEEKS BEFORE

•**Select a date** (and rain date) for the sale. Do not schedule the sale on a holiday weekend.

•**Call Town Hall** and find out if you need a permit.

•**Warn your immediate neighbors** so they have time to put up "no parking" signs on their property if they want to or put their cars in their garages to provide more parking.

•**Invite cosellers and assign them their own specific price tag** (red, blue, green, etc.) to be hung on their merchandise for easy record-keeping.

ONE WEEK BEFORE THE SALE

•**Schedule friends and family to keep an eye on things.**

•**Write and submit classified ads to your local newspaper and radio station.** Don't forget to put notices up around town, too. Use index cards or flyers and post them in supermarkets, libraries, etc.

•**Design garage sale signs and decide what street corners they'll go on.** Use large construction paper. Tape signs to telephone poles and trees with arrows pointing people in the right direction. Put some signs on the main road and some at intersections.

•**Decide if unsold merchandise will be taken back** or find a charitable organization that will pick up unsold goods.

•**Plan lunch for helpers and cosellers.**

THREE DAYS BEFORE THE SALE

•**Arrange for cosellers to bring their own tables and racks,** as well as bags and boxes for buyers to use to take merchandise home.

•**Price items intended for sale,** clean them, make minor repairs and tag them.

•**Create colorful banners to hang over displays**—Toys! Kitchen! Bath!

•**Go to the stationery store and buy cashier-station materials,** like receipts, a cash box, a hand calculator, etc.

•**Make name tags for cosellers and helpers.**

•**Buy enough plastic cups,** coffee, cream and sugar to be able to hand a cup to browsers.

•**Rig a small dressing room in the garage** so people can try things on.

ONE DAY BEFORE THE SALE

•**Review cashier procedures** and give helpers their assignments and schedules.

•**Have $50 in change in a cash box:** 15 $1 bills, four $5 bills, one $10 bill and $5 in change.

•**Make an arrangement for your pets to be out of sight and sound.**

•**Put garage sale signs around the area.**

•**Arrange merchandise by hanging clothes on racks,** having $10, $5, $1 and $.50 tables and boxes for rummaging clearly marked in advance with what is contained inside of them.

•**Place a "sale begins at 9 o'clock" sign on your door to discourage early birds,** but expect an onslaught by 9.

DAY OF THE SALE

•**Put on the coffee at 8 am.**

•**Have cosellers and helpers take up their positions.**

•**Lock the house or rooms where the sale is not taking place.**

•**Open for business.**

•**Periodically remove extra cash from the cash box.**

AFTER THE SALE

•**Count the money!**

•**Distribute the proceeds to the various cosellers.**

- **Return anything borrowed.**
- **Box up goods for return.**
- **Remove garage sale signs.**
- **Thank everyone and congratulate yourself!**

A garage sale is a shared experience that is always a lot of work, but potentially also a great deal of fun and enjoyment.

Great Products to Combat Clutter

Debbie Gilster, president and organizing consultant, Center for Growth and Productivity, 25002 Hollyberry Ln., Laguna Niguel, CA 92677. www.centerforproductivity.com.

It's a cinch to organize your home and office when everything has a place. *Try these quick and easy organizing solutions...*

COMPUTER SOFTWARE

- **Kiplinger's Taming the Paper Tiger.** This program makes paper files easy to find. To use, number each file. Then enter their names, locations and identifying keywords into the database. An Internet-like search engine determines the location of any item in seconds. Also use it to organize CDs, wines, videos, etc. *Features:* Printable reports..."to do" lists...label printer. The Monticello Corporation, 800-430-0794. $169.95. *www.thepapertiger.com.*

HANDY REMINDER

- **Parrot messaging switch plate.** Ordinary light switch cover contains a battery-powered voice recorder that stores up to a 20-second message. Press a button to record...flip the light switch for playback. Use instead of notes to leave a reminder for yourself...or a special message for a loved one. Requires no special wiring. $14.95. *www.stun-ningsales.com.*

UNDER-BED STORAGE

- **Bed riser.** Works with all angle-iron bed frames to raise the height of any box spring and mattress by up to 10 inches. *Result:* Plenty of under-bed storage space. Stacks & Stacks, SKU#5622, 800-761-5222. $32.99–$79.99. *www.stacksandstacks.com.*

GARAGE STORAGE

- **Interchange modular wall storage system.** Sturdy mounting on a wall to hold any of 11 interchangeable racks, hooks and hangers that lock securely in place. *Including:* Tool hanger, utility hooks, three-tier trays, vertical and horizontal bike hooks, cord wrap, hose rack, catch-all basket. Racor Home Storage Products, 800-783-7725. $8 to $20 per piece. *www.racorinc.com.*

ADJUSTABLE DRAWER DIVIDERS

- **Drawer organizers.** Sturdy clear or white plastic tabs are easily cut to size to create drawer dividers in any configuration—just score with a knife and snap. Use for organizing kitchen utensils, clothing, jewelry, etc. Available in 1″, 2″, 3″ and 4″ heights. Lifestyle Systems, 800-955-3383. $10 to $20 per drawer, depending on height. *www.lifestylesystems.com.*

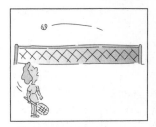

Building A Tennis Court

Ray Babij, tennis-court builder, Remsenberg, NY.

There are four types of tennis courts... clay, Har-Tru (pulverized green stone with a gypsum binder), asphalt and concrete. Clay and Har-Tru are soft and need daily maintenance. Asphalt and concrete are hard courts that require little upkeep.

- **Choosing the right court.** Soil and rock conditions can dictate the best type for your yard as much as your playing preference. Sandy soil with good drainage makes an ideal base for any kind of court. Heavy clay soil holds an all-weather court easily but requires additional excavation and filling for a soft court. Rocky areas may need blasting to create a proper base for any kind of court.

- **Construction time.** A tennis court needs time to settle, particularly the hard surfaces (asphalt and concrete) that might crack if the base were to heave. In the northern part of the country, where winters are severe, the ideal building schedule for hard courts is to excavate in the fall, let the base settle over the winter and finish the surfacing in the late spring or early summer. With soft courts, settling is less of a problem because cracks can be filled in with more clay or Har-Tru. A soft court can be built in six to eight weeks, with three weeks for settling.

• **Zoning and permits.** Property owners must provide an up-to-date survey of their property and be sure that the proposed court fits within the setback requirements—or get zoning variances if necessary. Contractors obtain the building permits. Many communities require fencing.

• **Costs.** Prices vary considerably from one part of the country to another. Special excavating problems create only one of the price variables. In general, however, a clay court with sprinkler system and fencing is less expensive than a similar Har-Tru court. All-weather courts (asphalt in the East, concrete in the West) are the least expensive of all.

• **Maintenance.** Soft courts must be swept and relined daily, sprinkled and rolled periodically and refurbished annually (or more often in climates where they get year-round use). Hard courts must be resurfaced every five to seven years. Many builders offer maintenance-service contracts.

Home tennis courts require much more space than is commonly believed. While the actual playing area of a court is relatively small (36 by 78 feet), adding the out-of-bounds areas pushes the total required to 60 by 120 feet, about one-sixth of an acre.

Safer Home Chemicals

Combustible liquids—gasoline, kerosene for backyard torches and charcoal lighter fluid—cause more deaths and injuries than all other summer chemicals combined. *Trap:* The combustible liquid could spill near someone who is smoking or near an open flame and ignite.

Another way people get hurt is by adding an extra dose of lighter fluid to boost an already lit fire. *Result:* The can may explode, scattering burning lighter fluid all over. *Recommended:* Put plenty of lighter fluid on the first time. If the fire doesn't catch, douse the whole thing with water and start over with fresh charcoal. Or better yet, buy charcoal that doesn't require lighter fluid.

Paint. In the warm summer months, many people paint or varnish furniture, decks, etc. *Caution:* If the label says "use with adequate ventilation," do the project outdoors. Opening windows and doors in the house does not provide enough ventilation. If you can't take the project outdoors (you're painting a room, for instance), use water-based paint, which doesn't require as much ventilation during use.

Jay Young, chemical health and safety consultant in Silver Spring, MD.

Keeping Your Home Safe

A multipurpose dry chemical unit is the best home fire extinguisher. Check the label to see what kinds of fires it's effective against. It should cover Class A (ordinary combustibles like wood and cloth), Class B (gases, greases, flammable liquids) and Class C (electrical fires).

Smoke detectors work best in a two-unit system. Place an ionization detector in the hallway outside your bedroom for a quick alert on a racing fire. Then install a photoelectric model downstairs in the general living area or the main stairway that will detect smoke from smoldering upholstery or rugs.

Aluminum wiring, which was used in two million homes and apartments built between 1965 and 1973, has caused more than 500 home fires in the past 10 years. *To check:* Ask the original electrical contractor, or look for an "AL" stamp on exposed wires in your basement. If you do have aluminum wiring, a qualified electrician may be able to make your house safe at a moderate cost. Never attempt repairs (even simple ones) on your own.

Consumer Adviser, Reader's Digest Association Inc., Pleasantville, NY 10570.

Oil- vs. Water-Based Paint

Water-based paint has many distinct advantages over oil-based paint. It dries in less than an hour, has no paintlike odor, doesn't show brush or roller lap marks as distinctly and makes for an easy soap-and-water cleanup. It also wears longer, is washable and holds color best. *Overwhelming choice:* Water-based paint (also known as latex or acrylic).

Stick with high-quality oil-based paint if the exterior surface is already painted with several coats of oil-based paint (alkyd resin). *Reason:* Latex expands and contracts more easily than oil does during the freeze-thaw weather cycle. This action may pull off any underlayers of oil-based paint that aren't locked onto the surface.

Latex exterior paints are ideal for exterior surfaces. *Why:* They allow the surface to breathe. And their flexibility during the freeze-thaw cycle enables them to adhere to the surface better. Latex house paint color has superior resistance to bleaching and fading. (If you have latex over an oil-based layer that is holding, continue with water-based paint.)

When painting over an already painted exterior surface, first rough up the gloss with sandpaper or a wire brush. This gives the smooth surface some tooth, on which the fresh paint can grip and bond. Make sure all chalking surfaces are clean and sound.

Before painting, scrub under the eaves and in protected spots with a solution of detergent and water. *Reason:* Salts from the air collect in these areas that are not washed clean by rain. Exterior paints won't hold.

Use latex paint for any interior jobs, even if it means covering existing oil-based layers. *Exception:* When there is a water-soluble substance underneath the oil. The water in latex softens these substances, which leads to peeling. Enough coats of oil-based paint usually shield the underlying calcimines or sizers from the water in the latex. *Test:* Paint a small area with latex. If there is no peeling within a couple of hours, continue with latex.

Neil Janovic, whose grandfather founded the paint and paper company Janovic Plaza Inc. in 1888 in New York City.

Painting Trouble Areas

Often, paint peels in one section of a wall or ceiling. *Causes...*

• **A leak making its way through the walls** from a plumbing break or an opening to the outside.

• **The plaster is giving out in that area** due to age or wear and tear.

• **The paint layers may be so thick** that the force of gravity plus vibrations from outside make the paint pop and peel in the weakest spot.

Fix: If it's a leak, find and correct it. Otherwise, remove as much of the existing paint as you can. Scrape away any loose, damp or crumbling plaster. Spackle and smooth the area. Prime and paint it.

For real problem areas: Spackle, then paste on a thin layer of canvas. Apply it as though it were wallpaper. Smooth it out so it becomes part of the surface. Then prime and paint it.

Best Color to Paint A House

Yellow houses have the most "curb appeal" and sell faster than those of any other color. Most people associate yellow with sunshine, optimism and warmth.

Leatrice Eiseman, color consultant and educator in Tarzana, CA. www.colorexpert.com.

Painting Pads

Originally made for coating wood shingles, pads are coming into general use. They are now available in a number of sizes and shapes for jobs such as edges and window trim or entire walls, indoors and out. Once the basic stroke has been mastered, most home painters find pads faster and neater than either rollers or brushes. Made of nylon fiber pile, pads leave a smoother finish than other applicators with both oil- and water-based paints.

How to Avert Structural Damage

Repair cracks in concrete as soon as you spot them. Look for them in the warm months, before the troublesome weather hits. The action of water, especially as it freezes and thaws, can quickly turn a small crack into a major one, possibly even resulting in structural damage.

Essential: First investigate and correct the cause of the crack.

New Shelter.

Protection from Storm Windows

See-through plastic windowpanes guard against breakage in hazardous locations such as storm and garage doors and basement windows. Use acrylic plastic one-eighth inch or one-quarter inch thick. Cut with a power saw fitted with a fine-toothed blade. Or cut by hand, using a scribing tool.

Roof Longevity

Slate or tiled roofs should last a human lifetime, as should terne (lead and tin) or copper sheeting. Asphalt shingles should hold out for 15 to 25 years.

Good precaution: After a roof is 15 years old, have a roofer inspect and repair it annually.

Modernize Your Home Heating

Heating systems that are more than a few years old need modernizing.

Gas: Install a stack damper and electric ignition to produce an average gas savings of 10%.

Oil: Older systems don't have a flame-retention head burner, which saves 15%.

Both systems pay for themselves in about three years.

Eleven Ways to Conserve Home Heating Fuel

There are certain things you can do to save money on heating. *Try these simple conservation ideas…*

1. Buy a new heating system. *Reason:* Systems more than 20 years old operate in the 65% efficiency range. New models average at least 80% efficiency. Increasing efficiency from 65% to 80% saves about $765 a year in a house that uses 1,700 gallons of heating fuel at $3 a gallon.

2. Service heating systems annually. *Point:* A 2% increase in efficiency will pay for tests and adjustments.

3. Reduce the hot-water heater setting to 120°F or lower. (Average settings range from 140° to 160°F.)

4. Minimize use of hot-water appliances.

5. Install automatic flue stack dampers on hot-water and steam-heating systems. They conserve heat by closing the flue pipe when the oil burner is off. *Potential savings:* 5% to 10%.

6. Install clock thermostats that automatically reduce heat at certain times during the day or night. *Potential savings:* If the clock thermostat is set to reduce the temperature from 70°F to 65°F for 16 hours a day, heating bills will drop 10%.

7. Use spot heating when needed.

8. Use draperies, shades and blinds to prevent heat from escaping. Minimize use of exhaust fans.

9. Insulate.

10. Use trees and shrubs as windbreakers.

11. Use humidifiers. *Reason:* Rooms with less than 30% humidity will feel chilly even when well-heated.

Heating and cooling use 70% of the energy. Water heating takes 20%. Cooking, refrigeration, lighting, etc., total only 10% of use.

Frank C. Capozza, manager of Frank's Fuel, a fuel distributor, N. Tarrytown, NY.

Weather Stripping

To test the airtightness of a window or door, move a lighted candle along its frame. If there is enough draft to make the flame dance, then caulk or weather-strip it. For a door, add weather stripping if you can slip a quarter underneath it.

Is Home Siding Economical?

New home siding of vinyl, aluminum or steel beautifies but does not save energy. The FTC has warned about advertising that claims adding siding helps lower fuel bills. *Exception:* Some insulating effect occurs when the siding is installed over sheets of formed plastic.

Special Telephone Secret

Carl Oppedahl, a New York City–based lawyer and the author of *The Telephone Book*. Weber Systems Inc.

A network interface is a special telephone jack that allows you to determine which wires are faulty when your phone goes dead—outside wires, which the phone company must repair at no cost to you, or inside, which the phone company may charge to repair.

Installation: If you want to install your own interface, buy the materials at a phone-supply store. If your phone repairman installs it, you must purchase the materials from him. *Tip:* To avoid charges for the visit, have the repairman install the interface when he is at your house doing other phone work.

How the interface works: When your wires go dead, simply plug a phone into the network interface. If you hear a dial tone, the problem is in the wiring on your premises. If there is no dial tone, something is wrong with the wires leading to your house. *Extra benefit:* If the problem is internal, the phone plugged into the interface will provide phone service until repairs are made.

Cost advantages: You are no longer susceptible to billing tricks of the phone company.

Example of such a trick: If you don't pay inside wire maintenance fees, phone repairmen often claim that the problem is in the wiring on your premises—when it's really in outside wiring. *Result:* The phone company charges you for the repairs and visit, which should be free.

Also: You can repair an internal problem yourself or have an electrician do the job, which is often cheaper than the phone company's work. And you no longer have to pay inside wire-maintenance fees, which cover the cost of any service call the phone company makes on the wires inside your house. Since these wires almost never break, you can save up to $50/year for maintenance you don't need.

Capping the Chimney Flue

Chimney problem—warm air leaks out, and birds nest in the flue. *Solution:* Install a chimney cap, which closes off the chimney flue at the roof. A long chain hangs down into the fireplace. To open the flue, pull the chain to release the spring-loaded cover. A tug on the chain closes the flue.

at a distance, and radiator covers should have ample holes at the top and bottom.

Home Energy Hints

Try these simple solutions to save money and energy…

• **Draft resistance.** Before winter sets in, trace drafts. A ¹⁄₁₆-inch crack beneath a door lets out as much warm air as a 4-inch-square hole in the wall. Check with your utility about local energy audit services to help find leaks and stop heat losses.

• **Cut kitchen heat loss by covering the range hood's vent** (when not in use, of course). Use a piece of ¾-inch Styrofoam encased in aluminum foil. Attach it to the hood with springs, or by fastening temporarily with duct tape.

• **Solar protection.** Keep insurance in mind when converting a home to even partial solar power. *Among the hazards:* Rooftop storage tanks that are too heavy for present structural supports…vulnerability of collection panels to hail, lightning, falling objects and vandalism …potential bursting of pipes if liquid freezes in heat-transfer systems.

Do-It-Yourself Heat Saver

Homemade reflectors placed behind your radiators provide more efficient heating.

Directions: Cut radiator-size sheets of quarter-inch-thick Styrofoam and cover one side with heavy-gauge aluminum foil. (Tape or staple it into place on the reverse side.) Slip the reflector behind the radiator, with the foil facing the room. The Styrofoam keeps the cold wall from absorbing heat, and the foil directs the heat out into the room.

For best circulation of radiator heat, keep the radiator fins well dusted and make sure that there is a free flow of air above and below the radiator. Drapes and furniture should be

Cooling the House Without Air-Conditioning

John A. Constance, licensed engineer specializing in industrial ventilation, Newtown, PA.

Ventilating fans can cool an entire house—or a single room—at a fraction (about 10%) of the cost of air-conditioning. The trick is knowing how to use them.

Unlike oscillating fans, which simply move air around, ventilating fans exhaust hot air while pulling in cooler air. You control the source of the cooler air by manipulating windows. During the day, for example, downstairs windows on the shady northern or eastern side of the house are most likely to provide cool air. All other windows should be closed and shaded from direct sun with blinds and drapes.

At night, lower-floor windows can be shut for security while upstairs windows provide cool air. The very motion of air, like a light breeze, has a cooling effect.

TYPES OF VENTILATING FANS

• **Attic fans** are permanent installations above the upper floor. They are powerful enough to cool the entire house. The opening to the outside must be as large as the fan-blade frame in order to handle the air flow properly. Louvers, bird screening and (particularly) insect screening all reduce the exhaust capacity of a fan. A doorway or other opening must allow the fan to pull cool air directly up from the rest of the house. Direct-connected fans are quieter than belt-driven fans. Some attic fans have thermometers that automatically turn them off and on when the attic temperature reaches a certain degree of heat.

• **Window fans** have adjustable screw-on panels to fit different window sizes. Less powerful than attic fans, they serve more limited spaces.

• **Box fans** are portable and can be moved from room to room to cool smaller areas.

PICKING THE RIGHT-SIZE FAN

Ventilating fans are rated by the cubic feet per minute (CFM) of air that they can exhaust. For effective cooling, engineers recommend an air-change rate of 20 per hour (the entire volume of air in the area to be cooled is changed 20 times every 60 minutes). To determine the required CFM rating for a particular room, calculate its volume in cubic feet. Then multiply this figure by 20/60 (⅓). *Example:* A room 20 feet by 15 feet with an eight-foot ceiling contains 2,400 cubic feet of air. This multiplied by ⅓ gives a CFM rating of 800 for a proper-size fan.

The CFM rating of an attic fan is determined in the same way. Total the cubic feet of the rooms and hallways you want cooled before multiplying by ⅓.

Air-Conditioning Secrets

John A. Constance, licensed engineer specializing in industrial ventilation, Newtown, PA.

Room air conditioners mounted in a window or through the wall are ideal for keeping small, comfortable havens cool against the worst of summer's hot spells. They can be more economical than central air conditioning because they are flexible—you cool only the rooms you are using. But even a single unit can be expensive.

Buy for economy. Tailor the size of the unit to the room. Oversize air conditioners cool a room so fast that they don't have time to dehumidify the air properly. Slightly undersize units are more efficient (and cost less to begin with). Check the energy-efficiency tags on different models for lowest operating costs.

To keep a room cool with minimum use of the air conditioner…

•**Limit the use of the air conditioner in the "open vent" setting**—it brings in hot outside air that the machine must work hard to keep cooling.

•**Protect the room from the direct heat of the sun** with awnings, drapes or blinds.

•**Close off air-conditioned rooms.**

•**Turn off unnecessary lights**—they add extra heat (fluorescent lights are coolest).

•**Turn off the unit if you will be out of the room** for more than 30 minutes.

•**Service room air conditioners annually to keep them efficient.** Replace filters, keep condensers clean and lubricate the moving parts.

Buying an air conditioner that is too large is uneconomical. *To find the most efficient machine:* Divide the BTU rating by the watts rating (also on the label). If the resulting number (the energy-efficiency rating) is eight or more, it won't run up your electric bill unduly.

Compare prices. Energy-efficient air conditioners cost more initially. Where use is heavy (the South) or electric rates are high (the Northeast), the price difference is probably worth the investment. *Bonus:* Energy-efficient air conditioners cool rooms faster.

Supplement central air-conditioning with a room air conditioner in the most-used room. Greatest saving is when only one person is home and the excess cooling isn't needed.

Home Emergency Checklist

Vital information about the house should be known by everyone in the family in case of emergency.

Key items: The location of the fuse box or circuit-breaker panel, placement of the main shutoff valves for the water and gas lines and the location of the septic tank or the line to the main sewer.

Also keep easily accessible: Records of the brands, ages and model numbers of the stove, refrigerator, freezer, dishwasher, furnace, washer and dryer.

Woman's Day.

Visible Address May Save Your Life

A clear address outside your house helps emergency vehicles (and visitors) locate you easily. *Complaint of firefighters and ambulance drivers:* Most street addresses are difficult to find and hard to read.

Solution: Put large figures where they are easily read from the center of the street at night during poor visibility.

Buying a Burglar Alarm

Home alarm systems, once mainly for the rich, are coming into widespread use. *Reason:* Locks aren't deterring burglars. Recent FBI figures show that 82% of the time, illegal entrance is gained through home doors, most often the front door.

Burglars just break open the door with their shoulders. Faced with a deadbolt or double lock, the burglar will use a heavy tool to take out the frame.

Best type of alarm: One that sounds off (not a silent alarm), so that the burglar is aware of it and alarm central (a security-company office or the local police) is alerted. This makes sense, since most burglars are youngsters ages 12 to 24 who live within an eight-block radius of the target.

Select a system with sensors on vulnerable doors and windows. The inexpensive alarm promoted at many electronics stores is not worthwhile. Good systems need a complex electrical tie-in in the basement as well as a control panel installed away from prying eyes and little children. Good systems can also switch on lights and TV sets and alert alarm central by automatic telephone dialing or a radio signal.

Have a secondary line of defense. This can be a few thin electronic pressure pads under rugs in high-traffic areas, or strategically placed photoelectric cells.

Choose a reputable, well-tested system. Two brand names are ADT and Honeywell.

Drawbacks: The greatest is the danger of continual false alarms. The police may ticket you if the family is to blame. Also, an alarm system needs regular testing and a routine for setting at night or when you're away.

Alarm systems can provide a false sense of security. The homeowner may not take all necessary precautions with locks or may leave the garage door partially open.

Secrets of a Professional Burglar

From my own experience as a successful burglar, and also from talking with hundreds of fellow inmates in prison for burglary, I've concluded that burglary is a psychological game. The only real deterrent is the realization that there is immediate danger to him, the burglar. Locks don't do this. Alarms don't do it. Hardcore doors don't do it. Only mind games really work. I'm not against good locks, sturdy doors and alarm systems. But if you rely 70% on mind games and 30% on hardware, you'll do much better in the end.

If a burglar sees warning signs, no matter how outlandish, on your house, he will think twice before breaking in. These signs should be handwritten, in large, clear print, on six-inch by eight-inch cards posted above each doorknob. Don't put them on the street or in your yard where passersby can see them. You don't want to give a burglar a reason to case your place and find out they are not true. You can make up your own wording. Just be sure the signs look fresh and new. *Some suggestions…*

• **"Danger: Extremely vicious,** barkless German Doberman." In his nervous frame of mind, a burglar probably isn't going to wonder if there is such a thing. He won't want to take the chance.

• **"Knock all you want. We don't answer the door."** Most burglars check to see if anyone's home before breaking in. About 95% of those questioned said they'd pass up a house with that sign.

• **"Carpenter: Please do not enter through this door.** My son's three rattlesnakes have gotten out of the cage and we've closed them off in this room until he returns, hopefully in a few days. We're sorry for this inconvenience, but we don't want anyone else to get bitten. The first is still in the hospital."

• **"Please stop!** We've already been forced to kill one burglar who was trying to get in while we weren't home. Please don't become the second." Like the barkless dog sign, this one seems outlandish. But a jittery burglar isn't going to stick around thinking up ways you could kill him while you're not home.

• **"Attack dogs trained and sold here."** Again, 95% said they'd be gone like a shot if they saw this sign. *Suggestion:* Have one engraved, and post it on your front door (so it can't be seen from the street).

Leave extremely large bones and two-foot-wide dog dishes near all entrances. Someone who's up to no good will think a very large dog lives there.

Paste stickers on the windows indicating that you have an alarm system. *Try motion-detector alarms:* "This building is equipped with laser-type motion-detector devices. Bodily movement inside will set off audible or silent alarm." Some 85% of inmates questioned said they'd pass up a house with this notice. *Also:* Paste alarm foil along windows. Put suction cups on the inside of windows and alarm-type bells on the outside walls.

Put fine gravel in your driveway or in gardens surrounding the house. This makes a lot of noise that burglars won't want to chance.

When you go away on vacation, don't tell anybody except the local police. Ask a neighbor to pick up your mail and newspapers and occasionally empty a small can of junk into your trash can. Close all shades, blinds or curtains. Leave one or two radios on. Have your outside lights on a light-sensitive switch and inside ones on an alternating timer. Put up your deterrent signs.

Buy an air horn (the kind small-boat owners use). If someone breaks in while you're at home, go to the opposite window and squeeze the horn. These horns can be heard for a mile over water. Everyone said this tactic would scare them off.

COMMON LOCK AND ALARM MISTAKES

• **Putting a deadbolt or other expensive lock** on a flimsy door that can be kicked in. *Also:* Thinking that this lock will do the trick. The burglar simply uses a bigger crowbar.

• **Not locking the door when you're home.**

• **Positioning a lock on a door with a glass window** in such a way that if the window is broken, the burglar can reach in and unlock the door.

• **Installing the burglar alarm on/off switch outside the house,** not inside it.

• **Forgetting to turn on your alarm.**

SOME BURGLAR-SURVEY RESULTS

• **85% were deterred by hearing a TV or radio in the house.**

• **75% were more likely to go through windows than doors.** (Sliding glass doors are easier to open than wooden ones.) *Remedy:* Storm windows. None of the burglars surveyed would bother with these at all.

• **85% cased out a house before hitting it.** *Recommended:* If you see a stranger hanging around, call the police.

• **Only 20% picked locks or tried to pick them.** *Why:* It takes too much skill. There are so many faster ways into a house.

• **63% cut the phone lines before entering.** *Remedy:* Put up a sign that says the police will be notified automatically if the phone lines are cut.

• **65% said that a large,** unfriendly dog would scare them away. *Most frightening:* Dobermans.

• **80% looked in garage windows to see if a homeowner's car was there.** *Remedy:* Cover your garage windows.

• **50% said that neighborhood security guards didn't deter them.**

•**72% made their entrance from the back.**

•**56% continued to burglarize if they were already inside** when they realized that people were at home but asleep.

Recommendations of A Master Locksmith

Menasche Sofer, All-Over Locksmith, Inc., 1335 Lexington Ave., New York City.

Traditional wisdom says there's no point in putting a good lock on a flimsy door. This is not true. In most cases you must prove forcible entry to collect insurance. If you have a poor lock, your cylinder can be picked in seconds. You're inviting your insurance company to give you a hard time.

THE BEST STRATEGIES

•**If you have a wooden door, get what the industry calls a police lock.** This is a brace lock with a bar that goes from the lock into the floor about 30 inches away from the base of the door. It can be locked from the inside, but you can get out easily in an emergency. *Also:* Get a police lock if your door frame is weak. It keeps the door from giving because of the brace in the floor. Even the best regular locks won't protect you if the whole frame gives.

•**If you're buying a door,** buy a metal flush door without panels and get an equally strong frame to match it. *What makes a good frame:* A hollow metal construction, same as the door.

•**On a metal door,** I like a Segal lock on the inside and a Medeco on the outside with a Medeco BodyGuard cylinder guard plate. If it's a tubular lock, get Medeco's Maxum. It gives you the option of a key on the inside, and you don't need a guard plate.

•**If your door opens out instead of in,** get a double-bar lock—one that extends horizontally on each side. With a door that opens out, the hinges are often exposed on the outside, allowing a burglar to remove the door from its hinges. With a double-bar lock he can't pull the door out.

OTHER IMPORTANT DEVICES

•**Plates.** Pulling out the lock cylinder is the burglar's easiest and most effective way of getting in. Most people put a plate over their lock and think that will take care of it. But most plates have bolts that are exposed on the outside. With a hollow metal door, the burglar can pull that plate away from the door with a wedge and simply cut the bolts. If the head of the bolt is exposed, he can pull it out slightly with pliers and snap it right off. *Remedy:* Medeco's BodyGuard. A cylinder and plate combination, it's a drill-resistant, one-piece unit with no exposed bolts, a sleeve to prevent burglars from chiseling the bolts and a hardened plate to protect the keyhole.

•**Jimmy bars.** Don't bother with them. They're psychological protection only. If you have a metal door, a good lock is sufficient protection. With a metal door, we recommend a jimmy bar only if the door has been damaged through a forcible break-in and is separated from the frame. In this case, the bar will straighten out the door and hide some of the light shining through. If you have a wooden door, a jimmy bar can actually help a burglar by giving him leverage. He can put a crowbar up against it, dig into the wood and break through the door.

•**Peepholes.** Get one that's as small as possible. Large peepholes use a one-way mirror that doesn't permit you to see around corners. And if someone hits that mirror while you're looking through, it could damage your eye. Small peepholes use a double lens, making it possible to see around corners. And if the small peephole is knocked off the door, it won't benefit the burglar. If a big one is knocked off, it creates a weakness in your security. *Recommended:* If you already have a large peephole, remove it. Have the locksmith bolt two plates on the door, with a smaller hole in the center to accommodate a small peephole.

•**Closets.** Let's say you want to protect a closet—not necessarily against burglars but against someone who might have a key to your house or apartment. Locking the closet isn't sufficient because most closets open out and have hinges on the outside, making it easy to remove the door. *Remedy:* A door pin. This involves putting the pin on the hinge side of the door and through a receiving hole in the frame. Anyone who cut the hinges off or removed the pins couldn't lift the door out.

- **Window locks.** The best window locks use a key, which makes them difficult to manipulate from the outside. Without a key, almost any window lock is vulnerable. *Best:* Try one with a heavy pin, which allows you to drill holes for either complete locking or three- or six-inch ventilation.

- **Window gates.** In New York and other cities, the fire laws prohibit window gates that lock with a key. *Remedy:* Gates with keyless locks. They allow you to get out easily, but a burglar can't put his hand through the gate to open it.

CHOOSING A LOCKSMITH

Go to locksmiths' shops to size them up. Make sure the store is devoted exclusively to the locksmith business and isn't just doing locksmithing on the side. Ask to see the locksmith's license if it's not displayed. There are a lot of unlicensed people doing business illegally. *Best:* Locksmiths who belong to an association—they keep up with the latest developments. Look for a sticker in the window indicating membership in a local or national locksmiths' association.

Best Place in Your House To Hide Valuables

John Littlejohn, manager of Abbey Locksmith, Inc., New York City.

Even if you have a safe, you still need a good place to hide for the safe key or combination. Obviously, it should not be hidden anywhere near the safe. And if you don't have a safe, you should hide your jewelry and other valuables where they won't be found.

RECOMMENDATIONS

- **Don't hide things in any piece of furniture that has drawers.** Drawers are the first place burglars will ransack.

- **Don't hide anything in the bedroom.** Thieves tend to be most thorough in checking out bedrooms. Find hiding places in the attic, basement or other out-of-the-way areas. *Best:* The kitchen. In 90% of burglaries the kitchen is untouched.

- **Don't be paranoid.** If you have thought up a good location, relax. A burglar can't read your mind.

GOOD HIDING PLACES

- **Inside the phony wall switches** and generic label cans sold by mail-order houses.

- **In a book, if you have a large book collection.** So you don't forget which book you chose, use the title to remind you (for example, *The Golden Treasury of Science Fiction*). Or buy a hollowed-out book for this purpose.

- **Inside zippered couch cushions.**

- **In the back of a console TV or stereo speakers** (thieves usually steal only receivers, not speakers) or in the type of speakers that look like books.

- **Under the dirt in a plant.** Put nonpaper valuables in a plastic bag and bury them.

- **Under the carpet.**

- **In between stacks of pots in the kitchen** or wrapped up and labeled as food in the refrigerator or freezer.

The best hiding places for household valuables are those that look completely innocent and, preferably, would be inconvenient to take apart. *Examples:* Inside an old, out-of-order TV or vacuum cleaner in the basement. In a pile of scrap wood beneath the workbench. In the middle of a sack of grass seed.

How to Hide Your Valuables by Linda C. Cain. Beehive Communications. Limited availability.

Best Safes

Valuable items require a burglar-resistant safe that's protected on all six sides. Such safes carry the Underwriters Laboratories rating TRTL30x6. The safes are rated by how tool resistant they are. The most common safes on the market—usually labeled TL15, TL30 or TRTL30—are protected only on the front face and door.

Safe Factory, a division of MegaSafe, NY.

Biggest House-Fire Danger Spot

Not the kitchen, as commonly believed, but the living room. Fires there account for the largest number of deaths year after year. *Safety measure:* Install a smoke detector in the living room.

Journal of American Insurance.

One smoke alarm isn't enough. *Recommended:* An alarm on each level of your home and in each bedroom.

International Association of Fire Chiefs, Fairfax, VA.

Easy Ways to Do Hard Things

Keep aluminum windows and doors in working order with simple maintenance procedures when you switch from screens to storm panels. *You should:* (1) Clean the channels where window panels slide up and down with the crevice nozzle of the vacuum cleaner or a tiny stiff brush. Spray with silicone lubricant. (2) Spray stiff spring locks with a moisture-displacing penetrating lubricant (WD-40, for example). (3) To prevent oxidation and pitting on frames, scrub with a detergent solution, rinse and coat with a good grade of automobile wax.

• **To unclog a sink drain,** first place a basin below the trap (the U-shaped drainpipe beneath the sink); the basin will catch water that runs from the trap. Then use a wrench to unscrew the plug at the bottom of the trap. Slip on a rubber glove and move a finger into the open trap to loosen any blockages. To complete the job, run a stiff wire into either side of the trap. Screw in the plug and tighten it with the wrench.

• **Sluggish sink drains respond to one of these treatments:** Remove the strainer. Pour several pots of boiling-hot water down the drain. Then run hot tap water down the drain for a couple of minutes. If this does not bring results, pour one cup of baking soda into the drain. Follow this with one cup of vinegar.

Cover the drain opening tightly for 20 minutes. Then run hot tap water down the drain. *Last resort:* A commercial preparation.

• **Prevent clogged drains by replacing the S-trap** in the drainpipe with a squeezable trap. One hard squeeze sends a drain block on its way. Available from hardware and plumbing-supply stores. Easily connected with a screwdriver.

• **To clean a burned pot,** first dampen it. Sprinkle baking soda on the charred area, and add a little vinegar. Let it stand for 20 minutes. The pot should then wash clean.

• **Alcohol stains on tabletops.** To remove white rings, rub gently in one direction with moistened cigar ash or superfine steel wool dipped in mineral oil.

• **Furniture scratches.** *For small blemishes:* Try toothpaste—its mild abrasive action is effective on minor scratches. *Deeper scratches or wide areas:* Use a blend stick, crayon, liquid shoe polish or paste boot polish. Apply toothpaste to even out the finish after coloring. Then wax with furniture polish and buff with a clean cloth.

• **Sticky drawers.** Rub the bottom rails with soap. If the rails are rough or worn, rub chalk on the drawer runners or sides or on the chest's rails or guides. Put the drawer back in and move it until it sticks. That spot will be marked by chalk. Sand or plane the sticky spot and then rub the area with soap.

• **Cutting down on dust.** Spray your home furnace filter with a no-wax dusting product that attracts and holds circulating particles. Then clean the filter regularly. Do the same with the air-conditioner filter.

• **Contact lenses lost in a carpet.** Place a nylon stocking over the nozzle of a vacuum cleaner and carefully vacuum the area. The lens will be pulled up onto the stocking.

Best Toilet Bowl Cleaner

In-tank toilet bowl cleaners containing calcium hypochlorite corrode the flushing mechanism. Moreover, these cleaners are of little use. All toilet bowls get dirty, and the best way to clean them is with a sponge or brush and a liquid cleaner.

Try a nonhypochlorite cleaner: Ty-D-Bol Blue is a good one.

How to Noiseproof Your Home

Noise intrusion is a constant and nagging problem in many buildings because of thin walls and badly insulated floors and ceilings. *Some solutions…*

• **Walls.** Hang sound-absorbing materials such as quilts, decorative rugs or blankets. *Note:* Cork board and heavy window draperies absorb sound within a room but do not help much with noise from outside. *Unique step:* Carpeted walls provide excellent sound-proofing. Some brands of carpet can be attached to the wall with adhesive. *Alternative:* Try a frame that can be attached to the wall. Insulation

goes on the wall within the frame, and then a fabric is affixed to the frame.

• **Ceilings.** Acoustical tile may be applied directly to the ceiling with adhesive. *Best:* A dropped ceiling of acoustical tile with about six inches of insulation between the new and existing ceiling is a good bet.

• **Floors.** A thick plush carpet that is laid over a dense sponge-rubber padding works well. *Key:* The padding must be dense, at least three-eighths of an inch thick. Your foot should not press down to the floor when you step on the padding.

Versatile Vinegar

This safe, natural and inexpensive product is a handy thing to have around the house, aside from its obvious usefulness in the kitchen. It can be used as a cleanser and a deoxidizer, an antiseptic for minor first-aid needs or a fluid (three parts vinegar and one part water) that keeps windshields both ice- and frost-free.

Antique Furniture Care

Use a room humidifier when central heating is on. (Dryness causes cracks and splits.) Keep furniture away from heat sources such as radiators, working fireplaces and direct sunlight. (Excessive heat will make it warp.) Use a clear, hard wax once a year, but avoid liquid or spray waxes containing silicon, which damages wood. Don't worry about any tiny bumps or scratches; they're signs of authenticity.

Diversion.

Top-Notch Home-Cleaning Secrets

Cheryl Mendelson, Esq., a graduate of Harvard Law School and author of *Home Comforts: The Art & Science of Keeping House*. Scribner.

When my home was undergoing major renovations, I found myself with some knotty cleaning questions. I couldn't find effective information for removing many stains or getting all the different surfaces of my home as clean as I wanted.

For answers, I consulted manufacturers, private businesses and craftsmen around the country. *Here is what I learned...*

KITCHENS

•**Sweeping.** Use a broom with even nylon or synthetic bristles. It collects dirt better than corn brooms.

Start sweeping at the walls, and move dirt toward the center so you push it the shortest distance. Don't lift the broom high off the floor after a stroke—this flings dirt into the air.

Store brooms with the bristles up. Otherwise bristles break or bend.

•**Coffee or tea stains on china,** plastic and glassware. Mix one-eighth cup of regular chlorine bleach with one cup of water. Pour into the bottom of your dishwasher before starting the wash cycle.

Important: Make sure nothing aluminum or silver is in the machine—it can become discolored.

BATHROOMS

•**Hardened soap scum on tiles.** Coat the entire surface with undiluted liquid detergent, and allow it to dry overnight. Wet the surface and scrub with a stiff brush and scouring powder. Rinse and buff with a bath towel.

•**Nonslip treads on bathtub floor.** Try Naval Jelly or KRC-7, a porcelain and tile cleaner (both available at plumbing-supply stores). These cleaners may remove mineral stains without eating away at the treads.

•**Rust around faucets and fixtures.** Use a powder containing oxalic acid, such as Bar Keeper's Friend or Zud (both available at hardware stores).

Important: Never mix these rust removers with chlorine bleach. The fumes are toxic.

•**Concentrate on the spots where fingerprints accumulate**—if you want to disinfect your bathroom in addition to just cleaning it.

Examples: Toilet handles, light switches and knobs on the shower door, medicine cabinet and door.

FURNITURE

•**Water rings on hardwood surfaces.** Try mildly abrasive substances, such as mayonnaise mixed with a bit of ashes or toothpaste. The secret is to rub gently for a long time—as long as 45 minutes—so you remove the stain without scratching the finish.

Afterward, wax the whole surface to even the finish. Use paste wax (sold at home centers and hardware stores). It is more protective than oils or liquid waxes.

•**Minor scratches on wood.** I use Old English Scratch Cover (sold at hardware stores). If in doubt about which color to use, start with a lighter color. Apply the product to your wiping cloth, not directly on the furniture.

•**Use the right dust rag.** Soft white flannel or cheesecloth is best because dust adheres to it so well. Dampen the cloth very slightly with water. For heirlooms and valuable antique woods, use distilled water to dampen rags. For carved furniture, china, ceramics, chandeliers and vases, use a small artist's paintbrush made from natural- or hog's-hair bristles.

UPHOLSTERY

•**Stains from eggs,** milk, chocolate. Rub with a solution of one tablespoon household ammonia and one-half cup of water.

•**Coffee, cola and beer stains.** Rub with a solution of one-third cup of white vinegar mixed with two-thirds cup of water. Avoid soap, which can set the stain permanently.

•**Ink stains.** Sponge with rubbing alcohol.

WALLS

•**Nonwashable wallpaper.** For grease stains, place an absorbent towel over the stain and cover it with an iron set at low for several seconds. For ink or pencil marks, try rubbing the wall with cleaning putty such as Absorene (available at home centers) or a wadded-up piece of fresh, soft, white bread.

• **Washable vinyl wallpaper.** For stubborn stains, such as crayon, tar or adhesives, use WD-40 (available in hardware stores).

• **Painted walls.** Mix a thick paste of baking soda and water. Dip your cloth in it, and rub marks very gently to remove fingerprints, crayon, etc.

CARPETS

• **Spills.** Use as little water as possible. Blot as much of the spill as possible with paper towels. Then, in a bowl, whip up a sudsy foam using water and mild detergent. For delicate carpets, I use Orvus WA Paste from Procter & Gamble (available at veterinary stores or feed stores and on-line).

Dip your brush into the foam, not the water. Brush stain lightly, then wipe off excess foam with a clean cloth. Rinse with a 50/50 solution of white vinegar and water. Then rinse with plain warm water. Blot thoroughly.

• **Use a vacuum with low dust emissions.** If you have asthma or other allergies, consider investing in a vacuum with a HEPA filter. Miele vacuum cleaners, 800-843-7231, *www.miele.com.*

WOOD FLOORS

• **Scuffs and heel marks on hard-finish or urethane-type floors.** Dampen a cloth with a small amount of mineral spirits (available at hardware stores). Rub gently in the direction of the grain.

• **Oil or grease stains on natural-finish floors.** Saturate a cotton ball with hydrogen peroxide, and place over the stain for several minutes. Saturate a second cotton ball with ammonia, and place over the stain for several minutes. Repeat until the stain is removed. Let the area dry, then buff with a soft cloth.

COMPUTERS

• **Keyboards.** Try rubbing alcohol or degreaser sprays (available at electronics stores) to clean off the grime.

• **Computer screens.** Make sure screen is off. Use a slightly damp cloth. Avoid those special-purpose towelettes sold in office-supply stores. They leave a soapy residue.

When You Need An Exterminator And When You Don't

Tom Heffernan, president of the Ozane Exterminating Co., Brooklyn, NY.

Clifton Meloan, professor emeritus, Kansas State University, writing in *Science.*

Bug problems can usually be solved without an exterminator. *Keys:* Careful prevention techniques, basic supermarket products and apartment-building cooperation.

Roaches are persistent pests that are the bane of apartment dwellers. The problem is not that roaches are so difficult to kill but that the effort has to be made collectively, by every tenant in a particular building. Roaches cannot be exterminated effectively from an individual apartment. If one apartment has them, they'll quickly spread throughout the building.

Most landlords hire exterminating services that visit during daytime hours when most tenants are at work. They wind up spraying just a few apartments, which is totally ineffective. *Recommended...*

• **Apartment dwellers have to get together,** contact their landlord and arrange for all apartments to be exterminated at the same time. If the landlord is uncooperative, the Board of Health should be notified. If you live in a co-op, the co-op board should make arrangements for building extermination. *Best:* A superintendent or member of the building staff should perform the regular exterminations, since he can get into apartments at odd hours when the tenants are not at home. A professional exterminator should be called only as a backup, in case of a severe problem in a particular apartment.

• **Incinerators that no longer burn garbage are a major source of infestation in large buildings.** In an attempt to cut down on air pollution, many cities have ordered the compacting rather than the burning of garbage. Garbage is still thrown down the old brick chutes, which have been cracked from heat, to be compacted in the basement. Roaches breed in these cracks, fed by the wet garbage that comes down the chute, and travel to tenants' apartments. *Remedy:* Brick chutes should be replaced with smooth metal chutes, which don't provide breeding places. *Also:* Compactors must be cleaned at least once a week.

• **Homeowners do not need regular extermination for roaches.** Since a house is an individual unit, a onetime extermination should do the job. Food stores are the major source of roach infestation in private homes. People bring roaches home with the groceries. Check your paper grocery bags for roaches before you store them.

• **Ants and silverfish can be brought under control** without professional help unless there is a major infestation. Don't call the exterminator for a half-dozen ants or silverfish. Try a store-bought spray first. *Exception:* Carpenter ants and grease-eating ants must be exterminated professionally.

• **Clover mites come from cutting the grass.** They look like little red dots. The mites land on windowsills after the lawn has been mowed and then travel into the house. *Remedy:* Spray your grass with miticide before cutting.

• **Spiders don't require an exterminator.** Any aerosol will get rid of them.

• **Termite control is a major job** that needs specialized chemicals and equipment. Call an exterminator.

• **Bees, wasps and hornets should be dealt with professionally.** Their nests must be located and attacked after dusk, when the insects have returned to them. If the nest is not destroyed properly, damage to your home could result. *Also:* Many people are allergic to stings and don't know it until they are stung.

• **Clothes moths can be eliminated** by hanging a no-pest strip in your closet and keeping the door closed tightly.

• **Flies can be minimized with an aerosol or sticky strip.** An exterminator is of no help in getting rid of flies. *Best:* Install screens on all the windows and doors.

• **Weevils and meal moths can be prevented by storing cereals,** rice and grains in sealed containers. *Also:* Cereals are treated with bromides to repel infestation, but the bromides break down eventually. Throw out old cereals.

There is no 100% effective solution to exterminating mice. *Try these alternatives...*

• **Trapping is effective unless you have small children or pets.**

• **Poison should be placed behind the stove or refrigerator,** where children and pets can't get at it.

• **Glue boards** (available in supermarkets) placed along the walls can be very effective. Mice tend to run along the walls because they have poor eyesight.

Many of the residual (long-lasting) sprays have been outlawed because they don't break down and disappear in the environment. The old favorites, DDT and Chlordane, are no longer permitted except for particular problems such as termite control. *What to use...*

• **Baygon and Diazanon are general-purpose,** toxic organophosphates meant for residual use in wet areas. They're recommended for all indoor insects, including roaches.

• **Drione is a nontoxic silica gel that dries up the membranes in insects.** Recommended for indoor use in dry areas only, it is especially effective against roaches.

• **Malathion is helpful in gardens,** but it should not be used indoors.

• **Pyrethrin is highly recommended,** since it is made from flowers and is nontoxic. It has no residual effect but is good for on-contact spraying of roaches and other insects. If there is a baby in the house, Pyrethrin is especially useful, since children under three months should never be exposed to toxic chemicals. Don't use it around hay-fever or asthma sufferers.

When buying products in the store, look at the label to determine the percentage of active ingredients. Solutions vary from 5% to 15%. The stronger the solution, the better the results.

Prevention is synonymous with sanitation. If you are not scrupulous about cleanliness, you will be wasting your money on sprays or exterminators. Moisture is the main attractor of insects. If you live in a moist climate, you must be especially vigilant. Coffee spills, plumbing leaks, fish tanks, pet litter and pet food all attract bugs. Clean up after your pets, and take care of leaks and spills immediately. If puddles tend to collect around your house after it rains, improve the drainage.

- **Word of mouth is the best way to choose a good exterminator.** Don't rely on the *Yellow Pages*.

- **Contracts for regular service,** which many exterminators try to promote, are not recommended for private homes. A onetime extermination should do the trick, but apartment dwellers must exterminate building-wide on a regular basis.

- **Rout roaches without poisoning your kitchen.** Boric acid or crumbled bay leaves will keep your cupboards pest-free. *Another benign repellent:* Chopped cucumbers.

- **Wood storage and insects.** Firewood kept in the house becomes a refuge and breeding ground for insects. *Risky solution:* Spraying the logs with insecticides. (When the sprayed wood burns, dangerous fumes could be emitted.) *Better:* Stack the wood (under plastic) outside and carry in only the amount needed.

- **To remove a bat from your house at night, confine it to a single room,** open the window and leave the bat alone. Chances are it will fly right out. Otherwise, during the day when the bat is torpid, flick it into a coffee can or other container. (Use gloves if you are squeamish.) Release it outdoors. Bats are really very valuable. A single brown bat can eat 3,000 mosquitoes a night. *Note:* Bats, like other mammals, can carry rabies. If you find a downed bat or you are scratched or bitten by one, call your local animal-control agency and keep the animal for testing. However, very few people have contracted rabies directly from bats. *More likely source:* Skunks.

Plant Poisoning

Plant poisoning among adults has increased alarmingly in the past decade. For children who are under the age of five, plants are second only to medicines as a cause of poisoning. *Prime sources:* Common houseplants, garden flowers and shrubs, as well as wild mushrooms, weeds and berries.

Most important rule: Never eat anything that you are not absolutely sure is safe. More than 700 US plants have been identified as poisonous when eaten, causing violent illness and sometimes death. *If you suspect someone has eaten a poisonous plant:* Call the nearest poison-control center and your doctor. Try to collect samples of the plant for identification.

Among the most common poisonous plants:

- **Garden flowers.** Bleeding heart, daffodil, delphinium, foxglove, hen-and-chickens, lantana, lily of the valley, lupine, sweet pea.

- **Houseplants.** Caladium, dieffenbachia, philodendron.

- **Garden shrubs.** Azalea, mountain laurel, oleander, privet, rhododendron, yew.

- **Wildflowers.** Autumn crocus, buttercup, jimsonweed, mayapple, moonseed berry, poison hemlock, water hemlock, wild mushrooms.

Indoor Plant Care

Spider plants are the champion indoor plant for fast growing, catchy looks and long life with little care. The leaf colors range from solid deep green to green-and-white stripes. *Fastest growers:* Plants with all-green leaves. A small plant fills out in four months. Hang it in a north window (flowers form faster in low light). Keep the soil damp and fertilize once a month.

Self-watering planters can tend your indoor garden while you are on vacation or simply save you time in regular maintenance. Based on the principle of capillary action, these nonmechanical pots come in a variety of sizes, shapes and finishes. They can be bought at garden centers or florist shops. Foliage plants with modest demands will stay sufficiently moist for as long as three months. *Names to look for:* Grosfillex and Natural Spring.

Home Remedies for Houseplant Pests

Use simple, natural solutions to eliminate common household insects. *For example…*

•**Red spider mites.** Four tablespoons of dishwashing liquid or one-half cake of yellow soap dissolved in one gallon of water. Spray weekly until mites are gone, then do so monthly.

•**Hardshell scale.** One-fourth teaspoon olive oil, two tablespoons baking soda, one teaspoon Dove liquid soap in two gallons of water. Spray or wipe on once a week for three weeks; repeat if necessary.

•**Mold on soil.** One tablespoon of vinegar in two quarts of water. Water weekly with solution until mold disappears.

•**Mealybugs.** Wipe with cotton swabs dipped in alcohol. Spray larger plants weekly with a solution of one part alcohol to three parts water until bugs no longer hatch.

Decora Interior Plantscapes, Greenwich, CT.

Ten Foolproof Houseplants

These hardy species will survive almost anywhere and are a good choice for timid beginners who don't have a lot of sunny windows.

•**Aspidistra (cast-iron plant).** This Victorian favorite, known as "The Spittoon Plant," survived the implied indignity in many a tavern.

•**Rubber plant.** Likes a dim, cool interior (like a hallway). If given sun, it grows like crazy.

•**Century (Kentia) palm.** A long-lived, slow-growing plant that needs uniform moisture. Give it an occasional shower to dust it.

•**Philodendrons.** They like medium to low light and even moisture but will tolerate dryness and poor light.

•**Dumb cane.** Tolerates a dry interior and low light but responds to better conditions. Be careful not to chew the foliage or your tongue will swell.

•**Bromeliads.** Exotic and slow-growing, they like frequent misting but are practically immune to neglect and will flower even in subdued light.

•**Corn plant (dracaena).** Good for hot, dry apartments.

•**Snake plant.** Will survive almost anything.

•**Spider plant.** A tough, low-light plant that makes a great trailer and endures neglect.

•**Nephthytis.** Will flourish in poor light and survive the forgetful waterer.

Edmond O. Moulin, former director of horticulture, Brooklyn Botanic Garden, New York.

Secrets of a Great Lawn

Less work makes a grassier lawn. *Mowing:* Set the blades to a height of two to two-and-a-half inches, and cut the grass only once a week. When the weather gets really hot, every other week is fine. *Benefits of taller grass:* Less mowing, stronger and healthier plants that spread faster, more shade to discourage weeds. *Bonus:* Let the clippings lie. They will return nutrients to the soil.

Other work- and lawn-saving tips…

•**Water only when there has been no significant rain for three or four weeks.** Then give a one-inch soak. (Use a cup under the sprinkler pattern to measure—it takes longer than you think.) Frequent shallow watering keeps roots close to the surface, where they are vulnerable to drought and fungus disease.

•**Use herbicides and insecticides only for specific problems.** Routine use weakens the grass and kills earthworms.

•**Sow bare spots with rye grass for a quick fix.** Proper reseeding should be done in late August or early September, when the ground is cooler and moister.

•**Apply fertilizer twice a year,** but not in the spring. September and November are the right months.

Gardening for Fun and Food

Sally Sherwin, editor of *Investment Cooking*.

Growing your own produce can save money. But even when it doesn't, you still get exercise, fresh air, tension release and vitamin-packed harvests.

Home gardeners feel deep satisfaction in making the salad or seasoning the casserole with freshly picked plants. The taste is incomparable. It also works more fresh vegetables into meals. The surplus can be frozen, given as gifts or sold by the children.

Where space is limited, grow a minigarden, indoors or out. Windowsills, balconies and doorstep areas can be used, as well as milk cartons, pails, plastic buckets and cans.

Gear planting to local weather conditions. Summer planting can still be done in June in most regions. Planning for fall crops can be started in early summer.

Proper spacing is very important. One sturdy plant is better than several weak ones. Crowding chokes root systems, causing spindly growth and poor production. Save packet directions for referral.

Look for hybrid bush seeds rather than vining ones to save space.

Seeds do not always have to be bought. Reasonably fresh dill, anise, fennel, coriander and other seeds already on the spice rack should grow. If not, they are too old to add much to food anyway and should be replaced. Plant sprouting garlic cloves, ginger eyes, onions and potato eyes.

Scoop out seeds from vegetables you've bought. Dry them a week or so before planting. Zucchini, summer squash, beans and peas are among the easiest. Or try tomato seeds, especially cherry tomatoes.

Buy seeds for growing vegetables that don't contain seeds—beets, radishes, carrots, swiss chard, mustard greens, scallions, celery, shallots, endive, brussels sprouts, kale.

Ruffled-leaf lettuces grow more easily and are much more nutritious than iceberg. Sprouting (stalk) broccoli is easier than head broccoli.

Consider grapes and berries. Though some take a while to get established, they bear more each year.

Gardening offers a change from the monotony of the supermarket. You can grow yellow tomatoes, ornamental purple kale, scalloped squash—all interesting variations.

Soil preparation is crucial for good results. Have the soil tested annually. Every state has a land-grant college that will test soil for a small fee. It will give abundant basic gardening advice, largely free, through its Cooperative Extension arm. Check state or federal government listings under Agriculture. There are even offices in some large urban centers. Many have helpful USDA Home and Garden Bulletins available. No. 202, *Growing Vegetables in the Home Garden,* and No. 163, *Minigardens for Vegetables,* are good starters. Some offices publish newsletters that give local planting suggestions plus listings of courses or talks about gardening. Get on mailing lists. Always be guided by local experts on the specifics, since weather can vary greatly even within a few miles.

Planting suggestions:

• **Minimize weeding with mulch** (hay or black plastic surrounding plants). It also helps retain soil moisture.

• **Companion planting can help insect control.** *Example:* Basil with tomatoes. (See organic gardening publications.)

• **Look into raised-bed or hill planting when space or soil is limited.**

• **Where light is limited,** put the smallest plants in front of the sun's arc, larger ones behind it.

• **Harvest often.** Many vegetables stop producing if allowed to mature fully.

• **Don't expect instant results.**

• **Vegetable seeds' life span.** *One to three years:* Hybrid tomatoes, leeks, onions, corn. *Three years:* Beans, carrots, peas. *Four years:* Chard, fennel, beets, standard tomatoes. *Five years:* Brussels sprouts, broccoli, cantaloupe, radishes. *To store seeds:* Seal packet with freezer tape. Mark with date and freeze in container.

Real Estate: Bargains From Banks

Malcolm P. Moses, attorney and president, Malcolm P. Moses & Associates, financial and management consultants, 3428 S. Hewlett Ave., Merrick, NY 11566.

Individuals or companies that want to buy real estate at distressed prices should search for banks with portfolios of foreclosures and repossessions, referred to as REO, or real estate owned. They're difficult to find, but the search can really pay off.

When commercial or savings banks foreclose on commercial property, they're often in a hurry to sell the property to remove non-income-producing assets (referred to as non-performing loans prior to foreclosure) from their books. If the real estate market is weak or the property is not prime, you have substantial leverage in negotiating with the bank.

Insiders, however, know that banks don't generally advertise real estate they want to sell. They usually find buyers through private contacts.

Three excellent ways to overcome this problem...

• **Ask loan officers at your bank** to put you in touch with colleagues in their real estate workout department. A workout officer who specializes in real estate is usually in charge of selling foreclosed property.

• **Use business contacts** to get introductions to real estate workout officers in other banks.

• **Make cold calls to bank real estate workout departments.** Lenders who are anxious to sell property will sometimes provide information about available real estate to total strangers. Be persistent and follow up. A property that a bank is not willing to take a hit on today may go on the block tomorrow. *Important:* Inquire if the bank intends to sell the property privately, or if it has already made a policy decision to dispose of the property at auction, or as part of a "packaged sale." Often they will waste your time when a decision not to sell the property privately has already been made. Once you've located a property for sale, there are certain things to bargain for.

PRICE AND FAVORABLE FINANCING

One bargain hunter I know of has been able to buy high-quality property for up to 50% of the original cost. Of course, the discount is biggest when the property is in a distressed area.

Banks often are willing to offer enticing mortgages to the purchasers of foreclosed property. But it's usually possible to go even further.

Good News for Home Owners

An IRS rule lets more taxpayers escape capital gains when selling homes they have lived in for less than two of the prior five years.

Taxpayers will be able to prorate excludable capital gains—$250,000 ($500,000 jointly)—if the two-year test isn't met for reasons that now include death of a household member... divorce or separation...job loss resulting in unemployment benefits...multiple births from the same pregnancy.

Those who sold homes without claiming a partial exclusion can file an amended return. Consult your tax adviser for more information.

Laurence I. Foster, CPA, PFS, consultant and former partner in the accounting and advisory firm of Eisner LLP, New York City.

5

Looking Great

How to Buy Clothes That Make You Look Good

It's a mistake to choose color to "go with" your hair and eyes. It's your skin tone that matters most crucially in your choice of color. That's what determines how a particular color looks on you. *More mistakes...*

Mistake: The idea that black will make you look slimmer. Black will make you stand out, particularly against any light background. (The walls of most rooms are light.) The more intense and dark your clothing, the larger you'll appear and the less likely to blend into the environment. *Another problem:* Black is usually draining, especially on men, who don't have the help of makeup to offset the pasty look that black gives. Most men should beware of very dark or black suits. *Similar problem color:* White, which tends to wash out the face and yellow the teeth. Soft ivory tones are somewhat better but look good on relatively few people.

Mistake: Sticking to one or two color groups because you think they are good for

you. Most people can wear many different color groups. It's the shade that's important. (There are some shades of your favorite color that can look deadly on you.) *The point:* Don't rule out entire color groups—all blues or all greens. Most people can wear certain shades of most color groups. *Exceptions:* There are a few color groups, such as orange and purple, that are really not good for many people in any shade.

Mistake: Failing to pay attention to pattern or weave. People who are short or small-boned should not wear big prints or checks. They can wear a small true tweed. Slender, smallish men and women are overwhelmed by heavy fabrics. Light wools are better for them than heavy worsteds.

Mistake: Not considering aging skin in choosing colors. Wrinkled skin is minimized by softer shades. Hard, dark, intense colors maximize the evidence of aging.

Mistake: Not allowing for the way environment affects your physical appearance. The colors and textures of your office or living room can

Adrienne Gold and Anne Herman, partners in Color-conscious, Inc., Larchmont, NY.

119

affect your looks for better or worse especially in a small room. The colors surrounding you determine the way in which the eye perceives your skin and even your features. Some colors will produce deep shadows, enlarge certain features or produce deep facial lines because of the way they interact with your skin tone.

Women's mistake: Changing makeup to "go with" clothes. Makeup should be chosen according to skin tone only. Using the wrong color makeup is worse than wearing the wrong color clothing.

Men's mistake: Misplaced affection for plaid and madras in sports clothes. Men tend to think they look terrific in these patterns. *Fact:* Most men can't wear them. *Reason for the disastrous choices men make in their sports wardrobe:* They are restricted, or restrict themselves, to conservative business clothes. A man rarely lets himself wear, say, a green suit to the office. *Result:* When men choose sports clothes, they go wild in the other direction, having had little practice in choosing dramatic colors that are suitable.

Mistake: Ignoring the effect of graying hair on complexion. Few men have the sort of skin that takes graying hair well. Men whose skin looks sallow next to graying hair should consider covering the gray.

Mistake: Thinking you can wear colors you ordinarily don't look good in because you have a tan. A tan does make you look healthier, but it doesn't change the basic effect certain colors have on your skin. With a tan, wearing colors you normally look good in is important because that's when those colors look better than ever. *Point:* Neither season nor fashion should dictate the colors of your clothing.

What Women Hate About What Men Wear

Letty Cottin Pogrebin, freelance writer.

No matter how differently women dress from one another, they are surprisingly unanimous about what looks good on men. To verify that hypothesis, an informal survey across the female stylistic spectrum was conducted. *The survey included all types of women:* Preppies in gray flannel Bermudas, ladies who wore gold lamé to lunch, dress-for-success executives in skirt suits, SoHo trend-setters flashing blue nail polish, dignified disciples of designer labels, overaged hippies with feathered headbands and no-nonsense types in polyester pantsuits with matching vinyl shoes and bags.

The result of this survey is a 10-point program:

•**Socks.** These were by far the most frequently mentioned item of annoyance. Socks, women say, must be long enough to cover the calf or "it's death to a woman's libido." Nothing is less titillating than a glimpse of hairy skin below the trouser cuff when a man wearing short socks crosses his legs (except maybe wearing socks to bed when otherwise naked). Also "out" are socks with clogs, black socks with tennis sneakers, white cotton socks with business shoes, and socks with holes in the heels.

•**Comb-overs.** Although not strictly a dress item, the habit of letting hair grow long at the side and combing it over a bald head was high on women's list of loathing. "Who does he think he's kidding?" they ask. "And when the wind blows, oh brother, if he could see himself!" Pulses may quicken over young men with full heads of hair, but women don't dislike baldness per se. They do dislike comb-overs and other compensatory acts of denial and bravado. They like men who like themselves.

•**Miami Beach macho.** Those who sold men on exposing five buttons' worth of chest and a medallion should be hanged at dawn by their own gold chains. Women hate that look. Even women who think men are nifty in manicures and pinky rings hate that look.

•**Misfits.** Women say clothes that don't fit advertise poor character traits. Either the guy doesn't really see himself, which means he is probably oblivious to all his other flaws, too, or he doesn't like himself enough to care how he looks, which means a woman will spend her life shoring up his self-image. Or he's got the Alexander Haig syndrome, choosing the pigeon-breasted tight-jacket look to give the impression that he's too big for clothing to contain him. Or he blames his buttons bursting in midair on shirt shrinkage (his wife's fault), not calories. Whatever the analysis, most women conclude that a man in poorly fitting clothes bodes ill for women.

• **Textures.** Passions run high. "Men shouldn't wear velour; it's like being with a stuffed animal." "Silk is arrogant. If a man has to wear a robe, only terry cloth is forgivable." Corduroy, yes! Rayon, no! Camel's hair, yes! Double knit, no! *Eventually, one rule emerges:* Men shouldn't shine. Anything synthetic that glistens is too glitzy and anything naturally shiny is "pseudo-regal." Or, as one woman put it, "Men need a matte finish."

• **Affectations.** Women opt for simplicity. They like their men unadorned, not gimmicky. "Playboy rabbit insignia drives me wiggo," said a normally subdued woman. "Full-dress fully grown cowboys look ludicrous on Lake Shore Drive," said another. *Also contemptible:* Men wearing one earring (not to mention two); initials on shirts; tie clips or lapel pins promoting a lodge, Lions Club, PT-109, the American flag or God; sweaters with reindeer ("I thought of establishing a moth colony to get rid of it"); leprechaun hats; and "anything Tyrolean."

• **Shoes.** This is an easy one. Whether women were partial to men in Guccis or Adidas, cordovans or bucks, glove-leather wing tips or crepe-sole Hush Puppies, none of them liked tassel loafers.

• **Color.** Anything goes—except the too-bright tones. For instance, heather green is great in a sport jacket, kelly green ghastly. For a sweater, buttercup yellow is warm and friendly, chartreuse off-putting. *General consensus:* If it stops traffic, stop wearing it.

• **Gestures.** If women understand the power of clothing better than men, it is because traditional female socialization teaches them to gain approval through their appearance. Women also know that clothing inspires attitudes in the wearer. An elegant gown can inspire even a child to act aristocratic. And women say certain items of clothing inspire annoying gestures in men. *The worst:* "Shooting cuffs"—the almost spastic movement with which a man pushes his arms out so that his sleeves show more of his

shirt cuffs (usually monogrammed and affixed with ostentatious cuff links). "The mirror sneak" —checking and rearranging his tie in every looking glass. "The hoist"—the unceremonious, vaguely obscene lifting of the waistband of loose trousers. *Women's advice on the subject:* Stop posturing, sit still and pay more attention to us.

• **Underwear.** Questions about boxer shorts versus jockey shorts and T-shirts versus sleeveless undershirts produced another quick consensus. The issue is settled by body type. The man with a "good bottom" and tight belly should wear jockeys. The well-muscled-shoulder man should wear sleeveless undershirts. Everyone else shouldn't. And if boxer shorts are what a man wants, women prefer that the ones with pictures and slogans be left to the little boys.

Proper Pants Fit

It's not the waist size but the rise (the measurement from waistband to crotch) that determines the way a man's pants fit, according to the head tailor at Brooks Brothers. A man 5 feet 6 inches tall or shorter needs a short rise. *Regular:* 5 feet 6 inches up to 5 feet 9 inches. *Long:* 5 feet 9 inches to 6 feet 3 inches.

Accentuate the Positive, Eliminate the Negative

There are many strategies women can use to minimize figure flaws during the summer season.

Top-heavy: Wear tunics that glide over the problem areas, V-necked blouses to make shoulders and bosom appear smaller, a diagonal-wrap one-piece bathing suit in contrasting colors, blousy tops (gathered at the waist).

Chunky: To suggest curviness, wear nipped-in waists and eye-catching belts, a blouson dress or drop-waist dress, a one-piece bathing suit with vertical or diagonal stripes.

Bottom-heavy: Pants that end below the knees to show shapely calves, classic pantsuit that falls smoothly in a straight line without pleats or cuffs, vertically striped wraparound dress, one-piece bathing suit with a colorful bra top and darker color below.

The Best Perfumes

The best perfumes for women to wear in the office are the lighter scents. This is particularly true for those with dry skin. *Reason:* Dry skin makes any perfume more pungent.

Avoid Oriental scents such as musk and heavy jasmines. *Reason:* Too strong.

Best Time to Use An Antiperspirant

To stay dry all day, it helps to put on antiperspirant at bedtime. The main ingredient (aluminum chlorohydrate) works by plugging sweat glands, and it does that best when they're dry for as long as possible. You're dry longest when you're asleep. To build up sweat protection, it's best to use antiperspirant every day. It takes up to eight days for an antiperspirant to reach a level of maximum effectiveness.

Kenneth Hiller, PhD, coordinator, Procter & Gamble Beauty Care Council.

The Best Soaps for Your Skin Type

Soft soap: Contrary to traditional wisdom, a soap with a high pH content, or high alkalinity, does not irritate normal skin. It does cause soap film, especially in hard-water areas. *Who should be cautious in choosing a soap:* The elderly if they have sun-damaged skin. Women who have overused makeup and soaps. People with very dry skin.

Best for these skin types: A petroleum-based, synthetic imitation soap. This type has gentler ingredients as well as added moisturizers.

Dangers of "Unscented" Cosmetics

Cosmetics labeled "unscented" can still cause the itchy, swollen skin known as dermatitis because they contain masking perfumes.

Best bet: Look for "fragrance free" labels on makeup and creams. Dab perfume only on clothes or hair.

American Academy of Dermatology, cited in *Women's Health.*

A Better Way to Beat Baldness

Now there's a better way to treat baldness. *New tool:* Tissue expanders—balloonlike rubber implants used to stretch the skin.

How they work: The bladder is implanted under the skin in the problem area, then injected with a saltwater solution. This produces a slight tension in the overlying skin. Once or twice a week more solution is added to maintain tension as the skin begins to stretch. After one to two months the bladder is removed and the skin is manipulated to cover the defect.

Tissue expanders have virtually limitless potential for reconstructive surgery. Essentially they give surgeons new skin to work with without the need for skin grafts.

Male pattern baldness: By removing a portion of hairless scalp and expanding hair-covered areas, doctors can redistribute hair to cover the entire head. Tissue expander treatment works better than hair plugs or skin grafts. *Drawback:* Patients undergoing tissue expansion of the scalp look odd during the two-month process. Privacy is essential.

Andrew Kleinman, MD, associate adjunct of plastic surgery at the New York Eye and Ear Infirmary in New York City.

Why Women Go Bald

Arthur Bertolino, MD, PhD, adjunct associate professor of dermatology and director of the Hair Consultation Unit at New York University School of Medicine, New York City.

About 30 million men and 30 million women in the United States go bald from natural causes. *Surprising:* Genetic malfunctions, illness, medication and stress can cause more women than men to go bald—sometimes irreversibly.

CAUSES OF HAIR LOSS

• **Temporary loss.** Women can suffer hair loss for weeks or months due to physiological stress and hormonal changes caused by any of these factors:

• Ingestion of particular prescription drugs, such as beta-blockers, vitamin A analogs (taken for acne) and thyroid supplements.

• Changes in hormonal levels—occurring, for instance, when a woman has a baby or stops taking birth-control pills.

• Overuse of cosmetic treatments such as dyes, permanents, etc.

• Severe illness and high fever.

• General anesthesia.

• Underactive thyroid.

• **Permanent loss.** This can be caused by the following conditions:

• Androgenetic alopecia, the most common cause of female balding, is thought to be a genetically predisposed oversensitivity to the male hormones active in every female. *Background:* The small amounts of male hormones can cause hair follicles to shrink, first making hairs grow finer and then preventing hair growth altogether. *Result:* Diffuse balding.

• Alopecia areata (a localized patch of hair loss) is an autoimmune disease in which antibodies damage hair cells. *Sometimes helpful:* Steroid treatments.

MAKING HAIR LOOK FULLER

• **Surgery.** Small sections of hair-bearing scalp can be transplanted to bald spots. *Caution:* These procedures are less effective for female balding than for the larger, unified patterns typical of male balding.

• **Minoxidil.** The lotion form of this drug is an effective treatment. The drug enlarges hair follicles so that thick instead of thin hair grows, a particularly effective approach for diffuse balding.

Drawbacks: Minoxidil works on only 25% of those who use it, and if treatment is halted gains are reversed.

• **Hairpieces and wigs.** These are still the safest and easiest way to cover baldness. Custom-made pieces of real hair are virtually undetectable.

The Secrets of a Great Shave

A good shave with a blade demands the best possible equipment and proper preparation of the beard. Blades and shaving creams are constantly being improved, so it pays to treat your face to the most up-to-date equipment available. *What to look for…*

Shaving cream: All types of cream (lather, brushless and aerosol in either lather or gel form) are equally efficient. Brushless shaving cream is recommended for dry skin.

If you like, buy three or four different kinds of shaving cream. Use different ones for different moods.

Blades: Modern technology makes the current stainless-steel blades a real pleasure to use. *The best type:* The triple blade.

Proper preparation: Wash your face with soap at least twice before shaving. This helps soften the skin, saturate the beard and remove facial oils. *Best:* Shave after a warm shower.

The secret of shaving cream is its ability to hold water on the hairs of the beard, which allows them to absorb the moisture. Thus any cream is more effective if left on the face for a few minutes prior to actual shaving. This saturation causes the facial hairs to expand by about one-third, which enhances the cutting ability of the blade. *One routine:* With the lather on your face, brush your teeth and then set up your razor and other equipment. Do other minor tasks while allowing the lather to soak the beard.

Except on the warmest days, preheat shaving lather in the can or tube by immersing it in hot water.

The art of shaving: The manufacturing process leaves a slight oily residue on the edge of the new blade. This can catch and pull the tender facial skin during the first couple of strokes. So start by trimming the sideburns, a painless way of breaking in the new blade. Always shave the upper lip and chin last. *Why:* The coarsest hairs grow here. Your skin will benefit from the extra minutes of saturation and wetness.

When you have finished shaving, rinse the blade and shake the razor dry. Never wipe a blade dry; this dulls the edge. When rinsing the blade, hold it low in the water stream for quicker results.

After shaving: Save money by skipping the highly advertised aftershave lotions. Use witch hazel instead. It is odorless, less astringent, leaves no residue and is better for your skin than most of the aftershave lotions.

What Dry Cleaners Don't Tell You

Joseph Boms, former assistant manager, Kless dry-cleaning chain, Brooklyn, NY.

The dry-cleaning process is not mysterious, but it is highly technical. After marking and sorting your clothes on the basis of color and type of material, the cleaner puts them into a dry-cleaning machine. This operates like a washing machine except that it uses special solvents instead of water. After the clothes have gone through the dryer, the operator removes stains from them.

A good dry cleaner will use just the right chemical to remove a stain without damaging the fabric. Pressing correctly is next—also a matter of skill. With some fabrics, the garment is put on a form and steamed from the inside to preserve the finish. After pressing, the clothing is bagged.

WHAT TO LOOK FOR

- **Suits** should be put on shoulder shapers.
- **Fancy dresses and gowns** should be on torso dummies.
- **Blouses and shirts** should be stuffed with tissue paper at the shoulders.
- **Except for pants and plain skirts,** each piece should be bagged separately.

TAKING PRECAUTIONS

- **Bring in together all parts of a suit to be cleaned.** Colors may undergo subtle change in the dry-cleaning process.
- **Check all pockets before bringing in your clothing.** A pen left in a pocket can ruin the garment.
- **Read care labels carefully.** Many clothes cannot be dry-cleaned at all. Do not dry-clean clothing that has printed lettering or rubber, nylon or plastic parts. If you're not sure, ask your dry cleaner.
- **Make sure your dry cleaner is insured** if you intend to store a large amount of clothing during the winter or summer months.
- **Examine your clothes before leaving them with the cleaner.** Point out stains and ask whether or not you can expect them to be removed.

For best results, tell the cleaner what caused the stain.

GETTING YOUR MONEY'S WORTH

- **Don't wash clothes and then bring them to the cleaner's for pressing.** The savings are minimal.
- **Don't try to remove stains yourself.** You may only make them worse. Bring stained

clothing to the cleaner as soon as possible. Old stains are harder to remove.

• **Ask if the cleaner will make minor repairs as part of the cleaning cost.** Many cleaners offer such services free.

• **Don't request same-day service unless absolutely necessary.** Rushed cleaners often do a sloppy job.

DAMAGE OR LOSS

• **If your cleaner loses or ruins a garment,** you should be reimbursed or given a credit. Most dry cleaners are neighborhood businesses where reputation is vital. You can damage a cleaner's reputation by giving the cleaner bad word of mouth. You might remind the store of this fact if there is resistance to satisfying your complaint.

• **If your cleaner fails to remove a stain you were told could be removed,** you still have to pay for the cleaning job.

• **If your cleaner dry-cleans a garment with a "do not dry-clean" label,** the store is responsible for ruining the garment.

• **If your cleaner ruins a garment that should not be dry-cleaned** but lacks the "do not dry-clean" label, responsibility is a matter of opinion. The cleaner may reimburse you to keep your goodwill, or you may have to complain to an outside agency.

• **The amount you will be reimbursed is always up for bargaining.** You will have to consider original value and depreciation, and whether you have a receipt.

MAKING COMPLAINTS

If you cannot get satisfaction from your cleaner voluntarily, most states have dry cleaners associations to arbitrate complaints. These associations go under various names in different states, so check with your local Department of Consumer Affairs. Be sure to keep all dry-cleaning receipts and other relevant information to substantiate your complaint.

Caring for Down

Down is almost spongelike in its ability to absorb moisture, oils and dirt, its worst enemies. But cleaning is hard on down and even harder on its owner. *Some maintenance tips for staving off cleanings...*

• **Sponge off the shell fabric as soon as possible after spotting.** Be sure to use mild soap and water.

• **Enclose comforters in removable sheet casings** that can be washed frequently. (These are available in most department stores.)

• **Let garments air-dry away from steam pipes,** sun or other heat sources before putting them in the closet. (Or put them in a large dryer at low heat with a clean sneaker.)

• **Patch tears, rips, or holes** in the shell with the pressure-sensitive tapes sold in sporting-goods stores until you can make a permanent repair with a fine needle and thread or have a professional make a "hot spot" repair.

• **Hang vertically channeled coats upside down** occasionally to redistribute the down.

• **Store clean down flat or loosely folded.** Wrap it in a breathable covering such as a sheet to protect it from dust, light and rodents.

WASHING DOWN

Care labels frequently recommend washing. (Gore-Tex® for example, is destroyed by dry cleaning.) Smaller items can be easily washed in a front-loading, tumble-type machine. Empty the pockets and close all the zippers, snaps and Velcro tabs.

Run the washer on medium cycle with warm water. Use half the amount of nonphosphorated soap or detergent recommended. Rinse twice to be sure the soap is all out.

Never use a top-loading agitator machine. It will take apart seams, fray internal edges and diminish the life of the garment by 75%.

For larger items, use the bathtub. Dissolve mild soap or detergent in warm water first. Then submerge the jacket or coat completely. Let it soak no more than 15 minutes. Let the water drain without disturbing the article, and rinse several times until the water runs clear. Don't twist or wring, but compress the excess water out before hanging the garment over a rack or several lines to dry. Be extra careful with comforters or you will tear the baffling, which is irreplaceable.

DRYING DOWN

Never a fast process, air-drying can take several days even in perfect weather. Be patient, and turn the article often. Home dryers are good only for small items such as vests and children's jackets. Larger items don't have room to fluff properly. Hot dryers can melt nylon zippers and even some fabrics. *Best:* Commercial dryer with a low heat cycle. Add a couple of clean sneakers (laces removed) or clean tennis balls and a large towel to break up the wet down clumps. Take plenty of change; the process requires several hours.

DRY-CLEANING DOWN

Professional dry cleaning may be the easiest way to restore good down clothing and bedding. However, there are traps in this. The best solvent for cleaning is a nonchlorinated petroleum product that is banned from most city cleaning establishments because of its flammability. Two companies* specialize in this preferred type of cleaning and take care of customers through United Parcel Service. Both also handle repairs and restylings.

Conventional dry cleaning, which is harder on the product, necessitates careful airing afterward to allow toxic fumes to evaporate.

Always spray clean garments with silicone water repellent yourself. Professional waterproofing is a dip that soaks the down. (Nylon shells will not take silicone spray or dip.)

*Down East, New York; Down Depot, San Francisco.

Cosmetic Surgery

Neal B. Schultz, MD, dermatologist with Park Avenue Skin Care, 1130 Park Ave., New York City 10128.

Every year thousands of Americans try the latest plastic surgery techniques designed to keep them looking younger longer. *Problem:* Each new procedure is only as good as the surgeon who administers it. And not being aware of the risks ahead of time could leave you emotionally as well as physically scarred.

How to decide whether you should have surgery: Consider your emotional need to have the procedure done, as well as the problems that may result from it. Then try to balance the two to determine what you should do.

• **Liposuction,** removing fat cells from the body to produce smoother contours, has been around for a few years. We're now discovering more of its many risks.

Problems: If too much fat and fluid are removed you can go into shock, bleed internally—or die. *Bottom line:* This is a cosmetic procedure that in the wrong hands could end in disaster. And even when it's performed correctly, it can cause dimpled or sagging skin.

CHOOSING A GOOD SURGEON

The success of any cosmetic procedure depends on the skill of the surgeon. *To find a good one...*

• **Call a teaching hospital in your area** and ask the staff for recommendations. *Reason:* Teaching hospitals offer much higher-quality control and peer review.

• **Talk to people who have had the type of surgery that you are considering.** See if they are happy with it and find out who their doctors are.

• **Choose a board-certified plastic surgeon.** *Note:* Although this is a form of quality control, it does not necessarily mean you will get the best surgeon. *Reason:* Plastic surgery is an art and to become board-certified, all you have to do is pass an exam. *Better:* Seek out a recommendation from someone who has had successful surgery.

• **Make sure the surgeon you choose has performed the procedure hundreds—** if not thousands—of times. And the surgeon should be able to give you the names of at least three satisfied patients. You should call them to verify the surgeon's results.

No More Facial Wrinkles

Neal B. Schultz, MD, dermatologist with Park Avenue Skin Care, 1130 Park Ave., New York City 10128.

Facial wrinkles are caused by a variety of factors, including heredity, excessive sun exposure and smoking. There are several different ways to have these wrinkles removed or minimized at a dermatologist's office.

LASER SKIN RESURFACING

This is suitable for treating lines and wrinkles of all depths. It is performed under local anesthesia.

How it works: A computer-controlled laser beam vaporizes the skin of the wrinkled area to a flat or almost flat surface. The surgeon using this technique halts the process when the lines disappear. Healing takes seven to 10 days. It is more rapid than dermabrasion and deep chemical peeling.

Follow-up: Usually there is no pain shortly after the procedure. During the first seven to 10 days of healing, the skin is bright red. After this period, the skin is pink—but the color fades over the ensuing weeks and months and is easily concealed with makeup.

While a significant part of the improvement in the wrinkles is visible one to two months after the procedure, improvement continues for six to 12 months after the procedure as new skin grows.

Important: During healing (until the pink color fades), it is essential to avoid the sun because sun exposure can cause the skin to heal with uneven color and cause serious damage.

SKIN PEELS

• **Dermabrasion.** The top layers of the skin are "sanded" off with a rapidly rotating wire brush. The treated area heals as new skin grows in.

This process removes wrinkles of all depths and can be done under local or general anesthesia. The procedure takes about one hour.

Results are less predictable than with laser resurfacing—except when performed by surgeons with exceptional experience. Some pain is experienced in the first few days after the procedure.

The skin that was removed grows back in one to two weeks, and your face's pinkness will disappear in about two to three months. The sun must be avoided during this time.

• **Deep peels are done with an acid.** The acid peels away the skin until the wrinkles flatten out. These peels are suitable for mild to moderately deep wrinkles. The skin that was removed grows back in seven to 10 days. Your skin's pinkness will fade over a period of two to three months. Here, too, avoid the sun.

Results of this type of peel are less predictable than with laser resurfacing because the depth of penetration of the acid solution is more difficult to control. There is also a greater risk of scarring and loss of color.

• **Glycolic and beta-peels.** The acid is painlessly applied for several minutes and then removed. These need to be repeated six to 10 times. The peels have little effect on wrinkles and are more suitable for treating uneven skin texture and skin tone.

• **Retin A is a wonderful drug that replaces a sallow color with some pinkness,** causing blood vessels beneath the surface to proliferate collagen formation (thereby plumping up the skin and filling out the fine wrinkles). It is used topically at bedtime in very small quantities. *Net results:* Removal of very fine crosshatch wrinkles, evening and removal of brown mottling that often results from prolonged skin exposure and refreshment of scaly dull skin while plumping it up and restoring some pinkness.

Problems: Treatment leaves you much more susceptible to sunburn. And too much Retin A can cause redness and peeling.

COLLAGEN INJECTIONS

Collagen injections fill out the wrinkles instead of burning or scraping them away. This is better for people with dark skin for whom the pinkness of raw skin would be more obvious and in whom there is a greater chance of discoloration from laser peels and dermabrasion. A six-week skin test is required to determine if there is an allergic reaction.

Drawback: The injected collagen lasts only a few months before wrinkles begin to reemerge. As a result, injections need to be repeated on a regular basis.

Liposuction Safety Net

Liposuction is safest when performed as an outpatient procedure under local anesthesia —in a doctor's office, not in a hospital. The doctor should be a board-certified dermatologic surgeon.

Avoid doctors who plan to extract large amounts of fat at one time...and those who perform multiple procedures at the same time.

Liposuction is usually safe, but serious complications do occur in rare cases—usually when general anesthesia is used. *These include:* Shock, blood clots, infection, bowel perforation in abdominal procedures.

William Coleman III, MD, clinical professor of dermatology, Tulane University Health Sciences Center, New Orleans, and leader of a study of 257 liposuction-related insurance claims, published in *Dermatalogic Surgery.*

Dangers in Personal-Care Products

Many beauty and hygiene products contain chemicals that can make you sick— or even kill you.

Cosmetics are often made from harmful substances. Lipstick may contain PVP (polyvinyl-pyrrolidone plastic), saccharin and mineral oil, all of which have caused cancer in animals. Formaldehyde, alcohol and plastic resins in mascara can cause irritation and burning and swelling of the eyes.

Solution: Use a natural lip gloss. If you must have color, stain your lips with beet or berry juice and brush colored clays (available at most natural-food stores) on cheeks and eyelids. Buy unscented, hypoallergenic mascara.

Debra Lynn Dadd, author of *Nontoxic Home.* Penguin.

Finger Beauty Danger

Nail-wrapping, glue-on false nails and nail augmentation can cause rashes, redness, scaling and swelling of the skin surrounding the nail or, worse, infection of the nail bed (skin beneath the nail) and even permanent loss of nails.

Problems: Cyanoacrylates, an ingredient found in nail glues, trigger allergic reactions. Infection-causing bacteria, fungi and yeast get trapped in the nail bed by waterproof nail-wrappings. Longer nails increase the chance of tearing the nail plate from the nail bed.

Solution: Halt use of products. *Better:* Keep nails a reasonable length and if a problem develops, dispense with enhancement techniques.

Paul Kechijian, MD, chief of the nail section at New York University School of Medicine, New York City.

Questions to Ask Your Plastic Surgeon

Neal B. Schultz, MD, dermatologist with Park Avenue Skin Care, 1130 Park Ave., New York City 10128.

Plastic surgery for cosmetic reasons is surrounded by a lot of hype. The fantasy that your life will be magically transformed by surgery can play into the hands of the unscrupulous. Although the overwhelming majority of plastic surgeons are competent and ethical, there are a few bad apples.

If you know which questions to ask both yourself and your doctor before you make a commitment to surgery, you'll save heartache —to say nothing of money.

WHAT TO ASK YOURSELF

Do I really need plastic surgery? You must be objective when you look in the mirror. Some people want surgery for a couple of wrinkles that are barely noticeable to anyone but themselves. Their vulnerability to the power of perfection may make them easy marks. *How it can happen:* Someone who thinks he or she needs a face-lift begs the surgeon to "just give me a little tuck." An unethical surgeon who is pushed, instead of refusing, may put the patient under general anesthesia, make a couple of incisions and sew him up. The patient then wakes up with two healing incision lines near his ears and thinks he looks great. In reality, he has paid up to $8,000 for virtually nothing. *Criteria to follow:* Would repair of an imperfection that bothers you enhance your well-being? Does that imperfection actually exist?

What do I want done and what will it accomplish for me? Although the psychological factor in cosmetic surgery cannot be overlooked, it must be approached realistically. Cosmetic surgery can improve your state of well-being—for some people, how they feel depends on how they look—but it usually does not change anyone's life. Many people blame all their difficulties on a particular physical defect. They delude themselves into believing that their difficulties will instantly be overcome if their physical defect is corrected.

How did you find your plastic surgeon? Did you fall prey to advertisements for low-cost surgery (with limousine service thrown in)? Like anything else, you get what you pay for. Stay away from high-pressure advertising. *Best:* Referral from other satisfied patients. If you don't know anyone who has had the type of surgery you want, ask your family doctor or internist for a recommendation. If you have a good relationship with your primary physician, there will be quality control. Your doctor can't afford to have his reputation damaged by recommending a bad doctor.

Have I asked for a second opinion? There's no other area where second opinions are more valuable. Only another doctor can confirm that you actually need the surgery and that the particular procedure your surgeon wants to do is reasonable for the result you seek.

WHAT TO ASK YOUR PLASTIC SURGEON

Realistically, what will be done? Not what can be done, or what you can hope for, but what you can expect. You'll also want to know what will happen if you don't get the result the doctor promises. How will he remedy that situation? Will you have to pay for the unsatisfactory job? Will he do a corrective procedure at no cost? Or will he say, "Sorry, I can't help you"? *Crucial:* Preoperative and postoperative pictures taken by the same photographer. Only with photos can you prove that you didn't get the promised result.

What is the chance of real damage, and if it happens, what might the extent of it be? Plastic surgeons aren't gods. They are physicians who have had extensive training in delicate repair of skin, but nobody can break the integrity of normal skin without leaving a mark. Plastic surgeons are only a bit like magicians. They leave marks in areas that are less conspicuous. But if you have a big growth in the middle of your cheek, you can't expect the doctor to cut it out without leaving a mark. *Other areas of concern:* The chances of infection and other complications.

Where will the surgery be done? Although many reputable plastic surgeons operate out of their own offices, surgery done in a hospital inevitably offers more quality control. There's much less room for nonprofessionalism in a hospital, where nurses and operating-room teams are provided by the institution and there is peer review of a surgeon's work. *Generally safest bet:* A doctor who is university-affiliated and teaches in a hospital or medical school.

May I see your book of before and after pictures? You may want to ask if you can contact a surgeon's other patients. But since this might violate confidentiality, he may only be willing to show you his patients' before and after pictures. If he offers you a whole book of good results, you can certainly feel confident.

Can the surgery be done in stages? A male model had a bad result on facial moles that a plastic surgeon had treated with liquid nitrogen. His skin had darkened, and there were brown spots and scars. The surgeon hadn't done a trial on one mole but had treated them all at one session. *Suggestion:* If you have many of the same defects, have one corrected first to see if you like the result.

Is there a less serious procedure that will produce a similar result? Very effective collagen injections available today eliminate both wrinkles and acne scars. Suction lipectomy can remove fat pockets. You may want to look into such lesser procedures before undergoing full-scale surgery.

How much will it cost? How much time will it take? How long will I be out of work or away from home? Ask whatever other questions concern you. Prepare a written list. No matter how many questions you have or how trivial you feel they are, ask!

Facts About Face-Lifts

Each year half a million Americans choose face-lift operations as a way to turn back the clock.

Factors that hasten this decline: Hereditary tendencies (some faces age faster than others)...cigarette smoking, which decreases blood flow to the skin...excessive use of alcohol...poor nutrition...lack of sleep and exercise. *Main culprit:* Sunlight. To keep skin smooth, stay out of the sun. When exposed, apply sunscreen lotion.

A face-lift is major surgery. *What is done:* The facial and neck skin are literally lifted from the underlying tissue and set back in place. This gives the face a smoothed-out appearance. *Possible complications:* Blood clots, hemorrhages under the skin, facial-nerve injuries, abnormal scarring.

Payoff: The operation removes wrinkles and restores firmness. But at best it makes the face look 10 years younger.

Avoid: A mini-lift in which the skin is pulled tight rather than lifted off the face.

Note: Most insurance policies do not cover elective cosmetic surgery.

6

Smart Consumer

Best Bargain Buying On the Internet

The Internet is chock full of bargains for consumers—with more appearing every day. You may have to hunt and search a little bit, but your efforts will generally result in big savings.

To get started, here are a few of the "best bargain" sites on the Web today.

And if these don't work for you, there are thousands of other Web sites that offer bargains...

AIRFARES

Airlines now offer unsold seats at steep discounts through their own Web sites and weekly E-mail "alerts" sent to subscribers.

Snag: The average consumer can't watch all these sites and E-mail lists. But the WebFlyer site will do it for you.

WebFlyer surveys the airlines' Web sites and E-mail lists and organizes the "best bargain" information from them in one place.

Tell WebFlyer the city you want to travel from, and it will list the best deals available—and give you discount prices for hotels and car rentals, too.

The WebFlyer site is run by Randy Petersen, the publisher of *Inside Flyer* magazine. The site also presents a wealth of other free travel information. *www.webflyer.com.*

AUTOMOBILES

Find a deal on a new or used car at Auto-web, the leading Internet car-selling service. It uses a network of dealers in the US. Enter the make and description of the car you're looking for along with your zip code, and you'll be offered a price from a dealer near you within 24 hours.

If you're not ready to buy yet, you can research different models at the site's "showroom,"

Patricia Robison, president, Computing Independence in New York City.

131

read product reviews and examine technical specifications. *www.autoweb.com*.

BOOKS, MUSIC AND MORE

You can order almost any book, CD, DVD or video in the world from Amazon.com, including very hard to find titles rarely found in conventional bookstores or "superstores."

You can also search for books of interest, get publishing details and read customer reviews. In addition, Amazon offers multiple ways to personalize the site using your preferences—for example, it will search for your favorite titles and get specific product information. *www.amazon.com*.

Alternative: The giant Barnes & Noble bookstore chain has its own Web site at *www.barnesandnoble.com*. It offers current bestsellers as well as thousands of used books, text books, CDs, DVDs and more.

COLLECTIBLES

If you want to buy or sell coins, stamps, antiques, jewelry, pottery and glass, dolls, sports memorabilia or any other collectible you have gathering dust, visit the eBay electronic flea market. It runs 24 hours a day, seven days a week.

At any given time there are more than *78 million* items available in more than 50,000 different categories. New categories are being added all the time. Items range from homerun baseballs to classic designer clothing. *www.ebay.com*.

INSURANCE

The InsWeb site can help you find the best price for life, health, auto, homeowner's and renter's insurance. Describe the coverage you want and the information will be submitted to a range of leading insurers. You'll receive quotes tailored to your needs, and you select the best.

The InsWeb site also gives a range of educational information, including auto and life insurance needs analyzers—work sheets to fill out that help you determine how much coverage you should buy. *www.insweb.com*.

INVESTMENT RESEARCH

Do you use a discount broker to save fees but miss the research that full-service brokers provide?

You may be able to find the best of both worlds. Morningstar, for instance offers extensive investment research on its Web sites, with a free 14-day trial.

For premium services: www.morningstar.com.

In addition, you can always obtain free investment information from Yahoo! Finance (*http://finance.yahoo.com*) or The Motley Fool (*www.fool.com*).

INVESTMENT TRADING

You can trade stocks and mutual funds in all American markets from your personal computer through the E*TRADE Web site, for as little as $6.99 per trade. Stock or fund shares can be paid for through electronic fund transfer.

E*TRADE offers margin accounts and lets you place market, limit, stop and stop limit orders, just as you would at a full-service broker. E*TRADE also provides market data, corporate data and other "intelligence" needed by investors. *www.etrade.com*.

TRAVEL

A unique "reverse auction" buying technique is offered by Priceline.com for travel items like airline tickets, hotel rooms, rental cars and more.

Key: Other Web sites search out the best prices offered by many different sellers (such as auto dealers or insurance companies). At Priceline.com, you set the price that you want to pay, and the sellers come to you—accepting or rejecting your price.

If an airline has an empty seat or a hotel has an empty room when you want it, you may get it at a price much lower than the airline or hotel would ever publicly offer it.

Priceline.com also offers tours, cruises and more. Check it out at *www.priceline.com*.

More Bargain Internet Shopping Sites

John Edwards, a technology writer based near Phoenix.

The World Wide Web has become the world's largest—and most diverse—shopping mall. Web merchants are selling products that range from pet food to diamonds, many—but not all—at prices that can't be matched by traditional retailers.

Here's a closer look at bargain shopping available on the Internet...

AIRLINE TICKETS

A variety of airline Web sites offer special deals to Internet shoppers, including...

- **American Airlines' "NetSAAver,"** *www.aa.com.*
- **Continental Airlines' "Specials,"** *www.continental.com.*
- **Southwest Airlines' "Click 'n Save,"** *www.southwest.com.*
- **United Airlines' "Special Deals,"** *www.united.com.*
- **U.S. Airways' "Specials,"** *www.usairways.com.*

Before you buy a ticket: Check Priceline.com (*www.priceline.com*), an Internet-based buying service that lets users name their price for airline tickets.

Shoppers simply post their request and guarantee the offer with a major credit card. Priceline.com then tries to find a seller who can fulfill the request—at no extra charge to the customer. *Note:* You have to commit to buying the ticket if they find it for you. It is not refundable.

Priceline.com also operates similar services for people who want to book a hotel room or rent a car.

CDs

- **Amazon** stocks more than one million books but also offers discounts on CDs, DVDs and videos. *www.amazon.com.*

CARS

- **Autobytel.com** helps Web surfers buy a new or used car or truck at the best possible price.

Shoppers specify the make, model and other relevant information for the vehicle they wish to purchase.

The information is then submitted to an Autobytel.com manager at a nearby dealership. Within 24 hours, the manager supplies the closest match and suggests a price. The shopper can then purchase the vehicle or look elsewhere for a better deal. *www.autobytel.com.*

- **MSN Autos,** has a nationwide network of dealers to help shoppers find the new or used car or truck they want at the lowest possible price. *http://autos.msn.com.*

HOTELS AND MOTELS

Many hospitality chains use their Web sites to promote weekend and other special rates...

- **Best Western's "Special Offers,"** *www.bestwestern.com.*
- **Embassy Suites' "Special Offers,"** *www.embassysuites.com.*
- **Hilton's "Featured Specials,"** *www.hilton.com.*
- **Holiday Inn's "Weekend WebSavers,"** *www.holiday-inn.com.*
- **Hyatt's "Featured Offers,"** *www.hyatt.com.*
- **Radisson's "Hot Deals,"** *www.radisson.com.*
- **Ramada's "Special Offers,"** *www.ramada.com.*
- **Ritz Carlton's "Promotions,"** *www.ritzcarlton.com.*
- **Wyndham's "Special Offers,"** *www.wyndham.com.*

HOME ENTERTAINMENT

- **Crutchfield** features a vast array of TVs, DVD and MP3 players, car stereos and other entertainment systems at prices that are generally competitive with those at leading superstores. Check out the "specials" area for impressive discounts on selected products. *www.crutchfield.com.*

APPAREL

• **Burlington Coat Factory** offers savings of up to 60% off department and other specialty-store prices on a large selection of designer and brand-name fashions, as well as linens and jewelry. *www.burlingtoncoatfactory.com.*

OTHER APPAREL SPECIALS

• **Eddie Bauer,** *www.eddiebauer.com.*

• **J.Crew,** *www.jcrew.com.*

• **Lands' End,** *www.landsend.com.*

• **L.L. Bean,** *www.llbean.com.*

BEST DEALS ON WEB PURCHASES

Comparison-pricing sites let you choose among retailers throughout the US. The sites are especially useful when shopping for computers and computer products. *Sites worth visiting…*

• **"CNET Shopper.com,"** *http://shopper.cnet.com.*

• **"Bottom Dollar,"** *www1.bottomdollar.com.*

• **"PriceGrabber.com,"** *www.pricegrabber.com.*

How to Avoid the Pitfalls Of Shopping On-line

Preston Gralla, a computer and Internet technology writer based in Cambridge, MA. He is author of *The Complete Idiot's Guide to Online Shopping.* Alpha Books.

The Internet is the ultimate shopper's paradise. Anything you could ever want to buy—from an abacus to a zither—is just a few mouse clicks away.

Shopping on-line is convenient and simple and you can save a lot of money, but…

Trap: Scams and con artists are everywhere on the Internet. Even savvy on-line consumers are vulnerable.

To avoid being ripped off on the Internet…

• **Never buy from a site that does not list its mailing address or phone number.** It's harder on-line than in the mall to know whether a store is reputable. A mailing address and phone number are important if you have problems with the merchandise you buy. You'll be able to complain and send it back.

• **Never shop a site that is not secure.** A secure site uses encryption technology to ensure that personal information—such as your credit card number and your address—is kept confidential.

Secure sites generally carry an icon that pops up when you log on. The icon looks like a lock. If no icon shows up, go to "Frequently Asked Questions" or "Help." Typically, secure sites explain their meaning of security.

• **Be especially careful when buying directly from individuals.** Most on-line shopping problems occur at auction sites where you are not buying from an established merchant but from an individual you don't know.

Self-defense: Before sending money to an individual, check the background of that person—or the company he or she says he represents. Even the most reputable sites take very little, if any, action against problem sellers. Buyers' complaints, however, may be listed for you to read and come to your own conclusions. If you're dissatisfied with a seller, you must take your own action against him. Some sites have an ombudsman who tries to sort out problems.

Strategy: For big-ticket items, use an Internet escrow service. This is an independent third party that acts as a conduit between the buyer and the seller. There are benefits to both buyer and seller. On eBay, for example, you would use Escrow.com, which charges a fee that varies according to the amount of the purchase and the method of payment.

Alternative: Ask the seller to send the item COD (and to pay the extra mailing cost if it's the first time you've dealt with him/her). Most sellers wait until the check clears before they ship the goods.

• **Don't give your credit card numbers** unless you're using a secure Web site. Check the Web address—a secure site will show "https" (the "s" at the end for "secure") rather than "http".

• **Don't give personal information,** such as a Social Security number, PIN number, etc., to anyone on-line. There's no reason a legitimate seller needs this information. Con artists who, in the past, used telemarketing and the mail, have now turned their sights to the Internet.

• **Read the fine print before signing up for a "free trial."** You usually have to give your credit card number in order to receive the offer. And usually you'll be billed for the item or service unless you cancel before a certain time.

There are many con artists playing the "free trial" game on the Internet. They will continue to bill you each month even though you've told them you don't want the product.

• **Watch for hidden costs on sales.** What appears to be a good buy may not be so good when sales tax and shipping costs are added in.

Example: A $25 book with a 20% on-line discount sounds great. But if shipping and handling add more than $5 to the cost, you'd be better off picking it up for full cost at your neighborhood bookstore. *Hidden costs include...*

• **Sales tax.** The sales tax moratorium imposed by the federal *Internet Tax Freedom Act* was signed into law in 1998 and has been extended until November 2014. Some states may tax on-line sales, so be sure to check the amount being charged on the purchase page.

• **Shipping and handling charges.** The majority of on-line merchants add on these charges. But costs vary widely. Be clear about how the items are being sent—first-class mail, overnight express delivery, etc.

• **Know your rights if something goes wrong.** *Always check the site's policies concerning...*

• Warranties. Does the warranty come from the site or the manufacturer?

• Return policies. Can you return the goods for cash or just for credit or exchange?

Caution: In most cases, merchandise bought on-line from retailers can't be returned to their retail stores. It must be returned on-line to the warehouse it was shipped from.

Recent development: Some retailers, such as the Gap and Macy's, will allow returns of Internet purchases at their retail stores.

• **Don't buy goods, stocks or services solely on advice from discussion boards or chat rooms.** It's too easy for con artists to self-promote on these sites by forging names and logging on multiple times.

• **Always thoroughly tour the site where you're planning on making a purchase.** See if the site offers product reviews that are honest and unbiased instead of merely sales pitches.

• **Protect yourself against Internet scammers.** Check out any seller with the Better Business Bureau *(www.bbb.org)* before you make a purchase.

Check with government agencies, such as the Federal Trade Commission *(www.ftc.gov),* and private agencies, such as the National Fraud Information Center *(www.fraud.org),* about any complaints against particular sites.

These sites are also good places to file complaints against Internet scammers (if you keep careful records of on-line purchases).

• **Stay away from too-good-to-be-true offers.** While scams aren't limited to cyberspace, they seem to be abundant there. *It's generally a good idea to steer clear of the following...*

• Work-at-home offers that promise instant wealth and success. You'll wind up paying for fees and materials. The people making money from these offers are the con artists who push them.

• Credit-repair services. They can't do anything you can't do yourself—free. If they offer you a second credit file (using a second Social Security number), don't deal with them. This practice is illegal.

Web Savvy

Beware—offers on Web sites are not considered to be offers in writing...and are not binding. Web sites can be easily changed, and you cannot prove what an offer was when you first saw it.

Bottom line: If you see a good offer on the Web, get a letter confirming it.

The late John Awerdick, an attorney who specialized in direct marketing, Hall Dickler Kent Friedman & Wood, New York City.

How to Buy Shoes That Really Fit

John F. Waller, Jr., MD, foot and ankle surgeon in private practice in New York City.

Shoes should provide a lot of cushioning to match the type of surface that the bare foot needs.

Poor: A rigid, so-called supportive shoe. Shoes should be loose and giving.

Good: The running shoe, the most physiological shoe made. Soft and malleable, it provides cushioning and a little bit of support.

Women: If you wear a high-heeled, thin-soled shoe, have a thin rubber sole cemented onto the bottom to cushion the ball of the foot.

•**Fit shoes with your hands, not with your feet.** There should be an index finger's breadth between the tip of the toes and the front of the shoe. Tell the salesperson to start with a half size larger than you usually wear and work down. The shoe shouldn't be pushed out of shape when you stand. The leather should not be drawn taut.

•**An ideal heel height for a woman is 1½–2 inches.** This is not a magic number, simply the most comfortable. If a man wore a 1½-inch heel, he'd be more comfortable than in the traditional ¾-inch heel.

•**Flat feet are not bad feet.** A flat, flexible foot is very functional. Most great athletes have them.

Problem: The shoe industry does not make shoes to fit flat feet. Look for low-heeled shoes that feel balanced. They should not throw your weight forward on the balls of your feet or gap at the arches.

•**Buy shoes in the late afternoon when your feet have had a full day's workout and are slightly spread.** Shoes that you try on first thing in the morning may be too tight by evening and generally uncomfortable for all-day wear.

How to Recognize Quality Clothes in Off-Price Stores

To take advantage of sales, discount designer stores or consignment shops, learn the details that signal first-class workmanship, label or no label. *Look for…*

•**Stripes and plaids that are carefully matched** at the seams.

•**Finished seam edges** on fabrics that fray easily (linen, loose woolens, etc.).

•**Generous seams** of one-half inch or more.

•**Buttons made of mother-of-pearl,** wood or brass.

•**Neat, well-spaced buttonholes** that fit the buttons tightly.

•**Felt backing on woolen collars** to retain the shape.

•**Ample, even hems.**

•**Straight, even stitching** in colors that match the fabric.

•**Good-quality linings** that are not attached all around. (Loose linings wear better.)

Designer Bargains For Women in Boys' Department

Not all the smart women shopping in the boys' department have sons. Many are just looking for bargains in shirts, sweaters, pants, jackets, robes and belts for themselves. Even designer boys' clothes may cost 20% to 50% less than similar items in the women's department. *How to size up boys' wear…*

Women's size	Boys' size
5/6	14 top, 29/30 pants
7/8	16 top, 30/31 pants
9/10	18 top, 31/32 pants
11/12	20 top, 32/33 pants

How to Buy Sunglasses

Be sure they are large enough. Light should not enter around the edges. *Best:* Try frames that curve back toward the temple. *Lenses:* Plastic is less heavy than glass. *Drawback:* It scratches easily. Clean with a soft cloth, not a silicone tissue.

To prevent glare: Greenish grays, neutral grays and browns are best. Other colors absorb wavelengths and upset color balance. *Test:* Try on the glasses. The world should appear in true color, but not as bright.

Good all-around choice: Sun-sensor lenses, which adjust from dark to light. For use near water, polarized lenses block reflected glare. An old pair of prescription lenses can be tinted to a desired density.

Best Eyeglass Cleaner

Use a piece of damp newspaper. There is less chance that it will scratch the lenses than cloth or facial tissue.

How to Choose the Right Hairbrush

The best hairbrush bristles come from boars. Their uneven surface cleans better than smooth nylon. *Stiffest:* Black bristles from the back of the boar's neck. Good for thick, heavy hair, these are the rarest and most expensive bristles. White bristles are better for fine and/or thinning hair.

Jan Hansum, Kent of London, quoted in *The Best Report,* New York City.

Best Mouthwash

Bad breath is cured best by mouthwashes that contain zinc. This is because the source of most mouth odor is sulfur compounds. The zinc mouthwashes negate these compounds for at least three hours. *Contrast:* Non-zinc mouthwashes attack bacteria. *Point:* Check the labels of mouthwashes for zinc.

Joseph Tonzetich, PhD, the late professor of oral biology, University of British Columbia, Vancouver.

Best Insect Repellents

Insect repellents vary in the amounts of active ingredients they contain and their effectiveness. *Active ingredients:* N, N-diethyl-m-toluamide (DEET) and ethyl hexanediol. *Most effective:* DEET. *Spray with high DEET level:* Off! Deep Woods (25%). *Lotion with high DEET level:* 3M Ultrathon (31%).

Best Sleeping Bags

Waterfowl down still offers the best warmth-to-weight performance as padding (or fill). But now the newer, lightweight, polyester-filled sleeping bags (in most above-freezing conditions) are preferred by campers on practical grounds. *Polyester's virtues...*

• **It keeps two-thirds of its insulating capacity when wet** (it absorbs very little moisture), and it dries much faster. Down is worthless when wet. It takes hours to dry and must be refluffed before the bag can be used again.

• **It's washable, even by machine.** Down bags are best dry-cleaned.

• **It's nonallergenic because it doesn't collect dust.** Down is a magnet for dust, the real cause of suffering for those who think they are allergic to it.

• **It's much cheaper than down.** Most polyester-filled sleeping bags cost about 50% less than comparable down-filled ones.

How to Buy a Mattress

The quality of sleep makes the quantity less important. To enable you to relax, your mattress must provide proper support for your body yet be resilient enough for comfort. The old-fashioned double bed gives each sleeper only 26 inches of space, about the same width as a baby's crib. The most popular size—queen—is seven inches wider and five inches longer than the old double bed. King size is an additional 16 inches wider.

Mattress prices depend on the materials, quality of construction, size, number of layers of upholstery and the store's markup. (Prices may be lower in small, neighborhood stores with low overhead.)

Standard mattresses have two different kinds of construction, innerspring or foam rubber. Top-quality innerspring mattresses have covered metal coils, cushioning material and an insulator between the coils to prevent them from protruding.

Foam mattresses are made of a solid block of urethane, high-resiliency foam or laminated layers of varying density sandwiched together. A good foam mattress is at least five to six inches high and feels heavy when lifted. A high-density foam mattress should last 10 to 15 years. Foam mattresses can be used on a wooden platform for extra firmness or with a conventional boxspring.

When shopping for a mattress…

•**Sit on the edge of the bed.** The mattress should support you without feeling flimsy, and it should spring back into shape when you get up. A reinforced border increases durability.

•**Lie down.** (If the bed is to be used by a couple, both partners should test it by lying down.) Check several different firmnesses in order to choose the one you're most comfortable with. Next, roll from side to side and then to the center. The mattress should not sway, jiggle or sag in the middle. If you hear creaking springs, don't buy it.

•**Examine the covering.** *Best:* Sturdy ticking with a pattern that's woven, not printed on.

•**Check for handles on the sides for easy turning,** small metal vents to disperse heat and allow air to circulate inside and plastic corner guards.

•**Up to 80% of the sleeper's weight is borne by the boxspring.** The finest mattress won't be effective unless it's accompanied by a boxspring of equal quality. When a new mattress is needed, both the mattress and the boxspring should be replaced to ensure that the support system is designed specifically for the mattress.

Queen-sized innerspring sets should be used in a sturdy bed frame with a footboard or in a six-leg heavy steel support. Twin and double sized can use a four-leg metal frame. A good innerspring sleep set should last 15 to 20 years.

There is no proven medical advantage to sleeping on a hard surface, so consider comfort as the key factor. According to Dr. Hamilton Hall, an orthopedic surgeon who specializes in techniques to relieve back pain, there is no single perfect mattress. "What's perfect for one person may be uncomfortable for another," he says.

Best advice: Buy only sleep sets made by a manufacturer with a good reputation and sold by a reputable dealer. Be very wary of advertised bargains.

Test of Well-Made Wooden Furniture

Is the piece stable when you gently push down on a top corner or press against the side? Is the back panel inset and attached with screws (not nails)? Do drawers and doors fit well and move smoothly? Are corners of drawers joined with dovetail joints? Do long shelves have center braces? Are table leaves well supported? Are hinges strong and well secured?

Better Homes & Gardens, Des Moines.

Test of Good Carpeting

Insist on density. Closely packed surface yarns and tightly woven backing make for carpets that wear and look good longer. Bend a piece of the carpet backward. If a lot of backing is visible through the pile, go for a higher quality.

- **Avoid soft plush textures** when covering moderate-to-heavy traffic areas.
- **Invest in good padding.** It absorbs shocks, lengthens carpet life and creates a more comfortable surface.
- **If cost is a factor,** compromise on the amount or size of carpet, not on the quality. Or choose lesser qualities for low-traffic areas.

Better Homes & Gardens, Des Moines.

Oriental Rug Test

Spread the pile apart. If you see knots at the bottom, the rug was made by hand. But sewn-on fringes are a clear machine-made giveaway.

Pasargad Carpets Inc., rug importer and manufacturer, Washington, DC.

Buying a Piano

The best sound comes from a grand piano, but new ones can cost a bundle. A smaller spinet, console or studio upright will provide satisfactory sound for most people and costs much less.

How to test a piano before purchase: Play it by running up and down the scales. High notes should be clean and crisp; low notes should resonate. If you are considering the purchase of a used piano, look for one that's 10 years old or less. Don't buy one that's more than 20 years old. Have a piano tuner check out a used piano.

Best Pots for Pot Roast

Pot roasts cook best in heavy-cast ironware. That's one tale that happens to be true, though it is mysterious. *Other iron-pot pluses:* They're energy savers, since they hold heat longer. And traces of iron released chemically into food (unlike nonferrous metals) are good for you, especially for those who suffer from iron-deficiency anemia. People with rare hemochromatosis (too much iron in the system) should avoid all food contact with ironware.

How Safe Is Food in Your Kitchen? by Beatrice Trum Hunter. MacMillan.

Best Toilet Seat

The standard toilet seat was the most uncomfortable of all those tested in a university's contest of designs. *A winner:* An elongated seat contoured to support the thighs and buttocks.

Report on tests made at Loughborough University, Loughborough, Leiceistershire, England, in *New Scientist.*

Buying Kitchen Knives

The best steel for knives is high-carbon stainless steel. It takes and holds a sharp edge well and resists discoloration. *Also good:* Carbon steel. And it is relatively inexpensive. *Drawback:* Carbon steel must be kept dry or it will deteriorate. *Worst:* Stainless steel. It is very difficult to sharpen. *Top brands:* Wusthof, Forschner/Victorinox, Henckels and Sabatier.

Appliances That Pay for Themselves

Jennifer Thorne Amann, director, buildings program with the American Council for an Energy-Efficient Economy, a nonprofit organization founded in 1980 to encourage energy efficiency. *www.aceee.org.* She is coauthor of *Consumer Guide to Home Energy Savings.* ACEEE.

The latest energy-efficient appliances can cost up to hundreds of dollars more than standard models. But many pay for themselves over their 12- to 20-year life spans. Virtually all major appliance manufacturers —even some smaller ones—offer energy-efficient models. Visit *www.energystar.gov* or *www.aceee.org* for details.

Important: Look for the blue "Energy Star" label when you shop for appliances. To earn this label, appliances must exceed government efficiency guidelines. Also keep an eye out for the Federal Trade Commission's yellow "EnergyGuide" label. This provides estimated annual energy consumption for an appliance based on typical usage.

REFRIGERATORS

The greatest progress in energy-efficient appliances has been made in refrigerators. Many models built before 1988 consume more than $100 worth of electricity a year. Those made in the 1970s can use as much as $200.

Current standard refrigerators save an average of $50 a year in electricity. Since many new refrigerators retail in the $500 range, a new unit will pay for itself in about 10 years. High-efficiency units can run on less than $40 a year.

Caution: The Energy Star and EnergyGuide labels can be somewhat deceiving with refrigerators. The units are compared only between similar models. Thus a 22-cubic-foot side-by-side refrigerator might earn the Energy Star label, while an 18-cubic-foot freezer-on-top unit might not, even though it uses far less energy.

Refrigerators with freezers on top or bottom tend to be about 7% to 13% more efficient than side-by-side models. An automatic ice maker installed in the door can reduce efficiency by up to 20%.

Small units are more efficient than larger ones—but one large fridge is more efficient than two small ones. Don't buy something so small that you have to put the old unit in the basement for extra storage. If you do need an extra refrigerator, buy a new one.

Helpful: Consumers often feel that throwing out a working refrigerator is wasteful. But virtually every part of an old refrigerator is likely to be recycled. It is more wasteful to continue using an energy hog.

WASHING MACHINES

The typical washing machine lasts 12 years or more and consumes about $800 worth of electricity during that time.

Some new machines consume less than half as much power, principally by using less hot water. Ninety percent of the energy used to wash clothes is to heat the water.

Buying an energy-efficient washer makes good financial sense. High-efficiency machines cost as little as $600—about $200 more than typical washers. They also deliver as much as $60 in annual energy savings, so they can pay for themselves over their lifetimes.

In addition to the energy savings, a high-efficiency machine should save 6,000 to 8,000 gallons of water per year, based on annual average family use of around 400 loads.

Front-loading machines typically are much more efficient than top loaders. They use less water, and their higher spin speeds remove more moisture, reducing the energy used.

Energy saver: Wash clothes in cold water whenever appropriate.

CLOTHES DRYERS

Many new dryer models have temperature or moisture gauges that automatically turn off the unit when clothes are dry. Moisture sensors located inside the drum tend to be more accurate than temperature sensors. These can reduce your energy costs by up to 15%.

A typical new dryer will consume $85 worth of power a year, creating an annual savings of perhaps $10. Over the expected 11-year life of a dryer, that is a total of $110.

Sensor models cost $150 to $250 more than base models. But given the energy savings, they come close to paying for the extra cost— and often do in areas where electricity is expensive.

Ask retailers which dryer models contain in-drum moisture or temperature sensors, or check for them yourself. They usually look like small, black patches located either in the back of the drum or near the lint filter.

Helpful: Replacing an electric dryer with a gas-powered model can reduce your energy bills to about 13 cents per load from about 35 cents, based on current average electricity.

DISHWASHERS

There is a debate regarding dishwasher energy efficiency. A number of models include a "soil sensor," which detects how dirty the dishes are and adjusts wash time and water usage. The potential energy advantage of this is obvious.

Manufacturers, however, can't agree on how much energy a soil sensor saves. The current Department of Energy tests are of little use because they test only with clean plates.

For the time being, it is difficult to say which models are best. A knowledgeable salesperson might offer some guidance. But if you need a dishwasher, check the Energy Guide and Energy Star labels. Even without soil sensors, new models tend to be much more efficient.

Helpful: Don't prerinse dishes. Newer, more efficient dishwashers let you save time, water, electricity and elbow grease.

Where to Buy Hard-to-Find Recordings By Mail

Musical Heritage Society, 1710 Highway 35, Oakhurst, NJ 07755. 732-531-7003. *www.musicalheritage.com.* The best place to buy rare classical recordings.

• **TimeLife.com,** Direct Holdings.com, Virginia Beach, VA 23479-1003, 800-950-7887. *www.timelife.com.* Selected masters as well as a large selection of country, rock, pop, R&B and soul, jazz, gospel and other music CDs.

Best Chocolates In the World

The finest chocolates in the world need be no farther than your mailbox. However, some chocolatiers ship throughout the US only from October through May. (High temperatures are too hard on good chocolates to risk summer shipment.)

• **Bissinger's Handcrafted Chocolates,** 4742 McPherson, St. Louis, MO 63108, 800-325-8881. *www.bissingers.com.* Chocolate-covered mints, malted milk balls and other specialities. Free catalog.

• **Martine's Chocolates** at Bloomingdale's, 1000 Third Ave., New York City 10022, 212-705-2347, *www.bloomingdales.com,* and at 400 East 82nd St., New York City 10028, *www.martines chocolates.com. Noteworthy selections include:* Assorted truffles of caramel with praline crunch, orange peel and coffee, among others. "Oysters," an exquisite blend of five Belgian chocolates—their secret recipe. No catalog.

• **André's Confiserie Suisse,** 5018 Main St., Kansas City, MO 64112, 800-892-1234. *www.andreschocolates.com.* Bold and rich Swiss-type chocolates. Call directly to be sent a free catalog.

• **Dilettante Chocolates,** Seattle 98102, 800-482-0281. Hand-dipped light or dark chocolates, truffles, marzipan and French butter creams. Catalog on-line at *www.dilettante.com.*

• **Dan's Chocolates,** 800-800-DANS. *www. danschocolates.com.* Dan's chocolates are hand-made in small batches in their Rhode Island factory. Because they are shipped directly to you, they are incredibly fresh.

• **Edelweiss Chocolates,** 444 North Canon Dr., Beverly Hills, CA 90210, 888-615-8800. *www.edelweisschocolates.com.* Liquored truffles and brandied cherries. Free catalog.

• **See's Candies,** 754 Clement St., San Francisco 94080, 800-895-7337. *www.sees.com.* Old-fashioned fudge.

• **Teuscher Chocolates of Switzerland,** 25 E. 61st St., New York City 10021, 800-554-0624. *www.teuscher.com.* They have chocolates called rusty tools (for their shapes) which are dusted with cocoa. The champagne truffles are justly popular. Free brochure.

Best Time to Drink Champagne

Vintage champagne should be drunk shortly after purchase. Sparkling wine does not improve with age, and it will deteriorate with prolonged refrigeration. *For proper chilling:* Use an ice bucket with ice and a little bit of water.

The Wine Spectator.

Easy-Opening Champagne

Opening champagne is easier if the bottle is chilled in a bucket of ice rather than in a refrigerator. If the neck of the bottle gets too cold, the cork won't come out. Then you lose the satisfying, dramatic effect of a forceful cork-popping.

Successful Meetings.

The Six Best Champagnes

Drinking a fine sparkling wine is one of life's truest pleasures. *Six of the best…*

• **Taittinger Comtes de Champagne**—vintage only. An exceptionally good rosé champagne. Taittinger also makes a fine blanc de blancs and a nonvintage brut.

• **Dom Perignon**—vintage only. This is probably the most widely acclaimed champagne, and deservedly so. Elegant and light, with delicate bubbles. The producer also makes, under its Moët et Chandon name, a vintage rosé champagne, a vintage champagne, a nonvintage champagne and a nonvintage brut.

• **Perrier-Jouët Fleur de Champagne**—vintage only. This house produces champagne of the highest quality in a particularly popular style. The wine is austere yet tasteful. It is also extremely dry without being harsh or acidic. Perrier-Jouët also produces a rosé champagne.

• **Louis Roederer Cristal**—vintage only. *Cristal's magic lies in its plays with opposites:* Elegant yet robust, rich taste without weightiness. Roederer also produces a sparkling rosé, a vintage champagne and a nonvintage brut.

• **Bollinger Vieilles Vignes Françaises**—vintage only. This is the rarest of all fancy champagnes. Its vines have existed since before phylloxera (a plant louse) killed most French grapevines in the mid-1800s. The wine is robust and rich-flavored. Bollinger also makes a vintage champagne and a nonvintage brut.

• **Dom Ruinart Blanc de Blancs**—vintage only. Produced by Dom Perignon in Reims rather than in Epernay, it is held in low profile so as not to compete strongly with its illustrious coproduct but is every bit as good. The wine is light (not thin), complex, very alive, yet velvety.

Grace M. Scotto, veteran of the wine business and former owner, Scotto Wine Cellar, Brooklyn.

Best American Beers

The Gourmet Guide to Beer by Howard Hillman. Facts on File.

The quality of beers varies almost as widely as the quality of wine…but the difference in price between the worst and the best is far narrower. Unlike wine, beer can be judged visually. Like wine, taste is the ultimate test.

How to tell a fine beer by sight: Use a tulip-shaped glass or a large brandy snifter. The beer should be at about 50°F (a bit warmer than refrigerator temperature). Pour it straight down the center of the glass. Side pouring is necessary only if the beer has been jostled or insufficiently chilled. *Now look for the three visual signs of excellence...*

1. Small bubbles that continue to rise for several minutes.

2. A dense head, one-and-one-half to two inches high, that lasts.

3. No trace of cloudiness.

After drinking, look for the clear "Brussels lace" tracery that should remain on the inside of the glass.

- **Best American regular beers.**
  - Anchor Steam Beer (San Francisco)
  - New Amsterdam Amber Beer (NYC)
- **Best dark beers.**
  - Prior Double Dark Beer
  - Sierra Nevada Porter
  - Sierra Nevada Stout
- **Best beers to go with meals.**
  - Kronenbourg (from France)
  - Kirin (from Japan)
- **To buy and store beer...**
  - Be sure the bottles are filled to within one-and-one-half inches of the top.
  - Buy bottles instead of cans. Avoid twist-cap bottles if possible.
  - Try to buy refrigerated beer that has not been exposed to fluorescent light.
  - Store bottles upright at 40°F to 50°F. Avoid agitating the bottles in transit or in storage. (For example, do not put them on the door shelves of a refrigerator.)
  - Do not store beer for long periods.
  - Do not quick-chill beer in the freezer.

Best Corkscrew

Waiter's corkscrew is 25% longer than the traditional model, resulting in greater leverage. This device is usually much more durable and also has a handy knife for careful removal of the capsule on bottles.

Grace M. Scotto, veteran of the wine business and former owner, Scotto Wine Cellar, Brooklyn.

Greatest White Wine

Alsatian white wines are among the greatest in the world, yet strangely go underappreciated, says *The Wine Advocate* editor Robert M. Parker, Jr. Dry, rich and full-bodied, they are closer to white Burgundies than to German Reislings. Great bargains include the Domaine Weinbach Reserve Pinot Blanc and the F.E. Trimbach Pinot Gris.

Connoisseur.

Best Sparkling Water

Time.

Connoisseurship apparently knows no limits. Many people who used to ask for whiskey by the brand do the same with sparkling water. Some may even distinguish among flavors, but not if ice cubes and limes are used. Differences are hard to spot, even when the waters are downed neat. But they do exist, as the following list indicates. *Brands of club soda and carbonated mineral water are ranked by preference and rated as follows:* Four boxes, excellent; three, very good; two, good; one, fair; zero, must suit tastes other than mine.

☐☐☐☐*San Pellegrino, Italy:* A real charmer with a lively, gentle fizz. Clear, springlike flavor is balanced and sprightly.

☐☐☐*Saratoga, US:* There's a bracing lilt to the soft fizz. The clear, neutral flavor has a slightly dry, citric pungency.

☐☐☐*Perrier, France:* Dependably neutral when cold, but a mineral taste develops. Overly strong fizz softens quickly.

☐☐*Poland Spring, US:* Fizz is a bit overpowering. Generally acceptable flavor with some citric-sodium aftertaste.

☐*Canada Dry, US:* Despite an overly strong fizz, this has a fairly neutral flavor with mild saline-citric accents.

☐*Apollinaris, Germany:* Strong, needling fizz and a warm, heavy mineral flavor that suggests bicarbonate of soda.

□*Calistoga, US:* After the gently soft fizz, it's all downhill. Musty, earthy flavor has salt-sodium overtones.

Seagram's, US: Sugar-water sweetness is a real shocker. Citric bitterness develops later. Moderate fizz.

Schweppes, US: A prevailing citric-saline bitterness makes this dry in the mouth. Fizz is extremely strong.

How to Select a Cigar

Fondle a fine cigar from tip to tip. It should feel supple and soft, never hard. *Avoid:* Cigars that have wrapper leaves with lumps or veins. Shop only at a tobacconist's store. *Favored:* Unwrapped cigars that have been kept under perfect storage conditions. They have better flavor than cigars sold in metal or plastic tubes.

Care of Videotapes

Do not rewind videotapes after use. Wait until just before playing them the next time. This flexes the tape and sweeps away any lingering humidity.

•**Store tapes in their boxes** to keep dust and dirt from reaching them.

•**Never touch the tape itself.** Oil and acid from the fingers do damage. Also, cigarette smoke blown on the tapes does them no good.

•**Avoid abrupt changes in temperature.** When bringing a tape into a heated room from the cold outside, allow half an hour for the tape to adjust to the change before playing it.

•**Never keep a tape in pause or still frame for more than a minute.** The video heads moving back and forth will wear down that section of tape.

The New TV Recorders— Pros and Cons of TiVo And Media Center PCs

Samir Bhavnani, consumer technology director at the NPD Group, a market research firm headquartered in Port Washington, NY. He is a member of several global advisory councils that provide feedback on new technologies to Dell, Lenovo, Panasonic and Toshiba.

Toni Duboise, senior analyst for desktop computing at the NPD Group, also was interviewed for information on media center PCs. She has 10 years of experience as a PC analyst.

The once wondrous VCR is practically an antique nowadays as TiVo machines, DVD recorders and even newer high-tech options for recording TV programs abound.

We asked two senior technology market research analysts to explore the pros and cons of the new devices...

DVRS ARE EASIEST TO USE

Today's digital video recorders (DVRs) record onto a computer-style hard drive for later viewing. There are different makers and models of DVRs, but TiVo is by far the best known.

Pros: Once you understand how a DVR works, you will find it easier to record programs with it than with a VCR—and it offers more flexibility. Simply select a program from an on-screen guide using the remote control, and follow a few on-screen directions. *You can...*

•**Instruct the DVR to find and record your favorite shows anytime they air.** The latest generation of DVRs can fit hundreds of hours of television programs on their hard drives.

•**Search for and record any movie** with a particular actor or director.

•**Program most TiVos remotely** through the TiVo Web site.

•**Watch one program while your DVR is recording a different one.**

•**Start watching a recorded program from the beginning** at the same time the DVR finishes recording the end.

Once the DVR gets to know your tastes, it can choose programs to record based on what your history of shows watched indicates you might enjoy. *Also…*

• **Playback is as simple as choosing recorded programs** from an on-screen menu with your remote control.

• **DVRs automatically make temporary recordings of any program you watch,** typically for up to 30 minutes, so you can pause and even rewind "live" programming, then fast-forward through commercials.

• **Some DVRs have an automatic "30-second skip" function** to make it easier to jump past recorded commercials.

• **DVR picture quality is as good as live television.**

Cons: Because DVRs record programs on a hard drive, you can't just pop out a recording and play it in a different machine somewhere else, as you can with VCRs. *Exception:* Some DVRs include DVD drives that allow you to record onto a DVD disk. You then can play the disk on your computer or any DVD player.

The second major drawback is cost. DVRs typically cost about $200, plus a subscription fee (usually $5 to $20 a month). A high-definition TiVo Series 3 costs $800 plus shipping if you order on-line.

Selecting a DVR: TiVo isn't just the best-known DVR—it is considered the easiest to use and most reliable. But DVRs offered by your cable or satellite television provider may be best for you. They might not be as well-designed as the TiVo, but if you buy or rent through your cable or satellite company, you're likely to get a subsidized price…better customer service…and a DVR designed to work seamlessly with your programming feed.

Important: If you have a high-definition television, make sure the DVR is designed to record high-def programming.

MEDIA CENTER PCS COMBINE COMPUTER AND RECORDER

Certain personal computers can record and play TV programs. These media center PCs provide all the functions of DVRs, and like DVRs, they record television programming onto a hard drive for viewing on a TV. But with a media center PC, there is no monthly subscription fee…and the hard drive is part of your home computer, not an independent unit.

Media center PCs offer access to a wealth of information that DVRs cannot. You can quickly call up movie reviews on your TV screen before deciding if a film is worth watching. Expect to spend $1,000 or more for a media center PC.

Satellite Television Systems

Margaret J. Parone, former senior vice president of communications, Satellite Broadcasting & Communications Association, 1730 M St. NW, Suite 600, Washington, DC 20036.

More than 27 million American households now own home satellite television systems. Today's DBS or C-band satellite television system owner enjoys the widest variety of entertainment programming available with access to over 250 channels of video programming and CD-quality picture and audio reproduction. Satellite system owners can also receive an additional 100 services from around the world. These systems utilize satellites that transmit programming signals with 5- to 17-watt transponders and require an average receiver antenna size of seven feet.

DIRECTV

Through the DIRECTV-brand DSS satellite system featuring an 18-inch satellite dish, consumers have access to over 200 channels of entertainment and informational programming, as well as digital audio services. DIRECTV is sold at popular consumer electronics stores and satellite dealerships across the country for around $100 to $250, plus installation and an additional monthly programming fee, which ranges from $29.99 to $104.99. There are a variety of sports and movie packages available as well. *www.directv.com.*

DISH NETWORK

DISH Network offers consumers monthly satellite packages that range from $19.99 to $94.99, and offers as well a number of premium packages for sports and movies. A receiver and 20-inch satellite dish start at around $200, and you can buy additional receivers on which you can view different stations with their DISH 500 system (unlike earlier dishes, the DISH 500 can receive two separate feeds). Like DIRECTV, DISH Network can be purchased at electronics stores and satellite dealerships. *www.dish network.com.*

What makes satellite television such an attractive alternative to other multichannel video providers?

• **Satellite television** delivers unparalleled studio-quality picture performance.

• **Satellite-delivered digital stereo** is considered to be the highest fidelity of any broadcasting transmission.

• **Compact state-of-the-art components** are highly user-friendly and easily operated by all members of the household.

• **Parental programming lockout** features allow parents to guide child viewing to pre-selected channels only.

When the industry was born in the late 1970s, the typical satellite system was manufactured in the basement of some enterprising entrepreneur or small manufacturing shop, and had an average retail price tag of around $35,000, if and when you could find them. Since that time, the satellite industry has seen increasing unit sales.

Over 5,000 professional satellite television retailers are located across the United States. Consult the local Yellow Pages for the names of area retailers. As with any large purchase, ask for a listing of references and shop around. There are about 20 different brands of receivers and dishes being manufactured today.

Certainly, the satellite receiving system is the most sophisticated video gear in the consumer's home today. No other component combination could come close to the technology needed to capture a microwave signal from over 23,000 miles in space, focus it, amplify, process and convert that energy to a flawless, ghost-free picture perfect for presentation on today's high-tech television.

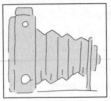

How to Buy a Used Camera Without Getting Stung

Ask for a 90-day repair warranty (never less than 30 days) and a 10-day, no-risk trial period. Use the 10 days to shoot several rolls of slide film at different combinations of shutter speeds, f-stops and lighting conditions. The enlarged, projected slides will reveal whether any features are defective.

Unneeded camera attachments: A motor drive is usually a waste of money unless you take a lot of sports or fashion pictures. Zoom lenses are good only for sports events. Their many glass elements tend to produce glare and internal reflections. *Good substitute:* A 250-mm telephoto that does not zoom.

Best Binoculars

The key to enjoying birding is a great pair of binoculars. Prices for good models start at around $150, and excellent models can cost as much as a few thousand dollars.

Considerations beyond just the price: Weight…magnification…and lens size.

Example: Binoculars labeled "7 x 35" create an image that appears seven times closer to you. The 35 refers to the size of the objective lenses, which are on the far side of the binoculars.

All else being equal, a pair of binoculars that is lighter and smaller is better for the beginner.

Budget-minded birders can buy a good, lightweight 7 x 35 pair for between $150 and $300. *Favorites…*

• **Canon 10 x 30 IS Image Stabilized Binoculars.** *Price:* $660.*

• **Vortex 10 x 42 Viper.** *Price:* $609.

*All prices are manufacturers' suggested list.

Before going out into the field, practice locating objects. Spot a target with your eye, then zero in with your binoculars. For comfort, you may wish to replace the binoculars' neck strap with a wider one.

Barry Kent MacKay, an avid birder in Markham, Ontario, who has written and illustrated numerous books on the subject. He is author of *The Birdwatcher's Companion*. Key Porter Books.

Best Fire Extinguishers

Look for an extinguisher rated ABC to fight the three most common household fires. Class A fires involve paper, wood and cloth. Class B, flammable liquids and gases. Class C, electrical equipment. Choose the most powerful unit you can easily carry and use. Power categories range from 1 (low) to 10, indicating what size fire the unit can fight. *Recommended:* An all-purpose ABC unit having a minimum power rating of 2-A:10-B:C.

Be a Smart Shopper

Buyer beware—the biggest bargains may not be uncovered by Web sites that compare on-line prices for books, CDs and other merchandise. Better sites—such as PriceSCAN *(www.pricescan.com)* and eSmarts *(www.esmarts.com)*—conduct broad Internet searches instead of restricting their listings to merchants who pay for the service. *However:* Local stores may offer even lower prices. Shipping costs are added to on-line orders...while sales tax is collected on in-store purchases.

Bottom line: Use Web sites as a tool to comparison shop—but not the only tool. When comparing prices, always make sure that the model number, size, etc. are the same. Buy only from reputable merchants.

Diane Rosener, former editor and publisher, *A Penny Saved,* Box 3471, Omaha, NE 68103.

Your Rights When You Buy "As Is"

Buying "as is" doesn't mean the buyer has no rights at all. "As is" clauses relate to quality, not to general class or description.

Example: If the buyer contracts to buy boxes of bolts as is, sight unseen, he or she won't be obligated if the boxes turn out to contain screws, not bolts.

Also, "as is" clauses don't override express warranties. They don't bar claims of fraud or misrepresentation. And they don't stop tort claims (personal injury actions if someone is injured by a defective product).

The late Dr. Russell Decker, professor emeritus of legal studies, Bowling Green State University, Bowling Green, OH.

How to Complain Effectively

Americans are not great defenders of their consumer rights. Two-thirds of the respondents in a major survey admitted to living with shoddy goods, incompetent services and broken promises. Only one-third of them had asked for redress.

People *should* complain. More than half of all consumer complaints result in some sort of satisfaction. (The psychological lift that comes with filing a protest is an added bonus.)

People don't complain because they think it won't do any good. *But there are effective ways to complain and get results...*

• **Have your facts straight before you act.** Be clear about dates, prices, payments and the exact nature of the problem.

• **Be specific about what you want done** —repair, replacement or refund.

• **Give reasonable deadlines for action you expect to be taken,** such as a week for store personnel to look into a problem. Deadlines move the action along.

•**Send copies of receipts.** Keep the originals for your records. File copies of all correspondence and notes (with dates) on any telephone dealings. Those records may be the pivotal factor if negotiations are prolonged or you must take your complaint elsewhere.

•**Be businesslike in your attitude** and project an expectation of a businesslike response.

•**Find out where you can go if the seller fails to make good,** and indicate your intention to follow through. Government agencies, such as a state attorney general's office, may need the very kind of evidence that your case provides to move against chronic offenders. Licensing boards or regulatory bodies are good bets for complaints against banks, insurance companies or professionals.

Additional recourse...

•**Consumer-action centers** sponsored by local newspapers and radio and television stations often get swift results.

•**Small-claims court.** If you can put a monetary value on your loss, you may get a judgment by suing in small-claims court. Collecting can be a problem (you must take the initiative yourself), but the law is on your side and the psychological benefits are enormous.

•**Trade associations** can be effective with their member organizations but not with outside companies.

Protect yourself before making large purchases or contracting for expensive services by dealing with reputable sellers. Companies that have been in business a long time have a vested interest in keeping their customers happy. Think about what recourse you will have if something does go wrong. A company with only a post office address, for example, will be impossible to trace.

What Goes On Sale When

If you're a serious shopper, you want to know when all the sales happen. *Here's a month-by-month schedule for dedicated bargain hunters...*

January:
  Appliances
  Baby carriages
  Books
  Carpets and rugs
  China and glassware
  Christmas cards
  Costume jewelry
  Furniture
  Furs
  Lingerie
  Men's overcoats
  Pocketbooks
  Preinventory sales
  Shoes
  Toys
  White goods (sheets, towels, etc.)

February:
  Air conditioners
  Art supplies
  Bedding
  Cars (used)
  Curtains
  Furniture
  Glassware and china
  Housewares
  Lamps
  Men's apparel
  Consumer electronics
  Silverware
  Sportswear and equipment
  Storm windows
  Toys

March:
  Boys' and girls' shoes
  Garden supplies
  Housewares
  Ice skates
  Infants' clothing
  Laundry equipment
  Luggage
  Ski equipment

April:
  Fabrics
  Hosiery
  Lingerie
  Painting supplies
  Women's shoes

May:
  Handbags
  Housecoats
  Household linens

Jewelry
Luggage
Outdoor furniture
Rugs
Shoes
Sportswear
Tires and auto accessories
TV sets

June:
Bedding
Boys' clothing
Fabrics
Floor coverings
Lingerie, sleepwear and hosiery
Men's clothing
Women's shoes

July:
Air conditioners and other appliances
Bathing suits
Children's clothes
Electronic equipment
Furniture
Handbags
Lingerie and sleepwear
Luggage
Men's shirts
Men's shoes
Rugs
Sportswear
Summer clothes
Summer sports equipment

August:
Back-to-school specials
Bathing suits
Carpeting
Cosmetics
Curtains and drapes
Electric fans and air conditioners
Furniture
Furs
Men's coats
Tires
White goods
Women's coats

September:
Bicycles
Cars (outgoing models)
China and glassware
Fabrics
Fall fashions
Garden equipment
Hardware

Lamps
Paints

October:
Cars (outgoing models)
China and glassware
Fall/winter clothing
Fishing equipment
Furniture
Lingerie and hosiery
Major appliances
School supplies
Silver
Storewide clearances
Women's coats

November:
Blankets and quilts
Boys' suits and coats
Cars (used)
Lingerie
Major appliances
Men's suits and coats
Shoes
White goods
Winter clothing

December:
Blankets and quilts
Cars (used)
Children's clothes
Coats and hats
Men's furnishings
Resort and cruise wear
Shoes

A Shopper's Guide To Bargaining

Sharon Dunn Greene, coauthor of *The Lower East Side Shopping Guide,* Brooklyn.

The biggest problem most shoppers have with bargaining is a feeling that nice people don't do it. Before you can negotiate, you have to get over this attitude. Some ammunition…

• **Bargaining will not turn you into a social outcast.** All a shopkeeper sees when you walk in is dollar signs. If you are willing to spend, he or she will probably be willing to make a deal. He knows that everybody is trying to save money these days.

•**Bargaining is a business transaction.** You are not trying to cheat the merchant or get something for nothing. You are trying to agree on a fair price. You expect to negotiate for a house or a car—why not for a refrigerator or a winter coat?

•**You have a right to bargain,** particularly in small stores that don't discount. *Reasoning:* Department stores, which won't bargain as a rule, mark up prices 100% to 150% to cover high overhead costs. Small stores should charge lower prices because their costs are less.

The savvy approach: Set yourself a price limit for a particular item before you approach the storekeeper. Be prepared to walk out if he/she doesn't meet your limit. (You can always change your mind later.) Make him believe you really won't buy unless he comes down.

Be discreet in your negotiations. If other customers can overhear your dickering, the shop owner will feel obliged to remain firm. Be respectful of the merchandise and the storekeeper. Don't manhandle the goods that you inspect. Address the salesperson in a polite, friendly manner. Assume that he will want to do his best for you because he is such a nice, helpful person.

Shop during off hours. You will have more luck if business is slow.

Look for unmarked merchandise. If there is no price tag, you are invited to bargain.

Tactics that work...

•**Negotiate with cash.** In a store that takes credit cards, request a discount for paying in cash. (Charging entails overhead costs that the store must absorb.)

•**Buy in quantity.** A customer who is committed to a number of purchases has more bargaining power. When everything is picked out, approach the owner and suggest a total price about 20% less than the actual total. *Variation:* If you are buying more than one of an item, offer to pay full price on the first one

if the owner will give you a break on the others. *Storekeeper's alternative:* You spent $500 on clothing and asked for a better price. The owner said he couldn't charge you less, but he threw in a belt priced at $35 as a bonus.

•**Look for flawed merchandise.** This is the only acceptable bargaining point in department stores, but it can also save you money in small shops. If there's a spot, a split seam or a missing button, estimate what it would cost to have the garment fixed commercially and ask for a discount based on that figure. *Variations:* You find a chipped hairdryer. When you ask for a discount, the manager says he will return it to the manufacturer and find an undamaged one for you. *Your reply:* "Sell it to me for a little less and save yourself the trouble."

•**Adapt your haggling to the realities of the situation.** A true discount house has a low profit margin and depends on volume to make its money. Don't ask for more than 5% off in such a store. A boutique that charges what the traffic will bear has more leeway. Start by asking for 25% off, and dicker from there.

•**Buy at the end of the season,** when new stock is being put out. Offer to buy older goods—at a discount.

•**Neighborhood stores.** Push the local television or appliance dealer to give you a break so you can keep your service business in the community.

Hate Shopping?

Most big stores have employees who'll do your shopping for you. You don't even have to be there. Call the store and ask for the personal shopper. *Stores that specialize in personal shopping:* Bloomingdale's and Saks Fifth Avenue in New York City, and Nordstrom in Seattle.

Buying from Door-to-Door Salespeople

Impulse buys made from door-to-door salespeople or houseware parties need not be binding. Under Federal Trade Commission rules, you have three business days to reconsider at-home purchases of $25 or more.

Recommended procedure: At the time of purchase, always ask for two copies of a dated cancellation form that shows date of sale and a dated contract with the seller's name and address. The contract should specify your right to cancel. *Note:* If you have received no forms, contact the nearest office for advice within three business days.

To cancel: Sign and date one copy of the cancellation form, and keep the second copy. *Hint:* As insurance, send the cancellation by registered mail (return receipt requested).

Sellers have 10 days to act. *Their obligations:* To return any signed papers, down payment and trade-in. To arrange for pickup or shipping of any goods. (Sellers pay shipping.) Pickup must be made within 20 days of your dated cancellation notice.

Reminder about picking up merchandise: You must make it available. If no pickup is made within the 20 days, the goods are yours. If you agree to ship the goods back and then fail to do so, or if you fail to make the goods available for pickup, you may be held to the original contract.

Note: The same rules apply at a hotel, restaurant or any other location off the seller's normal business premises. They do not apply to sales made by mail or phone, or to sales of real estate, insurance, securities or emergency home repairs.

Bargaining with a Mail-Order Firm

Discounts from mail-order firms are often possible. *How:* Wait for the catalog to be out for three months or so. Then phone and ask if the company will give you a 25% discount off the item you want. Many won't, but some that are trying to get rid of unsold merchandise will welcome the opportunity.

Sue Goldstein, author of *The Underground Shopper.* Great Buy Press.

How to Avoid Junk Mail

To avoid much of today's advertising mail, get in touch with the Direct Marketing Association. DMA's Mail Preference Service (including more than 500 major national mailing houses) can get your name off many computerized mailing lists. They also handle the telemarketing Do Not Call list. *www.the-dma.org.*

How to Get a Bargain at A Postal Service Auction

A US Postal Service auction is an exciting combination of Las Vegas and a flea market—you gamble for bargains and come out a winner or loser, depending on the effectiveness of your strategy. In the meantime, you've had lots of fun, and you just may pick up the buy of a lifetime.

The Postal Service holds regular auctions of lost, damaged or undeliverable merchandise every two to four months in all major US cities. Call the main post office in your city for time and date.

The merchandise that's available ranges from jeans and Oriental furniture to bottles of dishwashing detergent and microcomputers. In fact, anything that can be sent through the mail might turn up at a post office auction. *Items typically available:* Stereo equipment, TVs, radios, dishes, pots and pans, tools, typewriters, clothing, books, coins.

HOW IT WORKS

•**Items are sold by lot.** Similar articles are often grouped together, such as a dozen jeans, four typewriters or three radios. The items must be purchased together. *Suggestion:* Bring friends who might want to share a lot with you.

•**Lots are displayed the day before the auction.** Inspection is not permitted on the day of the sale, and viewing is all that's allowed. Lots are in compartments or bins that are covered with netting. Nothing (except clothing on hangers) can be handled or tested. *Suggestion:* Many compartments are badly lighted, so bring a flashlight to get a good look.

•**All lots are listed by number on a mimeographed sheet given out on the inspection day.** They are auctioned off by number, and each has a minimum acceptable bid listed next to it (never less than $10). But the minimum bid is no indication of how much the lot will sell for. Some go for 10 or more times the minimum bid listed.

•**All lots are sold "as is."** There is no guarantee of quality or quantity. Despite the disclaimer, the Postal Service is not trying to trick anyone into bidding high for damaged goods. It tries to mark items it recognizes as damaged. *Remember:* All sales are final.

•**You must pay the day before the auction to obtain a paddle for bidding.** Each paddle has a number on it, which the auctioneer recognizes as your bidding number. To bid, hold up your paddle until the prices being called by the auctioneer exceed what you are willing to pay. The cost of the paddle will be refunded if you don't buy anything. Otherwise it is applied to the purchase price.

•**You must deposit 50% of the purchase price in cash or certified check 30 minutes after buying a lot.** It is desirable to bring several certified checks instead of one big one.

•**Merchandise must be picked up a day or two after the auction.** You must bring your own container.

The bidding at these auctions is extremely unpredictable and quirky. There is absolutely no way of knowing how much a lot will go for. Some lots are overbid, while others go for the minimum bid, often with no obvious relationship to actual value. *Example:* At a recent auction, a set of inexpensive plastic dishes went for more than the retail price, while a much more valuable and lovely set of china dishes sold for less than the plastic ones.

Prices seem to depend on who is attending a particular auction and what they are in the market for. *Example:* In furious bidding at the same auction, a number of dealers bid up a record-album lot to $750. But no one was interested in a number of lots of Reed & Barton silver-plated flatware, which went for the minimum bid of $5 per place setting.

BIDDING TIPS

•**Go through the list of lots carefully while looking at the merchandise** and write down your maximum bids. During the actual auction, bidding is confusingly fast, with prices rapidly increasing by $2 at a time as bidders drop out. Listen to the bidding carefully, and don't exceed your maximum.

•**Sit in the back of the room so you can see who is bidding against you.** *Why:* If you're in the market for a particular item, you'll be aware of how many others are in the same market that day. Also, you can see people drop out of the bidding.

•**Take someone knowledgeable to the visual inspection,** especially if you're planning to bid on something like electronic equipment. Find out how much that particular piece is worth and calculate your top bid by including the cost of repair.

•**If you can't find someone who is knowledgeable,** stick to bidding on lots that you can see are in good shape. *Best bets:* Dishes, cutlery, pots and pans, hand tools, furniture, clothing sold by the garment (much of the clothing is sold in huge bins and can't be inspected).

For more information and a list of upcoming auctions, go to *www.usps.com/auctions.*

How to Bid and Win @ On-line Auctions

Reyne Haines, an antique-glass specialist, columnist for *AntiqueWeek* and a regular antique-glass appraiser on PBS *Antiques Roadshow*.

The rapid rise of the Internet has produced hundreds of auction sites. Despite the growing popularity of these on-line sites, buyers and sellers need to take steps to protect themselves.

Reason: The sites only serve as the middlemen. They say up front that they don't guarantee the items offered at auctions are as described. They also don't ensure that winning buyers will pay the amount they bid.

HOW ON-LINE AUCTIONS WORK

People who want to sell something through an on-line auction must first register with the auction site. Sellers provide the starting price and sometimes a "reserve price"—the dollar amount below which they can refuse to sell. And they list how long they want the auction to last, usually seven to 14 days.

An electronic photo of the item can be uploaded to accompany the item's description.

Buyers must also register and, on some sites, provide a driver's license number, Social Security number and date of birth to prove they are indeed who they say they are. Once the auction is over, the item is shipped, usually at the winner's expense, either immediately if the buyer pays by credit card or after a personal check to the seller has cleared.

DOING IT RIGHT

• **Watch out for skimpy descriptions.** Merchandise offered for auction will carry a description listing the history, condition, flaws, repairs and other important details.

If any part of the description seems to be missing—such as the date that the antique furniture was made—E-mail the seller requesting more information.

Once an item is sold, most auction sites will purge the description from the site.

Self-defense: Always save a copy of the description on your computer. When the item arrives, if it doesn't fit the description, you have recourse to return it to the seller and get your money refunded.

Some auction sites offer free insurance policies with up to $2,000 in coverage in case there is a problem.

Other than that, the auction sites do not guarantee an item's quality—or the reputations of either the buyer or the seller.

• **Read the feedback from previous buyers.** On most sites, buyers who have previously purchased items from a seller can report their experiences to the auction site feedback form. These "reviews" are available for all to read.

Better auction sites prevent shady sellers from having friends load up the board with positive comments by limiting access only to people who have bought or sold merchandise. Check to see if the auction site has such a policy.

• **Ask about the site's return policy.** While some sites require sellers to accept returns for any reason, others leave it up to the individual.

Legitimate sellers will give you at least three days after receipt of an item to notify them that you're returning it for a refund.

• **Stick to sellers who accept payment by credit card or check.** Beware of those who insist on money orders only.

By law, credit card companies must stand behind faulty merchandise or transactions paid for with their cards. Also, you can stop payment on a check.

• **Beware of snipers.** A sniper is someone who bids on an item moments before the bidding session closes.

Snipers might outbid you by as little as $1. Even if you're on-line at the time, there may not be enough time to submit a higher bid.

To prevent this problem, better sites have instituted a five-minute delay.

How it works: If a bid comes in within five minutes of the close, the deadline is extended an additional five minutes to give other potential buyers the chance to raise their own bids. This extension continues, five minutes at a time, until no more bids are received for one full five-minute period.

Caution: At sites that do not have a five-minute delay, never assume you're the only one bidding for an item—even if your bid is the only one listed on your computer screen.

•**Use automated bidding to stay in the action.** Better sites allow you to make an initial bid and then indicate privately a maximum bid. Then, if someone outbids your initial offer, the system automatically raises your offer in predetermined increments until it reaches your limit.

In the end, you may lose out on the item. But you won't spend more than you initially planned. You can always raise your bid higher than your set maximum if you want to.

FAVORITE AUCTION SITES

•**eBay.** The world's largest and most popular on-line auction site adds hundreds of thousands of new items daily. It sells more than half of everything offered for sale. Antiques, books, collectibles, memorabilia, stamps, trading cards. *www.ebay.com.*

•**uBid.com.** Brand-name, new and used computer and office equipment as well as jewelry and gifts, collectibles, apparel and more. *www.ubid.com.*

Gearing Up for Auctions

Depending on the kind of auction (country, indoor) and the type of merchandise sought (bric-a-brac, tools, furniture), assemble the appropriate gear. *Suggestions...*

•**Cash, credit cards or checkbook.** (Some auctions accept only cash.)

•**Pens, pencils and notebook.**

•**Pocket calculator.**

•**Rope for tying items to car roof.**

•**Old blankets for cushioning.**

•**Tape measure.**

•**Magnet** (for detecting iron and steel under paint or plating).

•**Folding chair and umbrella** (if auction is outdoors).

•**Picnic lunch.**

Internet Auction Fraud Protection

When buying at an Internet auction, protect yourself against fraud. Internet auction firms like eBay and uBid are perfectly legitimate, but some of the thousands and thousands of people who use them are not.

Safety: Use the "escrow payment" option that most auction firms offer to hold your payment until satisfactory delivery of the item occurs. Obtain and verify the name and physical address of the seller—don't deal with those who won't provide them. Ask about warranties and return policies.

Be wary of hard-to-verify claims, such as stories about antiques.

Be careful when buying from an individual —consumer protection laws that apply to businesses won't apply.

Holly Anderson, communications director, Internet Fraud Watch of the National Consumers League. *www.fraud.org.*

How to Avoid Lines and Beat Crowds

Marilyn Machlowitz, PhD, a New York City–based organizational psychologist and consultant, and the author of *Workaholics: Living with Them, Working with Them.* New American Library.

If time is scarcer than money for you, you might be willing to pay to add the equivalent of a twenty-fifth hour to your day.

Suppose your local museum offers free admission from, say, 6 pm to 8 pm one evening a week. I can guarantee that you'll have the museum to yourself if you go from 5 pm to 6 pm that night. Everyone else will be waiting for the stroke of 6.

Similarly, if your watering hole reduces the price of drinks during its happy hour from 5 pm to 7 pm, go after 7. (Unless, of course, you hope to meet someone, in which case you'll want to be there when it's most crowded.)

If you hate waiting in line, simply learn when places are least crowded and go then.

Some suggestions...

• **Movies are semi-deserted on Mondays,** since most people go out over the weekend. If it's a really hot film, the showing immediately after work is less likely to be crowded than the 8 pm or 10 pm show.

• **Bakeries are also almost empty on Mondays.** People start their diets promptly on Monday morning and forget them by Tuesday morning.

• **Banks are least busy before payday.** So go Thursdays if Fridays are payday where you live or on the 14th and 29th if paydays fall on the 15th and 30th.

• **Post offices aren't crowded on Thursday afternoons.**

• **Supermarkets have long lines 15 minutes before closing time** but no lines 15 minutes after opening.

If you're unsure about when your health club, swimming pool, laundromat or barber shop is least crowded, just ask the manager.

Learn which days you have two opportunities to do something rather than one. *Example:* If your favorite restaurant offers two dinner seatings some evenings and only one on others, your best bet is to aim for a two-seating night. Similarly, you're more likely to get into an evening theater performance on a day when there's also a matinee.

Another trick is to reverse the logical sequence of things. Almost everyone buys tokens or commuter passes before boarding the train. If, instead, you line up as you exit, you'll be on your way in no time. Also, take forms with you when you leave the bank or airport. Fill them out at your convenience

instead of struggling to complete them as you stand in line.

To minimize wasted telephone time, make your next appointment as you leave your dentist's or doctor's office. Make your next reservation as you leave a restaurant. You can do the same thing with your lunch companion or golf cronies as well.

If you hate being placed on hold, call before 9 or after 5. This is an old journalist's trick that almost guarantees that you won't be intercepted by a protective assistant. Learn the numbers of people's private lines. You can quietly copy these down when you're in the office, or you can ask. Most travel agents, for instance, know special numbers for reaching airlines and hotels. If all else fails, invest in a speaker phone. That way, at least, you can continue working while you hang on hold.

Clear Answers to Common Cell Phone Questions

Sasha Novakovich, cofounder and CEO of GetConnected.com, telecom price-comparison Web site, based in Boston. She is coauthor of *Consumer's Guide to Cell Phones & Wireless Service Plans.* Syngress.

Millions of Americans now have cell phones. But few know which plan is best or how to get good service. *Here are answers to the questions that current and prospective cell-phone users ask...*

What are cellular "family plans"? Are they good deals?

Each service provider's family plan is a little different. Generally, every member of your group—you don't have to be related—gets his/her own phone and phone number, but you all share the same pool of monthly minutes. There is only one bill.

Expect to pay the usual service rate for the family plan you select, plus about $10 per month for each additional phone. Calls *between* cell phones in a family plan typically are included in the monthly rate or offered at a flat fee.

Family plans can make sense if you do most of your calling among a small group of family members, friends or colleagues. But with everyone sharing the same minutes, it is easy to lose track of usage and wind up paying steep per-minute overcharges each month.

Be sure the "family" is stable. If you sign up with a girlfriend and then break up, you'll be stuck in a contract together.

Is there any way to get out of a long-term service contract without paying a big penalty?

Probably not. But there is no reason not to try, especially if the wireless provider has not lived up to the agreement. Have you received poor service? Have there been repeated overcharges on your bill? If so, document these problems carefully, noting times and places. Take this information to the service provider's nearest store. With enough evidence, the provider might agree to end the contract—or let you buy your way out for a lower amount.

If you don't get satisfaction at the store, call the provider's 800 number, and ask for the customer-retention department or the customer-loyalty program. Make note of the name and direct phone number of everyone with whom you speak, plus the order number for the transaction if the company agrees to end the contract.

Do cell phones cause cancer? How can I reduce the risk?

There is no scientific evidence that cell phones do—or don't—cause cancer.

You may be able to avoid potential radiation danger by using a cell-phone earpiece, which keeps the phone farther from your head. Earpieces are available from cell-phone manufacturers, service providers and electronics stores for anywhere from $8 to $100.

Service is spotty where I live. How can I improve reception?

You may want to switch service providers when your contract expires. Service providers don't all use the same networks. Your region might be better served by another company.

See which of your friends gets the best reception in the locations—home, office, route to work—and at the times you expect to use your cell phone the most. Sign up with that company.

Or ask the sales representative to let you test the service before you make a commitment. Wireless providers often let new customers cancel their agreements and return their phones within a few days if they have experienced poor service and have accumulated less than 30 minutes of call time. The customer has to pay for calls made. Confirm this cancellation policy before signing up.

Switching to a newer phone model also may help reception. But don't switch from a digital-and-analog phone to a digital-only phone—your reception might get worse. Old analog networks fill in the gaps where newer digital networks have not been built. Having a phone that works on both systems gives you more complete coverage.

Also, don't buy an internal antenna to add to your phone. It won't make a significant difference in reception.

Is it true that calls made from digital cell phones are more secure?

Not really. It is less likely that someone can eavesdrop on a call made from a digital cell phone than from an analog phone. But if privacy is important, use a corded landline.

Must I pay full price for a new phone if I lose or break my old one?

You can sign up in advance for cell-phone insurance, offered by service providers for about $3 to $8 per month. But unless you are prone to losing or breaking phones, it isn't worth the cost. Your warranty may cover breakage as well.

If neither insurance nor a warranty applies, ask your service provider what can be done for you. You may be able to buy a new phone at cost or get a discount if you extend your contract.

How do I find out how many minutes I have left each month?

Cell phones have call timers. To find the timer on your phone, check the "Call Log" section in the menu. Just reset the timer after each billing period ends.

Timers aren't perfect, though. Your timer may record a call as 10 seconds, but your provider may round it up to a full minute. And most timers don't distinguish between peak and off-peak use.

For a better estimate, go to your service provider's Web site. Many of them—such as Sprint, T–Mobile and Verizon—allow customers to check their minutes on-line for free.

Some providers charge if you *call* to check your minutes. For example, the time that Sprint customers use to dial in to check their remaining minutes will be subtracted from their monthly allotment.

What You Need to Know About Cell Phones

R. Michael Feazel, executive editor, *Communications Daily,* a magazine for the telecommunications industry.

Here is what to do if you're in the market for a cellular phone or service provider…

•**Pick a service plan before you pick a phone.** New cell-phone designs are so seductive that many people sign up with providers only if they carry the phones they want. That can leave you with excessive calling charges.

Consider before signing up…

•**The number of minutes you'll likely be on the phone** each billing cycle.

•**How often you'll use your phone outside your local region.** Long-distance "roaming" charges are expensive.

•**Phone size and options you prefer.**

Also, most people are unaware that if they decide to switch service providers, they will have to buy new phones.

Reason: While service providers sell identical-looking phones built by the same manufacturers, each phone is designed to access the network of one carrier—and one carrier only.

•**Don't sign a service contract that lasts longer than one year.** Some firms offer two- and three-year deals with what appear to be attractive rates. But considering how far prices have fallen and how much cell-phone technology has improved in recent years, any contract today will be a terrible deal three years from now. Also, any phone will be obsolete in three years.

Hiring a Private Detective

James Casey, private investigator and former New York City police detective, East Northport, NY.

Times have changed for private detectives. They're no longer breaking down hotel doors to snap incriminating photos for divorce cases. The modern private eye's bread and butter lies in serving the business world, in both security and personnel matters.

Private detectives are often effective in tracking down runaway children. A missing-persons bureau may have to worry about 30 cases at a time; a private eye can focus and coordinate the leads for a single client, giving the matter undivided attention. *Caution:* If the detective can't find a hard lead within three days but is eager to continue, he or she may be milking the client.

For three hours' work, a detective can devise a home security plan that will satisfy any insurance company, including itemized lists, photographs, locks and alarms.

How to choose one: Before hiring a detective, interview the person for at least 20 minutes to discuss your needs and how they'd be met. Be sure that the detective is licensed and bonded. A bond larger than the minimum bond might be advisable for a broad investigation covering several states or even a foreign country. To make certain the private eye's record is clean, check with the appropriate state division on licensing (usually the Department of State). And ask the detective for a résumé. The best detectives usually have ample experience. The best gauge is frequently word of mouth. Reputations are hard-won in this business.

Get Rid of Pain Cheaply

Inexpensive aspirin works as well as the most expensive brand. So always buy the least expensive. This is heard so often that it is a cliché. *Surprise:* It happens to be true. *Findings of a new study:* All brands contain the same amount of aspirin in each tablet. All dissolve at approximately the same rate. Each is absorbed into the bloodstream to start relieving pain in about the same length of time.

Coffee-Lover's Guide

Lyn Stallworth, a culinary-arts teacher, writer and author of *The Woman's Day Snack Cookbook*. Collier.

Which fruit product is most consumed by Americans? If you answered coffee, you were correct. The coffee bean is actually the pit of the round fruit of the coffee tree. (It's called a cherry by growers.)

Varieties: Two species account for most of the coffee we drink. Arabica, grown at high altitude and rich in flavor, is the larger crop. Robusta, mostly from Africa, is hardier but thinner in flavor.

IMPORTANT PRODUCERS

- **Brazil.** The quality ranges from indifferent to good. *Best:* Bourbon Santos.
- **Colombia.** Good to superlative coffees.
- **Costa Rica.** Arabicas, ranging from poor to great. Costa Rican coffees are rated by the hardness of the bean. Trust your coffee merchant or specialty store to provide strictly hard bean (SHB) or good hard bean (GHB), the mountain-grown best.
- **Jamaica.** Look for mellow, aromatic Blue Mountain.
- **Java.** The word *java* was once the slang for coffee. However, the finest trees were destroyed in World War II and replaced by robusta. Sturdy, rich, heady Indonesian arabica is now very scarce.
- **Kenya.** All of Kenya's crop is arabica—mild, smooth and round.

Roasting: Slightly roasted beans have little taste. Overroasted ones taste burned. Variations in roasting time affect flavor, but there is no right or wrong, just personal preference. Darker roasts are not stronger. The strength of the brew depends on the amount of coffee used.

SOME ROASTING TERMS

- **Light city roast.** Often called cinnamon. Can be thin.
- **City roast.** The most popular. Makes a tasty brew.
- **Full city roast.** Beans are dark brown, with no show of oil. Preferred by coffee-specialty shops.
- **Viennese roast.** Somewhere between full city and French roast.
- **French roast.** The beans are oily, and the color is that of semisweet chocolate. Approximates espresso but smoother.
- **Italian/espresso roast.** The beans are oily and almost black. Serious coffee, drunk in small amounts.
- **French/Italian roast.** Dark and full-flavored but not as bitter as espresso.

CHOOSING COFFEE

Most coffees are a blend of two or more varieties. A skillful blender balances the components.

Suggestion: Start with a coffee merchant's house blend. Like house wine, it must please a broad range of tastes and demonstrate the quality of the merchant's offerings. Go on to try many blends. Most merchants sell their coffees in half-pound or even quarter-pound amounts.

Best Place to Store Coffee

For fresher coffee, store it in the freezer. Frozen beans stay fresh longer than frozen ground.

The Washingtonian.

How to Roast Beans In Your Own Oven

Coffee beans can be roasted in any ordinary oven. Place the green beans in a perforated pan under the broiler (set at 350°F). Toss them every two minutes. For a light American roast, go for 10 minutes. For a dark Italian roast, figure 20 minutes.

The Washingtonian.

Herbal Teas Can Be Dangerous

Herbal teas sometimes counter the effects of prescription drugs or cause serious side effects. *Severe diarrhea:* Senna (leaves, flowers and bark), buckthorn bark, dock roots and aloe leaves. *Allergic reactions:* Chamomile, goldenrod, marigold and yarrow. *Cancer:* Sassafras. *Toxic (possibly fatal) reactions:* Shave grass, Indian tobacco and mistletoe leaves. *Hallucinations:* Catnip, juniper, hydrangea, jimsonweed, lobelia, nutmeg and wormwood. Be sure to read ingredient lists.

End-of-Season Barbecue Care

Soak grill in a plastic wastebasket with hot water, dishwasher detergent and a small amount of white vinegar to cut the grease. After about an hour of soaking, grease will almost rinse away—only a little scrubbing is needed. *For even easier cleaning:* Soak the grill after every use.

Gene Gary, syndicated home columnist, Copley News Service.

Best Videotaped Cooking Lessons

Linda Gassenheimer, a syndicated food columnist and author of many cookbooks, including *Dinner in Minutes.* Houghton Mifflin.

Amateur chefs shopping for their first cooking videos should buy tapes that specialize in food-preparation techniques rather than recipes. *Reason:* Most recipe tapes are rarely viewed more than twice—or until you've mastered the dish. Also, great recipes can be found in plenty of places today, from magazines to TV to the Internet.

But a good instructional tape will become part of your kitchen library, serving as a long-term reference guide. If the tape is especially good, you will learn something new each time you watch it. *My two favorite cooking-technique videos...*

• **The Way to Cook: Julia Child's Complete Cooking Course.** Six hour-long tapes hosted by the famed chef who patiently goes over the basics of preparing haute cuisine.

• **The Culinary Institute of America,** one of the country's top cooking schools, offers instructional tapes and DVDs in a wide variety of categories, including basic culinary skills and techniques of healthy cooking. *Average running time:* 30 minutes.

The Culinary Institute of America, *www.ciachef.edu/enthusiasts/training.* 800-888-7850.

Buying and Storing Cheese

Neil Hearn, former proprietor of The Cheese Shop, Greenwich, CT.

Believe it or not, it *does* matter where you buy cheese. You should go to an experienced cheesemonger because you should buy only cheese that is fully or almost fully ripened. Getting cheese to this prime state is a specialist's job. For example, our store buys Brie and Camembert 85% ripened. Then it takes us 10 days of expert care to bring it to eating condition. Supermarkets sell potentially good cheeses, but because they can't take the time to age them properly, the shopper is often disappointed. Any cheese is at its best when it is bought from a good cheese store in a perfectly ripened state and is eaten within hours.

How can you be sure all the different cheeses you might want for a party are at their best?

Visit your cheese shop a week or more in advance to make your choices. The proprietor can then have each variety ready at its optimal state—even pinpointed to a particular hour for serving it—on the day of the party.

What about the leftovers? Can they be kept successfully?

We find that cheese, if kept cool and well wrapped, doesn't really need that much care once it is ripened. We have mailed more than 5,000 packages of cheese and had only five complaints—and two of those were sent to the wrong addresses.

How do you store leftover cheese?

Wrap cheese "like a Christmas present" in plastic wrap or aluminum foil. Be generous with the wrapping, and tuck in the sides. A chunk of well-wrapped hard cheese will keep for more than a month in the refrigerator without losing much weight or moisture. If it develops surface mold, you can just brush that off.

Can you freeze cheese?

In most cases, yes, and the quicker you freeze it, the better. If you receive a gift wheel of Cheddar, Swiss, Muenster or Parmesan, for example, cut it into half-pound or one-pound portions. Make individual slabs, not wedges, so it will freeze evenly. Put the unwrapped slabs in the back of the freezer overnight. Take them out the next day, wrap them immediately and put them back into the freezer. The cheese should be good for six months. Let it defrost overnight in the refrigerator before you use it.

If you want blue cheese for crumbling over salads, we recommend refrigerating it unwrapped so it dries out a little. (Wrapped

blues—Stilton, Roquefort and Danish blue—will keep for several weeks refrigerated.)

Which cheeses are poor keepers?

The triple cremes, such as St. Andre and Explorateur. The higher the cream content, the greater the risk of change. When creamy cheese is frozen, crystals form.

What about the glass cheese keepers sold in many gourmet shops?

You put vinegar and water in the bottom, supposedly to preserve the cheese. We find that it gives the cheese an unpleasant vinegar odor.

Food-Storage Secrets

For many people, how long to store and keep foods is a guessing game. *If you've ever had to throw away food that's gone bad, these guidelines will help...*

• **Banana bulletin.** For many years now it has been okay to put bananas in the refrigerator, contrary to the still-popular 1940s Chiquita Banana jingle. (More sophisticated picking and shipping have speeded the ripening process.) Yellow bananas can be held at the just-ripe stage in the refrigerator for up to six days. Although the peel might become slightly discolored, the fruit retains both its flavor and its nutritional content. Green bananas should ripen at room temperature first. Mashed banana pulp can be frozen.

• **Nuts in the shell keep at room temperature for only short periods of time.** Put them in a cool, dry place for prolonged storage. Shelled nuts remain fresh for several months when sealed in containers and refrigerated. For storage of up to a year, place either shelled or unshelled nuts in a tightly closed container in the freezer.

The Household Handbook by Tom Grady and Amy Rood. Meadowbrook Press.

• **Storage times for frozen meats vary significantly.** *Recommended holding time, in months*:* Beef roast or steak, 12. Ground beef, 6. Lamb, 12. Pork roasts and chops, 8 to

*Based on a freezer kept at 0°F or lower.

12. Bacon and ham, 1 to 2. Veal cutlets and chops, 6. Veal roasts, 8 to 10. Chicken and turkey, 12. Duck and goose, 6. Shellfish, not over 6. Cooked meat and poultry, 1.

• **Keep an accurate thermometer in your refrigerator or freezer.** *Optimal refrigerator temperature:* 40°F for food to be kept more than three or four days. *For the freezer:* 0°F is necessary for long-term storage. *Note:* Some parts of the freezer may be colder than others. Use the thermometer to determine which areas are safe for keeping foods long-term.

• **Freezing leftovers.** *Raw egg whites:* Freeze them in ice-cube trays. *Hard cheeses:* Grate them first. *Soup stock:* Divide it into portions. *Stale bread:* Turn it into crumbs in the blender. *Pancakes, French toast and waffles:* Freeze and reheat in the toaster oven at 375°F. *Whipped cream:* Drop into small mounds on a cookie sheet to freeze and then store the mounds in a plastic bag. *Citrus juices:* Freeze in an ice-cube tray.

• **Freezing fish.** Make a protective dip by stirring 1 tablespoon of unflavored gelatin into ¼ cup lemon juice and 1¾ cups cold water. Heat over a low flame, stirring constantly, until gelatin dissolves and mixture is clear. Cool to room temperature. Dip the fish into this solution and drain. Wrap individual pieces of fish in heavy-duty freezer wrap. Then place them in heavy-duty freezer bags. Use within two months.

• **If you do your own food canning, preserve only enough food to eat within one year.** After that time, its quality deteriorates.

Freezing Vegetables From Your Garden

Some vegetables can be frozen and enjoyed any time. *A few that freeze well...*

Tomatoes: Cut out the stems and rotten spots. Squish each tomato as you put it into a big cooking pot. Boil the tomatoes down to about half their original volume. Then put them through an old-fashioned food mill, catching the purée and discarding the skins and seeds. Pour the purée into a large, deep metal baking pan and leave the uncovered pan in the freezer overnight. The next day, run some hot water on the bottom of the pan to remove the purée, place the block of purée on a chopping board and icepick it into small pieces. Bag and freeze the chunks (a few to each bag).

Zucchini: Peel and split it and scrape out the seeds. Grate coarsely. Stir-fry in butter or oil until half cooked. Follow the same freezing procedure as for tomatoes.

Greens: Boil, drain, squeeze the water out, chop to desired consistency and follow the same freezing process.

How to Become a Game Show Contestant...and How to Win, Too

Greg Muntean, a former game show contestant coordinator. He is coauthor of *How to Be a Game Show Contestant.* Random House.

Some people think that all they have to do to become a game show contestant is write to the address they see on TV.

When I was the contestant coordinator for *Jeopardy!,* we used to test 200 people a day who hoped to be on the show—and maybe we accepted two.

The odds were just as daunting when I worked on *Wheel of Fortune.* The other 99% of applicants never got a chance to be on the program, but many of them could have avoided rejection.

Here are a few ways to improve your odds of becoming a game show contestant during the interview process...

• **Be realistic about your talents.** Choose your game show according to your skills. At every game show I've worked, people would come to auditions even though it was obvious this was not their show.

At *Jeopardy!,* we had people come in and score a zero on the written test. They couldn't answer a single question.

Sitting on the couch at home, all game shows seem easy. That's the illusion. If people couldn't play along at home, they wouldn't watch.

But with five cameras, a studio audience and other competitors, it's not quite as simple. You need to be very good to hold up under that pressure. So on *Jeopardy!,* we made the written test to qualify as a contestant a bit harder than the actual questions in order to select only the best contestants.

If you're only competitive and not superior to the players you see on TV, you might not pass the test.

Strategy: Don't pick your show because it offers the most valuable prizes or even because it's the most fun to watch. There are word games such as *Wheel of Fortune*…trivia games such as *Jeopardy!,* and *The Price Is Right*…and a wide variety of puzzle word games. Spend some time determining which category—and which game—caters to your strengths.

Note: The best-known shows are going to be the hardest to get on as a contestant.

• **Know your show.** Once you've selected a game show that's appropriate for your skills, watch it on TV for a while. Don't just try to answer the questions. Look for details, such as the jargon the contestants use.

Examples: If your show is *Jeopardy!,* practice putting your answers in question form and pay attention to the betting strategies. For *Wheel of Fortune,* the jargon is "I'd like to buy a vowel"—and "Come on, $5,000."

These are the details to which the people playing at home tend to pay less attention than the games themselves. But if you don't know them, they can hurt how you do at the audition.

• **Be personable.** Once you're in the audition, few things matter as much as your personality. A *Jeopardy!* contestant is very different from a *The Price Is Right* contestant, but the basic element of pleasantness is always there.

• **Be as upbeat as possible.** Game show executives look for contestants who will make their programs seem exciting. Again, you need to know the show. If you're auditioning for *Jeopardy!,* you don't have to jump up and down…but if you're aiming for *The Price Is Right,* you should jump.

• **Don't take anything for granted.** Even if you've already passed the written test and the audition and have been called to the studio, you can still be cut from the show—for just about any reason.

Example: On one program, a contestant's contact lens was causing him to blink too much during the rehearsal. The producer insisted we cut him to avoid the possibility it would happen during the show.

The studio is really the final interview. And even if you're simply phoning the show to confirm your rehearsal, be upbeat and energetic. Game shows have more than enough qualified potential contestants. Don't give them a reason to reject you.

While you can be rejected for any number of problems, game shows try to find a diverse group of contestants. You are not likely to be turned down on the basis of race, gender, age or occupation.

• **Take the process seriously.** Game shows seem lighthearted on television. That's the idea—they're supposed to be fun to watch. But game show producers take these shows very seriously.

Treat the show's application process as you would an interview for a job. Dress nicely for tests and the interview…be ready to display a knowledge of the show…and consider your responses to potential questions before you arrive.

Example: On many shows, the host asks the contestants about their occupations or families…or to relate an amusing anecdote. Those questions come from interviews the contestant coordinators conducted earlier in the process.

Have an interesting story or two prepared, but try to tell them with a degree of spontaneity, just as you would answer questions about yourself during a job interview. If you manage to survive the show's selection process, you earn the right to join the real competition—the game itself.

How to win at least something…

The skills and knowledge you'll need vary from show to show, but there are some strategies that will improve your odds of bringing home a prize.

• **Study the system of prize distribution for the show in which you are interested.** These distribution systems can be as different as the games themselves.

Examples: On *Jeopardy!*, only the winner keeps his or her cash. The other contestants receive parting gifts. But on *Wheel of Fortune,* all the contestants keep what they've won.

Consider the prize system when you're planning your strategy. If coming away with something is more important to you than actually winning the grand prize, you can improve your odds by selecting a game show that has more than one winner.

• **Consider your prize goals.** Are you happy with any award…or are you in it for cash only?

Many shows offer only merchandise—not cash—while nearly all shows give the losing contestants parting gifts. On some game shows, those gifts can be significant. So if you see victory slipping away, it might be worth angling for the second-place.

All prizes, whether they are cash or merchandise, are considered earned income by the IRS—so they are taxed at the fair market value (the lowest price you may find in an ad or a store). If you win a $30,000 boat, your tax bill could reach five figures. Of course, you can choose to turn down a prize after the game, but that's probably not what you had in mind.

• **Be better prepared than your competitors.** If possible, familiarize yourself with the mechanical aspects of the game.

Example: One of our first $100,000 winners on *Jeopardy!* practiced at home with an improvised buzzer to improve his timing. When he was on the game show, he was able to buzz in before the other contestants and that was a big part of his success.

Also, if there's a home version of the show available—either a board game or a computer game—buy it and play it often.

Secrets of Contest Winners

Rich Henderson and Ann Faith, coeditors of *Contest Newsletter,* PO Box 536, Bethel, CT 06801. *www.contest news-letter.com.*

Cash, vacations, houses, cars, electronic equipment, cameras and much, much more are the dream prizes that keep millions of Americans doggedly filling out entry blanks and helping to lower the post-office deficit. More than $100 million worth of prize money and goods are dispensed annually through an estimated 500 promotional competitions and drawings.

Some dedicated hobbyists have been able to win as many as 50 prizes in a single year. *Lesson:* There is an advantage to a planned approach to overcome the heavy odds against each entrant.

Winning strategies…

• **Use your talents.** If you can write, cook or take photographs, put your energy into entering contests rather than sweepstakes. Since contests take skill, fewer people are likely to compete…improving your chances. Photography contests have the fewest average entries.

• **Follow the rules precisely.** If the instructions say to print your name, don't write it in script. If a three-by-five-inch piece of paper is called for, measure your entry exactly. The slightest variation can disqualify you.

• **Enter often.** Always be on the lookout for new sweepstakes and contests to enter. *Sources:* Magazines, newspapers, radio, television, store shelves and bulletin boards, product packaging.

• **Make multiple entries,** if they are permitted. The more entries you send in, the more you tip the odds in your favor. *A scheme for large sweepstakes:* Spread out your entries over the length of the contest—one a week for five weeks, for example. When the volume of entries is big enough, they will be delivered to the judges in a number of different sacks. The theory is that judges will pick from each sack, and your chances go up if you have an entry in each of several different mailbags. *Simple logic:* A second entry doubles your chances of winning.

• **Keep informed.** Join a local contest club or subscribe to a contest newsletter. Either source will help you to learn contest traps and problems—and solutions. They'll alert you, too, to new competitions.

• **Be selective.** You must pay taxes on items that you win, so be sure the prizes are appropriate for you. If you don't live near the water, winning an expensive boat could be a headache. (Some contests offer cash equivalents.)

If you do win, check with your CPA or tax lawyer immediately. You must report the fair market value of items that you win, whether you keep them, sell them or give them away. This can be tricky.

Some contests and sweepstakes ask you to enclose some proof of purchase or a plain piece of paper with a product name or number written on it. Obviously, since these competitions are designed to promote a product, the sponsors have a vested interest in your buying what they are selling. And many people assume that a real proof of purchase will improve their chances of winning. *Fact:* In a recent survey, more than half the winners of major prizes reported that they had not bought the sponsor's product.

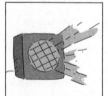

Radio Contests: More Than Luck

Bob Gross, who has won more than $10,500 in cash and prizes in radio contests.

Almost every popular radio station uses giveaways. Rewards include cash, cars, vacations and other prizes, ranging from record albums to TV sets. Playing the contests won't make you rich, but there's nothing like the thrill of hearing your name announced over the radio—as a winner.

Although chance plays the major role, you can greatly increase your odds of winning by understanding how call-in contests are run.

To begin: Pick a few stations that have entertaining contests and good prizes. Listen to each closely for a few hours, and phone in several times to get a feel for how the game is played.

The more contests you enter, the greater your chance of winning. The trick is to do this without spending your life on the phone. *The key:* Each program's disk jockey has a format that he or she follows closely.

Example: My prime listening time is from 11 pm to 1 am. By monitoring the same four stations, I have found that one station holds its regular contests at 42 minutes after the hour, another at either 15 or 45 minutes after the hour, another at either 5 or 35 minutes after the hour and another at 5 minutes of the hour. I tune in to those stations only at those times.

After the contest has been announced, several factors determine how quickly you should place your call...

• **The winning number.** The number of the winning call often corresponds to the station's location on the dial. For example, one station, at 95.5 FM, always rewards the ninety-fifth caller. If you dial right away, you'll be about number 20 (stations generally tell you your number when your call is answered). So wait 35 seconds before dialing. By the time the call goes through and the phone rings a few times (at least five seconds per ring), you'll be pretty close to call number 95. It usually takes the station 70 to 75 seconds to reach that call.

• **The number of lines at the station.** This helps determine how quickly they get to the winning number. A station with only two phone lines moves more slowly than one with 22. If you ask, most stations will tell you how many lines they use for contests.

• **The number of people answering the phones.** Stations that have two or more people handling the calls move more quickly than those where it's left up to the DJ. After you've played the contests a few times, you'll get to know the voices—and the number of phone answerers at each station.

•**Individual speeds.** Some DJs get the contest rolling quickly; others are slower. Get to know their habits.

There's always an element of chance. The difference between being caller number 94 and caller number 95 is a split second, and there's no way you can control that. But you can greatly increase the odds of winning.

Don't give up. If you get a call through and you're five or more numbers away from winning, hang up and try again. And don't let a busy signal discourage you. *Hint:* Many stations have a recording that says "Please try again later" if all the lines are busy. Stay on the line. Your call will be answered…sometimes in the middle of the recording.

Some DJs award the prize at random rather than counting through the calls to, say, number 95. Others announce that caller number two will win, so they don't have to answer 95 calls (and with such a low number, it's really no contest at all). Your only recourse in such a situation is to complain to the station's management. If lazy DJs know they've been caught, they'll improve.

Holiday Tipping Guidelines

The year-end holidays are a time when many people get into the spirit of giving. *For those people who help you all year long, here are some guidelines…*

Household help: The equivalent of a week's pay is standard. But much more elaborate gifts are appropriate for employees who have been in your service for a long time or to whom you are very close.

Newspaper deliverer: $5 to $25, depending on whether you get daily or weekend-only delivery.

Trash removal: $15 to $20 for each worker if it is legal in your community.

Mail carrier: While it is technically illegal to tip the mail carrier, many people give $10 to $20 to their regular carrier.

Day care workers: $10 to $25 per person for those who care for your children regularly, depending on the center's gift policy.

Baby-sitter: A gift certificate or a book for a regular sitter, or the equivalent of two nights' average pay.

APARTMENT DWELLERS

Superintendent: $30 to $100.

Doorman: $25 to $100.

Elevator operator: $15 to $25.

Concierge: $25 to $50.

Handyman: $20 to $30.

Porter: $15.

Garage attendant: $15 to $20.

If your building establishes a pool for tips that is divided among employees, you need only give an additional amount to those service people who have gone way beyond the call of duty for you this year.

OUTSIDE THE HOME

Restaurants where you are a regular customer: *Maître d',* $20 to $40. *Bartender,* $10 to $15. *Captain, waiter, busboy:* Divide the average cost of a meal among the three of them.

Beauty salon or barbershop: Give the owner-operator a bottle of wine or a basket of fruit. For employees who regularly attend you, $15 to $25 or the equivalent of a regular service.

Tailor or seamstress: $10 or wine or perfume.

Solving Consumer Complaints

Shirley Rooker, president, Call For Action, a Bethesda, MD–based international consumer hotline. *www.callfor action.org.*

There are ways you can get the results you deserve when lodging a consumer complaint. Evaluate the problem and decide what action you want taken, whether it's repairing or replacing the faulty product, getting a full or partial refund, etc.

Cars: Get a receipt every time your car is serviced. Without a record of the car's problems, your complaint will be worthless.

• **Call the person you dealt with initially and explain your problem and what you'd like done.** If that person is unable to help, proceed to the store manager. If the manager can't help, go to his or her boss, and so on.

Important: Be assertive, not aggressive. Aggressiveness puts the other person on the defensive and never helps your case in the long run.

• **Keep a detailed record of everything that transpires,** including the name, phone number and title of each person you talk with, and the date and content of each conversation.

• **If your problem still isn't solved, explain it in writing** and include a summary of what you'd like to have happen and a record of all the steps you've taken so far. Send it to the person ranked above the last person you've talked with, and follow up by phone.

• **If the company refuses to respond, contact your local consumer hotline,** the consumer protection office in your city or state or small-claims court.

FRAUDULENT COMPANIES

• **Ask for your money back with the realization that you probably won't get it.** Many of these companies operate for a short time in one area before moving on to another location and changing their name.

• **If they don't respond in a timely fashion** (in a few weeks), you should report them to the postal authorities, the Federal Bureau of Investigation, the Federal Trade Commission or any other state or federal organization that can put them out of business.

• **Protect yourself from fraudulent companies by avoiding prize offers with a price attached,** offers that sound "too good to be true" and offers that are only good if you send your check or money order "today."

Best Time of Year to Get A Good Deal on a Car

The best car-buying time is shortly before Christmas, when business tends to be slow and dealers are willing to take smaller profits.

Also good: The postholiday period into February, especially in cold-winter climates. *Best day:* A rainy Monday.

Consumer Adviser, Reader's Digest Association, Inc., Pleasantville, NY.

The ABCs of IPOs

Linda Killian, CFA and portfolio manager, Renaissance Capital, Two Greenwich Plaza, Greenwich, CT 06830. *www.ipohome.com.*

Spurred by the success of new Internet ventures, the number of companies that are going public is on the rise.

Despite the record number of deals, individual investors still find it difficult to obtain shares, as most IPO shares go to institutional investors.

HOW IPOS WORK

When a company first decides to go public, it selects an underwriter, which controls the issuance of shares. The underwriter then sets a price for the stock and sells the stock to its best clients in advance of its being traded publicly.

The sale of the stock by the underwriter to the public is called the Initial Public Offering (IPO). The price set by the underwriter is almost always less than the price at which the IPO will trade initially on the stock exchange. This is called the IPO discount, and it is why IPOs are so sought after by institutions and individuals. Many recent IPOs have attracted tremendous investor interest because the price of their shares soared in just the first few minutes of trading.

HOW TO INVEST

There are several ways individuals can participate in an IPO...

•**Sign up with a brokerage that is a major IPO underwriter.** The two big IPO underwriters are Merrill Lynch (800-637-7455)…and JPMorgan Chase (800-776-6061).

But just because you are a client at a brokerage doesn't necessarily mean that you have a shot at buying the stock of a company that is going public.

In order to do that, you have to be one of the brokerage's better customers—meaning, someone who trades frequently, has a high account balance, etc.

•**Sign up with the right small brokerage.** Another way to participate in an IPO is to become a client of a brokerage that specializes in underwriting IPOs in the sectors you favor and want to invest in.

If you like the technology and health-care sectors, the major underwriters of these IPO stocks are Deutsche Bank Securities (800-638-2596)…and JPMorgan Chase (800-776-6061).

Or you can sign up with a regional brokerage that underwrites IPOs.

Examples: William Blair (800-621-0687)… Raymond James (800-647-7378).

To find out which brokerages underwrite which deals, visit the Web site *www.ipohome.com.*

•**Put in a bid with a discount/on-line broker.** Until a year or two ago, customers of discount brokerages such as E*Trade, Fidelity and Schwab were unable to buy stock in IPOs.

But now these brokerages have teamed up with institutional underwriters to sell IPO shares. Generally, these IPO shares are reserved for customers who meet certain qualifications (large account balances, frequent trading activity, etc.).

Many people who buy IPO shares like to sell them shortly after to lock in fast gains.

To discourage *flipping*—or taking short-term profits—many discount brokers insist that customers hold shares for 30 to 90 days. Customers who sell sooner are often barred from participating in new IPOs for six months or longer.

On-line investors are unlikely to get more than 100 shares, however.

•**Buy the shares once they start trading.** Once the stock begins trading on the stock exchange, any investor can buy shares. However, investors should be cautious about jumping right in. Hot IPOs can double or triple in price on their first trading day, only to fall back later.

By waiting a few weeks to buy the stock of a company that has just gone public, you stand a much better chance of paying less for the shares.

SIGNS OF IPO QUALITY

Not all IPOs are worthwhile investments. *Here's what to look for…*

•**Large *spin-offs* of established companies.** A spin-off is a division of a public company that becomes independent by selling its own stock. The larger the division, the more shares are issued and the greater your chances of buying stock in the new company.

Most large spin-offs have established track records and histories of delivering higher annual earnings.

Many large spin-offs make particularly good IPOs because they are often good businesses that are not dependent on the parent company.

•**Clean preliminary prospectus.** Pay close attention to the section called "Management Discussion and Analysis of Financial Conditions." This section explains where the company's revenues come from and how the money is spent. Also read the section called "Risk Factors," which discloses potential problems. *What to look for…*

•Excessive executive compensation. We raise our eyebrows if management is paid more than $1 million a year—or if members of the board of directors receive more than $25,000 to $30,000 a year.

•The company expects to issue additional stock to finance operations. This means the initial offering isn't expected to raise enough money to meet the company's future needs.

•Management that holds a significant amount of stock. While every deal is structured differently, we like companies in which the average percentage of stock retained by management is at least in the high single digits.

•**Beware of dot-com IPOs.** Some people assume any Internet enterprise is a winner. But it's impossible to determine these companies' values. Be skeptical, especially if the company's only strength is its Web site.

7

Play Time

The Best Fly-Fishing Equipment and Where To Fish with It

Fly-fishing offers a rare opportunity to connect with creatures of beauty and power in extraordinary settings. Timing, patience and good companions all add to the joy of fishing.

Over the past eight years, as the number of fly fishermen in this country tripled to more than three million, we have entered a golden age of fly-fishing equipment. *How to get started...*

BUYING THE RIGHT ROD

A quality fishing rod is important. *Helpful:* Beginners should invest most of their start-up money in a good rod. A first-class rod costs $325 to $400. Most veteran fly fishermen own several different rods.

A good all-purpose rod is a "9-for-7"—a nine-foot rod with a seven-weight line. This rod will work for brook trout, steelhead, Canadian bass and pike, as well as larger trout in the Rockies. As long as you stick with a reputable rod maker—Fisher, L.L. Bean, Loomis, Orvis and Sage, among others—it is difficult to go wrong. *Other considerations about your rod...*

• **Material.** Bamboo rods are wonderful to look at but require considerable expertise to be wielded effectively.

Graphite rods have higher strength-to-weight ratios. A typical graphite rod might weigh only three ounces, compared to between four and five ounces for a bamboo or fiberglass rod. *Result:* Superior "feel" and responsiveness.

• **Style.** "Eastern" rods are more flexible and have slower casting action than other types of rods. This makes them ideal for beginners. They're best suited for catching smaller fish in smaller streams.

In windy conditions and bigger streams—such as those found in the Rocky Mountains

Howell Raines, Pulitzer Prize–winning journalist and former executive editor of *The New York Times*. He is author of *Fly Fishing Through the Midlife Crisis*. Harper-Collins.

168

or Pacific Northwest—stiffer "Western" rods can shoot out longer casts.

- **Portability.** With a total length of eight to nine feet, a two-piece rod is fine if you are driving to a stream. It will fit easily in the trunk of your car. But a three-piece rod is more convenient for air travel, since it can fit in a carry-on bag.

- **Line weight.** Rods are designated by the weight of the line they cast. Line weights range from Number 1, for tiny trout and panfish, to Number 15, for tarpon and marlin.

- **Economy.** G. Loomis, Orvis and Sage sell budget versions of their high-quality graphite rods with less expensive fittings. The reel seats and handles aren't as aesthetically fine as those of top-of-the-line models, but the rod functions almost as well.

OTHER EQUIPMENT

- **Reels.** An excellent reel is the Orvis CFO ($179 to $198), which is spool-milled from a block of solid aluminum and lasts indefinitely. Comparable reels are made by Abel and Lamsom.

For approximately $100, you can purchase good—but heavier—models by Cortland, Orvis Battenkill and Scientific Anglers.

- **Flies.** Excellent ready-tied trout flies are made by Orvis and L.L. Bean and cost less than $2 each. You'll want a combination of "dry" flies—for when fish are dimpling the surface for bugs...and "wet" flies—for when fish are feeding below the surface.

Basic assortment: Dry flies—Adams, Elk Hair Caddis, Light Cahill, Royal Wulff. Wet flies—Wooly Bugger, Hare's Ear Nymph, Pheasant Tail Nymph. *Better:* The Clouser Minnow that, in various sizes and colors, works for trout, bass, pike and saltwater fish.

GREAT FISHING SPOTS

- **Delaware Water Gap, Pennsylvania.** Water gaps—the places where big rivers come through big mountains—are ideal for their panoramic settings. Only two hours from New York City, the Delaware Water Gap offers some of the best trout fishing in the country.

More information: Aquatic Resources Program Specialist 717-626-9081.

- **Leeville, LaFourche Parish, Louisiana.** Atmospheric marshlands and a great spot for catching redfish (also known as channel bass)—a shallow-water ocean fish.

More information: LaFourche Welcome Center 985-537-5800.

- **Rapidan River, Virginia.** Like the Big Sur coast or the Grand Tetons above Jackson Hole, Wyoming, the Rapidan River is an ideal expression of its kind. It is an Eastern mountain stream plunging through hemlock forest. Since the Rapidan flows within the Shenandoah National Park, it is protected from development.

More information: Department of Game and Inland Fisheries 804-367-9369.

- **Snake River, near Jackson Hole, Wyoming.** Overwhelmingly beautiful scenery, lots of fish and a variety of conditions, from fast and deep channels to shallow flats.

More information: Wyoming Game and Fish Department 307-777-4600.

- **Yellowstone River, Yellowstone Park, Wyoming.** Even beginning fly fishermen may catch big fish at this premier protected cutthroat trout fishery.

More information: Yellowstone Park Information 307-344-7381.

WILD FISH

Many experienced fly fishermen prefer streams with wild—not stocked—fish. Stocked fish are those added to streams by park rangers for ecological and sporting purposes. Wild fish offer more fight and are harder to deceive.

In any waters, wild fish can flourish only if fly fishermen release every fish they catch. After 40 years of fishing, I do not own a single mounted fish. My photographs and memories are trophies enough.

Fishing Demystified

Rivers, lakes or open sea—if you know where to start looking, you can catch any fish successfully. *For example, bass tend to congregate...*

• **Near trees that have recently fallen into the water.**

• **In hot weather.** Under lily pads, especially in the only shallow spots around.

• **In consistently mild weather.** In backwater ponds and coves off the main lake. *Best:* Good weed or brush cover, with a creek running in.

• **Anytime at all.** In sunken moss beds near the shore.

Outdoor Life.

For fishing around a fallen tree, start at the top, using deep-running lures. Along the sides, use medium-running lures. Toward the base of the tree, change to shallow and surface lures.

Sports Afield.

For good year-round fishing, try Florida's east coast from Melbourne Beach to Fort Pierce. *Fall and spring:* Runs of snook, the delicious saltwater gamefish that weighs up to 30 pounds. *Winter:* Surf fishing for blues, big whiting and pompano, which many think is the best-tasting of all the saltwater fish. The nearby Indian River also provides good year-round fishing with light tackle.

Best Offshore Fishing

Barry Gibson, former editor, *Salt Water Sportsman*, and John F. Klein, a charter captain out of Sarasota, FL.

Face it. You've always wanted to play Ernest Hemingway for a day, your muscles straining, your face stinging from salt and sun, hair lashed by the wind, hooting and hollering in pain, exultation and glory as you engage in mortal combat with a colossus of the deep—man versus marlin.

Fact: Offshore fishing for big game fish requires the least amount of previous experience of any type of sportfishing. You don't have to rig your tackle, bait a hook, cast a line, or navigate. All you need is a good boat, a good captain, a competent crew and a strong back!

Once known as "deep-sea fishing" (a term now seen only in the brochures of tropical resorts), offshore fishing refers to sportfishing

for larger species—billfish (marlin, sailfish and swordfish), tuna, tarpon, cobia and shark. The US offers excellent fishing off all three coasts.

Chartering a boat: The procedure is similar everywhere. If time permits, visit the boat docks at sunset when charters return. See what kinds of fish are being brought in. Talk with the passengers. Were their previous fishing experiences and their expectations similar to yours? Did they have fun? Are they satisfied with their day's trip? Would they do it again?

Talk to the mates. Are they pleasant? Enthusiastic about the captain?

Next, inspect the boat. Is it clean and well maintained? Does it appear to have proper radio and safety equipment? Naturally, a boat will not look its best on its return from a day's fishing—but are the running gear and fishing tackle well kept? Or has tackle been stowed randomly, paint chipped, hardware corroded?

Many fishermen prefer an owner-operated boat to a vessel run by a salaried captain. In either case, check to see if the captain has been licensed by the Coast Guard.

Boats that carry six passengers or fewer are not required to pass an annual Coast Guard inspection, but they must carry mandatory safety equipment. Boats that have undergone a voluntary inspection will display a Coast Guard sticker. If you're planning to bring a child along, ask if junior-size life preservers are available.

If you expect to be able to keep your catch, check with the captain beforehand to avoid a dispute at the end of the day.

Expect to pay $300 to $400 a day for a private charter. In some areas, $600 to $800 is not uncommon.

Variations in costs depend largely on how far the boat must travel to reach prime fishing waters. In Boothbay, Maine, for example, you may have to travel only three to 10 miles offshore, while from Montauk, New York, 60 or 70 miles is not unusual.

Although some areas may offer half-day charters if the travel distance is not too great, it is more common for a good fishing trip to take a whole day.

Regardless of whether or not fish are caught, it is customary to tip the mate at the end of the day (and also the captain, especially if he is salaried and not the owner of the boat). The going rate is about 10% of the cost of the trip. Of course, as in any service business, a good catch and/or good service may inspire a more generous tip.

Party boats: For a less costly trip, though not necessarily a less enjoyable one, try a "party boat" or "head boat." These big, stable boats, equipped for a large number of passengers, range in cost from $15 or so for half a day to $20 to $30 and up for a longer trip. These boats are a great introduction for a beginning angler or for a fisherman who is new to an area. They offer wide variety and often concentrate on "good-eating" fish. *Disadvantages:* The equipment may be worn from continual use. (Don't hesitate to request another pole if you don't think yours is working right.) And you can't ask to go home if you're not having a good time.

On the Pacific Coast, some boats offer three-day to three-week trips for about $100 a day. They fish for numerous species along the Mexican coast. Passengers may keep their catch.

Most boats let you keep most or all of what you catch. The mate is usually happy to clean and fillet your fish for a small fee. But it is in very poor taste to ask the captain or the mate to clean your fish and then try to sell it on the dock. Take what you plan to eat and offer the rest to the boat. Keep your fish on ice in a cooler, being careful not to let your fillets come into contact with fresh water or ice.

ETIQUETTE

• **Dress appropriately.** Bring extra layers of clothing even if you are in the Florida Keys. It can be a lot cooler on the water than on land, and mornings are often chilly. Wear soft-soled boat shoes, polarized sunglasses and a hat, and bring a sunscreen.

• **Take precautions against seasickness.** Ask your doctor for medication ahead of time if you think you'll need it and begin to take it at least 24 hours before your departure. (This allows you to sleep off the early, drowsy part and be fully alert for your trip.) Medications for seasickness do not help if you wait until you are already queasy to take them.

• **Bring plenty of nonalcoholic beverages.** It is easy to get dehydrated while you are on the water. Also, bring any food you may want (it's a good idea to include a salty snack). Most charter boats do not supply food or drink, although many party boats have snack bars. *Note:* Although it is not in poor taste to enjoy a few beers over the course of a day's fishing, it is downright boorish, and frequently dangerous, to become drunk while on the water.

• **Limit the number of passengers.** Many people make the mistake of overloading a boat, hoping to split the cost. But on a charter boat with only one or two "fighting chairs," passengers take turns fishing. The more people on board, the fewer your turns to fish actively. As a general rule, a 28- to 30-foot boat accommodates four passengers comfortably. A 35-foot or larger boat can handle six.

• **Listen to the instructions of your captain and mate.** They have spent years studying an area, and they want you to catch fish. There are many differences in tackle, bait and techniques, and your favorite walleye lure may not be appetizing to a yellowfin tuna.

• **If you are a novice, say so.** Not only will the captain and mate appreciate your honesty, but they will best be able to help you if they have some idea of your previous experience.

• **Fish with an open mind.** The vacation day you have allocated for fishing may turn out to be a day fish are not feeding. Your guide isn't holding out on you.

Long-distance chartering: Many people don't have time to explore the docks of an area before they choose a boat. For recommendations by telephone, try calling a local tackle shop or the editors of a major outdoor magazine. (Resort hotels usually limit their referrals to the guides who service the hotel.)

Several travel agencies specialize (at no cost) in arranging fishing trips. *One good one:* Fishing International, Santa Rosa, California, 800-950-4242.

A few other pointers: Many captains will take "split charters." If you are traveling in a small group and would like to divide the cost of a charter, inquire at the dock for similar parties.

It is not polite, however, to ask a captain to find five other people to share your trip.

If you plan to take children, choose a charter that is geared toward variety fishing. Try a half-day charter first, and stay away from hard-core game fishing—it is boring just to watch Daddy fish all day!

Many of the favorite captains are booked solid a year in advance. Scout around early if you plan to fish in a new area.

SEASONAL SUGGESTIONS

•**April and May.** It's long-range party-boat season in Southern California. San Diego is the biggest port. Party boats in New York and New Jersey venture out for flounder, cod and other bottom fishing. Party boats and skiff guides are active in the Florida Keys.

•**June.** Head for the Gulf Stream from the Outer Banks of North Carolina to catch tuna and white marlin. It's big game billfish season offshore in the Gulf of Mexico from Louisiana to Texas.

•**July, August, early September.** In New York through New England, fish for giant tuna (up to 1,000 pounds!). It's peak season for white and blue marlin in North Carolina. There's excellent fishing in the Florida Keys (not crowded) for sailfish, bonefish and permit. Party and charter boats fish for salmon in the Pacific Northwest through Alaska.

•**September and October.** Catch bluefin tuna off Prince Edward Island before they migrate south.

•**October and November.** Big game fishing is winding down in the North and in the Gulf. But it's great for bluefish from Massachusetts through Chesapeake Bay.

•**September through November.** For a more glamorous trip, black marlin fishing is tremendous off the Great Barrier Reef in Australia or New Zealand.

•**December and January.** Winter is winter, even in the Florida Keys, but sailfish like the cold, rough seas. (Dress warmly.)

•**February and March.** The weather is very changeable in southern waters, so allow at least three to five days for a fishing trip. You may thus get one or two good days of fishing. There is still plenty of good fishing in the Carib-bean even though it is not peak season. Try for marlin and billfish in the Bahamas.

•**November through March.** Cabo San Lucas, Mexico, is prime for marlin, sails, dolphin (the fish, not the mammal) and roosterfish.

Good fishing! Once you try it, I bet you'll be hooked!

Great Wildlife Watching

Santa Cruz, California, Natural Bridge State Beach, 831-423-4609, where hundreds of thousands of monarch butterflies make their home from October through February…Sullivan County, New York, Eagle Institute, 845-557-6162, where more than 100 bald eagles winter from mid-December to mid-March…Florence, Oregon, Sea Lion Caves, 541-547-3111, where sea lions frolic year-round…Grand Island, Nebraska, Crane Meadows Nature Center, 308-382-1820, where hundreds of thousands of sandhill cranes and other waterfowl can be seen March to mid-April.

Diane Bair and Pamela Wright, coauthors, *Wild Encounters* (Willow Creek Press), writing in *Family Fun*, 114 Fifth Ave., New York City 10011.

Outdoor Programs For Young and Old

Great Camp Sagamore, a national historic site in New York's Adirondack mountains, offers a wide range of recreational and nature activities, 20 miles of hiking trails and a clear view of the Milky Way. Weekend and week-long programs include canoeing, history activities and llama trekking. Costs start at $199 per person.

Contact: Sagamore Historic Adirondack Great Camp, Box 40, Raquette Lake, NY 13436, 315-354-5311 or *www.sagamore.org*.

Mature Outlook.

How to Get Into Shape For Skiing

Being physically fit makes skiing more fun and helps prevent soreness and injuries. Getting ready for the slopes can be like your regular exercise regimen.

Muscle tone and flexibility: Stretching exercises keep your muscles long and pliable. They also warm muscles up for strenuous sports and help relax them afterward. Always stretch slowly. Hold the extended position for 20 to 30 seconds. Don't bounce. Do simple stretches. Rotate your head. Bend from side to side. Touch your toes. Lunge forward while keeping the back foot flat on the floor. Do sit-ups with your knees bent to strengthen abdominal muscles (they can take stress off the back).

Endurance and strength: Practicing any active sport, from swimming to tennis, for three one-hour sessions a week will get you into shape. Jogging builds up the muscles of the lower torso and legs. Running downhill strengthens the front thigh muscles, essential to skiing. Running on uneven terrain promotes strong and flexible ankles. Biking builds strong legs and improves balance.

Top 10 Skiing Resorts

An industry insider who has visited more than 120 North American ski centers during the past 22 years.

What makes one ski resort more exciting than all the rest? *According to our insider, it's the destination's diversity:* thrilling trails, cushy lodges and lots of after-ski activities. *The following are his North American favorites…*

•**Lake Louise, Alberta.** Probably the most outstanding scenery in North America. Canada's largest ski area with thousands of acres of bowl skiing, long tree-lined runs and high-speed lifts. Many enchanting and affordable ski lodges, including the spectacular Fairmont Chateau Lake Louise. 877-253-6888.

•**Snowbird, Utah.** One hour from Salt Lake City. Forty feet of snow each winter, plenty of difficult trails and a first-class spa. 800-232-9542.

•**Snowmass, Colorado.** Wide-open cruising terrain. Twenty-two lifts (seven of them high speed), 88 trails. Lodge lets you ski from your room to the lift. 800-923-8920.

Bonus: Trendy Aspen is only 10 minutes away by frequent, free shuttle bus.

•**Steamboat, Colorado.** Located above a quaint Western town, great mix of tree skiing and wide-open cruising trails. Has 142 trails and 25 lifts. Hot-springs-fed pools for bathing, horse-drawn sleigh rides. 877-237-2628.

•**Stowe, Vermont.** New England's tallest peak. 48 trails, modern lifts, improved snowmaking, great food and views. Cross-country skiing and night skiing. Twelve lifts (two high speed). 800-253-4754.

•**Sunday River, Maine.** Super-efficient lifts, snowmaking and grooming, plus all-ability terrain and lodging that allows you to ski to and from your door. Has grown to encompass 128 trails and three high-speed lifts. 207-824-3000.

•**Taos Ski Valley, New Mexico.** One of the finest ski schools. More than 100 trails, 12 lifts, abundant powder and sun 300 days a year. 866-968-7386.

•**Telluride, Colorado.** An expert's paradise, located above an old mining town nestled in a spectacular canyon. A modern ski-lodging development. 888-353-5473.

•**Vail, Colorado.** Largest single ski mountain in the US. Thirty-four lifts (many of them high speed), 5,289 acres of terrain, 193 trails and lots of powder, thanks to the high altitude. And, there are horse-drawn sleigh rides—including evening trips to local restaurants. 877-204-7881.

•**Whistler/Blackcomb, British Columbia.** Two mountains, 33 lifts, 8,100 acres of terrain, a mile of vertical descent that allows skiers to take their time winding down their choice of more than 200 trails. Has an enchanting base village with more than 100 shops. 877-932-0606.

When Sharpening Is Bad for Skis

Sharpening skis frequently to remove nicks and restore the edges can change their performance. Flat-filing the bottom reduces the thickness of the plastic base and makes skis more flexible. Side-filing can narrow skis and change the turning radius. For experts, this may be a problem, but most recreational skiers won't notice a difference.

Skiing.

How to Buy Ski Boots

The first rule in buying ski boots is, if a boot is not comfortable in the store, it will be worse on the slopes. *Proper fit:* Toes should be able to wiggle while the heel, instep and ball of the foot are effectively but not painfully immobilized. An experienced shop technician can expand the shell and modify the footbed and heel wedge. *Forward flex:* When you bend your foot, you should feel no pressure points on your shin or upper ankle. *Boot height:* A high boot spreads flexing loads across a wider shin area than low boots do. Most recreational skiers are at ease in a high boot with a soft forward flex. Low, stiff boots concentrate loads just above the ankle, which can be painful for the occasional skier.

Ski.

Golf Smarts

One way to improve your golf game while waiting your turn at the tee is to take some practice swings from the opposite side—if you are right-handed, take swings left-handed. Start slowly, and do not go more than 70% of your normal swing speed. Do the swings a few times on the first three or four holes of every round. Also do a few opposite-side swings at the driving range. They will help strengthen and balance your muscles, making it easier to hit longer drives.

Gregory Florez, golf trainer, Salt Lake City, quoted in *Men's Health.*

How to Play Better Golf

John Youngblood, author of *How I Went from 28 to Scratch in One Year Playing Once a Week at the Age of 70.* Price Stern Sloan.

I studied every prominent golfer who ever played the game and listed the techniques they shared. From this, I distilled my system, *Ultimate Golf Swing Fundamentals.* Within nine months, at the age of 70, I reduced my handicap from 28 to scratch.

How it works: The backbone of this system is a *stairstep* program. The principle is simple. I believe that the foundation of every sound golf game resides in putting.

The fundamentals for every succeeding swing—from the chip and pitch, through the irons, to the woods and driver—are the same. The only difference is that the golfer's stroke becomes successively longer.

According to the *stairstep* principle, the golfer must perfect every shot possible with a particular club before moving on to the next club, up the *stairstep.*

MORE ADVICE

In addition to practicing on the course's practice area (and doing it right), *I recommend the following steps for any golfers intent on sharpening their game:*

•**Play regularly.** In my turn-around year, I increased my frequency of play from once a month to once a week. I finally got to know my golf course, and could begin to aim my shots to areas where the following shots would be easier.

•**Do your golf exercises in front of a mirror.** I achieved a major breakthrough while swinging a 5-iron before a full-length mirror. *Don't be modest:* Dressed only in my shorts, I soon isolated my problem—a quivering of my right knee during my backswing, the source of my frequently errant iron shots. With proper exercise I developed control of my knee—and with it my iron game.

•**Never rush on the golf course.** Allow time upon arrival for your practice shots and putts. Once on the tee, visualize the shot to be made and the spot where you expect it to land. Concentrate on this spot—and not on anyone who may be watching you—as you stroke the ball.

•**Skip the practice swings before you hit.** Most people tend to tighten up with extra swings. It's better to relax and fire away.

•**Don't overswing.** Use a three-quarter backswing with your irons—and only a one-half backswing for your chips and pitches. You'll more than gain in control and accuracy anything you might lose in distance.

All About In-line Skates

Joel Rappelfeld, an in-line-skating instructor in New York City and author of *The Complete In-Line Skater.* St. Martin's Press.

In-line skates—skates with their wheels all in a row—have become very popular. More than a million pairs have been sold in the US, and sales are increasing each year.

Often called rollerblades, after the manufacturer Rollerblade, Inc., these skates…

•**Ride faster and more smoothly than conventional roller skates.** Because the wheels are in a straight line, the rubber makes less contact with the ground—avoiding more surface bumps and other obstructions. And because the wheels are under each boot, rather than at the four corners, they can't hit each other if your feet come close together.

•**Provide better ankle support than most conventional roller skates.** In-line skates have a polyurethane boot with an inner liner—much like a ski boot.

•**Provide excellent exercise.** Skaters burn up to 450 calories in 30 minutes.

In-line skates cost $100 to $500 a pair—about the same as conventional skates. Plan to spend at least $200. Cheaper models are less comfortable and have inferior wheels and bearings, which can slow down your progress in learning. *Learning how…*

The biggest risk is falling, usually from not knowing how to stop, or because of surface hazards—gravel, oil, etc. *Self-defense:* Wear knee and elbow pads, wrist guards and a lightweight bicycle helmet.

I also advise people to take a lesson or two before trying to skate on their own. Find an instructor through the shop where you buy your skates.

Protection: Find out how qualified the instructor is. *Ask questions:* How long have you been in-line skating? What type of training have you received from other in-line skating instructors? Do you have any related training and background in similar sports, such as ice skating, skiing or roller skating?

Tennis Pro Secrets

Psyching yourself up for a big point on the tennis court means employing a normal physiological mechanism—the adrenaline response. When adrenaline is pumped into our systems, we are stronger, faster and quicker for a brief period. *How to trigger the response:* Open your eyes wide and fix them on a nearby object. Breathe deeply and forcefully. Think of yourself as a powerful, aggressive individual. Exhort yourself with phrases like "Fight!" Try to raise goose bumps on your skin—they signal a high point. *Note:* Save this response for a key moment toward the end of the match. Psyching yourself up too often will leave you drained.

Tennis.

Tennis players often have trouble switching from one type of playing surface to another. Ease transitions by preparing. If you're moving to fast cement from slow clay, for example, practice charging the net before the switch. If it's the other way around, spend extra time on your ground strokes. Tactical adjustments should also be made in advance.

World Tennis.

WHEN YOU'RE FACING A SUPERIOR TENNIS PLAYER

• **Suspend all expectations.** Avoid thinking about the situation. Watch the ball, not the opponent.

• **Play your game.** Don't try to impress your opponent with difficult shots you normally never try.

• **Hit the ball deep and down the middle.** The more chances there are for your opponent to return your shot, the more chances there are for him/her to err.

• **Concentrate on your serve.** No matter how outgunned you may be, you can stay in the match if you hold your serve.

Choosing the Right Tennis Ball

Tennis balls come in four varieties. Heavy-duty, regular, high-altitude and pressureless. *Difference between heavy-duty and regular:* The felt cover. Heavy-duty balls have additional nylon to resist wear on hard courts. Regulars have more wool in the covering for play on clay courts. *Note:* Do not use heavy-duty balls on clay. They become slower as the nylon in the cover picks up dirt. High-altitude balls are for courts that are more than 5,000 feet above sea level. Pressureless balls are long-lasting, but they are heavier than most American players are accustomed to.

Save the slightly fluffier tennis ball for your second serve. The fluff lets the ball take the spin more easily than would a fresh, new ball or an old, bare one. Until the nap is fluffed, a new ball flies faster, skids farther and has less bounce.

Tennis.

How to Play Good Tennis After 40

Older tennis players can win and avoid injuries by using the right strategies and techniques. The late Pancho Gonzales, a former champion, advised playing a "thinking man's" game.

PANCHO'S PRACTICAL POINTERS

With age, it becomes harder to concentrate on the ball. *Recommended:* When hitting, watch the ball right up to the point where it hits the strings of the racket.

Aim for consistency rather than winners. *Common error made by older players:* Hitting too hard. For power and pace, shift your body weight forward on every stroke. At impact, the weight should be completely on the front foot.

Anticipate your opponent. *Example:* If you have hit a shot to your right, it will probably be returned to your left. Be ready to move left, but don't commit yourself until the ball has been hit.

Back swing: The "how" (straight back or a looping motion) doesn't matter as much as getting the racket back quickly and all the way.

BETTER STRATEGY

Try to swing the same way on every shot—both for consistency and deception. Your opponent shouldn't be able to tell from the swing whether the shot is hard or soft. *Not recommended:* The underspin slice. *Reason:* The ball travels more slowly, giving older players a better chance to reach it. *Better:* Flat shots deep to the corners.

• **Always change a losing game.** Try to lob frequently against opponents who are dominating plays, especially if they have a winning net game. Against winning baseline players, hit drop shots to force them to come in and play the net.

• **Save energy.** Take plenty of time between points and before serving. Don't go all out in a game that you are losing by a score of 0-40.

THE SERVE! THE SERVE!!

Work on a consistent second serve. The resulting gain of confidence will lead to improvement of the first serve.

When practicing the serve, spend time on the toss. *Suggestion:* Practice with a bucket placed where a perfect toss should fall.

Beware of the topspin serve. Though effective, it is hard on the back muscles.

Return serves as early as possible, and keep them low.

HEALTH AND CONDITIONING

Playing tennis twice a week or so isn't enough to keep in shape. Weekly running and other cross-training exercises are a must. Squeezing an old tennis ball a few minutes a day builds up arm muscles, and rope jumping improves footwork.

Rest before and after playing. Use a warmup jacket to speed the loosening of the muscles before play. During play, run with bent knees to reduce shock to knees. After play, apply lotion to the palm of your racket hand to keep it from scaling and blistering.

EQUIPMENT

Both the beginner and intermediate player would choose a graphite with fiber racket for its flexibility. The advanced player would choose a 100% graphite racket, which is more durable and stiffer. Older players will probably be more comfortable playing with lighter-weight rackets, and they also may improve their game by using a racket that has been strung loosely.

DOUBLES STRATEGY

A doubles team should agree on strategy and signals before playing. *Most important signal:* Net players must let their partners know when they plan to cross over to intercept the return of a serve. (A clenched fist behind the back is often used.) During this move and all other moves, both partners should be in motion, one to make the shot and the other to cover the exposed part of the court.

The weaker player should take the forehand court. This player should be assigned to serve when the wind and sun are behind the server. The weaker player should play closer to the net. *Reason:* It is easier to volley in this position.

In doubles, one player normally concentrates on setting up shots. The job is to hit the ball low in order to force the opponents at the net to hit up on the ball. The second player has the job of making the put-aways.

Picking the Right Running Shoes

Gary Muhrcke, proprietor of the Super Runners Shop, 337 Lexington Ave., New York City 10001.

You walk into a store, and the choices seem endless. Where do your feet fit in the race for the perfect pair?

There are five important things to look for in running shoes…

• **A heel counter stiff enough to hold your heel in place** and keep it from rolling in and out.

• **Flexibility in the forefoot area** so the shoe bends easily with your foot. (If the shoe is stiff, your leg and foot muscles will have to work too hard.)

• **An arch support** to keep the foot stable and minimize rolling inside.

• **A fairly wide base for stability and balance.** The bottom of the heel, for example, should be as wide as the top of the shoe.

• **Cushioning that compresses easily.** (Several different materials are used now.) The mid-sole area absorbs the most shock and should have the greatest amount of padding. However, the heel (which particularly for women should be three-quarters of an inch higher than the sole) needs padding, too. Too much padding causes fatigue, and too little causes bruising.

Running shoes do not need to be broken in. They should feel good the moment you try them on.

FITTING

• **Start with manufacturers' least costly shoes** and keep trying until you find the one that feels best.

- **Try on running shoes** with the same kind of socks you wear when you run. If you don't wear socks, try on shoes using pantyhose or ultra-thin socks.

- **Light people need less cushioning** than heavier people do.

- **If you have a low arch or tend toward flat feet,** pick a more stable shoe with more rear-foot control, called a "cement"-lasted or boarded shoe. ("Last" is the foot shape that the shoe is built around.)

- **For a high arch,** try a softer, more curved last (called a "slip" last).

- **Be sure you have adequate toe room** (at least one-half inch of clearance). Running shoes, particularly in women's sizes, run small, and women often need a half-size or even a full-size-larger running shoe than street shoe.

How to Buy the Right Bike

Commuters have special biking requirements. If you're in the suit-and-tie crowd, you'll want fenders to keep yourself clean. You may want a rack on the back for a newspaper or side racks for your briefcase. Bicycle sacks (panniers) are made of heavier nylon, with stiffeners to retain their briefcase shape. Although rubber pedals are less durable than steel, they'll help preserve your leather soles. And every city rider needs a topnotch lock. The U-bolt models by Kryptonite and Citadel are among the best.

WHAT KIND TO BUY

Touring bikes are right for most people. They have a longer wheelbase for a "Cadillac" ride. Racing bikes offer a "Fiat" ride. With their shorter wheelbase, you feel the road more, but you get better handling and efficiency.

The Japanese have learned how to make bikes better and more cheaply. A European bike of equivalent quality will cost at least 20% more. Although there are many different Japanese makes, they're all produced by one of two corporate families, so they're all about the same.

The best American bikes offer better frames, with superior materials and hand-craftsmanship. But you sacrifice quality on components.

CHOOSING PARTS

A good frame design for women is the mixte (pronounced *mix-tay*). Two parts run from the head tube to the rear axle for added stability. With longer skirts, many women can use a man's 10-speed, and they do. The men's models are lighter and stronger.

For those riders who find bicycles uncomfortable, an anatomically designed saddle may be the answer. These seats, made of leather with foam padding, feature two ridges to support the pelvic bones, with a valley in between to avoid pinching the sciatic nerve.

Mixte handlebars, which project almost perpendicularly to the frame, are good for all-around cycling, as are racing (or drop) bars. The traditional curved bars are not recommended for city riding. They keep you sitting erect, so your spine is jolted by each bump. And foam grips will absorb more road shock than standard cloth tape grips.

In buying a helmet, look for a low-impact plastic shell. In a typical biking accident, this will protect the head best. Some states require by law that cyclists wear helmets.

Padded bike gloves make good shock absorbers. Sheepskin bike shorts provide added comfort. Bike jerseys with rear pockets will keep your keys from digging into your leg with each push of the pedal.

Charles McCorkell, owner, Bicycle Habitat, 244 Lafayette St., New York City.

Female bike riders should point the seat slightly downward to avoid irritating the genital area. Men should point the seat upward to avoid problems such as irritation of the urinary tract and injury to the testes.

The Physician and Sportsmedicine.

- **Sizing up a new bike.** Straddle the frame with your feet flat on the floor. There should be an inch of clearance between your crotch and the top tube. *If you can't find an exact fit:*

Buy the next smaller size, then adjust seat and handlebar height. A frame that's too big can't be adjusted.

Best Ski Pants

Stretch ski pants look great, but not all models are warm enough—especially for the novice or intermediate, who burns fewer calories and generates less heat.

What to look for: High wool content (preferably with the wool floated to the inside, nearest your body)...terry lining (traps insulating dead air). *For those who get cold easily:* Highly insulated stretch pants, which have a three-layer sandwich construction, should do the job.

Ski.

Volunteering Opportunities

The web site for Action Without Borders includes a directory of more than 53,000 nonprofit and volunteer organizations in 165 countries, as well as postings of nonprofit jobs and internships. *www.idealist.org.*

Gourmet Cooking

Designed and managed by *Bon Appétit* and *Gourmet* magazines, Epicurious attractively features thousands of recipes, cooking suggestions, etc. *www.epicurious.com.*

Butterfly Watching

The web site for the North American Butterfly Association provides links to publications, information about local chapters, butterfly gardening...and more. *www.naba.org.*

How to Buy Sports Goggles

Some types of swimming goggles apply pressure in the wrong places. *Best:* Buy the kind with soft rubber rims around the eyes.

Racquet sports, particularly squash and racquetball, can and do cause serious eye injuries if players don't wear protective goggles of some sort. *Least effective:* Open goggles without lenses. *Best:* Polycarbonate lenses that have been tested to stop a .22 bullet at 20 feet in a lab test.

How to Choose Ice Skates

The most important feature in choosing skates is a stiff boot with a snug fit. Toes should reach the tip of the boot but lie flat. Lace the boot tightly through the toe area, very tightly through the instep and comfortably at the top. *To check the fit:* Walk. If your ankles wiggle even though the lacing is correct, ask for smaller or stiffer skates.

How to Choose a Canoe

Before buying a canoe consider what you're going to use it for, where you'll use it and how many people you'll be carrying. *For rocky rivers:* Get an aluminum or plastic hull. Rocks destroy fiberglass hulls. Royalex ABS plastic hulls (made by Old Town) are the most popular. *Disadvantages:* ABS canoes are more expensive than aluminum and are vulnerable to wear and tear on bow and stern. One remedy is optional skid plates. *Good starter boat:* The Coleman polyethylene plastic canoe, which you can assemble yourself.

Canoe.

Buying an Inflatable Boat

Inflatable boats are no longer considered toys. They are now reputable crafts with a variety of functions. Inflatables perform well with much less horsepower than that required by rigid-hulled boats.

They can be stored at home, saving winter storage costs and mooring fees. They're easier to transport. *What to look for:* A design with several airtight compartments, an inflatable keel, self-bailers, bow handles and fitted D-rings, lifelines, heavy-duty fitted oarlocks, wooden or antislip aluminum floorboards and bow-dodgers with windshields for added spray protection.

Public Land Recreation

More than 2,500 federal recreation areas are listed at *www.recreation.gov*. The site offers a searchable map and links to national reservation systems. In addition to sites run by the National Park Service and Bureau of Land Management, it includes recreation sites of the Tennessee Valley Authority, National Wildlife Refuges and more.

Camping Life.

For Digital-Music Lovers

Easy to download to your computer, there are hundreds of thousands of CD-quality digitized songs available. Search on-line music sites, download the songs, play them on your computer and load them onto your iPod or any solid-state portable music player designed for MP3. You can even record CDs. Check out *www.mp3.com* and *www.emusic.com*.

Walking Barefoot on Hot Coals

Walking barefoot over coals with no pain or burns has been used for centuries by gurus to demonstrate the power of mind over body.

Our observation: Coals are bad conductors of heat. Although the temperature of coal cores can reach 1,500°F, you can walk over them quickly without sustaining burns. *Experiment:* In a study at the University of California at Los Angeles, hundreds of students walked over hot coals without serious harm—with no training.

Paul Kurtz, MD, chairman of The Committee for Skeptical Inquiry, Box 703, Amherst, NY 14226.

Bingo Never Was a Game Of Chance

John "Dee" Wyrick, author of *Complete Authoritative Guide to Bingo.* Gambler's Book Club.

Most people play bingo as if it were a game of sheer chance—as if any set of cards had just as good a chance of winning as any other. They are mistaken. If you choose the cards you play correctly, you can significantly improve your odds of winning any bingo game.

My system works with straight bingo (where you must cover five squares in a row—vertically, horizontally or diagonally), coverall (a jackpot game, in which you must cover every square on your card) or any other variation.

Key strategy: To get as many of the 75 numbers as possible on a given set of cards. There are 24 numbers printed on every bingo card. (There are 25 squares, but the center square is a nonnumbered free space.) If you chose three cards at random, their 72 numbered spaces would represent only 49 different numbers—the other 23 spaces would have duplicate numbers.

It is possible, however, to find sets of three cards with no duplicates—with 72 different numbers. (Time permitting, players can choose their cards freely at the beginning of any session.) If you were to play such a set, you would be 25% more likely to win a given game than a player with a random set. Depending on the size of the prizes, that edge can translate into hundreds—or even thousands—of dollars of winnings within a few weeks.

Ironically, most players choose sets that are worse than random. They look for cards with one or two "lucky" numbers—7 or 11, for example. And they are especially drawn to cards where those lucky numbers are at the corners.

The results are devastating. In an average straight game with 1,000 cards in play, a bingo will occur after 15 numbers are called. That means that any given number—regardless of whether it is "lucky" or not—will be called in only one of five games. In those other four games, any set of cards with an uncalled "lucky" number is 25% less likely to win. (When a number is at a corner, it affects three lines—one vertical, one horizontal and one diagonal.)

Another advantage of choosing nonduplicating cards is that it makes it easier to keep track of the numbers you're covering—and harder to miss one by accident.

Example: If you are playing three cards on which there are no duplicate numbers, every time a number is called, you know you will cover a space. *Exception:* If the number is called on the N line, you will cover a space only 80% of the time because the center square, which contains the free space, is in the N line.

There are countless statistical systems favored by bingo players, but this is the only one I've found that generates consistent profits.

The only other live variable in bingo is the proportion of money collected that is returned to the players. Most operators hold back at least 50% for overhead and revenue. (The percentage is usually posted on the bingo sheets or somewhere in the hall.)

Other games, however, return as much as 75% to the players. The more money that comes back, of course, the better are your chances of coming out ahead.

State Lottery Winning Strategy

When playing a state lottery, it's a good idea to choose at least one number higher than 31. *Reason:* Many lottery players use number combinations based on birthdays, anniversaries and other dates. Since this group concentrates on numbers of 31 or lower, a winning combination with one or more higher numbers will probably be shared by fewer people.

Dr. Jim Maxwell, American Mathematics Society.

8

Planning a Party

How to Enjoy Holiday Entertaining

Although everyone is supposed to look forward to the holidays, it can be a season filled with stress and strain, especially for those who are hosting guests.

Everyone is likely to be overtired, overstimulated and overfed. Children come home from college, accustomed to being on their own. Parents arrive as houseguests. Divorcées/divorcés bring new partners. Patterns are changed and roles are shifted, and the results can be shattering.

If you are the host or hostess, there are things you can do (aside from leaving town) to minimize the strain…

• **Include nonfamily in your invitations.** *Reason:* Everyone is then on "party manners," and the snide comments, teasing and rivalries are held back. This is not the time for letting it all hang out.

• **Accept help.** Encourage your family and friends not only to make their favorite or best dish but to be totally responsible for it—heating or freezing or unmolding and serving. *Reason:* It makes everyone feel better. The afternoon or evening becomes a participatory event rather than one where one or two people do all the work and the rest feel guilty or, worse still, awkwardly attempt to help. (The quality of the meal, by the way, improves enormously.) The one who hates to cook can supply the wine or champagne.

The best baker can be responsible for dessert. A favorite pudding, a special way to prepare vegetables, a conserve—all are welcome. Even the most unaccomplished cook can wash, peel and slice a colorful assortment of raw vegetables.

• **Let the table itself set a mood of fun,** and banish the usual air of formality. Use place cards wisely, and make them with amusing motifs that are appropriate for each guest instead of using names. Or let one

---

Florence Janovic, writer and marketing consultant.

182

of the younger children make them with a sketch of each guest or hand lettering. Set them out with forethought. Make sure a particularly squirmy youngster is nowhere near an aunt who is known for her fussy table manners. If there are to be helpers, seat them so they can get up and down with ease. Put the famous spiller where the disaster can be readily cleaned up. If the light is uneven, seat the older people in the brightest section.

• **Put everyone around a table.** It creates a warmer, more shared meal than does a buffet, and it's amazing how tables can expand. *Hint:* Use desk or rental chairs, which are much slimmer than dining chairs. (Avoid benches for older folks.)

• **Borrowing and lending furniture,** such as tables, can help you to find room for everyone. It doesn't matter if the setup is not symmetrical or everything doesn't match. A Ping-Pong table covered with pretty new sheets can provide plenty of room, or you can have tables jutting into hallways or living rooms. Using oversize cloths from bolts of attractive cotton can be an inexpensive way to cover your tables.

• **Have some after-dinner games ready.** Ping-Pong, backgammon, chess and cards are among the favorites. You may want to buy the latest "in" game or a new word game. Often the games are never opened, but it is comforting to know that they are there, just in case. Bringing out old family albums can be fun, too.

• **Gift exchanging is really a potential hazard.** Children, especially, can grump all day if something they expected hasn't been forthcoming. Grandparents often ask what is wanted, but they may be unable to do the actual buying. Do it for them. A check is not a fun package to open. If you want to be sure no one overspends, set a limit. Or set a theme. Or rule out gifts altogether, except for the children.

Overcoming the Anxiety Of Giving a Dinner Party

Situational Anxiety by Herbert J. Freudenberger and Gail North. Avalon Publishing.

Hosts who constantly worry about whether everyone is "comfortable" or fear that their guests are not eating enough are suffering from the situational anxiety of a dinner party. Making the right preparations for the party will relieve these and similar anxieties.

Helpful: Define the goals of the dinner party. The main purpose may be to establish a professional connection or to bring together two people who may be attracted to each other romantically.

Eliminate anxieties by verbalizing them. *Example:* Fear that the guests will not get along. Ask your spouse or a close friend to listen while you describe your worst fears. Once verbalized, the actual possibilities will appear less of a problem than when they were vague apprehensions.

Specify that the invitation is for dinner. It's not enough to say that you are having a get-together at 7:30. Let people know about dress —casual, nice but not formal, formal but not black tie. While phoning, mention one or two of the other guests, what they do and, if possible, what they are interested in. If a guest is bringing a friend, don't hesitate to ask something about the friend. Is there anything special you should mention or avoid mentioning to this person?

Do not serve a dish you have never prepared before. Guests will enjoy what you prepare best, even if it is just plain steak and potatoes or a simple fish casserole.

Have everything ready at least an hour before the party. Take a relaxing warm bath or shower. Allow extra time to dress and make up, and give yourself an additional 20 minutes to sit quietly.

Suggestion: Arrange to be free from the kitchen when the first two or three guests arrive. They need the host's help to get the conversation going.

For the single host: Reduce last-minute anxieties by inviting a close friend to come over early, test the food and look over the arrangements.

Surviving the Cocktail Party Game

Letty Cottin Pogrebin, freelance writer.

In America, it's old news that everyone worships success, everyone litters and everyone lusts. But the deep, dark, dirty little secret that remains unspoken is that everyone hates cocktail parties.

Even people who give cocktail parties hate cocktail parties. They give them because it's the most efficient way to discharge a great number of social obligations in the shortest time at a cost ranging from modest to obscene. Trouble is, after you give a cocktail party your guests owe you a reciprocal treat and you have to go to their cocktail parties. And so it goes, year after year.

Here is a very simple plan to end the canapé competition: Fight back.

You can confess that you hate standing around like an asparagus stalk, watching the waiters' trays stripped bare by the guests clustered near the kitchen door while you chew ice cubes or OD on martini olives.

You can ask the American Medical Association to issue a warning against drinking while upright and shifting weight from one foot to the other and getting a chill from the condensation dripping from your glass into your sleeve and down your arm.

You can stand up in church, synagogue or group therapy and tell the truth about cocktail-party conversation (which is to human discourse what paint by numbers is to fine art). And the truth is that cocktail party conversation only suits people who have three sentences to offer on any given subject and prefer their listener's eyes to be sweeping the room as they speak.

You can send in your check without making an appearance at the next charity cocktail party. Better still, start a trend. Ask potential donors, "How much will you pay not to have to go to a cocktail party?"

Seasoned political activists can boycott cocktail parties and petition the great hosts and hostesses of the world to give, instead, a sit-down dinner for 10, a round-robin Scrabble tournament, an intimate tea dance, a computer gamefest, a book circle or a quilting bee—anything but the dehumanizing ritual of the cocktail party.

Admit it. Cocktail parties are like sex. Everyone believes everyone else is doing it better and having more fun. Cocktail parties are like medicine. They may be good for your career, but often the cure is worse than the illness. Cocktail parties are poor indicators of interpersonal success. People who are good at glib smiles and small talk are often lousy at life.

But suppose you can't avoid cocktail parties? How can you survive them? *Five tips…*

- **If possible,** attend with someone sociable and loquacious who will stand at your side and banter with passersby as you think about tomorrow's headlines.

- **Pick one interesting person,** someone who seems to be eyeing the clock as longingly as you, and spend the next half hour getting to know that person as though the two of you were alone in the world. Cultivate your savior with as much energy as you would a sex partner. If you choose well, time will fly.

- **Act as you would if the party were in your honor.** Introduce yourself to everyone and ask them about themselves head-on. People will be profoundly grateful for your initiative. They don't call you overbearing—they call you charming.

- **Tell the host you have an injured leg.** Then commandeer a comfortable chair and let people come to you. (They'll be glad for an excuse to sit down.) If no one does, find an oversize art book to browse through or indulge in a few fantasies.

• **Help the host.** You'd be amazed at how overwhelmed a party giver can be and how many small tasks need doing—even with hired help. You can pass the hors d'oeuvres, hang up coats, refresh the ice buckets, and generally free the host for socializing. What's in it for you? A chance to move around (some call it "working the room"), the gratitude of your host and a nice feeling of usefulness.

Secrets of Successful Party Givers

Mary Risley, founder of Tante Marie's Cooking School, San Francisco. *www.tantemarie.com.*

The kind of entertaining you do depends on the length of your guest list and the dimensions of your house. For 10 or fewer people, a sit-down dinner is appropriate. For 25, a buffet is usually better. As the numbers grow, open houses and cocktail parties become the options. Limits are set by the size of your living space and the hours of the party. A cocktail party is traditionally scheduled for the two hours before dinner. An open house—usually 1 pm to 4 pm or 3 pm to 6 pm—can accommodate more people. If your rooms for entertaining hold 90 to 100 people for a party, you can invite as many as 250 to an open house. *Trick:* Stagger the hours you put on the invitations.

If you want to entertain several disparate groups—family, business associates and/or social friends—consider giving separate parties on succeeding nights. It takes stamina, but it does save effort and expense in the long run. *How:* You buy one order of flowers and greens for decorating the house. You assemble serving dishes and extra glasses (borrowed or rented) just once. You arrange furniture one time only. And you can consolidate food, ice and liquor orders, which, in bulk, can save money.

You want people at a cocktail party to stay on their feet and circulate, so your living area probably holds more people than you think. Removing some furniture—occasional chairs and large tables—gives you space and keeps guests moving. Clear out a den or downstairs bedroom, and set up a food table or bar to attract guests to that room, too. If you have a pair of sofas facing each other in front of a fireplace, open them out so guests can easily walk around them. Use a bedroom or other out-of-the-way place for coats. (You can rent collapsible coatracks, hangers included.)

FOOD FOR ALL TASTES

Set up different foods in different parts of the party area. If you have open bars, put different drink mixes at each setup. A group drinking a variety of cocktails will not be able to congregate for refills in the same place. *Avoid bottlenecks:* Don't put a bar or buffet table in a narrow hall, for example, or at the back of a tiny room. To make the most of a small space, have waiters to take drink orders and a bartender to fill the orders in the kitchen or pantry. Waiters can also pass the hors d'oeuvres in tight quarters, avoiding the clustering at a food table.

Count on seven hors d'oeuvres or canapés per person. Some will eat less, but it will equal out between the dieters and the hungry folks who make a meal of the party. Stick to finger foods. You'll want a variety of eight to 10 canapés, but pass each separately, starting with the cold foods and bringing out the hot dishes later. Trays with a single selection look prettier and avoid the congestion that develops when each guest has to make a choice. For long parties where a turnover of guests is likely, arrange two cycles of passing food, so the later guests get the same fresh selection as the earlier guests.

LAY IN SOME LIQUOR

You know better than anyone what your guests like to drink. Chilled white wine is popular, as are mimosas (champagne and orange juice) for brunches and afternoon parties. Discuss amounts with your liquor dealer, and ask if you can return any unopened bottles and extras. It is often cheaper to buy mixers by the case. *A good nonalcoholic drink:* Half cranberry juice and half ginger ale over ice, garnished with a sprig of fresh mint and a slice of orange.

185

Ice: For a large party, you can get ice from an ice company. A 40-pound bag will be enough for 50 people. Get more if you are also chilling wine. Use a bathtub to keep the ice in. A bathtub full of ice and chilling champagne can in itself be a festive sight. Or you can decant from the tub to smaller ice chests for each bar. If the nearest bathtub is too far from the party area, buy a plastic garbage bin to hold the major supply.

ADVICE FROM OTHER EXPERTS

You cannot be a good host without hired hands to take care of the food and drinks. Your job is to keep the guests happy, meeting one another and circulating from group to group. At a minimum, you need a bartender to be in charge of drinks and someone else to be in charge of the food. The larger the party, the more help you will need. *Helpful:* A bartender at each setup, someone in charge of the kitchen, and one or more waiters to pass food and replace dirty ashtrays.

John Clancy, chef, teacher, restaurateur and author of several cookbooks.

• **For clear ice cubes,** boil the water first. Cool and then freeze it. (Clear ice cubes last longer because they have fewer air bubbles.) *To keep ice cubes separate:* Store them in a dry, chilled metal container in the freezer.

• **Separate the ice cubes for mixed drinks from the ice being used to cool the beer and soft drinks.** For the average cocktail party, figure on two-thirds of a pound of ice per guest; for a dinner party, one pound per guest. Ice for the cooling of mixers and soft drinks should be figured separately. For cooling large quantities, a combination of block ice and cubes is best.

Emily Post on Entertaining by Elizabeth L. Post. HarperCollins.

• **For the best beer service,** use a spotlessly clean glass or mug (soap, grease or lint can ruin the taste). Just before pouring, rinse the glass in cold water and shake it dry, or put it into the freezer for a few minutes to frost it. Open the beer bottle or can carefully, without shaking its contents. Tilt the glass and pour the beer down the side to start. Then straighten the glass and pour into the center. How much foam is enough? It's a matter of taste, but you control the amount by the distance you hold the beer container from the glass as you pour. The greater the distance, the thicker the head.

• **The fastest way to cool off a bottle of soda, beer or anything else** is to hold it under running cold water. It's faster than putting it into the freezer.

• **Pile the food high when laying out a party buffet.** Avoid perfect rows of food. After the first attack, the rows look depleted, but piles of food retain some form. Place all the main-course food on one table. Don't allow empty spots, even if it means adding extra dishes. Put the food as high as possible, with platters or baskets on top of sturdy overturned bowls to add elevation.

Planning a Big Family Party

Unplug the Christmas Machine: A Complete Guide to Putting Love and Joy Back into the Season by Jo Robinson and Jean Staeheli. HarperCollins.

Are you hosting a large family gathering? Because a reunion brings together people of all ages, it presents special challenges. *Ideas to make your party more enjoyable for everyone...*

• **Infants and toddlers.** Parents will appreciate a place to change diapers and a quiet room for naps and nursing. Let them know if you can provide high chairs, cribs, safety gates or playpens. *Toys:* A box of safe kitchen equipment. *Food suggestions:* Mild cheese, bananas, crackers, fresh bread or rolls.

• **Preschool children.** Set aside a playroom. *Best toys:* Balloons, bubbles and crayons. Pay an older cousin or a neighborhood teen to baby-sit.

• **School-aged children.** A den or basement room and board games, felt pens and coloring books will keep them happy. Put them in charge of setting and decorating a children's dining table.

•**Teenagers.** Most teenagers find family re-unions boring. For those who have to come, provide a room with a television, VCR/DVD player and a CD player. Teenagers may be shy around relatives they don't know. When they come out of hiding, give them tasks that encourage their involvement with others, such as helping out grandparents.

•**Older folks.** They need comfortable chairs where they can hear and see what's going on without being in the way. Some may also need easy access to a bathroom and a place to rest or to go to bed early. *Food considerations:* Ask if anyone needs a low-salt, low-cholesterol or special diabetic diet. Spicy foods are probably out. Make travel arrangements for those who can't drive so they don't have to worry about inconveniencing others.

Now that you've seen to individual needs, how do you bring everyone together? *Common denominator:* Family ties. Make an updated family tree and display it in a prominent place. If you have an instant camera, take pictures as people arrive and mount them on the appropriate branch of the tree.

Special: Ask everyone to bring contributions to a family museum. *Suitable objects:* Old photographs, family letters, heirlooms, written family histories, old family recipes. After dinner, gather around the fire and exchange family anecdotes. You may wish to record them.

Hiring Party Help

Whether you call them butlers or waiters/ waitresses, they help you with the fundamental chores of your cocktail or dinner party.

Duties: Take coats, tend bar, prepare snacks or meals, serve and clean up.

How many are needed: One helper serves a seated dinner party for 10 guests or a cocktail buffet for 20, if the host prepares the food. Hire two for groups of 30. For 40 or more, use four helpers.

How to find them: Word of mouth is your best bet. Contact a local college or bartenders' school for willing students.

Payment: At the end of the party.

Rates: Experienced workers earn more, and often charge higher rates for late-night and holiday work.

Caviar Secrets

Keep the tin of caviar in the refrigerator until 15 minutes before serving. Then open the lid and place the tin in a serving bowl of crushed ice. Spoon helpings carefully, since caviar takes on an oily quality if the eggs are broken. Eat with a fork. Accompany with lightly toasted triangles of thinly buttered bread.

Caution: Never serve caviar with onion, sour cream or chopped egg, or squeeze lemon over it. These detract from the pure flavor. *Best:* Burst the eggs between the tongue and upper palate. This releases the full taste properly.

Christian Petrossian, caviar importer, quoted in *Harper's Bazaar.*

Creative Summer Drinks

With only a bit more effort than it takes to make a vodka and tonic or to pour a soft drink over ice, you can create impressive summer drinks.

Single alcoholic drinks…

•**Wine cooler.** Put 2 teaspoons of sugar and 1 teaspoon of cold water into a 10- to 12-ounce highball glass. Stir until sugar dissolves. Add 1 tablespoon of orange juice and 4 or 5 ice cubes. Fill with chilled red or white wine. Garnish red-wine cooler with a lemon slice and white with an orange slice.

•**Bullfrog.** Mix 4 tablespoons of lime juice with 1 teaspoon of sugar in a highball glass. Add 2 ounces of vodka and 3 or 4 ice cubes. Fill with club soda and stir. Garnish with a lime slice.

•**Floradora.** Put 1 cup of crushed ice into a highball glass. Add ½ teaspoon of sugar, 3 tablespoons of lime juice, 2 ounces of gin and 1 tablespoon of grenadine or raspberry syrup. Pour in 2 ounces of club soda or ginger ale. Stir gently.

•**Iced Irish coffee.** Combine 1 cup of strong chilled coffee and 1 teaspoon of sugar. Stir. Put 2 tablespoons of whipped cream in the bottom of a glass. Pour in coffee mixture. Stir. Add 3 or 4 ice cubes and 2 ounces of Irish whiskey. Top with 2 tablespoons of whipped cream. (*Regular iced coffee:* Omit the whiskey.)

SINGLE NONALCOHOLIC DRINKS

•**Summer delight.** Put 3 or 4 ice cubes into a 10- to 12-ounce glass. Add 3 tablespoons of lime juice and ¾ ounce of raspberry syrup. Fill with club soda and stir. Garnish with fruit.

•**Saratoga.** Combine 2 tablespoons of lemon juice, ½ teaspoon of sugar and 2 dashes of Angostura bitters in a glass. Add 3 or 4 ice cubes. Fill with ginger ale.

PUNCHES

•**Fish-house punch.** In a punch bowl, dissolve 2 cups of sugar in 3 cups of lemon juice. Add a large block of ice. Add 1½ quarts of brandy, 1 pint of peach brandy, 1 pint of rum, and 1 quart of club soda. Stir well. Decorate with fruit. Serve in 4-ounce punch glasses. Makes about 32 servings.

•**White-wine punch.** Pour a 25-ounce bottle of white wine over a block of ice in a punch bowl. Add the juice of 1 lemon and the peel cut into strips. Sprinkle in 1 tablespoon of sugar. Stir. Add 2 ounces of brandy and 1 quart of club soda. Garnish each glass with a stick of cucumber. Makes about 15 four-ounce servings.

NONALCOHOLIC PUNCHES

•**Strawberry cooler.** Blend 1 pint of fresh strawberries with ½ cup of sugar in an electric blender. Add 2 cups of vanilla ice cream and 1 cup of milk. Blend again. Pour over a block of ice in a punch bowl and combine with 1¾ quarts of milk. Makes about 15 four-ounce servings.

•**Pensacola punch.** Combine 2 cups of sugar and 6 cups of water in a saucepan. Cook over low heat, stirring until sugar dissolves. Cool. Pour one 46-ounce can of grapefruit juice and 3½ cups of lime juice over crushed ice in a punch bowl. Add the sugar syrup and 1 pound of grapefruit sections. Garnish with maraschino cherries and mint sprigs. Serve in 8-ounce goblets. Makes about 18 servings.

BARTENDING TIPS

•**Measure accurately.** Use a double-ended measuring cup for pouring. One end is a jigger (1½ ounces) and the other is a pony (1 ounce). A dash is 3 drops.

•**Use superfine sugar.** The finest granulated sugar, superfine, dissolves quickly and easily. Confectioners' powdered sugar is not as good.

•**Develop your own specialty.** Experiment with recipes to create your own drinks. *Important:* With alcoholic drinks, don't be heavy-handed with the liquor—you'll spoil the taste and the effect of the drink.

Throwing Guests Out Gracefully

Close the bar. Glance at your watch occasionally. Stifle a yawn or two. Start emptying ashtrays and cleaning up. If subtle hints have no effect—tell the truth. Say you're exhausted…that you have to get up early the next morning…or simply that the party's over.

Emily Post on Entertaining by Elizabeth L. Post. Harper-Collins.

Putting Off Unwanted Guests

Favorite ploys of city dwellers who don't want to put up all the out-of-town relatives and friends who invite themselves—"We'd love to have you, but...The apartment is being painted...We will be out of town ourselves...The house is full of flu...My mother-in-law is visiting...The elevator is out of order... The furnace is broken and we have no heat or hot water [winter version]...The air-conditioning is out, and you know how hot and humid it gets here [summer version]."

Surviving Weekend Guests

Weekend guests can be a drag. They leave the lights on, show up late for breakfast and expect to be waited on. But the clever host or hostess graciously but firmly takes charge and doesn't allow guests to become a nuisance.

- **Be a benevolent dictator.** You can't run a house as a democracy. The host or hostess has the right not to be put upon. If someone is cadging an invitation when you'd rather be alone, suggest another time. You don't have to take a vote to decide on the dinner hour if there's a time that's most convenient for you. Some hosts post written house rules. For most households, though, verbal instructions are adequate.

If you live without servants, tell guests what you want them to do—pack the picnic lunch, bring in firewood. You'll resent them if they're having fun and you're not.

- **Don't let food preparation become a chore.** Plan sufficiently ahead to have options if you decide to spend the afternoon on the boat instead of in the kitchen. Have on hand a dish you can pull out of the freezer, or a fish or chicken that will cook by itself in the oven or crockpot and maybe yield leftovers for another meal.

- **Involve guests in preparation and cleanup.** If they volunteer to bring a house gift, ask for food. If guests have special diets that vary radically from your own, try to give them the responsibility for supplying and preparing their own food.

Breakfast can be a frustrating meal to coordinate. Even if you eat all other meals together, it's a good idea to give guests a kitchen tour and coffee-making instructions so they can fend for themselves when they wake up.

- **Lay out plans and options early.** *First:* Present your own fixed responsibilities and activities. Don't be embarrassed to do something without your guests. *Next:* Present optional activities for everyone. Mention anything you expect them to participate in. Discuss availability of transportation, facilities and other amenities.

Finally a pattern for the weekend will begin to emerge. Keep it flexible. Suggest ways to communicate changes and important information (a corkboard for messages, an answering machine, etc.).

- **Encourage independence.** Supply maps, guidebooks, extra keys. And provide alarm clocks, local newspapers, extra bicycles.

Even dictators can reward good behavior. Warm thanks, praise and other signs of appreciation go a long way toward encouraging more of the same. After all, a host or hostess can't punish bad guests...except by not inviting them back.

How to Throw a Very Successful Party

Penny Warner, author of *The Best Party Book—1001 Creative Ideas for Fun Parties.* Simon & Schuster.

A successful party isn't hard to put together once you get the formula down. *Unforgettable parties are the result of the clever mix of...*

- **A legitimate reason** (or plausible excuse!) for a get-together.

- **A carefully orchestrated plan.**

- **Creativity.**

BE A DIRECTOR

Your party will be different if you direct it, rather than just invite folks and hope for the best. *Examples...*

- **If you host a baby shower,** make it a toys-only or baby's-bath-only shower, and your guests will head eagerly to the stores now that you've eliminated guesswork.

- **Center a retirement party on the retiree's hobby,** say golf, and have guests wear golf clothes.

- **Turn a going-away party into a movable feast where friends pick up and travel together from house to house for each course.** Meet at the first house for drinks and hors d'oeuvres. Move on to the second for soup and salad. Travel to the third for the main course. Wind up at the fourth house for dessert and coffee...and a fond farewell.

PARTY CHECKLIST

Once you have chosen the reason for a party, you must get yourself organized.

You don't want to be expecting your first guest to come through the door, only suddenly to remember you forgot to buy ice. To avoid that kind of catastrophe, develop a "things to do and things to buy" checklist that is divided into four sections that help you organize your time and effort as the day of the party approaches.

Section 1: Three weeks before the party. Develop a guest list, create the invitations (and mail them), decide the menu, write a grocery list and hire any serving help you might need.

Section 2: A week before the party. Call guests who didn't RSVP, purchase the food and drinks, prepare food and decide what you're wearing.

Section 3: One day before the party. Clean the house, arrange and decorate the party room, pull out the serving dishes and confirm deliveries and caterers.

Section 4: The day of the party. Finish decorating and cooking, then set up everything, mentally "travel through" the party and get dressed.

INVITATIONS

Make your invitation a show stopper. *Best:* Homemade invitations. *Examples...*

- **For a birthday party,** go to your library and get a photocopy of the front page of a newspaper from the day and year your birthday guest was born. Design your invitation to the size of a column in the paper, paste your column over an old column and photocopy as many invitations as you need.

- **For a baby shower,** cut out small footprints on which you've written party details.

- **For a Christmas party,** make gingerbread people, each one decorated with edible glitter. Tie a card with details around the neck.

THEME FOOD

Offer theme food—and serve it with flair. *Examples...*

- **For a graduation party,** serve high-quality food cafeteria style...on trays.

- **For dessert at a family reunion,** have each family contribute an eight-inch-square cake decorated with the contributor's name on it, and place the squares together to form a show-stopping pièce de résistance.

- **Break out the wicker baskets,** old-fashioned tins and large seashells to serve food, rather than use ordinary or dull serving dishes. Food looks and tastes better when it is served creatively.

ACTIVITIES

Plan unusual activities. No charades. No board games. Sustain the mood of the party. *Examples...*

- **For a baby shower,** buy eight jars of baby food, remove the labels and have each guest taste and write down the flavors she thinks she has just tasted. The guest with the most correct answers wins a prize—perhaps a home pregnancy kit or a stuffed toy.

- **Create a great birthday videotape by having guests relate funny anecdotes about the honoree.** Play the tape during the party, and give the tape to the birthday boy or girl as a souvenir.

•For a family reunion have the oldest relatives tell their life stories.

DECORATIONS

A party without decorations is like a movie without a musical score—something is missing. Done well, decorations add immeasurably to the atmosphere and to the enjoyment of the people at the party.

And here's where the kids, a spouse and friends come in. Pass out assignments...to cut out legs and boots from felt and hang Santa's legs in the fireplace at Christmas...to create a basket of honeymoon items (cologne, mints, body paint, silk panties, videos) as a centerpiece at a bachelorette party...to collect and hang photos of the guest of honor from past to present (complete with captions) at a birthday party.

UNUSUAL THEMES

Every month of the year, there is a ready-made excuse to throw a party...

•January 6, Sherlock Holmes' Birthday.

•March 24, Harry Houdini's Birthday.

•June 7, Day of the Rice God.

•July 14, Bastille Day.

•September 26, Johnny Appleseed's Birthday.

Any excuse can be the perfect excuse for a party. *Examples...*

•An international evening where the guests bring dishes from the Old Country.

•A fashion-victim party where guests wear the unwearable.

•A ski party far from the slopes where the guests dress in snow-bunny or ski-bum apparel.

•An invite-a-friend party where each guest brings someone new to the group.

Put your imagination to work.

Parties don't have to be held in someone's house or in a rented hall. You can also create your own car road rally or biking party by designing your own map and clues along the way with a favorite restaurant as the ultimate destination.

You might also consider having everyone meet at a bowling alley, espresso bar or at a nearby dance studio.

9

Collecting and Hobbies

Secrets of a Famous Collector

Over the past 60 years, Roy Neuberger, founder and senior partner of the highly respected investment management house Neuberger Berman, has amassed a collection of outstanding American art of the 19th and (primarily) 20th centuries. Much of it is now in the Neuberger Museum of the State University at Purchase, New York. *Here are some of Mr. Neuberger's secrets of successful collecting...*

TRAIN YOUR EYE

•**Pursue formal study.** This is one way, but it's not the only one.

•**Look at art.** This is the best way to develop your taste. Go to galleries. Look in museums, but be selective. There are too many museums today. Their experts who select what's to hang aren't infallible. Visit New York City, the current art capital of the world.

•**Never stop learning.** There is always more to know.

WHAT TO BUY

•**Unknown artists.** Buy someone you have never heard of before. This is especially good if you don't have much money. Names that are unfamiliar could turn out to be popular after a while.

•**Noninvestments.** I don't think of art as an investment. People should buy art because it's good for them and fulfills them. If art is meaningful to people, their judgment is likely to be sound, and then art could turn out to be a good investment.

•**Individuals, not schools.** Artists are individuals.

•**Be skeptical.** A lot of expensive, phony non-art masquerades as art.

WHERE TO BUY FINDS

•**Consultants.** Banks are charging 2% for their services as investment counselors on art.

Roy Neuberger, Neuberger Berman, New York City.

192

It's better to pay attention to an art critic whom you trust.

- **Dealers.** No matter how informed you become, a smart, honest dealer is important.
- **Local exhibitions.** There are good artists everywhere in the country.

Important: You can collect better if you're a good walker. Stay in top physical condition and get around.

Art as an Investment

Quality is the main factor at every level of the art market. It determines both purchase price and liquidity. The best items appreciate most when the economy is flush and maintain their value best in a recession.

The key to success is knowledge about art and the market. Knowledgeable collectors who follow their own intuition and buy what they like usually do better than investors who follow elaborate strategies.

Most experts agree that investors should never invest more than 10% of their assets in the art market. And art should be a long-term investment. Plan to keep an item for at least five years to get the best return. *To learn the market...*

- **Visit dealers.** Prices of comparable items can vary.
- **Attend auctions.** Dealers usually set their prices according to current auction prices.
- **Subscribe to auction catalogs.** Auction houses such as Sotheby's *(www.sothebys.com)* and Christie's *(www.christies.com)* annually publish prices brought by major items sold during the year.
- **Consult with experts.** Museum curators, dealers and art scholars can be very helpful, especially in assessing the work of lesser-known artists. Most will give free advice about a specific work. Never make a major purchase without consulting an expert.

Most works of art are bought and sold at private galleries and auction houses. A good dealer has a large selection of works pre-selected for their quality, whereas auction houses sometimes have to dispose of less worthy items. With a dealer, there is no waiting for a purchase time as there is for an auction, but a purchaser can still take time to reflect. A good dealer is willing to share knowledge, stands behind what is sold and often has an exchange policy. Ask a museum curator for the name of a reputable dealer.

For a knowledgeable collector, auctions present an advantage—comparable items can often be bought for less than from a dealer. *Primary advice:* Buy what you like, but buy quality—the best examples that you can find and afford.

BUYING GUIDELINES

- **When there is a preference for oil paintings in the art market,** drawings and sculpture will be better buys.
- **Less popular subjects**—some portraits, animals, religious paintings, violent subjects—are often less expensive.
- **Paintings that are under or over the most popular size** (two feet by three feet to three feet by four feet) tend to cost less.
- **Works that are not in an artist's most typical or mature style are usually less expensive.**
- **Avoid what's currently stylish.** Investigate the soon-to-be stylish.
- **Works of Western art that are not attributed or authenticated can be inexpensive,** but they are bad investments. A work with an authentic signature and date is always worth more than one without them.

COLLECTING CONTEMPORARY ART

At least 120,000 people in this country think of themselves as serious artists. Among them, fewer than 500 will ever see their works appreciate in value. Most of these artists are either very well known and very expensive or reasonably well known and reasonably expensive.

Works by artists who have not yet received the recognition they merit are affordable now and might appreciate in value. These artists are likely to be included in group exhibitions but may not have been shown alone. In private galleries, their paintings may sell for $5,000 to $20,000 and their drawings for $250 to $1,500. If the artist does not have a dealer, as the more famous artists do, you might be able to save 50%—the dealer's commission—by buying directly.

Large quality paintings by relatively unknown artists can be found for as little as $800. If you choose well, you can get a significant work of art, help support a deserving artist and, if you are very lucky, watch your work's value escalate.

Great Antiques Are Cheaper than Good Modern Furniture

Judith H. McQuown, author of many investment books. She also writes about shopping, antiques and travel.

Antique furniture is a better buy than modern reproductions. For example, a modern reproduction of a Georgian mahogany bowfront chest can cost over $5,000, yet the originals frequently sell at auction for $800 to $1,000.

Antique furniture also "stores" value better than modern reproductions do. Like a new car driven out of a showroom, even expensive modern reproduction furniture becomes "used" as soon as it's delivered. Offered for resale, it generally brings one-third or less of its original cost.

In contrast, antique furniture retains its value. If you buy a Georgian mahogany chest at auction for $1,000, change your mind and consign it to the next auction, it will probably fetch around $1,000 again. Allowing for commissions at both ends, you'll have lost $200. But if you hold on to that chest for two or three years, you may see an increase in value. And the longer you keep an antique piece—barring your

buying at the top of a vogue and selling at its bottom—the more valuable it will become. It's a much better investment than its modern reproduction, which can cost you $3,000 to $4,000 and bring you only $1,000 to $1,200 if you should decide to resell it.

Furniture buyers should look for simple lines and consider their space limitations. Buy basic shapes. You won't get tired of looking at the pieces, and they'll be easy to sell if you move or redecorate. Some antiques are especially suitable for small apartments—for example, drop-leaf tables (often with a drawer underneath for silver and linens) and nests of tables. Very large pieces are often sold at low prices because most people don't have enough room to accommodate them. Similarly, tall chests sell for less than low chests because people can't hang pictures above them.

When buying antique furniture at auction, look closely at the catalog's glossary and definition of terms. Christie's, for example, distinguishes among "A George II mahogany chest of drawers, mid-18th century" ("the piece is essentially of the period and has not been significantly altered or restored"), "A George II mahogany chest of drawers" (*no date:* "the piece is essentially of the period and has been significantly restored or altered") and "A George II-style mahogany chest of drawers" ("the piece is an intentional copy of an earlier design").

Antique furniture should be examined carefully before purchase. For chests and desks, check the drawers to make sure they move properly, and check the alignment of the runners. Check tables for structural stability. Federal and Empire tables on a central pedestal are frequently top-heavy and wobbly. Open a drop-leaf table to see whether its leaves lie flat or are warped. Are the leaves the same color? Or has the table been sitting in the sun so that one or more leaves have faded?

Inspect upholstered furniture very carefully. If the upholstery is in good shape, the rest of the piece is probably sound or has only minor damage that can be repaired easily. Keep in mind that professional reupholstering adds at least $500 to $600 to the cost of a chair and $800 to $1,200 to the cost of a couch.

Other repairs: Any reputable auction house or antique dealer can recommend a good cabinetmaker and tell you what should be repaired and approximately how many hours it should take.

Even first-timers can learn a lot by asking auction-house personnel a few questions…

• **Has this piece been repaired or altered in any way?**

• **Were the repairs done well or badly?**

• **Will it need work? If so, what should be done?**

What kind of antique furniture comes up at auction? Just about everything that was made after 1650 in the US, England, Europe and the Orient. This furniture is less than museum quality, and there is a lot of it around.

Antiques: Spotting The Real Thing

Here are helpful guidelines to ensure you get the antique you think you're paying for…

• **Wedgwood.** The only way to determine if a piece of Wedgwood is old or recent (assuming it bears the impressed mark of "Wedgwood") is by close examination of the raised relief molding. The earlier works have greater depth and more delicacy.

• **Porcelain.** The Chinese made porcelains a thousand years before anyone else did. Pieces that were copied at a later date may also have had the original identifying marks copied. (The Chinese didn't do this to deceive but rather to pay their respects to the skill of their ancestors.) Only a real expert can distinguish between the old and the very old.

• **Pewter.** The alloy of tin and other metals is easily identified by its color and appearance, which are more mellow and subtle than silver or silver plate. If a piece called pewter is marked Dixon or Sheffield, with a number on its underside, it is not pewter at all but Britannia metal, a substitute.

• **Ironstone.** Mason's ironstone, found largely in jugs made for the home and in dinner services, is the original only if the words "Mason's Patent Ironstone China" appear in capital letters on the bottom.

• **Enamels.** A dealer offering Battersea enamel does not necessarily mean a snuffbox or needle-and-thread case made at the small factory at York House, Battersea, between 1753 and 1756. The term has come to be used for old enamels made mostly in other English towns in the 18th century. However, the piece could also have been produced within recent years in a factory in Birmingham, or even in Czechoslovakia. The originals are of copper, surfaced with an opaque glass that was then hand-decorated with inked paper transfers taken from copper plates.

• **Silver.** An old Sheffield plate will show the copper where the silver plating has worn off. This generally means that the piece was made before 1850. Once a piece has been resilvered by modern electroplating methods, it is just about impossible to differentiate it from other kinds of silver.

• **China.** The patterns are not always an indication of age since copyright is a relatively new idea. In years gone by, one porcelain maker cheerfully borrowed the pattern of a predecessor. The only way to cope with the resultant identification problem, say the experts, is to look carefully until you become savvy enough to recognize a Staffordshire printed earthenware plate by the flowers of its border.

• **Collecting in general.** When looking around, always be on the alert for items whose design is basically sound. In this way you have the best chance of picking up the so-called antiques of tomorrow. Meanwhile, since more and more Americans have become collectors, and the supply of items made before 1830 (an arbitrary cutoff date between antiques and nonantiques) is limited, the value of any *good* old piece increases.

Best Antique Shops In NYC

Depending on your taste, there's something for every antique shopper in Manhattan. *Some great shops to visit...*

ART DECO

• **Dalva Brothers,** 53 E. 77th St., 212-717-6600. *www.dalvabrothers.com.* Mainly 18th-century French antiques, including porcelain sculptures, but you can also find a few fine Italian and English pieces here.

• **Howard Kaplan Designs,** 240 E. 60th St., 646-443-7170. *www.howardkaplandesigns.com.* A treasure trove of French, English and American pieces. They also feature his original pieces.

• **Kentshire Galleries,** 37 E. 12th St., 212-673-6644. *www.kentshire.com.* The place for formal English antiques. Eight floors of first-quality English, ranging from Queen Anne through the Edwardian periods. Extensive collection of antique accessories and jewelry plus estate jewelry.

• **Malmaison Antiques,** 343 E. 74th St., 212-288-7569. Excellent collection of French empire furniture, American furniture from the 1930s and 1940s plus Art Deco.

• **Newel Art Galleries,** 425 E. 53rd St., 212-758-1970. *www.newel.com.* An eclectic collection of formal furniture and a diverse collection of Decorative Art and Art Moderne.

• **Florian Papp,** 962 Madison Ave., 212-288-6770. *www.florianpapp.com.* In business since the turn of the century, with three floors of fine 19th-century furniture.

19TH-CENTURY AMERICAN FURNITURE

• **Didier Aaron, Inc.,** 32 E. 67th St., 212-988-5248. *www.didieraaron-cie.com.* English, French and Italian furniture.

OTHER SPECIALTY SHOPS

• **Leo Kaplan Antiques,** 967 Madison Ave., 212-355-7212. Eighteenth-century English pottery and porcelain. Large selection of antique and contemporary paperweights, English and French cameo glass and Russian enamel and porcelain.

• **Lillian Nassau,** 220 E. 57th St., 212-759-6062. *www.lilliannassau.com.* The best place in the US to buy Tiffany glass. Also has a fine collection of Art Nouveau and Art Deco glass and accessories.

• **James Robinson Inc.,** 480 Park Ave., 212-752-6166. *www.jrobinson.com.* Antique silver, china and glass, and a fine collection of antique jewelry.

• **Minna Rosenblatt,** 961 Madison Ave., 212-288-0250. Large collection of original Tiffany lamps and Tiffany glass and other antique glass, plus a lovely collection of French cameos.

• **A La Vieille Russie,** 781 Fifth Ave., 212-752-1727. *www.alvr.com.* Specializes in Imperial Russian Fabergé accessories and jewelry.

Collecting American Folk Art

The late Robert Bishop, founding director of the Museum of American Folk Art, New York City.

American folk art was discovered in the 1920s. Although there were a few pioneer museum exhibits, and a group of collectors founded the museum that was to become the Museum of American Folk Art in 1961, it didn't take off until recent years. Folk art has become increasingly popular for many reasons, including the country-furniture boom, its compatibility with modern design and the recent rise in Americans' appreciation of things American.

WHAT IS FOLK ART?

Folk art is difficult to define. It ranges from three-dimensional objects, such as copper weather vanes and carved wooden decoys, to native oil portraits and fanciful quilts. Traditionally it was created by immigrants who continued to use inherited design motifs—the Germans in Pennsylvania, the English in New England. But artisans outside of immigrant communities produced work that falls into this category, too. *Common denominators:* It is created by and for common folk, and it is utilitarian but has an aesthetic quality that elevates it beyond mere functionality.

Although country furniture is often classified as folk art, it really isn't. The country wood-worker is a professional.

THERE ARE THREE KINDS OF COLLECTORS

• **Antique collectors** who use folk art as decoration.

• **Fine-art collectors** who also collect folk art.

• **Those who collect folk art** as an investment.

HOW TO BEGIN

• **Visit galleries and museum exhibits that feature your special interest.**

• **Go to antique shows.**

• **Talk with antique dealers.** They are better informed than anyone in the field and are willing to share their information.

WHAT TO BUY

Acquire quality. It's better to buy one good thing than a lot of inferior pieces that will never be aesthetically pleasing and won't appreciate.

Specialize. Become knowledgeable in one particular area in order to be an effective competitor in the marketplace. But be flexible. It's shortsighted to say, "I don't collect that," and pass up something you really love.

Prices have skyrocketed in the past several years and are still high. But most folk art is still accessible to collectors who are just starting out. *Helpful:* Lots of 20th-century folk art is worth looking into. Ceramics, sculpture, quilts, textiles, paintings and other crafts are being produced all over the country. The problem is sorting out the quality. *The trick:* Look at enough good things to develop your eye.

CAVEAT EMPTOR

Anyone who is making a major purchase should ask for a written guarantee. It should include a description of the piece, the name of the maker, the period and disclosure of all restoration. The guarantee should specify that if any of the information proves to be incorrect, the piece can be returned for full refund.

Collecting Bronze Sculpture

Alice Levi-Duncan, Jody Greene and Christopher Burge, Christie's, New York City.

In the world of our grandparents and great-grandparents, no home was without its bronzes. J.P. Morgan and Henry Clay Frick collected them, and even families with modest incomes could afford these commercially produced pieces.

A recent revival of interest in sculpture of all kinds has created a lively market in old bronzes as well. They are plentiful, decorative and easy to take care of with a feather duster.

COLLECTING CATEGORIES

• **Academic or salon sculpture.** These realistic 19th-century bronzes from Europe and America were cast in a variety of subjects—portrait busts, prancing putti of India, laboring peasants and nudes. They provide a good starting point for beginners. *Important sculptors:* Jean Baptiste Carpeaus, Jules Dalou, Achille d'Orsi.

• **Animal sculpture.** A school of French artists led by Antoine-Louis Bayre produced sculptures of horses, dogs, lions and hunting scenes that are prized for their fine modeling and realistic movement. *Important artists:* Pierre-Jules Mene, Georges Gardet, Emanuel Fremiet, Alfred Dubucand. Attractive pieces are available starting at about $100, though name artists command more. *Examples:* A Mene bronze of two pointers sold for $1,100. A gilt-bronze, *Ostrich Hunting in the Sahara* by Dubucand, brought $4,620.

• **Art Nouveau and Art Deco.** Popular with collectors who specialize in all designs of these periods, these styles are subject to current fashion. Art Nouveau prices have leveled off after a period of inflation. Art Deco is still in and expensive. Bronze and ivory figures of exotic dancers by Demetre Chiparis recently brought $30,000. More modest Art Nouveau and Art Deco pieces, particularly by American designers, can be found for $500 to $5,000.

Many Deco bronzes are of athletes. "Pushing men" bookends are typical and popular.

• **American West sculpture.** The peak of this craze has passed, but prices are still high for this area of Americana. Frederic Remington's *The Norther* sold for $715,000. But this was the last available cast of a rare edition, and Remington is considered to be a major artist. Western sculpture by other artists is a less secure investment, but of course it is also less expensive.

• **Impressionist and Early Modern.** Bronzes by established artists of this era are considered to be fine art rather than decorative objects and are available only through auctions and galleries. Works by Rodin, Daumier, Degas, Maillol, Picasso, Henry Moore, Brancusi, etc., have proved to be sound investments, but they are extremely expensive—from $100,000 to millions of dollars.

• **Museum specialties.** Medieval, Renaissance, Baroque, Oriental and African bronzes require study and connoisseurship and attract only a few independent collectors. Expert advice is essential if you consider buying one of these pieces.

WHAT AFFECTS VALUE?

• **Fame of artist or founder.** Signatures or foundry marks should be crisp and clear. (Fakes abound.)

• **Edition.** A rare and limited edition is more valuable than a common one. *Problem:* Records of most 19th-century bronzes are sketchy. Many pieces were cast literally in thousands. And the records vary for established artists. Remingtons are carefully documented, including casts made by his family after the artist's death (called estate editions). Rodins, on the other hand, were made in several different foundries, and few records exist, providing a ripe market for forgeries or pirated editions. Estate editions, though authentic, are not as valuable as those supervised by the artist.

• **Condition.** Original condition is preferable. However, it is acceptable to have 19th-century bronzes repatinated or repaired in a reputable foundry if necessary.

• **Size.** This is a matter of fashion. Generally, the demand (and prices) are greatest for very large pieces appropriate for outdoor settings.

SPOTTING FAKES

Valuable bronzes, even those of contemporary artists like Henry Moore, have frequently been forged. The most common method is to make a "surmoulage" casting from the original. The fake will be slightly smaller than the original, since bronze shrinks as it cools, but the differences are minuscule. Fakes may also vary in color, weight and clarity of detail.

Danger signals: Bronzes that have been epoxied to a marble base so you can't check the hollow interior. An unnaturally even "Hershey-bar brown" color. Color that can be removed with nail-polish remover or scratched with a fingernail. A ghost impression around the signature or foundry mark. Air bubbles, bumps and craters around the base (good 19th-century craftsmen would have hand-finished such imperfections).

Seek expert advice as you learn the field. Stick to dealers and auction houses that guarantee the authenticity of the works they sell. *Make sure your receipt is specific:* "One bronze signed Henry Moore" says just that. It does not say the piece was made by Henry Moore.

BOOKS ON BRONZES

• ***Bronzes* by Jennifer Montagu,** Octopus Books Ltd., New York, 1972, out of print.

• ***A Concise History of Bronzes* by George Savage,** International Thomson Publishing, New York, 1969, out of print.

Collecting Art Deco

J. Alastair Duncan, formerly of Christie's; Herve Aaron, Didier Aaron, Inc.; Nicholas Dawes, antiques dealer; and Fred Silberman, Fred Silberman Gallery, all of New York City.

Art Deco is a design style that burst onto the international scene in the 1920s. (Its name comes from the 1925 Paris *Exposition International des Arts Decoratifs et Industriels*.) The sleek modern lines of the style appeared in architecture, furniture design, fabrics, posters, book covers, silver, glass, ceramics, clocks, boxes, cases, enamelware, jewelry and even clothing. Flamboyant and optimistic in the prewar years, it came out of Art Nouveau and melded into Art Moderne, a more industrial, machine-age fascination with technology and new materials, such as plastics and chrome, in the 1930s. Art Deco motifs were Egyptian, Mayan, cubistic and futuristic. The craftsmanship was superb.

Art Deco was rediscovered by collectors in the late 1960s, and prices escalated in the 1970s. Then, as with many other antiques and collectibles, the market softened in the 1980s, particularly for mass-produced items in good supply. When collectors and dealers sensed that Lalique was becoming cheap again, they started a new wave of buying, and the price roller coaster started up again.

Furniture by an Art Deco master like Emile Jacques Ruhlmann or lacquerwork by Jean Dunand (most famous for furnishings on the liner *Normandie*) has not weakened in price. The workmanship and rarity of such attributed pieces keep them at a premium. A record was set at a Christie's auction in 1997—the item was a 1916 Ruhlmann cupboard marqueted with ivory and ebony, which sold for over $650,000. You may still find chairs (and sometimes tables) for under $10,000 by Louis Sue and Andre Mare, Jules Leleu and Dominique. American names to look for are Donald Deskey (responsible for much of the Radio City Music Hall decor) and Paul Frankel.

For the beginning collector: Look for well-built wooden furniture. It was properly dried and crafted in the 1920s, using such rare woods as amboyna and black macasser ebony, which won't be seen again.

For the serious investor-collector, only signed, handmade pieces of great quality are safe buys for the future.

Mass-produced 20th-century decorative arts may not be an investment, but they are great fun to have. Charming design and good quality control make Art Deco household and personal items competitive with contemporary merchandise. Art Deco table silver, cigarette holders, ladies' compacts, perfume bottles, jewelry, boxes, lighters and other small items have great flair and affordable price tags. Some consider Art Deco low-quality art, but it has a sense of humor and great style.

Collecting Color Posters

Robert Brown, co-owner of the Reinhold-Brown Gallery, New York City.

Posters caught the public's fancy in the 1880s and have retained a fascination for collectors ever since. The development of cheap color lithography led to that first wave of artistic posters, most of which were designed for advertising. From 1880 to 1900, French, Belgian, English and American artists left their mark on the medium. *Best known:* The French Art Nouveau artists Toulouse-Lautrec, Mucha, Cheret and Steinlen.

German artists turned out the finest posters from 1900 to World War I. *Leading light:* Ludwig Hohlwein, who did posters for clothing stores and theatrical events and a famous series for the Munich zoo.

American posters came to prominence during World War I. *Uncle Sam Wants You*, the recruiting poster showing a determined Uncle Sam pointing toward the viewer, is an unforgettable image. *The artist:* James Montgomery Flagg. He and Howard Chandler Christy produced many of the most famous posters of their day. Today an Uncle Sam poster can sell for hundreds of dollars.

The work of French artist A.M. Cassandre stood out during the period between the two World Wars. *His most popular contributions: The Nord Express* and other train posters done between 1925 and 1932. His widely reproduced and imposing *Normandie* was completed in 1936.

Posters of note since World War II include those of Ben Shahn and the San Francisco rock posters of the 1960s.

The categories for collectors encompass various subjects, such as circus, theater, ballet, movies, music halls and both World Wars. *Best buys:* Automobile posters (except those for American cars, which are not of very good quality). *Star:* The Peugeot poster by French artist Charles Loupot.

Posters in constant demand: Those connected to avant-garde art that combine strong typographic design with photomontage. *Rare finds:* Work from the 1920s associated with the Bauhaus, the Dada movement and Russian Constructivism. Constructivist film posters made between 1925 and 1931 usually measure about 40 inches by 28 inches. *Classic example:* Any of the few advertising the film *The Battleship Potemkin.*

Beginners should look at Japanese posters made from the mid-1970s to the present. *Also recommended:* Post-World War II Swiss posters for concerts and art exhibits.

Best: Stick to recent foreign posters made in limited editions and not distributed beyond their place of origin.

Poster condition: Creases and small tears in the margin are acceptable. Faded posters are undesirable. (The quality standards are not quite as stringent for posters as they are for prints.)

Collecting American Quilts

Barbara Doherty, co-owner of Pineapple Primitives, Brooklyn, NY.

Appreciation of American-made quilts has grown greatly in recent years. *Most sought after:* Amish or Mennonite quilts. Prices start at $1,000. Many are made in somber colors (black, purple, dark blue) with a geometric design. They look striking in modern interiors. The quilters were forbidden by their religion to use flowers or other frivolous designs or decoration. However, they often tricked sterner members of the sect by backing their quilts with patterned fabrics.

Does this patterned fabric add to the overall value? No. The fine stitching and the sophisticated color schemes are the spectacular features of an Amish quilt. Incidentally, you will find a deliberate mistake, such as one square in a color that clashes with the rest of the scheme, in every quilt. This symbolizes that only God is perfect.

Are most Amish quilts old? Actually, most of them were made in the 1920s and early 1930s. Quilts older than that will have worn out from use.

Are they entirely handmade? No. Most borders were put on by machine. (Sewing machines were in use as early as 1840.)

Are the Amish and Mennonites still making quilts? Yes, but unfortunately they now use a combination of cotton and polyester fabrics. Even the cottons aren't the same. The old ones were vegetable-dyed, which gave special richness to the colors.

What other kinds of quilts are desirable? White brides' quilts, which are very rare. Fine patchwork with tiny pieces. (Tiny pieces, if expertly sewn, add to the value of a quilt.) Appliqué, in which a tulip, a basket or some other motif is cut out and sewn on separately. Trapunto, quilting with a raised effect made by outlining the design with running stitches and then filling it with cotton.

How do you judge a quilt? By design, color harmony and needlecraft. However, mediocre design with wonderful stitching can be outstanding. So can a quilt with less fine needlework but marvelous pattern or colors. The ideal is to find great taste and great workmanship together.

Is it possible to find large quilts? Once in a while you'll see one that's 100 inches wide, but most are in the 72- to 78-inch range, and often square. Quilts are rarely a standard size. If you have a very fine quilt, don't use it on a bed. There's too much risk of wear.

Where are quilts found now? The best buys are in the Midwest, particularly in Ohio and Missouri, but also in upstate New York and other more remote rural communities. Search at auctions and antique fairs.

How are quilts displayed? They are used as wall hangings, which is what most dealers advise. Dramatic colors and designs are the qualities that you should look for in a quilt you would like to use as a wall hanging.

How do you care for a quilt? If you hang it behind glass, it must never touch the glass. To frame a quilt, treat it like a fine print, and back it with acid-free paper. Never display a quilt in direct sunlight—colors fade, especially the reds. To store, roll it (don't fold) to prevent wear cracks. Wrap it in acid-free paper. Avoid old quilts with brown materials. Something in the mordant (the dye-setter) or the dyes themselves causes the brown to disintegrate.

How do you clean a quilt? No dry cleaning, ever. The solvents are too strong. If you must wash the quilt, do it in the bathtub with a dishwashing detergent such as Joy. Then rinse the quilt many, many times with distilled water. But sometimes you may have to leave it dirty. Don't tamper with rust stains or with blood stains (made by pricked fingers) that were not washed out right away.

Collecting Coins

Dr. Martin Groder, business consultant to a coin dealership in Chapel Hill, NC.

Coin collections fall into two categories—those done for the fun of it and those undertaken by collector-investors who mix value with the fun.

Collectors who are only looking for a pleasant hobby usually restrict themselves to inexpensive coins. *Basic procedure:* Obtain the standard books and buy albums in which to mount the coin purchases. Join clubs and attend shows to build up expertise at your leisure.

Collector-investors approach their coins with a higher level of commitment. *Main difference:* They spend significant amounts of money in the hope of reaping financial rewards.

SALIENT FACTS

• **The market for US Treasury-minted coins was once fairly steady since only collectors bought and sold.** But starting in the mid-1960s, noncollecting investors began to move cash in and out of the market, buying and selling coins as speculative investments much as they might stocks and bonds. This injection of volatile money transformed a relatively steady market into one of cycles, with booms and busts. Speculation increases demand for investment-grade coins, which makes those that are extant more and more valuable.

• **Experienced collector-investors and dealers often use their expertise to take advantage of the novice investor.** *Result:* Thousands of new collectors find that they are stuck with inexpensive junk when it is time to sell.

HOW TO AVOID BEING SKINNED

• **Study well before making major money investments.** There are a number of books about each major US coin series. These volumes discuss the historical background of the coins. *Examples:* How well the coins were struck and the condition of the dyes when the coins were made. The rare and common years for the coins and dozens of variations that make each coin distinct from others. The books often give values for the coins, but these are usually out of date. For the latest figures, consult the coin collectors' newsletters. *Point:* Learn all you can about a coin before investing. This background knowledge helps keep you from being cheated by a fast-talking dealer.

• **Learn from dealers.** Get acquainted with several to gain a sense of them as people. Be alert to their willingness to protect beginners from their own errors.

• **Do not depend on the advice of dealers for long.** To wean yourself away, spend lots of time at coin shows and auctions. Learn to identify and grade individual coins and note their sale prices. Subscribe to and study the literature read by professionals.

Crucial advice: Sell part of your collection every year. This shows you whether or not you knew what you were doing when you bought.

What to sell: Duplicates for which you have better samples. Coins from periods that no longer interest you. Samples that have lost their fascination.

Why should you start or rebuild a collection now? In the late 1970s and into 1980, a major speculative boom shot prices far beyond sustainable levels. After some panic selling, many paper profits disappeared. Now the market is pretty well cleared of all excess pricing. The boom drove away many novice and casual collectors as prices soared. But these people started drifting back into the marketplace as coins became more affordable.

Preservation: The value of a coin does not depend entirely on the market cycle. It can drop rapidly from poor handling or cleaning, or even from coughing on the coin. *Best:* Check with dealers and consult literature on the best methods of preservation. *Avoid:* Plastic holders made from polyvinyl chloride (PVC). This material breaks down with time and releases an oil that oxidizes the copper in coins, turning them green and oily. *Note:* Although damaged coins can be cleaned, they never look the same to an experienced eye.

Collecting Chinese Porcelain

Andrew Kahane, Andrew Kahane Ltd., New York City.

There have been times when fine Chinese porcelain has outpaced stocks, bonds and the money market, with an annual appreciation of 15% or more. A 14th-century pilgrim flask sold at a Doyle auction in 2003 for $5.8 million. This was the highest price ever paid for a Ming dynasty Chinese porcelain.

Chinese porcelain is pottery that contains the mineral products kaolin and feldspar (for translucency) and is fired at very high temperatures. Manufacture began in the late 10th century.

Why are dynasty names, such as Ming, used? Porcelain study is organized historically, and these names place an object in time. *The*

dynasties: Northern Sung (960–1127), Southern Sung (1127–1279), Yuan (1280–1368), Ming (1368–1643) and Ch'ing (1644–1912). Also, names of certain rulers within dynasties are used, especially for the 17th and 18th centuries. *Example:* K'ang-hsi (1662–1722). K'ang-hsi blue-and-white ware is highly prized.

Are there ways for a beginner to identify a period by the shape or color of an object? It is a complicated subject that demands a lot of looking. However, there are a few broad generalizations. The earliest porcelains are the white wares of the Northern Sung dynasty, termed Ting. The first blue-and-whites appear in the Yuan period. They are called Mohammedan blue, because both cobalt and the techniques used to fashion the wares were imported from Persia. The floral and figural decorations on porcelain with a predominant background color (Famille Rose, Famille Noire, Famille Verte, etc.) are 17th and 18th century. The monochromes (pure yellows, celadons, oxbloods, peach blooms, etc.) are basically developments of the 18th century. They were extremely popular with collectors in the early part of this century.

What is most sought after now? The highest prices are for early Ming (15th century) blue-and-white pieces bearing a reign mark. In recent years, a very strong interest for reign marks has developed. The reign mark or seal was placed on the object as a sign of deference or goodwill. In Ming pieces, they are crucial. *Example:* A hypothetical good early Ming blue-and-white vase will bring $100,000 if marked. Unmarked, it will go for around $30,000.

How much do chips or cracks affect value? Very much, in today's market. Steer clear of anything that's the slightest bit damaged, underfired or overfired.

Is it possible to begin collecting without paying a great deal of money? Yes, indeed. For the new collector, transitional blue-and-white ware, which was made in the 17th century, between the end of the Ming and the beginning of the Ch'ing dynasties, is still reasonable. A hypothetical sleeve vase (flaring and cylindrical) made between 1640 and 1650, with some nice incised decorations, should cost $2,500 or more in perfect condition. That is not very much to pay when you consider the price of other antiques of equal artistry.

Another relatively modest way to start: Export wares made for European and American markets, especially those bearing family arms or marks. They were made from the 18th into the 19th century, often as tea or dinner services. Prices could run from about $200 for a small plate up to $5,000 to $8,000 for a fine tureen. It is fun to do research on the family arms and to track them down to the year the porcelain was commissioned.

Is it difficult to care for porcelain? As long as you don't drop it, porcelain is very durable. Use reasonable caution, and wash it in soapy water.

What is the state of the market? Strong. *Example:* In a recent Christie's auction, a blue-and-white moon flask from the Ming dynasty (Yongle period) sold for $1.1 million—double its low estimate.

What are the best reference works on Chinese porcelain? There are hundreds of books on the subject, but the following are unequaled for anyone who is seriously interested in the field. They can be found on-line and in good libraries.

•***Chinese Ceramics, A New Comprehensive Survey from the Asian Art Museum of San Francisco*** by He Li (New York, 1996).

•***Chinese Pottery and Porcelain*** by S.J. Vainker.

•***A Handbook of Chinese Ceramics*** by Suzanne G. Valenstein.

•***Underglaze Blue and Red: Elegant Decoration of Porcelain from Yuan, Ming and Qing*** by Wang Qingzheng.

•***The Chinese Potter*** by Margaret Medley (London, 1976).

•***Chinese Blue and White Porcelain*** by Duncan Macintosh (London, 1994).

Collecting Pewter

Price Glover, antiques dealer and specialist in pewter, New York City. *www.pricegloverinc.com.*

Pewter appeals to collectors for both its handsomeness and its history. Because of their classic styles and satiny, silver-gray finish, pewter pieces also lend themselves well to decorative display.

Although pewter has sometimes been called the poor man's silver, fine pewter has always been esteemed. Basically, pewter is tin alloyed with lead, copper, bismuth and sometimes antimony. The proportions of metals vary according to the maker, but generally a lower proportion of lead (and subsequently lightness) means higher quality.

The most sought-after pewter in the US is American pre-19th century, both for its scarcity and the general fever to collect Americana. American craftspeople melted down damaged or badly worn pewter for recasting into new pieces. Constant remelting, heavy use and eventual discarding left little to survive. Since so few 17th- and early-18th-century American pieces are available, most collectors concentrate on post-Revolutionary War pewter.

The great scarcity has caused prices to escalate. A rare 1740 tankard sold for $15,000 at a recent auction. (Auctions with sizable collections of 18th-century pewter are also infrequent.) A late-18th-century plate or a small liquid tavern measure, however, might be found for $300 to $500.

Pewter was still made in the early 19th century, but in order to compete with the growing popularity of pottery and glass, some makers began adding antimony to their alloy. The result was a harder metal, adaptable to the refined patterns of silver. Called Britannia metal, this pewter was extremely popular until the mid-19th century. To a purist collector of pewter, though, it lacks the attraction of the traditional pewter.

By the mid-19th century, mass-production methods and the process of electroplating made silverplate more affordable, and pewter production died out. A collector might find pewter that was once silverplated with the plate later removed, but it is not as desirable as the original pewter.

Twentieth-century pewter pieces are not valued by collectors.

Beyond American shores, pewter has a truly ancient history that goes back to the Bronze Age. Pewter production has thrived in England since the Middle Ages. An astute collector may manage to find English pewter from as early as the 16th century. Imported by American dealers, 17th- and 18th-century English pewter is far more available than its American counterpart. It also commands about half the price of comparable American pieces, even when the English piece is as much as 75 years older. As American pewter becomes rarer, the urge for collecting English pewter seems likely to increase. Off-the-beaten-path antique stores in England are a source of bargains for the knowledgeable collector. So far, most European pewter is valued at only a fraction of English pewter's worth.

Design, good condition and an absence of discoloration are important considerations in evaluating pewter. The most important factors are age and origin. Touch marks imprinted on pewter are highly prized. Such symbols make it possible to date pieces and to determine if they are American (sometimes even the region is identified), English or Continental. However, Early American craftspeople often copied British symbols or stamped "London" on their wares to mislead the public. And some early pewter was not marked at all. The multitude of signs, hallmarks and makers' signatures makes reference-book research a necessity for the serious collector. Since fakes and forgeries are common, experts advise buying only from a very reputable dealer.

Early pewter was cast in heavy molds and then finished on a lathe. The finishing left shallow grooves called skimming marks on the pewter. When a handle was attached, the linen support placed under the handle left the impression of its weave. Hammer marks on the underside of a plate rim also indicate early craftsmanship. *Learning:* Most museums with Early American collections have displays of pewter that can be very informative for a beginner.

Collecting Antique American Clocks

Chris Bailey, curator of the American Clock & Watch Museum, Bristol, CT.

Clock collecting goes all the way back to 15th-century Europe, a time when royal patrons commissioned ornately jeweled timepieces. In America, quality clock making began in colonial times, and collecting by the affluent got an early start. A major display at the Columbian Exposition of 1893 was of colonial clocks.

MAJOR COLLECTING CATEGORIES

• **Tall-case clocks.** The earliest American-made clocks are over seven feet high and are popularly known as grandfather clocks. (Collectors call them tall-case clocks.) The earliest had square dials. Later versions have arched dials, often with pictures or moving figures that show the phases of the moon. Late-18th-century clocks may have wooden works. *Names to look for:* William Claggart, Peter Stretch and Simon & Aaron Willard. Prices for tall clocks range from the low thousands to several hundred thousands.

• **Banjo clocks.** In the late 18th century, banjo-shaped wall clocks were created. The earliest ones are now as valuable as tall-case clocks made in the same years. At one auction, an elaborate early-19th-century banjo clock by Lemuel Curtis sold for $15,000. One of uncertifiable make sold for $2,000.

• **Shelf clocks.** In the early 19th century, these more affordable clocks appeared. About two feet high, they fit comfortably on the mantel. Their mass-production methods, devised by Eli Terry and Seth Thomas, were America's main contribution to the clock industry. A good shelf clock can cost from $200 to thousands of dollars.

WHAT MAKES CLOCKS VALUABLE?

• **The best clocks have,** besides age and beauty, all their original parts in good working order. Cases must also be in good condition.

• **Replacements or repairs should have been expertly performed** using methods and materials of the clock's period. With proper restoration, a clock maintains its quality.

• **Signatures and labels** of esteemed clockmakers enhance value. But fine unsigned clocks also command good prices.

• **Embellishments to conform to a current fashion** detract from a clock's worth.

• **Scarcity is not synonymous with value.** Some fine clockmakers made many clocks, all of which command high prices because of quality, not rarity.

STARTING OUT

Veteran clock collectors have been described as one of the most canny groups of collectors. Fortunately, the novice can acquire information easily. Many good books are available in public libraries. Museum collections are a useful guide to variety and high quality. The National Association of Watch and Clock Collectors (*www.nawcc.org*) is a resource that has chapters nationwide, a bimonthly journal and research services.

For serious beginners, the best way to buy is through a reliable dealer who will give a written guarantee that the clock can be returned.

Clocks are no longer a good high-return, short-term investment. But quality clocks, especially tall-case clocks, will retain their value and grow with inflation. Even some pre-World War II clocks may be of collecting value. Two contemporary American clock companies, Chelsea and Howard, are still making limited quantities of high-quality clocks that may turn out to be the desirable antiques of the future.

For Big Band Enthusiasts

There is an Internet site that features recordings of big bands and jazz from the 1920s, 1930s and 1940s—plus biographies of many musicians of that era. The Past Perfect site is at *www.pastperfect.com*.

Michael Daly, cofounder and managing director, Past Perfect, Grange Mews, Station Rd., Launton, Oxfordshire OX26 5EE, United Kingdom.

Collecting Old Watches

Dr. Walter D. Bundens, former president of the National Association of Watch and Clock Collectors, and William Scolnik, dealer in antique watches, New York City.

Clocks were reduced to portable size in the early 1500s, when the first watches, highly decorated pendants, were proudly worn as fine jewelry. Technical advances in the 1870s, coupled with the newly chic long waistcoat (watches were slipped into convenient pockets), led to more practical timepieces. Two hundred years of innovations and refinements culminated in the precision instruments beloved by collectors today—primarily European, handcrafted mechanical watches made between 1700 and 1900.

EUROPEAN WATCHES

• **Decorative watches** have decorative cases with lids that close (called hunting cases) or unusual shapes and scenes or designs in engraved or repoussé gold, enamel or jewels.

• **Complicated watches** have intricate technical mechanisms for functions other than telling time. Some watches tell the month, day, year, phase of the moon, international times or even sidereal time. Others have alarms, timers or musical chimes. Watches were made with chronographs, thermometers and compasses—and one, sold for $1,350, had a built-in roulette wheel. A most popular type of watch, called a repeater, strikes on the hour, quarter hour or even minute, when a button is activated. Automata have moving figures that perform on the hour or quarter hour on demand. An erotic version was offered for almost $8,000. Always popular are skeletonized watches, whose movements are visible through clear cases. Some of these may sell for under $1,000.

• **The rarest of the rare.** It is the dream of every serious collector to own a watch by Abraham-Louis Breguet, an innovative French watchmaker of the late 18th to mid-19th centuries. Every watch he made is unique and distinctive. Only a small percentage of his known output has been accounted for. In 1895, a Breguet watch cost the equivalent of about 20 houses. Generally, one would sell for $20,000 to $150,000, and many fakes are around.

• **Other names to look for.** Patek-Philippe ("the Rolls-Royce of watches"), Frodsham, Rolex and Audemars Piguet.

AMERICAN WATCHES

• **Railroad watches.** Conductors and engineers of the late 19th century were dependent on their watches to keep to their timetables. These are the most popular collectible type in America. Often large and plain, and always accurate, they were expensive a century ago. *Names:* Waltham, Elgin, Howard, Illinois "Bunn Special," Hamilton and Ball.

• **Dollar watches.** Inexpensive, mass-produced pocket watches from the 1920s and 1930s are still cheap and easy to find. With few exceptions, dollar watches will probably never be highly valued, but they can be lots of fun for the beginning collector. *Exceptions:* Watches made for the World's Fairs (Chicago 1893, New York 1939 and others) or novelty watches like Mickey Mouse or Buck Rogers, currently selling for hundreds of dollars.

• **Top of the line.** Before 1915, many American watch companies made a "top of the line" model in limited quantities, numbered and inscribed that rivaled or even outshone contemporary European models. Collectors can learn to recognize these through reading and research.

• **Recent watches.** While the quartz watches hold little interest (so far) for collectors, early electric watches—the first Hamilton electric, for example—are sought, as are watches from Cartier or Tiffany made through the 1940s.

WHAT ADDS VALUE?

A famous maker or model. Degree of complication. Amount of purity of gold (or silver). Number of jewels. A low serial number (look inside). The beauty of case and movement. Condition. (Watches should be in working condition or repairable. Repairs must be done in the style of the original.)

WATCHES AS AN INVESTMENT

Prices of fine antique watches are soaring. At Christie's spring 2005 auction, an 18-karat gold, 1961 Patek-Philippe wristwatch with perpetual calendar and moon phases sold for more than $1 million, and an 18-karat pink gold, 1948 Patek-Philippe chronograph wristwatch with perpetual calendar and moon phases sold for $336,000.

Inexpensive watches are available wherever old jewelry is sold. When you consider purchasing an expensive watch, however, be sure to consult an expert. Estate auctions are generally good sources.

FOR THE BEGINNER

Membership in the National Association of Watch and Clock Collectors includes two publications: *The Bulletin* and *The Mart* (in which members buy, sell and trade watches —a wonderful source). The association also maintains a museum, a lending library and a new computerized "horological data bank." For more information, visit *www.nawcc.org.*

Collecting Native American Silver Jewelry

Teal McKibben, collector and owner of La Bodega de Rael, Santa Fe, NM, and Carl Druckman, researcher and consultant in Indian jewelry, Santa Fe, NM.

In the late 1960s and early 1970s, Native American Indian silver jewelry, previously collected by a small coterie, began to capture the interest of the general public. Count on a 10% to 15% annual appreciation on the value of fine old and contemporary pieces.

Learning the ropes: Look at photographs, go to museums, read. Expect to make a few mistakes. You have to do some impulse buying, then go home, study what you bought and profit from the experience.

Background: Indians of the Southwest are the major producers of silver jewelry. *Most talented and prolific:* Navaho and Zuni. *Also on the market:* Limited amounts of Hopi (known for overlay work) and Santo Domingo (turquoise and shell, sometimes combined with silver or gold).

• **Navaho first-phase jewelry.** The Navaho were the first Indians in the Southwest to work with silver. They learned the craft from the Spanish-Mexicans in the mid-1860s. *Ornaments made for their own use or for trading with other Indians:* Concha belts, najas (bridal decorations), bracelets, squash-blossom necklaces. *Characteristics:* Primitive, simple design with Spanish influence. The quality of silver is often not good, and hairline cracks may be visible. *Cost:* Very expensive.

• **Navaho second phase.** Starting in about 1890 to 1900, they began to use ingots. They embellished traditional designs and used more turquoise. Coral from Europe was introduced around 1910 to 1920.

• **Early tourist jewelry.** This covers 1910 to 1940. Produced for barter with white traders, it included belts, bracelets, boxes, lipstick cases, ashtrays and cigarette holders.

• **Zuni.** After the 1920s, the Zuni began to make silver inlaid with coral, turquoise, mother-of-pearl and jet. They developed the cluster style (clusters of symmetrically shaped stones). They also devised channel work, which is silver strips, typically with beading, outlining shapes in which turquoises are inserted. Generally, Zuni jewelry is more delicate than Navaho.

Since there is very little jewelry on the market from the 1800s, start by buying early tourist jewelry. *Secret:* Buy what can be worn by you or someone close to you unselfconsciously. *Reason to choose:* Because you love the piece.

What to look for: Quality of stones, weight of silver, stamping, craftsmanship and soul. *Problem:* It is difficult to find outstanding examples of all these elements in one piece.

• **Contemporary silver.** If the artist is well known, you often pay more for a new piece than for an old one.

• **Sources.** Flea markets, antique shows, local arts-and-crafts galleries. *Best possibilities:* Indian sidewalk markets on the plazas in Santa Fe and Albuquerque…shops in pueblos and trading posts on reservations.

Collecting Antique Jewelry

Rose Leiman Goldemberg, author of *Antique Jewelry: A Practical and Passionate Guide* (Crown Publishers) and *All About Jewelry* (HarperCollins).

Antique jewelry satisfies a love of the past and the appreciation of fine craftsmanship. It fulfills the expectation that quality jewelry should give pleasure for a long time. In addition, some of the most beautiful and unusual gems and designs can be found in antique pieces.

INVESTMENT: NEW VS. OLD

Despite the fact that the markup on new jewelry is as much as 100%, resale value declines the minute a piece is purchased. Unless a new piece has gemstones that will at least double in value, its worth will decrease drastically in a short time.

Antique jewelry is, of course, also marked up for retail. However, other factors besides gemstones help stabilize and increase its value. Setting, workmanship, style, rarity and history all determine price. Time enhances rather than diminishes value. Excellent antique jewelry nearly always rises in value.

BUYING

Knowledge is essential. Many antique dealers are not well informed about jewelry. Look for a dealer who is long established, and seek personal recommendations from other jewelry collectors.

Browsing to compare prices and learning what you can from books are basic. Auctions can be instructive, but novices are better off out of the bidding until they have some expertise.

PERIODS OF DESIGN

Jewelry styles may overlap decades or be so classic that they are repeated from one era to another. However, one of the most important things to learn is the dominant periods of design. Pieces made before the 18th century are extremely scarce, very expensive and usually impractical to wear. *The following historical periods are the major sources of available antiques...*

Georgian: Jewelry from the early 1700s to approximately 1830 looks different from any other style in history. Its characteristics are well worth studying. Comparative rarity and aesthetic appeal keep its prices high.

Although Georgian gold jewelry appears to be substantial, it is light in weight. Stones were often foiled (backed with colored metal) to enhance their hue. Glass gems, cut and polished as carefully as real ones, were often set in silver. The brilliant-cut diamond was new to the era and popular, but all precious and semiprecious stones were used, as well as natural Oriental pearls, coral and ivory.

Victorian: From 1830 to the turn of the century, a great deal of jewelry was made, and much of it still survives. Victorian jewelry is characterized by massive pieces of heavy gold and silver. Colorful stones and impressive parures (matched sets) were common. Jewelry with sentimental messages was highly popular.

Most available Victorian jewelry is English-made. American-made jewelry, though simpler in design, is scarce and apt to be higher in price.

Art Nouveau: At the end of the Victorian era, the flowing, sensuous lines of Art Nouveau emerged to dominate design. Jewelry became graceful, slender and feminine. Sterling silver was often used, and popular stones were muted in color or even colorless.

Many odd stones were also used, and iridescence was highly regarded. Opals, mother-of-pearl, horn and shell were common. Craftspeople aimed for unique designs. Fakes and reproductions are common.

Art Deco: From World War I to about 1940, the angular, shiny designs of Art Deco came into vogue. Its clean geometric lines and contrasts of black and white are still appealing and very wearable. Onyx, enamel, white gold, crystal, diamonds and jade are characteristic. Although such jewelry is not old enough to qualify as truly antique, the continuing popularity of Art Deco has caused prices to escalate.

CONDITION

Never buy a piece solely because it is old. Antique jewelry should be in good or perfect condition. Damaged jewelry has little resale value.

A 10X jeweler's loupe is essential for the serious collector. Check for glued-in stones, thin ring shanks, and poorly mended or broken parts. Signs of repair or alteration are drawbacks. The jewelry should be very close to its original state. Avoid jewelry that has been put together from various pieces, such as earrings from bits of a necklace.

CARING FOR JEWELRY

If a piece breaks or wears out, it should be repaired by a jeweler who is an expert on antiques. Generally, the less repair the better.

When cleaning, be gentle. When in doubt, do nothing. Avoid overzealous polishing or electronic cleaning. It can be damaging, and it destroys the wonderful patina of age. Soapy water will do for most pieces, but read up on the care and composition of a piece before trying anything.

REAL OR REPRODUCTION?

Honest reproductions are acceptable—but be alert for deception. A reproduction is apt to show signs of haste in its construction. Modern touches such as safety catches are often giveaways. If more than one sample of a certain piece is on display, be leery—few identical pieces survive.

How to Buy Jewelry at Auction And Save

Judith H. McQuown, author of many investment books. She also writes about shopping, antiques and travel.

Clearly, "cutting out the middleman" can save jewelry shoppers thousands of dollars on just one purchase. This is especially true of single diamonds. D color,* the marker of internally flawless stones, sell at auction for much less per karat than the high figures reported in newspapers and magazines. Furthermore, many auction diamonds come with Gemological Institute of America (GIA) certificates that show the weight, color and clarity of the stone.

Expert advice on how to buy at auction depends in part on what you're interested in. If you're buying contemporary jewelry, where the value of the piece lies almost 100% in the gemstones, it's most important to do a little arithmetic to calculate the value of the stones. Divide the presale estimate by the total weight of the stones.

The size of the stone—separate from its weight—affects prices as well. *Example:* Two diamond bracelets may have equal total weights, but the bracelet that has fewer and larger stones will be worth more and will sell for more.

For antique jewelry, where condition can count far more than design, workmanship or the intrinsic value of the gold and gemstones, the rules differ. Reading the description of the piece in the auction catalog and seeing it are far more important. Such words as *repaired, altered, cracked* or *later additions* can lower the value of the piece drastically. Joyce Jonas, former director of the jewelry department of Phillips, New York City, recommends careful examination of the piece before purchasing. According to Jonas, "The most important investment you can make is a 10X jeweler's loupe, which costs less than $25. Carry it with you whenever you're examining jewelry. Look at the front. Look for alterations—the front of a brooch may be pink gold, but the pin in

*D is the highest rating.

back, added later, may be yellow gold. That reduces the value. Look for marks of soldering repair. Gold solder, if used carefully, will not alter the value of the piece. Lead solder, which leaves gray marks, can reduce the price by 50%. Condition is crucial."

Auction houses are legally bound by their catalog descriptions. Look for listed imperfections (often printed in italics), such as *stone missing, stone cracked, lead solder marks, repaired, enamel worn, later additions,* etc. More pleasantly, catalogs also note the shape and weight of large stones (sometimes with GIA diamond ratings), karat of gold (if not listed, it's 14K) and whether a piece is signed. Descriptions are often so detailed that collectors who become familiar with catalogs can visualize the pieces.

If you're planning to buy frequently, make friends with the auction-house jewelry curators. They will often point out the merits or flaws of a piece and can advise you on the maximum reasonable bid. Subscribe to and keep catalogs and lists of prices paid at auctions. They are excellent reference tools in helping you decide how much to bid at future auctions.

When it comes to bidding itself, there are pros and cons to attending the auction in person versus leaving a written bid. Many people, realizing their susceptibility to auction-fever overbidding, find that it's wiser to have a written bid. Others, including many dealers, prefer to attend in person so that they can better control their bidding. Delaying a bid until just before the hammer comes down can get you a piece for a lower price. *Strategy:* If you sit in the rear of the room, you'll be able to see who's bidding against you.

Auctions are generally advertised in the weekend "Arts and Leisure" or "Style" section of major newspapers: *The New York Times, The Boston Globe, The San Francisco Examiner, The Washington Post,* etc. The ads list viewing dates and times (usually three or four days before the auction), as well as the date and time of the auction itself.

Says one collector of antique jewelry, fingering her diamond bracelet, "I could never afford jewelry unless I bought at auction. And I get such a wonderful feeling when I see jewelry in stores that's vastly inferior to mine for thousands of dollars more."

Collecting Carved Chinese Jade

Simone Hartman, collector and co-owner of Rare Art galleries, New York City, Dallas and Palm Beach.

For centuries, jade was the precious gem of the Chinese nobility, and carved jade pieces have long been one of the most important facets of Chinese art and antiques.

Collecting jade is almost as venerable an activity as the art of carving it. Today the center of collecting is the West, where most of the finest antique jade carvings are now found.

Both for aesthetic satisfaction and the potential appreciation in value, jade collecting is attracting wider attention in the US. Good antique jade is still available.

TRUE JADE

Only two minerals, nephrite and jadeite, can truly be called jade. They are very similar but have slightly different compositions. Jadeite was virtually unknown to the Chinese before the 18th century.

Although jade is tough (difficult to shatter), it is not as hard as such gemstones as rubies and emeralds. It can scratch more easily. (Jadeite is the preferred form of jewelry because it is beautifully colored and harder than nephrite.) It is the toughness of jade that lends itself so well to precision carving and accounts for the survivability of antique jade.

To most people, jade means green. However, a great variety of colors are available. Jade is found in natural shades of blue, lavender, white, red and brown as well as green. One of the most prized types of nephrite is called mutton fat for its lustrous grayish-white color with tinges of pale green.

Small jades that are old, historically important, unusually colored and beautifully carved can command steep prices. However, a collector who begins with an investment of several hundred to $1,000 can find a valuable, small jade carving that is 100 to 300 years old. Besides being a fascinating work of art (owners seem to develop an intimate relationship with their small jades), a fine piece is likely to increase in value (with reservations due to uncertain economics).

A good recommendation often followed by new collectors is to specialize. The collector might narrow a collection to only zodiac animals or flowered snuff bottles.

Best: Simple and handmade.

A good carver has made use of the different patterns and textures of the raw material. Even imperfections become part of the design. Much of the carving done in Hong Kong today is machine-powered. Experts feel that something is lost in the process and that the result is often too elaborate. However, Hong Kong is still a source of fine, hand-carved contemporary pieces.

Much of modern jade has been dyed to alter or enhance its natural color. And much "jade" is not jade at all. The commonest substitute is serpentine.

A buyer should beware of both intentional deception and honest mistakes. In addition, jade is very hard to date. Even museum experts can find dating a piece problematical. A trustworthy dealer offers on the bill of sale a description confirming that the item is what it is presented to be.

Attending auctions of Chinese art is one way to learn possibilities and prices. Museum collections also offer a way to survey some of the finest examples of jade workmanship. The Metropolitan Museum of Art in New York City has on permanent display the most impressive pieces from the Bishop Collection, one of the best jade collections in the world.

Collecting Stamps

Bruce Stone, president of Stamp Portfolios, Inc., Stamford, CT.

How much of an initial investment is required if you just want to collect for fun? Not much for starters, and that's one attraction of the hobby. Unlike coins, which are fairly expensive individual items, you can get started in stamps for about $20.

How does one start? By going through a learning curve. Consult the *Yellow Pages* for stamp shops in your area. Meet the owners. Find out about the weekend shows, called *bourses*. Subscribe to philatelic publications.

What are some collecting areas? Topicals are an excellent way to begin. If you have an interest in aviation, for instance, zero in on stamps depicting airplanes. Space stamps are a hot topical. Tropical fish are also popular.

First-day covers are another way to collect. Covers (envelopes) have the stamp canceled at first date of issue, from the town that is issuing for that particular stamp. (*Example:* The cover for the 75th anniversary of flight was issued at Kitty Hawk on December 17, 1978.) Covers bear a cachet (engraving) related to the subject. They are pretty and inexpensive, but they really have no long-term investment value.

Will they appreciate quickly? Slowly, because modern covers are issued in such quantity. Scarcity and historical importance are the key factors in philatelic value. Of course, if you could find a cover dated September 9, 1850, mailed from California, it would bring over $100,000. That's the date California became a state, and such a cover is prized.

How high do prices go? A collector paid $1 million for The Blue Boy, issued at Alexandria, Virginia, in 1846. This is actually a stampless cover. The postage stamp was invented in England in 1840 but not established in the US until 1847. Before that, letters were either franked (passed by official signature) or paid for on the receiving end.

What about stamps as an investment? Stamps seem to be recession-proof. Between January 2, 1978, and December 31, 1980, the Dow rose 2%. A cross section of 86 classic US stamps rose 85% in value during that same period. Demand for the supply of quality US stamps is great. The number is finite. There are more than 20 million collectors in the US. (Incidentally, over 95% are males. No one has explained that.)

How do you care for stamps? Investment stamps should be kept in a vault and not handled. Hobby stamps are slipped into glassine mounts for safety and arranged in albums.

What's the difference between a stamp collector and a philatelist? In a word, knowledge. A philatelist reads and has an eye toward a specific goal. The choice is limited only by imagination.

Collecting Autographs For Profit

The late Charles Hamilton, founder of Charles Hamilton Galleries, Inc., New York City, the first auction house in the US devoted exclusively to autograph material.

Autograph collecting is not limited to signatures. Collectors look for letters, manuscripts, documents and checks—anything signed or written by someone of interest. Most popular are presidents, composers, authors, scientists, black and feminist leaders and movie stars.

A doctor who is a music lover, for example, may concentrate on the correspondence of famous composers regarding their health. Many collectors strive to complete a "set," such as Pulitzer Prize winners or Mexican War generals.

The classic set of autographs to collect, the signers of the Declaration of Independence (known simply as "Signers"), also contains the most famous of rarities—the signature of Button Gwinnett, a Georgia pig farmer who perished in a duel less than a year after the signing. Genuine examples of Gwinnett's signature (he is frequently forged) have been auctioned for $150,000. A brief receipt signed by Gwinnett brought $100,000 at auction in 1979, the record price paid to date for a single signature.

Inexpensive and easy to find are signatures and signed promotional photographs of many entertainers and athletes, and signatures that have been clipped from the letters or documents they were once part of (a common practice in the 19th century). Complete letters or documents are much more desirable. A handwritten letter, manuscript or diary with historical interest is most valued of all.

WHAT AFFECTS VALUE

•**Content or context.** This extremely important factor brings history alive, thus ensuring enduring worth. A letter or journal by an unknown person describing field conditions during the Civil War is of far greater interest than a note from a famous person saying "Sorry, I can't make it on Tuesday," or "Here's the autograph you requested." Many collectors, especially youngsters, begin by writing to living noteworthies for their autographs. It is preferable to ask an original, thought-provoking question that will elicit a written reply instead of a form letter or a glossy photograph. Even a short response that reveals something of the personality of the writer will be of greater value later on.

Collectors of presidential signatures often prefer examples that date from the term of office. Ironically, it can be harder to find a signed, handwritten letter from a modern president (starting with Theodore Roosevelt) than from one of our "forefathers."

Reason: The advent of the proxy signature, the typewriter and the autopen. A signed, handwritten letter from President Ronald Reagan (during his administration or after) sells for $15,000. But signed typewritten letters from Ronald Reagan before he became president sell for $50 to $500, depending on their content.

•**Rarity.** The collector must learn what is scarce or common in his or her own field. Abraham Lincoln signed thousands of military appointments during the Civil War, but complete letters and signed photographs are rare.

Charles Dickens seems to have written letters daily throughout his long life, while Edgar Allan Poe's signature tempts the finest forgers.

•**Demand.** This has more to do with fashion than with fame. Even a figure as revered as Sir Winston Churchill could easily follow his predecessor, David Lloyd George, into relative obscurity as public attention shifts. A rare contract signed by ragtime composer Scott Joplin was sold for $5,000, outpricing a comparable piece by Beethoven.

As a general rule, villains outsell good guys. A John Wilkes Booth signature outprices Lincoln's, while Lee Harvey Oswald's is worth more than JFK's. Murderers' and Nazis' signatures are likely to remain popular.

•**Condition.** The strength and clarity of a signature, size and length of the material, condition of the paper and postal markings, among other variables, all affect the value of a piece. *Important:* Do not attempt repairs yourself. Never use cellophane tape on old papers.

•**Display.** The value of any collection can be enhanced by creative, attractive framing. Even inexpensive signatures take on new life when mounted with a portrait of the subject. Contemporary newspaper clippings, program covers or tickets, reproductions of documents and artwork can make exciting companion pieces of autograph material, as can early daguerreotypes, engravings, posters or other historical ephemera. Striking graphic design adds to the fun, and for this, a skilled professional framer is necessary. *Examples:* Irving Berlin's autograph, mounted on a background of red, white and blue stripes with his photograph and the original sheet music to *This Is the Army.* A check signed by Orville Wright, mounted next to an early photograph of his airplane. A Bela Lugosi autograph, set against a black cutout of a bat, beneath an early still from *Dracula.*

INVESTING AND THE MARKET

Unlike other collecting areas, there has been no slump in the market for autographs. Record prices continue to be set. This seems to be due to our increasing awareness of the importance of our cultural heritage, along with the desire to preserve as much as possible in this age of the telephone.

For investment purposes: Specialize in several areas at once. Perhaps interest in the American West will decline, while the astronauts hold their value—or vice versa. Select your purchases for the interest of their content or their relevance to a historical event. Don't be afraid to pay healthy prices for important material.

Private dealers and auction houses who will vouch for the authenticity of their material are the best sources for important pieces. A thorough knowledge of one's field is necessary to be able to recognize chance finds should they occur. Be careful of inscriptions in the flyleaves of old books, a favorite ground for the forger. Check the drawers in antique furniture, and don't throw out old family papers before consulting an expert.

For further reading: *Collecting Autographs and Manuscripts* by Charles Hamilton. Modoc Press.

Collectors' organization: Universal Autograph Collectors Club (UACC), Box 1205, Welaka, FL 32193. Publishes the bimonthly journal *The Pen & Quill. www.uacc.org.*

Collecting Maps

Ruth Shevin, the late map specialist at the Argosy Gallery, New York City.

Mapmaking goes back to at least 2300 BC, which is the date of the earliest known clay picture of how to get from one place to another—found in Iraq. We know that the ancient Chinese made sophisticated silk maps, Eskimos carved maps in ivory, the Incas etched them in stone and prehistoric Europeans drew them on cave walls.

Collectors revere maps for a number of reasons. Many old maps are beautiful (all early world maps are fanciful as well) and very decorative. Historians look for changing political boundaries, documents of military campaigns or journeys of early explorers. Homebodies like to trace changes in their country or city layout over the years.

• **Early maps.** Maps from the Middle Ages—now seen in museums and libraries—were more symbolic and religious than realistic. World views included imaginary places or vast expanses of terra incognita, often with remarkable creatures to match. These delusions and distortions are the delight of collectors, but their rarity makes them irreplaceable treasures.

Maps for practical purposes began to proliferate in the 15th century with the establishment of printing. Explorers needed up-to-date guides to the oceans and lands of the world. They helped to chart new areas and revise old standards. Although it is possible for a collector to find a 16th-century map, it will cost in the thousands. Prices for 17th- and 18th-century maps—most are pages from bound atlases—will vary according to scarcity and demand. Good reproductions of such maps, while handsome and interesting, are of no investment value, so collectors must be careful of their sources.

• **19th-century maps.** Fine examples of these more recent world or local maps can be bought for less than $100. Some come from atlases. Others are official maps used to define states or territories. US Geological Survey maps, published since 1879, indicate elevation, roads, swamps, railway stations and churches. Many early city maps show landmark buildings in addition to the streets. Particularly popular at the moment are maps of the American West.

• **20th-century maps.** Even early 1900s maps are of little value so far. Dealers do not yet carry them, so the interested collector must cull flea markets and garage sales.

DETERMINING VALUE

Rarity, authenticity, beauty and condition make a map valuable. Even maps that were run off on printing presses in great numbers can become quite scarce over time. The paper they are printed on is fragile, for they were never meant to endure. When a map gets out of date, for whatever reason, it faces what one expert calls "a dangerous interval of vulnerability" during which it has no value in contemporary, practical terms and yet arouses little interest in the scholar or historian. Not many maps survive that interval.

Determining the authenticity of old maps is difficult. The best protection is knowledgeable dealers who stand behind what they sell. (A good dealer will also search for specific maps for you.) Although beauty is in the eye of the beholder, condition is an obvious asset to an old map. Creases hurt a map, so potential collectibles should be stored flat.

LEARNING THE ROPES

A beginning collector must start by browsing and reading. Most major libraries have cartography sections with a variety of maps and books on mapmaking that can help you zero in on the types that most interest you. A good general book on the subject is *The Mapmakers* by John Noble Wilford (Knopf). Many libraries also have dealers' catalogs that can give you a sense of what is available and the going prices.

Great Britain is the world center for map collecting. In the US, a few major dealers specialize in maps, and interest here is picking up rapidly. A directory of antique-map dealers is available on-line at *www.cosmo graphy.com*.

Collecting Firearms

R.L. Wilson, historical consultant for Colt Firearms Division.

Firearms are among the oldest and most distinguished collectibles. (Henry VIII was a keen collector, as were George Washington and Thomas Jefferson.) And because firearms have been made since the 14th century, the field is vast. No individual can be expert in every aspect.

Most US collectors concentrate on Americana. For the past 40 years, they have tended to specialize—even down to a single gun series. A collector might choose the Colt Single Action Army group, the guns you see in Western movies, for example. They were called "the peacemakers" and "the thumb busters." The US Army adopted this series as a standard sidearm in 1873.

What are the criteria for collecting? Aesthetics play a great role. The finer guns are exquisite. The engraving can be compared with the work of Fabergé. Historical relevance is important, and so is condition. But quality and maker count more. Even excellent condition cannot make an ugly gun desirable. Add the allure of fine mechanics and also romance. Can you imagine Buffalo Bill without his six-shooters and Winchester rifles?

Who were the leading makers? The big four are Colt, founded in 1836; Remington, founded in 1816; Winchester, founded in 1866 but really dating from 1852, the same year as Smith & Wesson. (The last two companies trace their origin to the same firm.)

What about guns not from those firms? Many are very desirable. Tiffany was big in the gun business until 1911. And the Kentucky rifle (in excellent condition) is a classic collectible. These date from the early 18th century and continued to be made for about 100 years. They were made in small workshops, often by wonderful craftsmen. Kentucky rifles sell for $5,000 and up. One of them, circa 1810, sold for $103,500 in November 2004.

Are pairs more valuable than singles? Yes, indeed. *Also triplets:* A rifle, a revolver and a knife made as a set, for example.

Some collectors specialize in miniatures. These tiny weapons were a test of the gunsmith's art, and they were made for fun. (You can fire the little guns, though it's not advisable.) A society of miniature collectors exists.

Modern engraved guns are also very collectible. In the past few years, they've become a $25-million-per-year business. Colt, Remington and Winchester (among others) make these specialty firearms. The craftsmanship is magnificent. Some are the equal of anything done in the past. These are not replicas, and owners do not discharge them. One reason for collecting modern firearms is assurance of authenticity. However, after 1840 most US firearms were given serial numbers. If you own a weapon made after that date, a factory may have it on record.

How do you care for a collection? Rust is the great enemy. Try a light film of oil. Put on a pair of white cotton gloves, spray oil on the palm of one glove and rub the gun with it. If you use a rag, sweat from your hand will eventually mingle with the oil.

Should fine weapons ever be fired? Never! Well, hardly ever—only if the antique arm is not of much value. Black powder, outdated in the 1890s, is still available for shooting today. It is corrosive to metal and scars wood. If you do wish to shoot antique-type guns, you should buy replicas. About $100 million is spent on them annually. Even if black powder isn't used, wear and tear on the firearm lowers its value. Excessive refinishing or polishing is also not recommended.

Do you need a license for antique guns? Generally not, if they were made before 1898, the federal cutoff. But check with local authorities.

Gun collecting is expensive. How much should you spend? A few hundred dollars at the least—you can find very good sidearms from the 19th century for that price. However, before you invest any money, spend several hundred hours studying. There are over 12,000 books on the subject, but you should begin with the basic *Flayderman's Guide to Antique American Firearms and Their Values* by Norm Flayderman (Krause Publications).

Collecting Old Trains

Alan Spitz, owner of The Red Caboose, New York City, and Bruce Manson, editor emeritus of *Train Collectors Quarterly.*

Many children remember the thrill of receiving their first model train set. Some people like to recapture the excitement as adults, by collecting model trains as either a hobby or an investment or both. Certain old model railroad cars and sets have become so expensive that counterfeiters are making forgeries. Although most collectors are train buffs who belong to model railroad societies throughout the country and often attend "train swaps," the collectors also include some famous names. The late newscaster Tom Snyder was a collector, as are Graham Claytor, former secretary of the Navy, and Mick Jagger, who occasionally buys Lionel.

Finding bargains is difficult. Don't expect to discover valuable old train sets at garage sales or country auctions. Train collecting is a well-explored area. A price guide to all old Lionel cars is available, *Greenberg's Guide to Lionel Trains: Pocket Price Guide 1901-2006,* by Bruce C. Greenberg (Kalmbach Publishing).

Top collectors' items in the US consist primarily of pre-World War II standard-gauge Lionel cars. (Standard gauge refers to the 2⅛-inch width popular before the war.) Lionel stopped making the large-size sets in 1939 because the metals were needed for the war. Afterward, all trains were smaller. Other makes collected include American Flyer and Ives. (Both of these firms eventually merged with Lionel, so there is not such a large pool of items.) Marx was the manufacturer of smaller, cheaper trains that were sold through Woolworth's and other variety stores. They were eventually bought by Quaker Oats, and the line was discontinued. Marklin, a German manufacturer that began making trains in 1856, is the most prominent European producer.

The highest price on record for a model train is $110,000, paid for a Marklin brass gauge I "circus train," which was sold at auction in 2004. More expensive purchases may have been made privately, but there is no record of them.

The age of trains does not necessarily determine their price. Scarcity and demand are more important factors. *Example:* Any Lionel train with a Disney motif is likely to be very valuable. Lionel made an entire Disney circus train. In this case, the market is not limited to train buffs. Circus memorabilia collectors and Disney collectors also covet these trains.

Another rarity: Lionel made a special train for girls in the 1950s. The locomotive was pink and the caboose was blue. It sold poorly, and Lionel did not produce very many. Some dealers painted the trains black to get rid of them.

Those that are still pink and blue are therefore very valuable.

Reproductions: There are counterfeiters who may also call themselves restorers because they rebuild damaged trains. These trains are not very valuable. Some may be as much as 75% restored, in which case they are, for all intents and purposes, counterfeit. The most valuable trains are "in the box" or in mint condition. Since many trains were made of a zinc alloy called Zamac, which frequently became contaminated with other substances and disintegrated, many cars are partially original and partially restored.

How to tell: Lettering on counterfeit and restored pieces is usually stamped instead of using the old decal lettering. *Another telltale sign:* Original Lionel trains were dipped in paint. People should look for marks and imperfections in the paint job. Today, people spray-paint the cars, so it is easy to tell the difference. Other differences are more subtle, and it takes a great amount of expertise to distinguish a reproduction from an original.

Modern pieces: Manufacturing for the collector has become an important part of Lionel's business now. *Example:* The GG1 was first put on sale in 1956 for $49.95. When Lionel remade it in the 1970s, the list price was approximately $320. Not many parents spend that much on children's toys, but an investor might be interested.

Specializing: Many serious train buffs specialize in a single item, such as Number 8 locomotives or a certain kind of boxcar. There is a broad spectrum.

Displaying trains: While many collectors like setups (tracks on which the trains run), collector's items should be kept on display shelves.

Collecting Seashells

Jerome M. Eisenberg, director, Royal-Athena Galleries, and William Gera, The Collector's Cabinet, both in New York City.

She sells seashells by the seashore—and in cities, museum shops and through the mail. You can buy your shells or you can have the pleasure of finding them yourself. You needn't worry about investment, auctions or authenticity. Shell collecting is a just-for-the-fun-of-it hobby.

Begin by collecting as many types of shells as appeal to you. This way you can learn their names and become familiar with the distinctive qualities of each type. Most collectors are eventually drawn to one or two species and narrow their scope.

Prices within every species can range from 25¢ to several thousand dollars. But it is easy to put together a very broad collection of several thousand shells for $1 to $10 apiece, with an occasional splurge into the $20 to $25 range.

MOST POPULAR SPECIES

- **Cones (Conus).** Cone-shaped shells that exhibit an astonishing variety in pattern and color. One, *Conus bengalensis,* brought the record price ($2,510) for a shell sold at auction. At the time, it was only the fourth specimen known. However, several more were found shortly thereafter. It may now sell for $400 to $750, which is a warning to would-be investors. *C. textile:* Named for its wonderful repeating pattern, which resembles a Diane von Furstenberg knit. *C. marmoreus:* The model for a well-known Rembrandt etching.

- **Cowries (Cypraea).** Very rounded shells, with lips rolled inward to reveal regularly spaced teeth. Naturally so smooth, hard and glossy that they appear to have been lacquered, they are often considered the most pleasurable shells to handle. *Cypraea aurantium:* Deep orange—a classic rarity. The famous tiger cowrie, *C. tigris,* is speckled brown and white. *C. mappa:* Striking pattern resembles an antique map.

• **Murexes.** Swirling shells favored for their pointy spines, though many are delicate and hard to store. *Murex pecten (Venus comb):* Spectacular curving spines. *M. palmarosae:* Rose-branched murex, has floriate tips. *M. erythrostomus:* Has ladylike white ruffles and a luscious pink mouth.

• **Scallops (Pectens).** Shaped like ribbed fans in surprisingly intense reds, oranges, yellows and purples.

• **Volutes (Voluta) and Olives (Oliva).** Equally popular species. Best-loved classics are the triton *(Charonia tritonis)* and the chambered *Nautilus pompilus.*

Choose live-collected specimen shells in perfect or near-perfect condition, without natural flaws or broken spines or tips. Avoid lacquered shells and ground lips (an edge that has been filed will feel blunt rather than sharp). A label should accompany each shell, with its scientific name and location information.

Dealers have a worldwide selection of shells, access to professionally collected deep-sea varieties and experience in identifying tricky species. Dealers advertise in shell-collecting periodicals, and most sell through the mail or on-line.

Clubs provide contacts to trade with, up-to-date information on species, travel opportunities and techniques for cleaning and storage. Check the Internet or contact the nearest natural-history museum to find a local club.

The most colorful shells are found near coral reefs in tropical waters. Many areas offer special arrangements for shell collectors, from boat trips to uncombed beaches to guided snorkeling or scuba diving. Much of Southern California and Australia's Great Barrier Reef are closed or limited for environmental reasons.

Sanibel Island, Florida, is the best-known shelling spot in the US. It is especially well geared to the collector. Contact the Chamber of Commerce for on-line information, *www.sanibel-captiva.org.* Costa Rica offers both Atlantic and Pacific varieties, with pre-Colombian ruins as an added attraction. The Philippine Islands are known for their many local dealers and good values, as well as for fine beachcombing, snorkeling and diving. Cabo San Lucas, Mexico, on the southern tip of the Baja Peninsula, and the Portuguese Cape Verde Islands off Senegal offer great shelling.

Of course, you need never go near an ocean to start a fine collection of seashells. If camping in the mountains or dining in Paris is more to your taste, just bring along your copy of *Hawaiian Shell News.*

Great Web Sites For Train Lovers

The Web site Trains.com, *www.trains.com,* offers links to sites for train lines in the US and overseas plus train organizations and railroad museums. Railpace, *www.railpace.com,* is the Web site for *Railpace Newsmagazine*—which focuses on the northeastern US. Railserve, *www.railserve.com,* has links to everything from model railroading to rail passenger lines worldwide. *Railway Preservation News, www.rypn.org,* is an on-line magazine about railway history and preservation.

Nancy Dunnan, publisher, *TravelSmart,* Box 397, Dobbs Ferry, NY 10522. 800-FARE-OFF, *www.travelsmartnewsletter.com.*

Collecting Dolls

Collectors of fine art and antiques have discovered dolls in recent years. Dolls have surpassed coins in popularity and are now the world's second-largest collectible. (Stamps are number one.) The attractions are not only the investment potential of dolls but also their aesthetic appeal and cultural and historical significance.

Most collectors concentrate their attention on the "golden age of doll making" from 1840 to 1920, on modern dolls from 1920 to 1950, on artists' dolls from 1910 to the present or on such contemporary dolls as Shirley Temple and Barbie.

The doll market does not suffer from recession as do coins and stamps. *Reason:* Doll collectors are accumulators. Coin collectors don't buy multiples of the same thing, except for examples in better condition or for trading, but doll collectors do. One collector with 50 Brus (valuable French dolls) has 12 of the same size and mold number, yet each one is different because they are handmade and hand-decorated.

Dolls have "presence"—recognizable characteristics and humanlike personalities. As collectors grow more sophisticated, they become more aware of these distinctive characteristics and can recognize dolls they have seen before.

GOOD BUYS IN OLD DOLLS

• **German character dolls made between 1900 and 1917** by Simon & Halbig or Kammer and Reinhardt.

• **All dolls made by American artists.** The Georgene Averill baby has doubled in value in recent years.

• **Kamkins dolls made by Louise Kampus.** Buy any that is reasonably clean.

• **Kewpie dolls** (not figurines) are all good investments.

NEW DOLLS WITH POTENTIAL

• **Original creations** of members of the National Institute of American Doll Artists.

• **German dolls by Kathe Kruse.**

• **Steiff stuffed animals** (keep the tag and pin that come with them).

ADVICE TO NEW COLLECTORS

• **Educate yourself.** People who are in a hurry make mistakes. Become familiar with dolls. There are several excellent museums. *Leading ones:* The Strong Museum in Rochester, New York, and the doll collections at the Smithsonian Institution in Washington, DC.

A better way to learn about dolls: Visit stores and antique shows where you can touch and handle the dolls.

Guidelines: Many dolls are easy to identify because most manufacturers of bisque dolls numbered them. (Bisque is a form of china

introduced in 1870 and used extensively until 1940.) But get a guarantee when you buy. Anyone who purchases a valuable object should be able to sell it back at any time. However, a guarantee is only as good as the dealer.

Dangerous buy: A damaged doll. You can't go wrong paying $500 for a damaged Bru doll worth $8,000—the parts alone are worth that. But don't pay $5,000. A damaged doll will always be a damaged doll.

Many people have dolls stored in attics, basements or closets. One woman heard a description of a rare doll on television. She realized she had just thrown away a similar doll. She retrieved it from the trash can and sold it for $16,500, an American record for a doll sold at auction.

George and Florence Theriault, Dollmasters, Annapolis, MD.

• **The 1959 Barbie doll that cost $3 may now bring up to $10,000**—but only if it's in mint condition, with original striped bathing suit and gold earrings. And if you've lost the box, you've lost half the value. *Rule of thumb:* The more common the doll, the better shape it must be in.

Collecting Comic Books

Michael Feuerstein, owner of M&M Comics, Nyack, NY.

Comic books sell for as little as 15¢ each and for as much as $75,000. It is estimated that there are over 100,000 collectors in the US.

When did comic books begin? There were comics in the 1920s, but they were reprints of newspaper strips. The first "super-hero" comic book, *Action Comics No. 1*, was issued in 1938. The early books had 64 pages, with five or six stories featuring different heroes, and sold for 10¢.

What are the criteria for establishing worth? The first issue of anything is going to be the most valuable. The spread in price between the first issue and the second one is always great. A first issue may be worth $100 and the next only $35.

Condition is extremely important. Ten years or so ago, you'd have paid twice as much for a comic book in mint condition (practically untouched) as for a well-read one. Now if a mint book is worth $1,000, the same in well-read condition brings only $200. Mint condition is particularly important for books from the 1960s.

Scarcity also determines value. Books from the 1930s and early 1940s are rarest. Fewer were issued, and wartime paper drives prompted patriots to donate their collections.

How do you define scarce? Scarce is under a hundred known copies. Under 25 is considered rare.

How is a collection built? Usually collectors will try to get every issue of a particular title. It isn't easy, but the chase is part of the fun.

How do you decide on a title? Often nostalgia. Older collectors want comics from the Golden Age, from 1938 to 1956. After that, it's the Silver Age, starting with *The Flash*, a new character, in 1956.

How should one buy contemporary comics with an eye to future collectibility? Look for a good story line, superior artwork and popularity with fans. But what ultimately will determine a comic book's collectibility is its physical condition, scarcity and desirability. These factors are impossible to predict. So collect comics that you like, and keep them in great condition.

What about cartoon animals and other categories? The Walt Disney characters, especially those drawn by Carl Barks, appeal to specialists. A few of the scarcest sell for thousands of dollars. *Big Little Books*, small, thick and hardbound, may range from $3 to $350. *Classic Comics* appeal to some older collectors. There's a trap in the *Classics*. They were used in schools and reprinted every six months from the original plates. The dates were not changed. Many people who think they have originals actually have valueless reprints.

How should comic books be stored? Upright, in a box of some sort. Never store them flat—the spines of the bottom books will become crushed. Also, you must handle them all to get at the lower ones. For valuable books, use inert plastic mylar cases.

Collecting Baseball Memorabilia

The late Louis Ehrenkrantz, president of Ehrenkrantz King Nussbaum Inc., New York City.

When most people think of collecting baseball memorabilia, they think first of cards. Cards with players' pictures have been issued since the early days of the game, first by tobacco companies and more recently by chewing gum companies.

It's too late, from the viewpoint of investment, to collect cards. Recent cards will probably not be a collectible in the future.

Look back to the last era when people identified with baseball as the true national game, the late 1950s. Collect game programs, autographs and *Baseball Registers* from that time. For example, if you were a Dodger fan as a kid, you might like to have a number of old Ebbets Field programs.

An item that has gone up in value every year for the past 25 years is a publication called *The Baseball Register*. It's put out by *The Sporting News* and is a record of everything that happens in the major and minor leagues in a single year, including the results of every game played. Like any good investable book, it's rare. There's only one first edition. (The 1981 *Baseball Register* is bound to be worth something—a game-by-game record of the craziest season that ever was, and a whole history of the seven-week strike.)

Autographs from 1930 to 1950 are desirable, especially from good players who didn't give them out too freely. That said, Jackie Robinson and Babe Ruth both gave away a lot of autographs, but their signatures can still fetch thousands of dollars.

Buy autographs only from authorized dealers so you'll know they're not fakes. But you can buy game programs, *Baseball Register*s and old baseball magazines from anyone. They're self-explanatory.

Cards are not the repositories of our memories anymore. What is? Television. For earlier fans, radio. Old audiotapes by announcers Red Barber and Mel Allen would be worth a fortune.

Collecting Antique Playing Cards

Antique playing cards are amusing, interesting, inexpensive and, possibly, undervalued (worthwhile ones may start as low as $50). But collect them only for sheer pleasure...a buyer might be hard to find.

Popular Sheet Music

David A. Jasen, vice president of the New York Sheet Music Society and author of *Rags and Ragtime*. Dover Publishing.

The mass production of sheet music of popular songs is a uniquely American commercial phenomenon that started in the early 19th century and began to wane only with the popularity of the phonograph record at the time of World War I.

Few titles or editions of the 2 million songs published in the past 150 years are of investment value. An early printing of *The Star-Spangled Banner* (1814) is worth about $35,000. Civil War songs are valuable because of their scarcity.

And original printings of Scott Joplin rags can bring as much as $2,000 at auction because jazz buffs have recognized the musical importance of 1890s ragtime tunes.

But most sheet music is collected for fun— by era, by subject, by composer or by the artwork on the cover. At one time the staple of home entertainment, sheet music was popular music that could be easily played on the piano and sung in groups, and it reflected the popular culture of its time.

Early-19th-century songs told stories of romantic love, tragic death, home and mother. Minstrel-show music was catchy and sentimental (like Stephen Foster's songs).

After the Civil War, songs were topical: *The Price of Meat Is Going Up Again* is just one example. Typical lyrics discussed the stock market, sports fads, inventions and social scandals. Sheet music became big business in the 1890s with *After the Ball* by Charles K. Harris, a best-seller that earned up to $25,000 a week.

The sheet-music industry was concentrated on New York City's 28th Street, dubbed Tin Pan Alley. Songs at the turn of the 20th century could sell a million copies or more, and these songs are the ones that are now most frequently collected.

Where to find sheet music: There are few dealers who specialize in it. Flea markets, thrift shops and even garage sales are good places to start. Be prepared to plow through dusty cartons. Ephemera shops usually carry some sheet music.

Offers are made in the newsletter of a national collectors' group. For more information, contact the New York Sheet Music Society at *www.nysms.org*.

Collecting Stock Certificates

Edward Mendlowitz, CPA, partner, WithumSmith+ Brown, 1 Spring St., New Brunswick, NJ 08901. *www. withum.com.*

One type of certificate is "live" certificates, representing ownership in a company. These have wonderful engraved designs, called vignettes. (The New York and American Stock Exchanges require that all certificates carry a genuine engraving and a design with tones. This makes counterfeiting more difficult.) There are advantages to owning a single share in a company. You are on the company's mailing list and receive all financial information, including the annual report, which can be a collectible.

For someone starting a current collection, the following is recommended: One share each of Playboy Enterprises, Wells Fargo, Lion Country Safari, International Bank Note and Toro. These beautifully engraved stock certificates represent the New York and American Stock Exchanges as well as over-the-counter trading. Also, International Bank Note's annual report is quite a work of art.

Another collection you might want to start is of used, canceled stock certificates. Certain certificates are part of American financial history. For example, you might find an American Express certificate that was issued in the 1860s and signed by Mr. Wells and Mr. Fargo, then president and secretary of the company, respectively. (Many people's major interest in certificates is the autograph.) Millard Fillmore, John D. Rockefeller and Jay Gould once signed stock certificates.

One valuable certificate: Standard Oil, signed by John D. Rockefeller, which is worth approximately $4,500.

Old certificates needn't cost a lot of money. You can buy 20 to 30 for around $50. Some collectors specialize. They'll collect only oil companies or railroads, or only New York railroads, but you don't have to specialize. You should collect certificates for the fun of it as well as for the investment value.

Collecting Celebrity Memorabilia

Pamela Brown Sherer, Sotheby's York Avenue Galleries, and Julie Collier, Christie's, both in New York City.

Do you remember Rosebud, the sled that meant so much to Orson Welles' character in the 1941 film *Citizen Kane?* Rosebud means a lot to well-heeled movie buffs, too—the sled fetched $60,500 (including the buyer's fee) at Sotheby's New York.

Collectors have long cherished relics of the famous, and a market in celebrities' artifacts is well established. It was sparked by auction houses that found a willing market for television and movie memorabilia.

EXAMPLES

Christie's East, New York, sold a pair of ruby slippers worn by Judy Garland in the 1939 film *The Wizard of Oz* for $165,000 in June 1988—and sold again in May 2000 for $666,000. Few movies are strong enough in themselves to draw high prices for props or clothing. What could vie with the ruby slippers? Probably only a very recognizable item, such as a gown (in good condition) worn by Vivien Leigh in *Gone With the Wind.*

A Walter Plunkett costume sketch of Vivian Leigh in *Gone With the Wind* sold for $35,000 in April 2005. At a Profiles in History auction, Margaret Hamilton's Wicked Witch of the West hat from *The Wizard of Oz* sold for $54,625.

Who collects: A mixed group—friends of the famous as well as fans. Investment is always a consideration, but it takes a backseat to nostalgia.

The future: Hollywood memorabilia and collectibles will continue to be a hot market.

Collecting Butterflies

Michael Berman, The Butterfly Company, NY.

Papillon, *Schmetterling, farfalla, mariposa*—in almost any language, the word for butterfly trips across the tongue like the flitting, colorful creature it describes. Butterflies were held in lofty esteem by the ancient Greeks and by the early Christians, who saw in them symbols of the human soul.

The common names for some favorite butterflies range from painted ladies, jezebels, and jungle queens to emperors, rajas and Apollos. Ironically, these short-lived symbols of transient beauty, once captured and carefully mounted in a collector's cabinet, retain their shimmering colors for centuries, like frozen rainbows.

The lover of lepidoptera (butterflies and moths) must also be a lover of labels. There are 140,000 species of lepidoptera, about

20,000 of them butterflies. If the prospect of learning 20,000 scientific names is enough to give you butterflies in your stomach, you will understand why most collectors specialize in one family of butterflies (lepidopterists generally agree on 15 basic families) or further limit themselves to one genus or even to one species. Within any family, the price for a single specimen can range from less than $1 to several hundred dollars. Only extreme rarities sell for $1,000 or above. Females may be more costly than males because they are often left in the field to breed.

MAJOR COLLECTING CATEGORIES

•**Morphiodae** (Morphos) are the most popular (and flashy) butterflies to collect. The Morpho genus is conveniently small, about 80 species. What attracts collectors is their intense color—a dazzling, metallic blue that reflects light like satin, changing from deepest navy to royal blue to icy turquoise as one moves past them. Other morphos, patterned like watered silk, appear to be translucent white until, as one moves closer, they show subtle, opalescent colors, such as mother-of-pearl.

Examples: The large Peruvian morpho didius, an iridescent blue outlined in black, is extremely popular. A female, in softer pastels, sells for more.

•**Papilionidae is a family of about 700 species.** Particularly sought are the various swallowtails and the *Ornithoptera,* or "birdwings," including the largest-known butterfly, *Ornithoptera alexandrae.*

•**Nymphalidae contains several thousand species.** *Some of the subgroups most favored by collectors: Vanessidi* (vanessas), *Charaxes* (rajas), *Argrias* (a rare and expensive genus) and many others equally showy and varied, with colors, patterns and wing shapes resembling laces, leaves, Rorschach tests, stars in a night sky, maps, Dubuffet designs in magic marker, animals' eyes and Florentine bargello. An extreme rarity is the African species *Charaxes fournierae,* which may be worth more than $1,000 per pair.

Butterfly values are determined almost exclusively by their rarity. In this era of ecological abuse and species protection, this can be a tricky business, however, and it doesn't always work the way one might expect. For example, the *O. rothschildi,* for years worth $150 per pair, may only sell for $20.

Reason: A few years ago, it was bred in captivity and then released by the government, so it has become fairly common. Of course, the inverse is more often true. Fire or construction can wipe out a habitat in a short time. (The top price ever paid for a single butterfly was $2,436 brought by an *O. allotei* from the Solomon Islands at the 1966 sale of the Rousseau Decelle collection.)

Sets of 10 or so different butterflies are available for very little from hobby shops and on-line or mail-order dealers. The new collector must learn to mount specimens in open-wing position. Mounting equipment and instructions are available from the same sources.

Butterflies are usually kept in flat cases with glass or Plexiglas dustcovers that can be stored away from the light. A small container of mothballs in the storage area prevents other insects from attacking the collection. Some species, including many morphos, have greasy bodies that can harm the delicate wings. After the butterfly is mounted, the body can then be replaced with a dab of glue.

Buy only perfect specimens. Be sure each comes with its identification and date and location of capture for your labels.

The International Butterfly Book by Paul Smart is a good source of information. It's out of print but is available in many libraries.

Appraising Your Valuables

Valuable items worth over $100 should have written appraisals every two years. Replacement values change with current-day economics.

American Society of Appraisers, New York City. *www. appraisers.org.*

Buying and Selling Collectibles on the Internet

Malcolm Katt, a Millwood, NY–based antique dealer, also owner of Millwood Gallery, which specializes in militaria.

The volume of business on the Internet's collectible auction markets has exploded, and for very good reasons. *Collectible trading on the Internet gives you…*

• **Secure, anonymous, cheap and effortless access** to collectors all over the world.

• **The chance to view pictures of the thousands of items that are for sale** in your special field of collecting—no matter how quirky it is.

• **The opportunity to make a few extra dollars**—or a few thousand.

• **A fascinating entrance to the information superhighway**—if you're not there yet.

• **The possibility of developing friendships** through E-mail exchanges with other collectors.

If you're a serious collector, you may have to go on-line. (It has been estimated that within the next five years, 50% of all collectible sales will take place over the Internet.)

Fact: The world's largest Internet trading service, eBay, was started in September 1995 as a way to help its founder's girlfriend sell her collection of Pez dispensers. (The company went public in September 1998. The founder became a billionaire in only three years!)

BUYING AND SELLING ON-LINE

Popular Internet auction sites are…

• *www.ebay.com*

• *www.amazon.com*

eBay is the biggest by far. Millions of people have used eBay to buy and sell merchandise in thousands of categories—from Beanie Babies to books. Every day there are millions of "page views," that is, viewings by potential buyers checking out wares.

What does it cost? On-line auction companies typically charge an "insertion fee" for listing an item and a commission based on the selling price, plus other fees.

There are several software programs available to help sellers manage on-line selling. Check at a computer- or office-supplies store.

To be a buyer on-line: Register at one of the auction sites. Fill out an on-line application that includes your name and mailing address. You should never have to reveal your Social Security or credit card number. *Details…*

• **You are described on-line** only by a code name you have selected.

• **The highest bidder is notified by E-mail** and contacted by the seller to arrange payment.

• **Payment is made directly to the seller** by check or money order.

SAFEGUARDS

The buyer has the ability to verify the seller's honesty by checking a "feedback" rating. So, you can avoid dealing with individuals whose ratings raise questions.

Sellers receive positive, negative or neutral comments from previous buyers.

On eBay, if a seller has too many negative comments, he or she can be terminated from using the service.

Keep in mind that reputable sellers give the buyer the opportunity to return the item if unsatisfied for a valid reason.

On-line escrow services for expensive items are also available.

There is no fee to view, bid and buy on-line. The seller pays the insertion fee and commission. Buyers typically pay for postage and insurance.

BUYER BEWARE

Just like written descriptions, a photo seen on a small screen does not always reveal damage or problems that the seller has overlooked.

Remember that buying on-line is no different from buying in person. Often the seller is ignorant of what he is offering or is purposely deceitful. As always, *buyer beware.*

Portrait Photography Secrets

People are the most popular subject for photography. People pictures are our most treasured keepsakes. There are ways to turn snapshots of family and friends into memorable portraits.

TECHNIQUES

•**Get close.** Too much landscape overwhelms the subject.

•**Keep the head high in the frame as you compose the shot.** Particularly from a distance, centering the head leaves too much blank background and cuts off the body arbitrarily.

•**Avoid straight rows of heads in group shots.** It's better to have some subjects stand and others sit in a two-level setting.

•**Pose subjects in natural situations,** doing what they like to do—petting the cat, playing the piano and the like.

•**Simplify backgrounds.** Clutter is distracting. *Trick:* Use a large aperture (small f-stop number) to throw the background out of focus and highlight the subject.

•**Beware of harsh shadows.** The human eye accommodates greater contrast of light to dark than does a photographic system. Either shadows or highlights will be lost in the picture, usually the shadowed area.

FOR OUTDOOR PORTRAITS

•**Avoid the midday sun.** This light produces harsh shadows and makes people squint. Hazy sun, often found in the morning, is good. Cloudy days give a lovely, soft effect.

•**Use fill light to cut shadows.** A flash can be used outdoors, but it is hard to compute correctly. *Best fill-light method:* Ask someone to hold a large white card or white cloth near the subject to bounce the natural light into the shadowed area.

•**Use backlight.** When the sun is behind the subject (but out of the picture), the face receives a soft light. With a simple camera, the cloudy setting is correct. If your camera has a light meter, take a reading close to the subject or, from a distance, increase the exposure one or two stops from what the meter indicates.

•**Beware of dappled shade.** The effect created in the photograph will be disturbing.

FOR INDOOR PORTRAITS

•**Use window light.** A bright window out of direct sun is a good choice. However, if there is high contrast between the window light and the rest of the room, use filter-light techniques to diminish the shadow.

•**Use a flash.** A unit with a tilting head allows you to light the subject by bouncing the flash off the ceiling, creating a wonderful diffuse top lighting. (This won't work with high, dark or colored ceilings.)

•**Mix direct light and bounce flash.** An easy way to put twinkle in the eyes and lighten shadows when using bounce light is to add a little direct light. With the flash head pointed up, a small white card attached to the back of the flash will send light straight onto the subject.

•**Keep a group an even distance from the flash.** Otherwise the people in the back row will be dim, while those in front may even be overexposed.

Hot-Weather Hazards To Camera Gear

Humidity is the summer photographer's nemesis. *Here are some defensive maneuvers…*

•**Don't open new film until you are ready to load and shoot.** (It is packed in low-humidity conditions in sealed packets.)

•**Have exposed film processed as soon as possible.** Don't leave it in the camera for long periods—it may stick.

- **Use slow advance and rewind to avoid moisture static.**

- **Keep equipment dry with towels or warm (not hot) air from a hair dryer.** Store film and gear with silica gel to absorb excess moisture. (Cans of silica gel have an indicator that turns pink when the gel is damp. They can be reused after drying in the oven until the indicator is blue.)

Modern Photography.

How to Take Much Better Pictures Outdoors

Susan McCartney, an international freelance photographer who conducts workshops at the School of Visual Arts in New York City. She is the author of *How to Shoot Great Travel Photos* and *Nature and Wildlife Photography: A Practical Guide to How to Shoot and Sell.* Allworth Press.

You don't need magical skills to be a nature photographer. Even without sophisticated equipment, you can come away with wonderful pictures of landscapes, plants or animals. *What you need to take great photos...*

PATIENCE

Nature photography is a contemplative activity. You cannot rush nature. You cannot make animals or a landscape do anything. For the best pictures, you must settle in and observe.

Types of questions to ask yourself: How is a flower affected by the play of sun and clouds or by passing breezes? How does a landscape change with the light from dawn to dusk?

Example: When I recently visited the Grand Canyon, I watched one person after another march up to the rim, stand with their backs to this marvel, have a friend take their picture and then move on. I sat on the rim of the canyon for the entire day, photographing at intervals and watching the play of light and clouds. I took the best pictures at sunset.

LOVE OF THE SUBJECT

The first challenge is to become familiar with your subject through repeated exposure. African safaris and trips to Yellowstone National Park are wonderful opportunities, but you can also profit from less-expensive trips.

Where to start: A local park, zoo or woodland. For plants and flowers, a nearby botanical garden will do fine. Choose the subjects that most fascinate you, and "stalk" them like a hunter.

Caution: Avoid the woods during deer-hunting season. My own career was almost ended by a potshot in the Allegheny National Forest.

AWARENESS OF LIGHT

The best time to take photographs of nature is during the early or late day hours, when the low sun enhances the subject. *How to take advantage of the low-angle light...*

- **To produce dramatic pictures from even the simplest camera**—position yourself so that the light is coming diagonally over your shoulder onto the subject.

- **When shooting a landscape or the texture of animal fur,** bird feathers, fish scales or flower petals—position yourself so that the light is hitting the subject from the side. Side lighting reveals texture.

- **When you want to create a halo of light around animals or flowers or show the translucency of insects and plants**—position yourself so that the low sun is behind the subject. Be careful that the sun doesn't hit the camera lens directly.

Useful for all nature photos: Soft light that is diffused by thin clouds or light mist any time of day.

To be avoided: "Top" light from overhead summer sun, which casts shadows that record almost black on film. As a rule, I will not shoot if my shadow is shorter than I am.

EQUIPMENT

You can take good nature pictures with virtually any camera as long as you know its limitations. In fact, I have seen very good shots from point-and-shoot and even disposable cameras.

For serious nature photographers, a good tripod is an important accessory. It is absolutely essential for use in low light with long expo-sures or for close-ups made with slow small apertures and shutter speeds for maximum depth of field. It will minimize blur caused by camera shake when shooting with telephotos and zoom lenses.

OVERCOME YOUR LIMITATIONS

It is valuable to look at nature photographs taken by the masters to see the elements that make up great pictures.

Even more important is experience. Like driving a car or playing the piano, nature photography requires specific physical skills and quick reflexes. As you practice and experiment, those skills will become second nature—allowing you to seize those magical photographic moments.

Most common error: Viewing a subject—such as a landscape—through your eyes, and then barely glancing through your view-finder before taking the picture. The camera's translation from three to two dimensions will change the view.

Exercise: Train yourself to look at every-thing through your viewfinder, closing your other eye if necessary.

Personalized Photo Albums

Upload photos to Tabblo.com, and create photo pages, or "tabblos," using simple tools to move, edit or add text to your photos. There are dozens of style combinations. Once you have created a page you like, you can share it with friends, print out a high-resolution copy or order a print or book.

Great Photos the Easy Way

Load *Photobot* on your computer, and the program automatically searches for and enhances photos. It fixes red eye, brightens dark photos, corrects color and more. Any change can be undone if you don't like it. Cost: $29.95. *Information:* Tribeca Labs, 646-383-4608, *www.photobot.com.*

Guide to Digital Camcorders

David Kender, editor-in-chief of Camcorderinfo.com, a camcorder review and information Web site based in Somerville, MA. *www.camcorderinfo.com.*

Digital video "camcorders" offer bet-ter picture quality than older analog technology...the option of storing and editing movies on a computer...and the abil-ity to send video clips over the Internet. Very good digital camcorders now are available for $400 and great ones for $1,100 and up.

The benefits and drawbacks of each format and a comparison of features...

•**MiniDV camcorders record picture and sound data digitally on small cassette tapes.** *Best for:* Consumers who want the low-est price without sacrificing much video qual-ity. *Benefits:* Picture quality is strong. Tapes are relatively inexpensive. *Drawbacks:* The tapes start to wear out after two or three re-record-ings. The typical playback method—attaching the camcorder to a TV by a cable—is less convenient than some other formats. Fast-fowarding and rewinding are relatively slow processes.

Best pick: *Canon Elura 100.* An easy-to-use camcorder at an attractive price. It captures vivid colors...works better than most camcord-ers in low light...and unlike many camcorders in this price range, it has an audio input jack to attach a microphone. $400.*

•**MiniDVD camcorders record to small disks.** *Best for:* Those who want to be able to play back their videos with ease. *Benefits:* The disks can be played on most DVD players and computer DVD disk drives, making them convenient. Fast-forwarding on a disk is much

*Prices are manufacturers' suggested retail.

quicker than on a tape because you jump to chosen scenes. *Drawbacks:* Disks are relatively expensive. Picture quality is slightly inferior to that of miniDV camcorders of a similar price. Disks are hard to edit in some popular editing programs because of the variety of file formats the camcorders use.

Best pick: *Sony Handycam DCR DVD405.* Captures sharp images with wonderful colors, and it's a snap to learn how to use it. $870.

• **Hard disk drive (HDD) or flash memory camcorders record to fixed internal hard disk drives** or removable memory cards or sticks. To play back the HDD recordings, you can connect the camcorder to a TV or computer. For a flash memory camcorder, you put the memory card or stick in a computer or a TV that accepts it. *Best for:* Those who want an extremely easy-to-use camcorder with no worries about changing tapes or disks. *Benefits:* HDD and flash memory are a snap to use. *Drawbacks:* Image quality is weaker than with miniDVs. If a hard disk drive fails, you may not be able to retrieve your recordings.

Memory sticks and memory cards are more expensive than miniDV tapes and miniDVDs, but they can be reused thousands of times.

Capacity: HDD camcorders typically record for more than seven hours or, in some models, more than 24 hours. Flash memory camcorder capacity varies, depending on the recording mode and storage capacity of the memory card or stick.

Best pick: *Sony DCR-SR40 30-Gigabyte (GB) HDD Handycam.* One of the easiest-to-use camcorders. Image quality is respectable, though you could do better if you are willing to spend hundreds more. $600.

HD MODELS

If you have a high-definition television and are willing to spend $800 to several thousand dollars on a camcorder, select a high-definition model in one of the three formats above. Your images will be substantially sharper, with up to four times the resolution.

Best pick: *Canon HV20 MiniDV.* Sharpness and color performance rival those of $4,000 models. $1,100.

10

Retirement Planning

Everything You Need to Know About Social Security

Social Security was enacted in 1935 to—in the words of Franklin D. Roosevelt—"give some measure of protection to the average citizen and to his family against the loss of a job and against poverty-ridden old age." Today, the Social Security system is broader than Roosevelt could have imagined.

WHO CAN COLLECT?

• **You don't have to work a day in your life to collect benefits.** Nearly 30% of all Social Security benefits are paid to spouses and dependents of workers.

• **A spouse can collect benefits based on a worker's benefits.** The spouse must be at least age 62—or any age as long as the spouse is caring for the worker's child who is under age 16 or disabled. Benefits may be as much as 50% of the worker's benefits.

Note: Spouses who worked can collect on their own earnings. Benefits will be figured both ways (worker's benefits or spousal benefits) and the *larger* benefit will be paid.

If appropriate, you can collect benefits based on the earnings of your second spouse (or your own earnings if they result in a larger benefit).

• **If you have a child, benefits may also be payable to him/her.** Who qualifies? A minor child who is under 18...or 19 and a full-time high school student...or 18 or over with a total disability that began before 22. His benefit is 50% of yours.

Two or more children? *Each* of them could receive a 50% benefit. However, there is an overall limit on family payments ranging from

Andy Landis, author of *Social Security: The Inside Story*. Course Technology. Mr. Landis was formerly a field representative with the Social Security Administration and served as an economic security representative for AARP.

1.5 to two times a worker's full retirement benefits.

•**You don't have to be married to collect spousal benefits.** You may qualify as a "former spouse" and collect benefits on the basis of your ex-spouse's earnings. You qualify if you are at least age 62, the marriage lasted at least 10 years and you are currently single.

Benefits can begin if the ex-spouse worker is at least age 62 (whether or not collecting benefits). You'll get 37.5% of the worker's benefits if you are age 62, or 50% of benefits if you are age 65 or older.

•**Widow(er)s and surviving divorced spouses may also collect benefits** if they are at least age 60. The percentage of benefits, which can be as great as 100% of what the worker would have collected, depends on the age of the widow(er)/surviving ex-spouse and whether that person is caring for the worker's child who is under age 16 or disabled. Survivor benefits can also be paid to certain children and dependent parents.

•**You can collect benefits if you're disabled.** Nearly 10% of Social Security benefits are paid to disabled workers who are under the retirement age.

Eligibility requirements for collecting this benefit are strict. The worker must have done substantial work before the disability (worked a certain number of quarters). *And the disability must be…*

•A medically determinable physical or medical impairment…

•Which is expected to result in death or last for at least 12 months…

•And prevents a person from engaging in any substantial gainful activity.

Note: Medical standards for disability are stringent, and it generally takes about four months or longer before benefits will begin.

WHEN TO COLLECT

•**Collecting at the earliest retirement age may result in greater lifetime benefits.** Starting to collect benefits at age 62 instead of waiting until the normal retirement age results in a reduction of monthly benefits (for example, 80% of the benefit you would receive if your full retirement age is 65).

But—because you're collecting benefits for three extra years, you may wind up with more benefits in the long run. Only if you collect benefits for more than 15 years will you fall behind those waiting till age 65.

People in poor health or with poor family medical histories may want to consider taking benefits as early as possible. Those who have reason to believe they'll live past age 77 may want to wait until 65 to start collecting Social Security benefits.

•**Delaying the start of benefits can mean a bonus.** For each year past your full retirement age that you wait toa start collecting, you get a bonus. *The amount of the bonus depends on the year you were born, as follows…*

Year of birth	Bonus each year
1931–1932	5%
1933–1934	5.5%
1935–1936	6%
1937–1938	6.5%
1939–1940	7%
1941–1942	7.5%
1943 and later	8%

Example: You reached the normal retirement age in 2006 (you were born in 1941). If you wait until you're 70 to start benefits, you'll receive a total bonus of 37.5% (5 x 7.5%). So, if benefits at 65 years, two months, would have been $1,300 a month, you'd start your benefits at age 70 at $1,788 a month.

Note: No additional bonus accrues after 70. However, your benefits will be increased if you earn more in the years after age 70 than in your earlier working years.

WORKING AND BENEFITS

•**You don't have to stop working to collect retirement benefits.** You can continue to earn money and collect full benefits as long as you don't go over the earnings limit for the year.

Those people who attain their full retirement age can earn any amount without a reduction in benefits.

•**Retiring before you start benefits may not reduce them.** Benefits are based on your "average lifetime earnings" which are your 35 best years of work after 1950.

Remember that only the maximum "wage base"—the amount of wages that the law sets each year as the maximum amount from which Social Security taxes will be taken—is taken into account.

Example: In 2008, you earned $100,000. The wage base is $102,000. Earnings are treated as $102,000.

If you have less than 35 years of work, the shortfall will be treated as "zero years" yet averaged in.

Example: You worked 25 years and earned the maximum amount in each of these years. In figuring your benefits, you'll have 25 years at the maximum, plus 10 "zero years."

Bottom line: If you've already earned the maximum in at least 35 years, retiring or working part-time before starting benefits won't much affect the amount you can collect.

If you haven't earned the maximum or worked long enough, then continuing to work may help to increase your benefits.

How to Pay the Lowest Tax on IRA/Qualified Retirement Plan Distributions

Louis Wald, vice president, tax advisory department, Merrill Lynch, New York City.

The primary rule to remember is that any money taken out of the account is taxable income. Therefore, it's best to take out only as much as you have to. Any large distribution can put you in a high tax bracket, and you lose the benefit of tax-free earnings whenever money is taken out of the fund.

Qualified retirement plan distributions get a better tax break for those born before 1936. Benefits may even qualify for 10-year averaging. This method results in large savings.

Distributions after a taxpayer's death are also taxable, and there may be an estate tax.

WHEN IS DISTRIBUTION REQUIRED?

You must begin to distribute your account by April 1 of the year after the year you reach age 70½ unless, with a qualified plan, you keep working. (Contributions to an IRA must stop—except for rollovers and Roth IRAs—even if you're still working, but you can still contribute to a spousal account for a nonworking spouse who is under age 70½. Contributions to a qualified plan may be made at any age.)

You can withdraw the entire account in a lump sum, but you don't have to. You must, however, withdraw enough each year to distribute the entire account during your life expectancy at that time (or the combined life expectancies of you and your spouse if your spouse is more than 10 years your junior) as shown on IRS life-expectancy tables. *How to figure the minimum withdrawal...*

Look up your life expectancy in the IRS table to find your applicable divisor. Let's suppose you're 71 years old (your spouse isn't 10 years your junior), so your applicable divisor is 26.5. Divide the account balance on December 31 of the prior year by the applicable divisor. Then repeat the process each succeeding year, using the applicable divisor shown for that year.

If you withdraw less than you should, there's a 50% penalty on the difference. *Example:* You withdraw only $2,000 in a year when the minimum required is $8,000. You can be penalized $3,000 (50% of the $6,000 difference).

You do, however, get a tax break. The minimum requirement is based on the account's value as of December 31 of the year prior to the distribution, but you don't have to take it out until December 31 of the distribution. The account's earnings for the year are tax free and remain in the account.

Example: The account balance on December 31, 2007, is $100,000, invested at 8%. In a particular year, you're required to withdraw ⅒. By December 31, 2008, the account will have grown to $108,000, but you have to take out only $10,000.

Tax-Time Relief

If your Social Security benefits are subject to income tax, you can voluntarily elect to have the tax withheld from them by the Social Security Administration (SSA). That way, you won't have to come up with cash to pay the tax on April 15. Call the IRS at 800-829-3676 and ask for Form W-4V, or go to the IRS Web site at *www.irs.gov.* Fill out the form and file it with your local SSA office.

Edward Mendlowitz, CPA, partner, WithumSmith+ Brown, CPAs, 1 Spring St., New Brunswick, NJ 08901. *www.withum.com.*

Retirement Savvy

Plan your retirement date carefully if you have a traditional *defined benefit* pension plan. Formulas usually base the amount you get on length of service, wages and interest rate at the time you retire. Some plans credit you only for the last *completed* year of work, so you may want to work a *full* final year.

For lump-sum options: Know the date your company changes the interest rate used to figure the benefit. Base your exit date on whether the rate is likely to go higher or lower. The lump-sum amount is higher if rates go down...lower if rates go up.

Note: These factors do not arise in defined-contribution plans, which are more typical.

Avery E. Neumark, Esq., CPA, director of employee benefits and executive compensation, Rosen Seymour Shapss Martin & Co., a New York–based accounting firm.

Two-Month Interest-Free Loan from Your Own IRA

Generally, IRA borrowings are prohibited. But it is possible to move funds from one IRA to another, as long as the transfer is completed in a 60-day period.

Benefit: You have use of the funds for 59 days.

Warning: The exact amount you take out of the first IRA must be placed in the second one within the 60 days. And you can use this device only once a year.

IRA Procrastination Doesn't Pay

Make your full contribution on the first business day in January of the tax year rather than on the April 15 deadline of the following year. (For example, a working couple contributing just $6,000 in January of the tax year will have $75,000 more after 30 years—at an 8% return—than they would if they waited the extra 15½ months.)

Gold Coins and IRAs

Uncle Sam's newly minted gold coins are the only collectibles that can be included in an individual retirement account.

Cost: The spot price of gold plus about a 55% premium (less-than-one-ounce coins carry a higher charge).

Big IRA Tax Trap

Steven G. Lockwood, tax attorney and president, Lockwood Pension Services, Inc., New York City, writing in *Ed Slott's IRA Advisor,* 100 Merrick Rd., Suite 200E, Rockville Centre, NY 11570.

An IRA may be taxed at rates as high as 80% after the IRA owner's death if proper planning is not done—so it can be a big mistake to try to provide for heirs by leaving them IRA savings.

Tax traps: IRAs are fully subject to federal estate tax at rates as high as 45% in 2008. Funds withdrawn from IRAs by heirs also will be subject to federal income tax at rates as high as 35%. And state and local estate and income taxes may apply—creating a combined tax rate as high as 80%.

Planning mistakes: Not worrying about estate taxes on an IRA because...

• **You know you can leave it to a spouse estate tax free.** *Snag:* The IRA will be taxed when your spouse dies.

• **Only a total of assets up to $2 million in 2008 ($3.5 million in 2009) can be left free of estate tax.** *Snag:* "Hidden" assets, such as life insurance proceeds, retirement accounts and appreciation in a home, may push you over the limit.

Best: Meet with an estate-planning expert to plan how to minimize the tax bill. *Ideas...*

• **Consume IRAs, or leave IRAs to charity for an estate tax deduction,** and instead bequeath to heirs capital gains assets they can take income tax free with stepped-up basis.

• **Set up an estate-tax-free life insurance trust** with single life insurance or second-to-die life insurance to pay estate taxes that will be due on IRA savings at death.

Ensure IRA Heirs Get Their Share

If you want your IRA to pass to the heirs of a beneficiary who dies before you, make sure your IRA beneficiary forms clearly state this. (Most don't.)

Problem: Say you name two or more of your children as beneficiaries of your IRA and one dies before you. That child's family may receive nothing from the IRA. All the funds will go to your surviving children.

What to do: File a special beneficiary form with your IRA trustee to give the heirs of a deceased beneficiary a share of the IRA.

Seymour Goldberg, Esq., CPA, Goldberg & Goldberg, PC, 100 Jericho Quadrangle, Jericho, NY 11753.

The Deferred Commercial Annuity Trick

Irving L. Blackman, CPA, retired founding partner, Blackman Kallick Bartelstein, LLP, 10 S. Riverside Plaza, Chicago 60606. *www.taxsecretsofthewealthy.com.*

Few people have heard of the deferred commercial annuity (DCA), which is a completely legal personal tax shelter that can contribute greatly to an individual's retirement wealth.

How it works: An individual pays one or more premiums to an insurance company in exchange for the right to receive annuity payments beginning at some future date. The insurance company then invests the premium proceeds and credits the earnings to the investor's account.

TAX BENEFITS

• **Earnings accumulate in the account tax free until they are distributed.** They can thus be reinvested later to produce more tax-free earnings.

• **When the annuity is paid, a portion of each payment is tax free.** That's because a portion of each payment represents a return of the original premiums. Tax is due only on the earnings of the premiums that are paid out.

• **If the annuity is paid after the recipient retires,** the portion of the annual payment that is taxable will probably be taxed at lower rates.

A DCA can be set up in addition to an IRA, and there is no limit to the amount of money you can put into it. DCA contributions are not deductible the way IRA contributions are, but a DCA is still such a good deal tax-wise that the government does not want you to begin collecting payments from one too soon. So withdrawals from a DCA taken before age 59½ are subject to a 10% penalty.

Early-Withdrawals-from-IRA-Accounts Loophole

The 10% penalty tax on pre-age 59½ withdrawals from IRAs does not apply if the money is taken out in the form of an annuity —that is, in a series of payments over one's life expectancy or the joint life expectancies of a couple. This loophole can be put to good use if there is a fair amount of money in your IRA, say $100,000, from the rollover of a company pension plan.

Edward Mendlowitz, CPA, partner, WithumSmith+ Brown, CPAs, 1 Spring St., New Brunswick, NJ 08901. *www.withum.com.*

War Widows' Benefits

The *Veterans Benefits Act of 2003* stipulates that the spouses of deceased veterans who lost VA survivor benefits when they remarried may be eligible for Dependency and Indemnity Compensation (DIC) benefits if they are no longer married.

Important: Benefits are not restored automatically—you must reapply and give proof of the termination of a subsequent marriage. The amount you receive is dependent upon the veteran's date of death.

For further information: Call the Department of Veterans Affairs, 800-827-1000.

Ken McKinnon, public relations spokesperson, Bureau of Public Affairs, 2201 C St. NW, Washington, DC 20520.

Social Security Card Secret

Few people know it, but the first three digits of a Social Security number are a code for the state in which the card was issued. This code, which can be used to confirm a place of birth or an employment history, is not public knowledge. However, many private detectives have the key to the code and will crack the Social Security number for a fee.

The late Milo Speriglio, director and chief of Nick Harris Detectives, Inc.

Five Kinds of Pay That Are Exempt from Social Security Taxes

One type of pay is wages paid that are to a child under 18, when the parent's business is a proprietorship. Wages paid by a corporation are subject to tax. *The others...*

• **Loans taken out from the company by an employee or shareholder.** But be sure the loan is fully documented so that there is no doubt about its legitimacy. If the IRS concludes that the loan will not be paid back, tax will be imposed. The loan must carry an interest rate equal to 110% of the applicable federal rate at the time of the loan. The IRS will announce this rate monthly.

• **Health insurance payments made into an employee accident,** health or medical reimbursement plan.

• **Educational benefits that add to an employee's on-the-job skills.**

• **Moving-expense reimbursements when a move is job related,** the new job location is at least 50 miles farther from the worker's former home than the old job, and the worker stays at the new job site for at least 39 weeks during the next year.

Consultants Don't Always Have to Pay Social Security Taxes

A retired executive continued to work for his company as a consultant and a member of the board of directors. The IRS said he had to pay Social Security taxes on the fees the company paid him. *Tax Court decision:* For the executive. He was not self-employed in the trade or business of being a consultant and board member. *Key facts:* The executive had agreed not to work for any other company after retirement. He did no work for any other company. His duties as a director took up about six hours of his time each year.

Fred W. Steffens, TC Memo 1981-637.

Bigger Social Security Income for Wife Who Never Worked

M aking your wife a partner in your business could boost her ultimate Social Security retirement benefits. As a partner, the wife now has self-employment income. When she reaches retirement, her benefits will be based on that income. This could far exceed the 50% of her husband's retirement benefits that she would get if she had no earnings of her own on which to compute her Social Security entitlement.

John J. Tuozzolo, associated with the firm Collins, Hannafin, Garamella, Jaber & Tuozzolo, PC, 148 Deer Hill Ave., Danbury, CT 06810.

Protect Your Social Security Rights

Barbara Weltman, an attorney in Millwood, NY. *www.barbaraweltman.com.* She is author of several books, including *The Complete Idiot's Guide to Starting a Home-Based Business,* 2nd edition. Macmillan.

C heck the amount of annual earnings recorded under your name and number in the Social Security Administration's files every three years. It's harder to correct mistakes after this.

Why? You may have thrown out your own earnings records once the three-year limitation period on IRS audits has expired.

How to check your records: Review the statement sent to you three months before your birthday. If you don't receive a statement, request Form SSA-7004, *Request for Social Security Statement.* (Get Form SSA-7004 by calling 800-772-1213. Or download the form from its Web site at *www.socialsecurity.gov.*)

If you find a mistake: Suppose the statement says you earned $5,000 in 2006 when, in fact, you earned $50,000—call the number on the statement (800-772-1213). If the problem cannot be corrected over the telephone, you may be instructed to write to the Social Security Administration.

• **Ask SSA to update your statement immediately.**

• **Ask them to send you a new statement** so you can confirm that the correction has been made.

Social Security Secret

C ollecting Social Security early can pay off. Even though benefits are reduced, you won't lose out—at least not for a long time. *Example:* If full benefits are $750 per month for retiring at age 65, you can get reduced benefits of $600 a month by retiring at age 62. You'd have to collect full benefits for 12 years to make up the $21,600 you'd receive during the three years of early payments.

Changing Times.

Social Security Secrets For Those Under 65

Dan Wilcox, formerly a disability program specialist, Social Security Administration, Disability Programs Branch, New York.

It's your right as a working person to apply for disability insurance from the Social Security Administration if at any point you're unable to work because of a mental or physical disability. Before applying, you should know how the system works, who is eligible and what kind of medical criteria a decision is based on. When dealing with any government agency, the more you know before you walk in, the better are your chances of walking out with what you want.

There are two disability programs under Social Security. One is the needs-based program, Supplemental Security Income Program. SSI is basically a nationalization of welfare benefits for the unemployable. The other, which applies to working people, is the basic insurance program that you pay into as the FICA tax—old age and survivors disability insurance (OASDI).

Although the disability criteria for acceptance are the same under both programs, you don't have to prove financial need for OASDI. You're eligible if you've worked and paid into the system for 20 quarters out of the last 40 (five years out of the last 10) and have the necessary years of work credit, depending upon your age. If your last day in the system was 10 years or more ago, you're not eligible for disability benefits now, though you may eventually be eligible for retirement benefits.

Benefits are based on what you've paid into the system.

The system works as follows...

• **The first step.** File an application with your local Social Security office. You'll be interviewed by a claims representative, who will ask you some basic questions about your disability. *For example:* What is the nature of it? When did you stop working? How does it interfere with your daily activities and ability to work? Which doctors and hospitals have treated you?

You'll be asked to sign medical releases so Social Security can obtain information from your medical sources. The interviewer will also note any evidence of your disability that he observed.

• **This material is sent to a trained disability examiner at a state agency,** who will contact your medical sources.

• **If the medical information you have submitted isn't sufficient,** the agency will send you to a consulting specialist, at the government's expense, and this information will become part of your file.

• **If you've met the medical disability requirements** (which are extremely stringent), you'll be granted benefits. But you can still be found disabled even if you don't meet the medical requirements. Age, past work experience and education are also taken into account. Anyone over 50 is put in a special category because his vocational outlook is less favorable. A 55-year-old construction worker with minimal education who suffers from mild heart disease might be eligible—he can't do his past work and probably wouldn't be able to find another job. Another construction worker of the same age and disability, but with more education and skill, might be expected to find light or sedentary work. The approach is individualized throughout the process.

• **The final eligibility decision is made and signed by the disability examiner,** together with a physician who works for the state (not the consulting physician).

• **If benefits are denied,** you can either appeal the decision or reapply.

Social Security's definition of medical disability: The inability to do any substantial, gainful activity by reason of any medically determinable physical or mental impairment that can be expected to result in death, or that has lasted or can be expected to last, for a continuous period of not less than 12 months. To meet the definition, you must have a severe impairment that makes you unable to do your previous work or any other gainful work that exists in the national economy. *How to prove it...*

• **It's crucial that your doctor submit very precise medical information,** including all test results—the same kind of information a doctor would use in coming up with a diagnosis and treatment plan. Social Security won't accept your doctor's conclusions. It wants the medical evidence that led to the conclusion.

• **Social Security has a long list of impairments under which your disability should fall.** The listing, broken down into 13 body systems, covers about 99% of the disabilities that people apply for. This listing outlines exactly what tests must be met for eligibility. *Examples:* An amputee is eligible only if he has lost both feet, both hands or one hand and one foot. Angina pectoris victims must show certain results on a treadmill test and/or a number of other listed tests. *Helpful:* You and your doctor should take a look at the listings before you apply. If your doctor answers in sufficient detail, you might avoid a visit to the agency's consulting physician.

FILING AN APPEAL

When benefits are denied, a notice is sent. A brief paragraph explains the reason in general terms. At that point you can go back to the Social Security office and file for a reconsideration, which is simply a review of your case.

If the reconsideration is denied, you can take your case to an administrative law judge within Social Security's Office of Hearings and Appeals. You don't need a lawyer for this hearing, but many people do have one. At the hearing you present your case, review the evidence in your file, add other relevant evidence and personally impress the judge. The reversal rate at this level is fairly high (40% to 60%).

If denied at this hearing, you can go to the Appeals Council and then up through the courts. The chances of reversal improve at each level. Most people just go up to the administrative law judge level. If they're turned down there, they file a new claim and start all over. Often delay works in a claimant's favor, since disabilities may worsen over time.

• **Look into state disability programs.** If your disability is temporary, you might be covered by your state. State programs bridge the gap for people who have been disabled for less than a year. *Be aware:* Many state disability programs and private insurance companies require that you apply for Social Security first before you can collect from them.

• **File soon.** Don't wait until you've been disabled for a year. There's some retroactivity (up to 12 months), but the sooner you file, the better.

• **Call the Social Security office before going in.** You can save yourself a lot of trouble. Find out first what you should bring with you and which are the best days and times to come in.

• **Ask at your local Social Security office for the Listing of Impairments,** or look them up in the library. Request the Code of Federal Regulations—see 20 CFR 404 and 20 CFR 416.

When You Retire as a Consultant

A longtime executive of a company plans to retire but also plans to continue working for the company as a consultant. As a consultant, he'll be paid an hourly rate. The amount of consulting work to be done isn't fixed. *IRS ruling:* The retired executive will be considered to have separated from service with the company in spite of the fact that he'll continue to do consulting work. Thus the payout from his company's retirement plan will qualify as a lump-sum distribution and get favorable tax treatment.

IRS Letter Ruling 8635067.

Financing a Retirement Home

Maureen Tsu, CFP, San Juan Capistrano, CA, quoted in *Where to Retire*, 5851 San Felipe St., Suite 500, Houston 77057.

When buying a retirement home, a key decision you will have to make is whether to purchase it with cash or finance it with a mortgage.

Many people prefer the security of buying with cash and then not owing any debt on their home.

Drawback: Using so much cash may leave you cash poor and limit the lifestyle you can afford in retirement.

Contrast: Buying a home with a mortgage can leave you with more spendable cash. The debt on the home can be paid off or refinanced upon your death.

ISSUES IF YOU DECIDE TO FINANCE WITH A MORTGAGE...

• **Can you obtain tax benefits from deducting mortgage interest?** Do you have enough total deductions to itemize deductions? Are you in a high enough tax bracket to make it worthwhile?

• **Can you invest the cash saved by buying with a mortgage** to earn a higher after-tax rate of return than you will pay on the mortgage?

• **Are you willing to have your estate deal with the debt on your home by selling it,** or by having heirs refinance it at your death?

ISSUES IF YOU BUY WITH CASH...

• **Will you have a way of tapping your equity in the home** to raise cash in an emergency?

• **After spending cash on the home,** will you have enough money to enjoy a comfortable retirement lifestyle?

• **Will your estate eventually have to sell the home for cash**—so that you might as well take the cash while you are alive by financing the home?

Best: Consider these issues before you retire, while you are still working. You will have more options and a stronger credit standing to make any arrangement you finally choose.

Get Back the Tax Paid on Excess Social Security Benefits

If you paid tax on Social Security benefits that you received, then were told you had to repay some of the benefits because you had too much income during the year, is there any way you can get back the tax you paid?

Answer: Yes. File an amended tax return, Form 1040X, for the year in which you paid the tax. On it, report your accurate income total for the year—excluding the benefits you had to repay. You'll get your refund.

Retire in Alaska

Alaska is a tax haven for retirees who don't mind the cold. There's no state income tax or sales tax. Residents also share profits of the state's oil industry, receiving annual disbursements ($2,069 in 2008). Residents age 65 and over receive generous exemptions from property taxes and are exempt from car registration fees. Most cities, including Anchorage and Juneau, have no local sales tax.

R. Alan Fox, editor, *Where to Retire*, 5851 San Felipe St., Suite 500, Houston 77057.

All About "Top-Heavy" Retirement Plans

A "top-heavy" retirement plan, whether maintained by a corporation, a partnership, or a sole proprietorship, does not qualify for beneficial tax treatment unless certain conditions are met.

Meaning of top-heavy: More than 60% of the plan's benefits go to key employees. *These are:* Officers of the company, over-5% owners, over-1% owners earning more than $150,000 and employees with the 10 largest ownership interests in the company.

To qualify a top-heavy plan for tax purposes, the employer must...

• **Vest* benefits faster.** Either 100% vesting after three years of service or six-year graded vesting (with even faster vesting for employer matching contributions).

• **Provide minimum benefits for non-key employees.** In determining these minimum benefits, Social Security can't be taken into account. *For a pension plan:* The benefit must be at least 2% of pay for each year of service (but not more than 20% of average annual compensation). *For a profit-sharing plan:* 3% of the pay.

*A benefit is "vested" when the employee's right to that benefit can't be forfeited.

How Safe Is Your Pension?

The late James E. Conway, president of The Ayco Corporation, Albany, NY.

B e proactive with your retirement plans. *Here's how to check on the safety of your retirement income...*

For employees of public companies: Basic information is included in the firm's annual report. Usually the size of a firm's unfunded pension liability and the size of its past service liability are disclosed in footnotes. More detailed information is available in the financial section of the firm's 10K report, filed with the Securities and Exchange Commission.

For employees of private companies: Everyone who is in a qualified plan (one approved by the IRS under the Code) has the right to obtain information about his or her pension from the trustees of the plan. They may be either internal or external trustees. The average person may not be able to decipher the information. If you can't, then take it to a pension expert, actuary, lawyer or accountant for an analysis. Whether you are examining pension information of public or of private firms, you are seeking the same sort of basic information.

The size of a company's liability for retirement payouts is not as important as the assumptions about funding these liabilities. Like a mortgage, these obligations don't exist 100% in the present. Concern yourself with how the company expects to fund its liabilities.

TYPES OF LIABILITIES

• **Unfunded pension liabilities.** The amount a firm expects to need over the next 20 to 30 years to supply vested workers with promised pension benefits. These figures are derived from various actuarial assumptions.

• **Past service liabilities.** Created when a company raises its pension compensation. For instance, a company may have been planning to provide 40% of compensation as a pension. One year it may raise that to 45% and treat it retroactively.

TROUBLE SIGNS

• **A poor record on investing.** Compare the market value of the assets in the pension with their book value. If book value is more than market value, the trustees have not been investing wisely. *Point:* If the fund had to sell those assets today, there would be a loss. I would also get a bit nervous if the fund is still holding some obscure bonds or other fixed-income obligations issued at low rates years ago.

• **Funding assumptions are overstated.** Actuaries have myriad estimates on how long it takes to fund pension plans and what rate of return a company will get.

WHAT TO LOOK AT

•**Time frame.** This should not be too long. If the firm is funding over 40 years, I would want to know why and how, since 10 to 20 years is more customary. *Reason:* We don't have a crystal ball, and the investment world will be different in as little as 10 years from now. Assumptions made on 40 years may not hold up at all.

•**Rate of return.** If a company assumes a conservative 6% to 7% or less right now, you can be comfortable. If the assumed rate is 10% or more, I would want to know how it plans to meet that expectation for the entire fund over the long run.

•**Salary and wage scales.** The company should be assuming an increase in compensation over years. Most plans have such provisions. It must start funding now for future salary increases.

•**Assumptions about the employee turnover rate.** These should be consistent with the historically documented turnover of the company. If a firm has a very low turnover rate and assumes a 4% turnover, the company will be underfunded at some time. Estimates should be conservative.

To assess your own status in a corporate pension plan, see what benefits you are eligible for. Many people have the illusion that they are eligible for a maximum pension after only a few years. In truth, companies couldn't afford to fully include people who have such short service. They may offer some token pension for such service. But most people are not fully covered until they have worked for the firm for 10 or even 20 years, and then they might be covered only to the extent of their accrued pension to date, not the full pension expected at normal retirement. With so much job-hopping in the past two decades, an individual's pension-fund status may be much less than imagined.

Employees of troubled or even bankrupt companies need not panic. Trustees of the plan have an obligation to the vested employees. The assets of the plan are segregated, and no creditor can reach them. In fact, as a creditor the corporate pension plan can grab some corporate assets under certain circumstances. And if there has been gross mismanagement of pension funds, stockholders of a closely held company can be held personally liable.

The Mistakes in Retirement Can Be Avoided

Alexandra Armstrong, CFP, chairman, Armstrong, Fleming & Moore, Inc., financial advisers, 1850 M St. Suite 250, Washington, DC 20036. She is coauthor of *On Your Own: A Widow's Passage to Emotional and Financial Well-Being.* Kaplan Professional Co.

When it comes to retirement planning, what are the mistakes people make most often? The most common one is waiting too long to plan for retirement. Sometimes, a couple in their early 60s comes in and wants to know how things will look when they retire at age 65. All I can do is look at their financial assets and their current spending...and speculate what their situation will be when they retire. It certainly doesn't leave much time to accumulate assets.

•**What puts blinders on such people? A company pension plan?**

A feeling they have a house and enough to live on? No. Usually it's fear that they do not have enough...so they refuse to look at the facts.

•**When people wait that long to start their retirement planning, how can you help?**

First, cut back on current spending and save more—fast. Most people don't budget because they hate counting every penny. If you're going to crash-save for retirement, you simply have to do it.

•**Aside from saving more, what else can late-starters do?**

Change where they plan to live when they retire. Moving to a less expensive part of the country is one of the best ways to get by on less in retirement.

Caution: Make your move for sound reasons…not merely because it's somewhere you spent a few pleasant vacation weeks. If you don't know anybody who lives in that community before you move, that could be a big mistake. Too often what happens is that retired people sell their homes…buy in the new place…discover they don't like it…but can't afford to move back home.

•What's the smart way to make such a retirement move?

Test out a community. Rent out your current home for a year…and rent where you think you might like to move.

Caution: Don't make your move based on where your children live. There's the risk that a relationship with children that's great long-distance may not be so great when you live close to one another.

•What other big retirement mistake is being made?

Taking money out of an IRA too soon. Many people start taking money out at age 59½ because that's the first time they can withdraw from an IRA without facing a 10% penalty.

Unless your IRA is your major source of retirement income, you don't have to start withdrawing from retirement accounts until the year after you turn 70½. The longer you compound that money without paying current taxes on it, the better off you will be. During those 12 years, you could double your money.

•What about planning to live on Social Security and a company pension?

Don't count too much on either Social Security or your pension. More and more of Social Security will be taxed and may not be indexed to inflation—or it may be discontinued. And most company pensions are fixed. The monthly pension check may be worth only half as much in real dollars within 10 years after retirement. Think seriously about saving some of that pension income during your early retirement years because you may need that money later on.

•What's the most common mistake you see in investing retirement money?

Too many people invest entirely, or primarily, in fixed-income securities once they retire. That was fine when people retired at 65 and died at 70. Now they retire at 60 or earlier and live to 90-plus.

People used to figure their expenses would go down when they retired. But the reality for people who have to live on retirement income for 10, 20 or 30 years is that their expenses will go up.

Therefore, you want to invest to produce a rising stream of income during retirement. Think of total return…with your capital and your income stream continuing to build while you're retired.

•What about long-term-care insurance, to pay for a nursing home, as part of retirement planning?

A catastrophic illness requiring a nursing home stay can quickly deplete retirement savings unless you have insurance to cover your costs.

If you have over $1 million in assets, you can probably use this if you need long-term care at home or in a nursing home. If your assets are $100,000 or less, you'll probably qualify for Medicaid to handle those expenses.

People in their early 50s can generally find good long-term-care insurance for about $900 a year that will pay $100 a day plus up to 5% a year inflation adjustment…for 20 years. These policies are much improved over those first offered years ago. Premiums are deductible within limits.

Deduct Stock Losses Without Selling Your Shares

Examine your portfolio for stocks and securities that have gone down in value. Their sale will produce losses that can be used to offset capital gains and other taxable income. *Problem:* You may not want to sell the securities. What should you do? *Use one of the following strategies that allow you to lock in losses while substantially retaining your current investment position…*

1. Double up by purchasing a matching amount of the same securities you already own. Hold the new lot for 31 days, then sell the old lot. You get your tax losses on the sale of the old lot, yet emerge with the same investment you started with. Your tax losses may far outweigh the cost of carrying a double position for 31 days.

2. Sell and buy back the same securities, but be sure to wait 31 days before making the repurchase. Again, you get your losses while retaining your position. *Caution:* If you don't wait the full 31 days before making the repurchase, the loss won't be recognized.

3. Repurchase similar securities immediately after you sell the old ones. You don't have to wait 31 days to secure your losses. What is considered similar? (1) Stock of a different company in the same business. (2) Bonds of the same company with a slightly different maturity date and coupon rate.

Good News for Home-Owners

An IRS rule lets more taxpayers escape capital gains when selling homes they have lived in for less than two of the prior five years.

Taxpayers will be able to prorate excludable capital gains—$250,000 ($500,000 jointly)—if the two-year test isn't met for reasons that now include death of a household member… divorce or separation…job loss resulting in unemployment benefits…multiple births from the same pregnancy.

Those who sold homes without claiming a partial exclusion can file an amended return. Consult your tax adviser for more information.

Laurence I. Foster, CPA, PFS, consultant and former partner in the accounting and advisory firm of Eisner LLP, New York City.

Moving? Consider Capital Gains Rules

Not only do many US states have different income tax rates, they also have different rules for taxing capital gains. *For example, if you move to…*

•**A high-tax state like New York,** where capital gains are taxed at ordinary income rates, you may want to take a capital gain before the move.

•**A low-tax state like Florida,** which has no income tax, you may want to defer taking a gain until after you move.

Opportune timing of a large gain around a move may save you thousands of dollars—and may even pay for the move.

For more information, visit the "Retirement Living Information Center" at *www.retirement living.com.*

Barbara Weltman, an attorney in Millwood, NY. www.barbaraweltman.com. She is author of several books, including The Complete Idiot's Guide to Starting a Home-Based Business, 3rd edition. Alpha.

11

Crime Prevention

Financial Aid for the Mugging Victim

Financial compensation programs for mugging victims are available throughout the US. This compensation can cover both medical expenses and lost earnings. However, most of these programs utilize a means test that eliminates all but lower income victims from compensation. In addition, the victim's own medical unemployment insurance must be fully depleted before state compensation is granted.

•**Workers' compensation may cover you** (up to two-thirds of your gross earnings in New York State) if you were mugged on the job or on your way to or from company business during your workday. It will not cover you while traveling from home to work and back.

•**Homeowner's policies may cover financial losses suffered during a mugging.**

•**Mugging insurance is an idea whose time has come.** This insurance is available in New York. It covers property loss, medical care and mental anguish. If successful, this type of coverage may become available in other states.

•**A lawsuit may be successful if it can be proved that the mugging was the result of negligence.** *Example:* The celebrity Connie Francis was attacked in her room at a major motel chain. She won $2 million in damages by proving that the motel's security system was inadequate.

•**The Office for Victims of Crime (OVC) provides resources.** A division of the US Department of Justice in Washington, DC, this federal agency is a national clearinghouse for emerging victim issues and resources, which are available around the clock. Crime victims have access to a criminal justice library, information specialists to answer questions,

Lucy N. Friedman, PhD, former executive director, Victim Services, a domestic-violence prevention agency, New York City.

products and on-line services. Contact 800-851-3420 or go to *www.ojp.usdoj.gov/ovc/ovcres/welcome.html.*

Personal Protection For Executives

A bodyguard may be advisable if your company is becoming very controversial or getting involved in an area that is receiving a great deal of attention. Otherwise, unless an executive has gotten a personal threat, violence against executives is so rare that personal protection isn't necessary.

Oliver B. Revell, former manager of the FBI's criminal investigation operations, quoted in *Personnel Administrator.*

How to Outsmart Muggers

Ken Glickman, consumer editor, *Bottom Line/Personal,* Stamford, CT.

G etting mugged these days is a real and personal threat, not something that happens only to other people. Not only must you prepare yourself, but your entire family should be taught how to act to survive an attack. If only one member of a group that is held up responds badly, all of you might be hurt.

Fortunately, most muggings are simple robberies in which neither the criminal nor the victim is hurt. However, the possibility of violence is always there.

First rule: Cooperate. Assume that the mugger is armed. No matter how strong or fit you are, you are no match for a gun or knife. *Remember:* Your personal safety is far more important than your valuables or your pride.

SPECIFIC RECOMMENDATIONS

• **Follow the mugger's instructions to the letter.** Try not to move too quickly or too slowly—either could upset him/her.

• **Stay as calm as possible,** and encourage companions to do the same.

• **Give the mugger whatever he asks for.** Don't argue. But if something is of great sentimental value to you, give it to him, and then say, "This watch was given to me by my grandfather. It means a lot to me. But if you insist, I will give it to you."

• **When he has all he wants of your valuables,** ask him what he wants you to do while he gets away—stay where you are, lie face down, whatever. If he dismisses you, leave the scene immediately, and don't look back. Don't call the police until you are in a safe place.

Most criminals are not anxious to hurt you. If there is no violence, the police are not likely to pursue the offender. Mugging is like a job to many practitioners. If you respond in a businesslike way with a minimum of words and gestures, it will probably be over quickly and without injury.

SOME IMPORTANT DON'TS

• **Don't reach for your wallet in a back pocket without first explaining what you plan to do.** The mugger might think you are reaching for a gun.

• **Don't give him dirty looks or make judgmental remarks.**

• **Don't threaten him with hostile comments.**

• **Don't be a wise guy or a joker.** Even smiling is a dangerous idea. He may think you are laughing at him.

• **Don't try any tricks like carrying a second empty wallet to give to a mugger.** This common ruse could make the mugger angry. Some experts even recommend that you carry at least $25 with you at all times to keep from upsetting a mugger. Muggers are often as frightened and inexperienced as you are, which is why it is important not to upset them.

If you're assaulted, scream *Fire!* People are more likely to come to your aid than if you shout *Help!*

Limiting Larceny Losses

The two safest places for a wallet are in the jacket breast pocket and front pants pocket. Insert the wallet sideways so it's harder for a pickpocket to remove. Leave unnecessary credit cards at home. Don't put all your money in the same pocket. Always have some cash to give to a mugger. Don't keep your keys with your wallet or with any other form of identification.

Crime Prevention Manual for Business Owners and Managers by Margaret Kenda. AMACOM.

Pickpocket Deterrents

Pickpockets work in pairs. One is the stall and the other the pick. The stall distracts the targets by bumping into them or otherwise detaining them. The pick takes advantage of the moment of confusion to lift a wallet or a purse. Pickpockets carry newspapers in their hands to conceal the stolen goods. They stand too close to you. And they wear caps to keep people from seeing their eyes, which makes future identification more difficult.

Precautions: Men should not carry their wallets in their back pockets. Women should keep their bags zippered shut. Hold the bag under your arm. When you're walking with someone else, keep the bag between the two of you.

Andrea Forrest, president, Preventive Security Services, New York.

How to Catch a Thief

If you witness a crime in progress, report it immediately. Waiting even a minute or two makes it nearly impossible to catch the perpetrator in the act. In general, most crimes last only a few minutes.

Instant Revenge Against Obscene Phone Caller

Forget blowing a whistle into the receiver or slamming down the phone—this only serves to antagonize the pest.

Better: Electronic voice boxes, available with a preprogrammed joke script by comics such as Henny Youngman and Jackie Mason. Hold it up to the phone, press a button and have the last laugh. Available through many novelty mail-order houses.

Breaking In on a Burglary

If you walk in on a burglar by accident, just asking an innocent question may defuse potential violence. *Example:* "Oh, you're the guy who's supposed to pick up the package, aren't you?" If at this point the burglar tries to run away, it's smart to step aside.

Crime Prevention Manual for Business Owners and Managers by Margaret Kenda. AMACOM.

If an intruder is in your house when you arrive, resist the temptation to yell or otherwise provoke a confrontation. You then become an obstacle to the burglar's escape, escalating the chances that you may be hurt. *Better:* Go as quickly and quietly as possible to a neighbor's and call the police from there.

How to Protect Yourself from Crime. DIANE Publishing.

How to avoid walking into your home while a thief is there: Leave a $10 or $20 bill conspicuously placed, near the door. If the bill is gone when you walk inside, someone else may be there. Leave at once and call the police.

Venture.

Where to Hide Your Valuables

Bill Phillips, a lock expert who writes on security and safety issues. He is the author of *Home Mechanix Guide to Security: Protecting Your Home, Car & Family.* John Wiley & Sons.

To decide where to hide valuables, you need to understand exactly how burglars operate. The worst room to use is the master bedroom—the place where most people like to hide things. Thieves are likely to start right there. Burglars usually know just where to search both in the master bedroom and in other rooms—including the kitchen, where they are almost sure to check the cookie jar.

But thieves are in a hurry. They rarely spend more than 20 minutes in a house. You can take advantage of a burglar's haste to get away before he is detected by storing valuables in stealth devices. These hiding places take a thief a long time to locate.

• **The wall outlet safe* has a tiny compartment, and it requires installation.** But if you choose a color and style indistinguishable from your real outlets, there's little likelihood of its being detected. The sockets accept plugs, so you can plug in a combination

*These and other stealth devices are available at home improvement centers, some hardware stores and from a number of security catalogs.

battery/outlet clock radio with a light-up dial and actually run it on batteries. Or, you can install the outlet safe in a child's room. This is usually the last place thieves look, but also the place people don't like to hide valuables lest children get at them. They won't, though, if the fake outlet is behind a piece of furniture. And a thief probably won't, either—especially if you insert convincing child-safety clips in the sockets.

• **The flowerpot safe.** A real, plastic flowerpot with a hollowed-out hidden compartment within. The compartment is no larger than a small juice glass, but it makes a pretty safe place to keep a necklace and earrings or other valuables, as well as a few large bills.

• **Book safe.** Especially effective if you have lots of real books to hide it among. *Recommended:* Models hollowed out from actual books. You can't order these by title, but unlike a wooden fake book this model will age exactly like a real book.

• **Safe cans.** *These are facsimiles of popular canned products:* Shaving creams, cleansers, spray cans, etc. As stealth devices they are well-known to thieves. But they come in a wide variety of designs, and new ones appear all the time. *Best:* Spend extra money for a weighted model, since one that feels too light could betray its real use.

12

Points of Law

Collecting on a Judgment

After getting a judgment, many people find that they have spent much time and money and gone to a lot of trouble to get a worthless piece of paper. Estimated projections of the percentage of judgments that are collected in full are very low—according to some lawyers. Few people are willing to go to the trouble and expense of pursuing a reluctant debtor. To make winning a judgment worthwhile, it is important to know what to do and what to avoid.

BEFORE YOU SUE

The biggest problem with judgment collection is suing the wrong entity. For instance, Joe at Joe's Garage puts a defective part into your car. You sue Joe but later find out that the XYZ Corporation owns his shop. Even though Joe owns every piece of stock in XYZ, your judgment is not collectible out of the corporation's assets.

SOME GUIDELINES FOR A SUCCESSFUL SUIT

• **Don't sue a firm just because its name is on a sign outside a place of business,** or the person you assume owns the business. Always check further. *Example:* A large national fast-food chain has a number of restaurants in New York City that are not owned by the chain but by another large food corporation.

• **Check with the local county clerk's office,** business-licensing bureau, department of consumer affairs or police department to find out the actual name in which the business is registered.

• **Sue where the assets are.** The service person who did the damage, the franchise owner, the corporate owner or the parent corporation may all be liable if you can prove wrongful involvement. Sue whichever entity or entities have enough assets to pay your judgments. You can sue more than one.

Kenneth D. Litwack, attorney in private practice in Bayside, NY, and formerly the director of the Bureau of City Marshalls and former counsel for the New York City Sheriff.

246

FINDING ASSETS

Unless your judgment is against a well-established corporation, you may have to deal with a debtor who will not pay voluntarily. Hiding assets is the most popular method of avoiding payment. These assets must be uncovered in order to collect.

• **If you have ever received a check from or given a check to the debtor,** you may have a clue to the whereabouts of the debtor's bank account.

• **If you have a judgment against someone who owns a home,** check the county's home-ownership records in that area of residence.

• **If you have won a judgment against a business,** go personally to the business location to see what equipment and machinery are on the site.

• **If the judgment is large enough,** hire an agency to do an asset search. Before paying for a professional search, find out what the agency is actually going to do to uncover assets and what results you can realistically expect to achieve.

• **Watch out for fraud.** To avoid creditors, an unscrupulous company will often go out of business in one name and start up the same business the next day with a different name—on the same location and with the same equipment. To collect on your judgment you will need a lawyer to prove that the transfer of assets took place for the purposes of fraud.

HOW JUDGMENTS ARE COLLECTED

Judgments can be forcibly collected only by an enforcement officer (a local marshall, sheriff or constable) or sometimes the court clerk. You are responsible for informing the officer where to find the debtor's assets.

COLLECTION PROCEDURES

• **Property execution.** The officer seizes any property that is not exempt and sells it at auction to pay the debt.

• **Income execution.** The officer garnishes a debtor's salary. You may collect 10% to 25% of take-home pay, depending on state law. For an income execution, you must tell the officer where the debtor works.

COLLECTIBLE PROPERTY*

• *Exempt from collection:* Household and personal items, including furniture, stoves, refrigerators, stereos, TVs, sewing machines, clothing, cooking utensils, tools specifically used for a person's trade.

• *Collectible items:* These include motor vehicles, valuable jewelry, antiques, real estate, bank accounts, business equipment, stocks, bonds and the like.

• **A home lived in by the debtor is exempt up to a certain amount** (which varies from state to state). *The major problem in collecting on a home:* Many are jointly owned by married couples, which limits the creditor's right to have the house sold if the debt is only against one of the parties. But if only the debtor owns it, you can have it seized, sell it and return the exempt amount.

OUT-OF-STATE COLLECTIONS

Under the US Constitution, judgments are reciprocal from one state to another. If you have a judgment against an individual or business in one state that has assets in another, you or your lawyer can have the judgment docketed (registered) in the state in which the business is located or the state in which you wish to collect. The judgment is then viable in both places at the same time and can be collected in either. A judgment can be good for as long as 20 years, depending on the jurisdiction, and in some instances can be renewed by the court for an equal amount of time.

GETTING HELP

• **Legal help is recommended** if you are suing for an amount that exceeds the small-claims-court limit. After you win the judgment, your lawyer may arrange an asset search for you or recommend an agency to do one.

Collection agencies are not recommended. They deal mostly with large accounts and not with one-shot cases. *Also:* A collection agency can only dun a debtor in a formal, legalistic way to convince him to pay voluntarily. After assets have been uncovered, only an enforcement officer can actually collect.

*These are general guidelines. Details vary from state to state. Check with the local marshal or other enforcement officer for more information.

About Company Lawyers

If you're asked to discuss something about your job with the company attorney, you can't assume that all statements you make will be kept confidential. As a matter of fact, in most cases the lawyer would be violating his duty to his client (the company) if he even reminds you that your statements may be reported to company officials.

Exception: If the lawyer has represented you on some personal matter, such as drafting your will or handling some traffic tickets, then he or she might have a duty to explain the situation to you and point out that he is not representing you in this instance.

American Bar Association Journal.

Lawyer–Client Caution

Lawyer–client privilege may be lost if a third party sits in on the conversation. *Trap:* When a complicated financial matter is to be discussed, the lawyer may want an accountant or a banker, for example, to sit in. But since the third party cannot claim the lawyer–client privilege, confidentiality is lost. *Better way:* Have the lawyer hire a financial expert to sit in as an employee, or have the lawyer talk to the expert separately.

Nonclients Can Sue Lawyers

The owner of some shares of restricted stock needed a letter from a law firm in order to sell his shares. It took 10 months for the firm to issue the letter. Meanwhile, the price of the shares dropped significantly. But when the shareholder sued for damages

caused by the delay, the lawyers thought they had a solid defense. *Their argument:* We were the lawyers for the company whose shares were being traded, not for the shareholder. Since the shareholder was not our client, we did not owe him any duty. He has no basis for suing us.

Court: The shareholder is entitled to sue. He need not be a client to recover if he can show that the firm deliberately favored some shareholders by promptly issuing the letters that let them sell their stock while delaying the issuance of letters to others.

Singer v. Whitman & Ranson, 186 NYLJ 35, at 12.

When to Sue a Lawyer For Malpractice

The legal profession is entering its own malpractice crisis. The number of suits against attorneys being brought by clients is increasing, and the availability of malpractice insurance is decreasing.

Ground rules for considering a suit against your lawyer…

• **Where malpractice is charged in connection with litigation,** the client must show that the litigation would have ended with a result more favorable to the client if it were not for the attorney's neglect.

• **Where the attorney fell below the standards of skill and knowledge** ordinarily possessed by attorneys under similar circumstances, expert testimony is needed to support this charge. And the standard may be affected by specialization (which raises the standard of care required), custom and locality. Locality and custom can't lower the standard, but they may be used as a defense to show that the procedure or law involved is unsettled.

Some of the best ways to avoid malpractice charges…

• **See that there is good communication between lawyer and client.**

• **Avoid a situation where a lawyer is handling serious matters for personal friends.**

The tendency is to deal with friends in a more casual, informal way.

●**The attorney should give an honest opinion of each case, good or bad.** The client shouldn't press him for a guarantee as to the result.

●**All fee arrangements should be specified in writing.**

●**The attorney should spell out the scope of his responsibilities,** including appeals, and a limit should be placed on costs.

●**The agreement should provide for periodic payments** unless the matter is one involving a contingency fee and for withdrawal if there is a default in payment.

Cost of Bankruptcy

The court fee for a Chapter 7 action—a straight discharge of debt—is $299. The more complicated Chapter 13 bankruptcy is $274, and Chapter 11 is $1,039. Attorney's fees vary by case and location.

Robert H. Bressler of the law firm Bressler and Lida, New York.

Avoid Lawsuit Loans

If you are a plaintiff in a personal injury lawsuit, think twice about obtaining a presettlement cash advance. Someone who obtains one repays the advance only after receiving a favorable settlement. Most lenders will offer cash advances between $500 and $25,000.

Major drawback: Some companies charge a fixed fee, but others charge as much as 15% a month from the date the check was issued. You could end up owing fees that exceed the amount of the cash advance. While firms justify the fees because of the risks they face, in reality these companies offer money only in cases when the plaintiff almost certainly will win. If you have no other way to obtain cash and want

a presettlement advance, get offers from several firms and select the one that charges the least. Also ask your lawyer to review the terms.

Aaron Larson, attorney in Ann Arbor, MI, who specializes in civil appellate cases and litigation consulting.

Helpful Resource

Download forms (wills, powers of attorney, etc.), find a lawyer, use the extensive directory of legal information and services at *www.alllaw.com.*

Durable Powers Of Attorney

Peter J. Strauss, Esq., partner in the law firm of Epstein, Becker & Green, PC, New York City, and a fellow of the National Academy of Elder Law Attorneys. He is coauthor of *The Complete Retirement Survival Guide: Everything You Need to Know to Safeguard Your Money, Your Health, and Your Independence.* Facts on File.

Suppose an accident or illness robs you of your ability to look after your money. What will happen? Can someone do it for you?

Trap: If you don't make arrangements for money management before you run into trouble, your family will have to get a court to appoint a guardian to handle your affairs. This is time-consuming and costly. Depending on where you live, it could cost $2,000 to $5,000— and significantly more if anyone contests the guardianship.

You can prevent the need to go to court by having your lawyer put together a legal document called a "durable power of attorney," in which you name someone to handle your affairs in the event you become unable to do so.

THE BASICS

In a *durable power of attorney*, you name someone to act as your agent (also called an *attorney in fact*) to make your bank deposits, pay your bills, file your tax returns and handle your other financial matters. It's called *durable power* because it remains effective even though you become incapacitated. You can name a single agent or multiple agents. You can name your spouse and one of your children for this role.

Caution: Specify in the document whether multiple agents can act independently of one another or must act together. As a practical matter, independent action is simpler. But you can require the agents to agree with each other for certain actions, such as making gifts of your property.

Whom you should name as your agent: The person you name must be someone you have complete confidence in. While the agent holds a fiduciary position that requires he or she follow certain rules of conduct, there's no court looking over the agent's actions.

It's generally a good idea, of course, to name someone who's good at handling money. Trustworthiness, though, is more important. The agent can always seek financial advice from an accountant or other financial adviser.

Important: Name a successor agent, too—in case the first named agent is no longer able to act.

HOW TO CREATE A DURABLE POWER OF ATTORNEY

You can use a preprinted one- or two-page form available in most stationery and office-supply stores.

Caution: Be sure the form is the current version approved under your state's law.

The form contains a long list of basic powers provided under state law, including power to...

- **Sell your home.**
- **Make retirement plan benefit choices.**
- **Buy and sell stocks,** bonds and mutual fund shares.
- **Initiate lawsuits on your behalf.**

Additional powers: You may want to supplement the powers listed in a printed form with others.

Example: If your finances are complicated but you want to keep your property in your name for now, you may want to set up a trust that is unfunded. You can give your agent the power to fund the trust you've set up if you become incapacitated.

Other supplemental powers may include...

- **Creating, amending or revoking a trust.** In addition to funding a trust you've already set up, your agent may be able to create or change a trust. Not all states permit this action. States that do require the power to be clearly spelled out in the power of attorney and existing trusts may also have to include language allowing an agent to amend or revoke them.
- **Gift giving.** You can empower your agent to make gifts to himself and his family —something that can be beneficial for your estate planning.

It's generally not a good idea to make this power open-ended (there's a possibility that if he dies before you, the IRS could charge that he had a general power of appointment over all of your property and his estate would then be taxed on all of your assets).

Limit the power to the annual gift tax exclusion ($12,000 in 2008) or, if you've routinely been making gifts, to this level of gift giving. For larger gifts, exercise of the power should require consent of a third party.

After you've included the powers you want and named the agents to act on your behalf, make sure the form is properly signed (executed).

What constitutes proper execution varies from state to state.

After execution: Send a copy to each bank, brokerage firm and other financial institution you deal with asking whether they'll recognize the power of attorney in the event of your incapacity. Some states require banks to recognize them or face penalties. By getting a letter from each institution as to whether it will honor your power of attorney, you'll be able to overcome objections or take other action before it's too late.

Alternative: Have a lawyer draw up a durable power of attorney for you. Since the form is fairly simple, the cost is modest—or is part of the overall fee that you will be charged for planning. The lawyer will make sure that the form includes all special powers for your situation and that the form meets your state's law.

SPECIAL CONSIDERATIONS

Now that you know the basics, you may have special circumstances to address...

- **Property owned in more than one state.** If you have homes in New York and Florida, for example, be sure to have forms drawn up in each state. This will ensure that the forms are drafted and signed in accordance with each state's laws.

- **Psychological barrier.** If you're not comfortable with giving up control of your money, use a *springing power of attorney*. This is available in many (not all) states. The form is signed now, but comes into effect only upon the occurrence of a specified event.

Caution: Make sure the event is measured by an objective standard. For example, don't make the event just "disability," because this term is ambiguous. Instead, make the event a written certification by one or two physicians that you are unable to manage your affairs.

- **Your agent is a nonfamily member.** While a relative will act as your agent without any compensation, a nonfamily member, such as your accountant, will generally expect payment for services. Be clear about the fees. Specify your arrangement in the document itself or in a side letter.

Be sure the power of attorney authorizes the agent to write checks to himself so there's no fiduciary conflict.

- **Revoking the power.** When you recover, you can end the agent's power to act on your behalf. This is called a *revocation.* Keep track of all financial institutions and others who have copies of your power of attorney so you can notify them of your revocation.

OTHERS IN FAMILY

If you have aging parents, suggest that they sign durable powers of attorney if they haven't already done so.

Uncharitable Charities

Generous people who donate to charities like to think they're helping a philanthropic cause and people in need. Very often this is not the case. Often the only cause being helped is the charity itself—or its officers.

Problem: There are no federal guidelines specifying the amount of funds charities must channel toward their cause. As long as some of the money raised goes to the charity's cause the organization can still call itself a charity. Because of "creative" accounting practices used by charities and professional fund-raisers, it is often difficult for donors to assess how well a particular charity is performing.

Background: According to the standards developed by the Council of Better Business Bureaus, each charity must apply at least half of all income to its particular activities. Fund-raising activities are not to absorb more than 35% of the contributions received by the charity. Because of incompetence or outright fraud, many charities flout these guidelines.

To protect yourself: Before donating to a charity, contact the local Better Business Bureau or the state charities registration office in your area. In addition, it is important to obtain examples of how the charity has benefited the cause during the past years. If you're told what it plans to do...remember, big plans for the future do not count!

The Washington Spectator.

13

Computer Savvy

How to Get Started On the Internet

ot so long ago, few people had even heard of the Internet. Today, it is an integral part of the lives of millions, young and old, at home and at work. Today, many cell phones are referred to as "smart phones" because they allow you to access the Internet.

Recent estimates put the number of Internet users worldwide at approximately one billion. If you're not already among them, you're missing one of the most significant communications revolutions ever to shake the planet. The Internet literally places all the information resources of the *world* at your fingertips. *Bonus:* You can use the Internet to find and communicate with people who share your interests. Until you explore the Internet, you can't begin to comprehend the breadth or depth of all it offers. There's really

not much required. All you need is a system, a connection…and some basic curiosity.

THE BASICS

For most users, the *system* is synonymous with *computer*. Any new computer you buy today is Internet-ready. *Included in the computer package are…*

• **Modem, cable/DSL or wireless card** for connecting to the Internet.

• **E-mail program.**

Expect to pay approximately $400 or more for a new Internet-ready computer.

Minimum requirements in a basic Microsoft Windows Vista/XP system…

• **Intel Pentium processor.**

• **2 GB of memory.**

John R. Levine, coauthor of *The Internet for Dummies, Tenth Edition* (Wiley Publishing, Inc.) and an Internet Web host, consultant and lecturer.

252

- **250 MB of free hard-disk space.**
- **CD-ROM or DVD-ROM.**

MSN®TV2 service brings E-mail and Web access to your television. *Cost:* Monthly service starts at $21.95 for an unlimited number of hours to access the Web. The receiver and equipment sells for $199.95. *More information:* 866-901-4882.

NO-RISK INTRODUCTION

Most public, college and university libraries have one or more computers that are connected to the Internet. You can use these to sample how the Internet might benefit you before making any significant investment.

Before any system can connect with the Internet, it must first connect with a server, which is owned and maintained by an Internet provider.

YOUR CONNECTION

Servers are your gateway to the Internet, and charge a monthly fee for the privilege. You have a couple of choices, but the basic package you get from any Internet service provider (ISP) is about the same. *You get...*

- **User name and password** (which you make up).
- **CD-ROM** loaded with the required software tools for getting you on the Internet.
- **E-mail account.**
- **Access to the Internet.**

Most providers offer unlimited access, but some impose a surcharge after you've exceeded a set number of hours.

Average cost: Around $15 a month (depending on provider and services).

America Online (AOL) is the best known of the commercial on-line services. Others include EarthLink and the Microsoft Network (MSN).

Well organized, they offer subscribers the company's unique content, events and services along with the Internet connection.

INTERNET SERVICE PROVIDERS

If all you want is access to the Internet and none of the many other options that services such as AOL provide, an Internet service provider (ISP) may be a better bet than a commercial on-line server. As the name implies, its only service is connecting you with the Internet and providing technical help over the telephone when you have problems.

You're probably best served by a local ISP familiar with the local operating environment. Check the *Yellow Pages* under "Internet Service Providers."

Other choice: Your local cable company, which may now be an Internet provider.

The cable modem access ISPs provide is considerably faster than basic telephone connections, but costs about twice as much.

The quality of service from ISPs can vary greatly, so carefully consider these points for comparison...

- **Make sure you can connect by a local call.**
- **Find out how many hours of Internet access the monthly fees allow you.**
- **Ask if there are surcharges in addition to the monthly fee.**
- **Ask about the speed and types of connections the provider's system supports.**
- **Find out the number of users the ISP can handle at any given time.**

Put these questions to the Internet service provider's customer/tech support line. Polite, informative answers are a good sign.

Caution: Be wary of any ISP that has a tech support line that is always busy or doesn't answer calls.

Get recommendations: Your best insight into the provider will come from other users. Ask around and find out how satisfied they are with the service, and what, if any, problems they may have had.

JOINING THE REVOLUTION

Before you can connect to the Internet, you must create an account. The software supplied by your ISP reduces account creation to simply filling in the blanks with basic information about you and your system configuration.

You'll need to give a "user name," a password of your choice, the name and possibly a number address of your Internet provider and the addresses of its E-mail and news servers.

This takes only a couple of minutes to complete. If you have any trouble, the provider's tech support will guide you through the process.

Once your account is established, making the connection to the Internet is as simple as launching your Internet browser or E-mail program—just click on the provider's icon.

Once the Internet connection is established, your browser fills the screen with a "home page." You can change it later, but first time out it's usually the home page of your ISP or the supplier of your computer or browser.

Helpful: Every location, or site, you'll find on the World Wide Web has a name that is set up like *www.whatyouwant.com*. If you know a Web site address you want to visit, just type it on the address bar of your browser and hit "enter" on your keyboard.

The best way to understand the way the Web works is simple—just start exploring.

Learn to use search engines. They can locate whatever you want on-line. Try *www.yahoo.com* or, better still, *www.google.com* or *www.excite.com*.

Experiment with a few research projects. Track down information on a medical condition a relative is concerned about or a recipe that you have always wanted to try.

What Computer Salespeople Don't Tell You

There are so many variables to consider when buying a computer. *Be sure you don't get distracted and miss these important points...*

• **Burn in your computer by leaving it on for the first two weeks you own it.** If there are any electrical problems, most will surface during this period (when the machine is under warranty). *The good news:* Eighty percent of electrical circuits that survive a burn-in will last for many years to come.

The Personal Computer in Business Book by Peter A. McWilliams. Doubleday.

• **Water does not damage computer hardware** provided the equipment is cleaned and dried within 12 to 24 hours after wetting. *Most important:* The wet components should be washed down with demineralized water to remove any contaminants and then dried with a fan or ordinary hair dryer.

Ron Reeves, Factory Mutual Engineering and Research, quoted in *Computer Decisions.*

Computer Self-Defense

Relieve arm or hand fatigue or cramping while at the computer by frequently stretching wrists and forearms.

To stretch wrists: Extend one arm straight out in front of you and point fingers upward, gently pull the fingers back toward you with your other hand, hold 10 to 15 seconds.

To stretch forearms: With one arm extended, point fingers downward and gently pull fingers toward you with the other hand, hold 10 to 15 seconds. Switch arms and repeat.

It's also important to stretch your eyes. Do this by focusing on an object far away—on the other side of your office or outside.

Francesca Gern, acting executive director of the International Weightlifting Association, founded by a group of physical therapists to promote proper weight-lifting techniques.

Maintenance-Contract Caution

Computer-maintenance contracts that can be canceled after a year by either side (the general practice) may seem to provide desirable flexibility, but actually benefit the vendors. They often threaten to cancel in order to raise prices above the agreed level.

Solution: Amend the standard contract so it calls for a minimum period of guaranteed renewable maintenance of at least several years.

Best Computer for College Students

A laptop model, which can be transported easily to lectures or the library. Consider units with four- to six-gig hard drives and 64 megs of RAM.

Also important: A modem with send/receive fax capabilities for on-line and research purposes. Ask at the university computer center where student discounts on computer equipment can be found.

Adam Robinson, cofounder of The Princeton Review, a New York–based program that helps students do well on standardized tests. He is author of *What Smart Students Know: Maximum Grades, Optimum Learning, Minimum Time.* Crown Publishing.

How to Find Low-Cost Computer Assistance

John Edwards, a computer industry analyst and writer on high-tech subjects, based in Gilbert, AZ.

Although the days of free lifetime telephone support for users of new computer software are rapidly vanishing, there are still many low-cost—or no-cost—ways that computer users can get help with the increasingly complicated hardware and software products on the market today. *Here are some examples...*

- **Contact a user group.** User groups come in many shapes and sizes. Some organizations are dedicated to a specific type of computer, operating system or program. Others encompass a wide range of interests. Visiting a user group can put you in touch with people who can help you solve a wide range of computer problems.

You can locate user groups in your area by typing "computer user groups" into a search engine like Google or Yahoo! In addition, the Association of Personal Computer User Groups has a worldwide on-line directory of user groups. Go to *www.apcug.org* for more information.

- **Computer books.** You can find a troubleshooting book for virtually any computer product. Many of these books are structured in a question-and-answer format and are similar to the references used by the people who staff vendor telephone support lines.

- **Diagnostic programs.** These products allow your computer to help you pinpoint a variety of system problems. *Recommended...*

- **CheckIt Portable.** Helps Windows users resolve problems related to the installation and configuration of hardware add-ons. Users can also ask questions, such as, "What would happen if I installed this device on my system?"

TouchStone Software Corp., 978-686-6468.

- **Norton Utilities.** Offers a wide range of diagnostic routines to test such devices as mice, keyboards, speakers and system boards. The software can also check for viruses, diagnose the computer's current status and recommend necessary repairs or maintenance.

Symantec Corp., 800-441-7234.

- **On-line support.** Many computer companies offer customer support directly on the home page—users simply choose from a menu of help files. If you're experiencing a problem with a particular computer product, contact the manufacturer or software publisher and inquire whether the firm offers on-line help.

- **On-line services.** The leading commercial on-line services offer two types of support—direct links to manufacturers, and forums that cater to users of a company's products. A direct link allows users to type specific questions to a service representative, usually at no charge beyond the cost of using the on-line service. The forums are essentially virtual user groups, allowing participants to network with—and seek solutions from—experienced users.

- **The Internet.** The Internet's World Wide Web is rapidly becoming a key site for no-cost user support. Software support varies greatly between various suppliers. While some firms will supply detailed, specific replies to customer queries transmitted via the Internet, others simply offer searchable help libraries.

You can find the Internet address of just about any hardware or software company by conducting a search on either the Lycos (*www.lycos.com*) or Yahoo! (*www.yahoo.com*) Web search engine.

When a Free Computer Is Not a Good Deal

Free computer deals from Internet service providers aren't a bargain. Computers may be low-end models...service may cost more than that of other providers...and if service proves unsatisfactory, you may be stuck for the length of the contract. Other firms give away a computer if you fill out detailed personal-data forms allowing them to target you for ads. Ads are on-screen constantly, and you must use the computer at least 10 hours a week.

Bottom line: With many basic computers available for around $400, you may be best off buying your own.

Audri Lanford, PhD, coeditor, *Internet ScamBusters*, *www.scambusters.org*, an on-line newsletter about Internet fraud.

Basic Internet Terms

Before you surf the Web, it's a good idea to learn a few basic computer terms. *Here are a few you should know...*

• **Browser.** This software application allows you to move about and access information over the World Wide Web. The most popular browsers are *Microsoft Internet Explorer* and *Firefox*.

• **CD-ROM.** A form of computer media, similar to a compact disc, that contains large amounts of information, including software applications. In order for this information to be accessed, a CD-ROM disc must be played on a CD-ROM drive or a DVD drive.

• **Microprocessor.** This refers to the central processing unit, the mind of the machine. May be described in terms of speed, like 1.5

Gigahertz (GHz) as well as by a name, such as Pentium 4 or G4.

• **Modem.** A device that enables one computer to communicate with another, over phone lines or cable. An internal modem is built into your computer, while an external modem must be connected to the computer.

• **RAM.** Random Access Memory, the built-in memory a computer uses to run software and perform tasks.

• **Server.** A computer that provides some service—such as access to information—to other computers, called clients, linked to it over a network.

• **Web site.** A specific location on the Internet that contains a set of information, including text and graphics. In order to reach a Web site, you must know its Web address (*www.nameofsite.com*).

Computer Safety

Never run an unsolicited computer program or open an attachment that arrives attached to an E-mail unless you know *for sure* what it is.

Trap: It may be a "Trojan horse," a malicious program that the creator hopes you will naively run. A Trojan is different from a virus in that it does not reproduce by itself—but if you run it, it may destroy files or steal information such as passwords.

Caution: Don't even run programs E-mailed from friends without verifying what they are—a Trojan-infected computer may attach copies of the data on the computer to all E-mail it sends out without the computer owner knowing it.

Safety: Install a good antivirus program. It will defend against Trojans, too.

Tatiana Gau, chief trust officer and senior vice president, America Online, 22000 AOL Way, Dulles, VA 20166.

Have No Fear Of Viruses

Fear of Internet viruses is overblown. Established Web sites scan constantly for viruses and are usually quite safe. Any file you download from an Internet site should be scanned automatically by your computer's antivirus software. Most viruses come from E-mail attachments.

To be safe: Never open any E-mail attachment whose title ends in *.com*, *.exe* or *.doc* unless you are expecting it. Guard against infected files by scanning them with antivirus software before using them. *Favorite protective software:* The most current version of Norton AntiVirus.

Larry Schneider, owner of Accent on Computers, a consulting firm, Box 11, Cos Cob, CT 06807.

How to Isolate Junk E-Mail

Get more than one E-mail address when you go on the Internet. Have one address for family and friends, a second for business and a third you use on the Web and in open discussion groups—this one will draw a lot of junk E-mail.

Have your E-mail sorted by address. That way you'll keep your family and business mailboxes clear of junk. Most services, such as Yahoo! and Hotmail, offer free E-mail so it's easy to have multiple addresses.

Harry Newton, author of *Newton's Telecom Dictionary*. CMP Books.

Easy Learning

An easy way to learn computing is to get on the Internet at the library—many offer training and access at little or no cost. Or contact the nationwide SeniorNet organization, which offers a variety of computer training courses. 408-615-0699, *www.seniornet.org*.

Bruce W. Miller, computer trainer, Greenwich, CT.

Download Faster

Make Web downloads faster by setting your browser to download pages without pictures and animation. These enhancements—which rarely have anything to do with content—can slow downloads significantly.

Smart Computing, 131 W. Grand Dr., Lincoln, NE 68521. *www.smartcomputing.com*.

Web Browser Savvy

If your Web browser crashes—or the screen image looks strange when you try to look at one particular page—try loading the page using another browser. If that crashes, too, the page file is probably defective. If the page does not load on the other browser, make sure you are using the latest version of that browser. Older versions may not support some newer features of Web pages.

John Edwards, a computer industry analyst and writer on high-tech subjects, based in Gilbert, AZ.

Secret to Better Web Browsers

More important than which Internet browser you use—get the latest version. Most people use Microsoft's *Internet Explorer* or *Firefox*. To get the best performance from the browser you choose, visit the company's

Web site—*www.microsoft.com* or *www.fire fox.com*—every other month to see whether a new version is available.

Downloading is free—and now quite easy. For fast downloading and browsing, use a high-speed modem or cable/DSL service. Also, make sure your system meets the minimum requirements.

Bruce Judson, coauthor of *Hyperwars: 11 Essential Strategies for Survival and Profit in the Era of Online Business.* Simon & Schuster.

For Seniors, Too

Seniors who would like to learn how to use the Internet can take classes at over 240 learning centers sponsored by SeniorNet, a nonprofit organization of adults age 50 and older.

SeniorNet shows older adults how computer technologies and access can enhance their lives. The organization offers discounts on computer-related products and services. It also publishes a quarterly newsletter and a variety of instructional materials. Seniors may also participate in on-line communities to discuss hundreds of topics.

For more information: 408-615-0699 or *www.seniornet.org.*

Use E-Mail More Effectively

It is great for sending data and getting an answer. But it is not a substitute for conversation. If you feel a call would be a good idea, trust your instinct and use the phone, not your computer.

Jeff Davidson, professional speaker, Chapel Hill, NC, and author of *Breathing Space: Living & Working at a Comfortable Pace in a Sped-Up Society.* MasterMedia Publishing.

How to Set Up and Run Your Own Web Page

Bud Smith, coauthor—with Arthur Bebak, founder of Netsurfer Communications—of *Creating Web Pages for Dummies, 7th Edition.* John Wiley & Sons.

You don't have to be a high-tech wizard to design a Web page these days. A number of Web publishing services provide free space and tools to make it easy to create your own site.

In less than one hour, you can design a page that announces a recent birth...tells about your favorite pastime...posts your résumé or vacation photos...or describes your business.

GETTING STARTED

Technology needed to get started...

•**Computer** that has at least a 300-megahertz processor and 1.5 GB of RAM.

•**56 Kbs modem,** which comes with most new computers and dials your connection to the Internet. If you have to buy it separately, a modem costs under $100.

•**Internet Service Provider (ISP),** which allows you to connect to the Internet. *Cost:* Around $20 per month for unlimited service.

Examples: America Online (*www.aol.com*, 800-392-5180) and AT&T Worldnet (*www.consumer. att.com/plans/internet*, 800-967-5363).

•**Web browser.** A browser is software that allows your computer to read Web pages.

Examples: Microsoft Internet Explorer (*www.microsoft.com/windows/ie/default.asp*) and Firefox (*www.firefox.com*) are widely used browsers. Both can be downloaded free at their Web sites.

PLANNING YOUR SITE

Before creating your Web page, visit other Web sites for design ideas. *Steps to take...*

•**Visit a search engine's Web site,** such as AltaVista (*www.altavista.com*) or Yahoo! (*www.yahoo.com*). Enter the name of the subject that your Web site will cover.

The search engine will list all of the Web pages it can find on the subject. Then click on each title that appears in blue. The Web pages will come up on your screen.

• **Make notes on what you like and dislike about each site.** *While you're "surfing" the Web, notice that most pages are made up of the following elements...*

• Background—the color or pattern of the page.

• Headline appears at the top and tells visitors where they are in a site.

• Text is the body of the page on your screen.

• Graphics include pictures, company logos or other artwork. They add color and life to a site.

• Links are connections between two documents or sites. *Examples...*

☐ External link is text or a graphic that, when clicked, connects you to a page outside the Web site on your screen.

☐ Internal link connects you to other pages within the Web site on your screen.

☐ E-mail link is text or a graphic that, when clicked, sends mail to an E-mail address.

As you look at other sites, write down the features you would like to include on your site. Your site may consist of one page or a number of pages linked together.

Also write down the Web addresses of the sites to which you would like your site to be linked. You'll be asked to enter them when you design your site.

DESIGNING YOUR SITE

A number of Web publishing services offer free space and Web page design tools. *Leading services that allow you to create a Web site at low or no cost...*

• **Homestead** (*www.homestead.com*).

• **Tripod** (*www.tripod.lycos.com*).

• **Yahoo! GeoCities** (*http://geocities.yahoo.com*).

All share a similar sign-in process and are easy to use. Each of the services walks you through the entire design process, which consists of about 15 to 20 steps. *Each service will also prompt you to do the following...*

• **Register your site.** You'll be asked to enter personal information—your name and E-mail address. You may also be asked to choose a category for your site.

• **Name your site.** In most cases, the name you enter for your site cannot exceed 26 letters and cannot include punctuation marks. The actual Web address of your site will contain the name of the on-line service with which you are registered.

Example: If you name your site "My Home Page" on Tripod, the address that visitors will type to open your page will be *www.tripod.lycos.com/myhomepage*.

Most Web publishing services that charge a fee will provide you with a more official address that includes your Web site's name plus *.com—www.myhomepage.com*.

• **Choose a template.** Templates are preformatted pages that allow you to insert text or graphics. Most templates have a theme, such as a photo album, a personal page or a business page.

You'll also be asked to select a background color or pattern as well as the color of the text.

• **Add text.** Since most people don't like to read long paragraphs on a computer screen, use short sentences to convey messages easily and clearly.

• **Add graphics.** Most services allow you to download images from their clip art galleries, free of charge.

Alternatively, you may download images—and text—from your computer's hard drive onto your site.

When adding images to your page, always provide a text description of each image. Some users with slow Internet connections disable their computer graphics displays in order to speed up download time. Such users won't be able to view your images, but they will be able to read your descriptions of those images.

• **Add links to other pages within your site or to your favorite Web sites.** You may also want to add a link that allows visitors to send you E-mail.

• **Add other elements.** Some services allow you to add special elements to your sites.

Examples: Homestead, Tripod and Yahoo! GeoCities all let you add "hit counters" that show the number of people who have visited your Web site. They also provide "guest books," which list the E-mail addresses of visitors to your site.

• **Publish your site.** You can officially post your site on the Web by clicking a box on the screen labeled "publish" or "upload." After this process is complete, anyone can access your site.

EDITING YOUR SITE

Don't let your site go stale. Making timely changes and adding pages often will keep visitors coming back.

Web publishing services may remove your site from their servers if you don't edit it or if no one visits.

Very Useful Web Sites

The World Wide Web offers a plethora of information—from exercise instruction to language translators. *Here are some helpful sites...*

- **Best bank rates.** Search for the best bank interest rates on CDs nationwide. This site gives banks' toll-free numbers and links to their Web sites. *www.bankrate.com.*

- **Lowest airfares.** Find the cheapest fare to your destination...then book on-line. This site includes many exclusive discounts—not just the deals that are offered by airlines. *www.cheaptickets.com.*

- **Speedier homework.** *B.J. Pinchbeck's Homework Helper* links students to quality reference sites on history, math, science, etc. Has links to on-line encyclopedias and dictionaries. *www.bjpinchbeck.com.*

- **Smarter vocabulary.** This free E-mail service sends subscribers a new word daily with definition, pronunciation, usage examples and fun facts. *Weekly themes:* Nautical terms, mythology, etc. This is a painless way to learn words to prepare for the SATs. *www.wordsmith.org.*

- **Find a classmate.** Look up long-lost friends from your high school or college... then send them messages by E-mail. *www.alumni.net.*

- **Find a pet.** Directory of cats and dogs available at animal shelters nationwide. Search by zip code for a pet that meets your needs. Listings include the animal's name and age... description of its personality...some even have the animal's photo. *www.petfinder.com.*

- **Happier, healthier pets.** Expert advice on caring for dogs, cats, birds, fish, reptiles and other animals. *www.petsmart.com.*

- **Find lawyers fast.** Names, local bar associations, legal referral services and community organizations that provide legal assistance. *www. abanet.org/lawyerlocator/searchlawyer.html.*

- **Genealogy toolbox.** Directory of genealogy resources with links to more than 60,000 resources. Software for research. *www.geneal ogytoolbox.com.*

- **Golf information.** Courses worldwide, equipment, instruction...and tee times at more than 100 courses in the US and Europe. *www. golf.com.*

- **Zagat's restaurant guides.** Restaurant reviews plus maps and driving instructions— for free. *www.zagat.com.*

- **Yoga.** Easy-to-follow instructions for yoga exercises. Lots of other health and fitness information. *yoga.about.com.*

- **Biggest job-hunting Web site.** Lists more than 1,000,000 jobs in the US and abroad... skills assessment tools...chat rooms...career advice. *www.monster.com.*

Free Internet Access Isn't Always Free

Brenda Mack, administrative officer, Federal Trade Commission, 600 Pennsylvania Ave. NW, Washington, DC 20580.

Sometimes it seems as though you're getting a great deal—and you're not. *This is true with Internet providers, so be sure to check the fine print...*

- **Find out how long the trial period lasts.** If a company offers 500 free hours and the trial period is one month, you would have to be on-line more than 16 hours a day to reach 500 hours. But some firms start the clock as soon as you sign up.

• **Understand cancellation policies.** Some services allow on-line cancellation. And some others require a phone call—and they may be difficult to reach.

• **Be sure a provider has local access numbers**—so you avoid long-distance calls.

Helpful: A Federal Trade Commission alert on free Internet service offers, which is available at *www.ftc.gov.* Click on "Computers & the Internet."

Useful Sites

There is a wealth of information available on the Web. *You just have to know where to look...*

• **Comprehensive medical information.** Specific diseases...insurance...health organizations...hospitals...and many other topics. *www.healthfinder.gov.*

• **Free legal forms.** Search the database for thousands of forms and documents—power of attorney, sample contracts, state court documents, etc. *www.findforms.com.*

• **Vacation planning...**

• Tourist bureaus—*www.officialtravelinfo. com.*

• Family-friendly travel ideas—*www.the familytravelfiles.com.*

• Global security update—Daily updates on potential trouble spots, plus a list of reported security incidents and crimes in various countries around the world. The US Department of State established this site as an advisory for students and business employees traveling abroad. *www.osac.org.*

• **Learn the lingo.** Directory of more than 2,000 language-related Web sites. On-line lessons...translations...more. *www.ilovelan guages.com.*

• **Holidays.** Celebrations arranged by date, religion and country. *www.earthcalendar.net.*

• **Volunteer your time.** Directory of charitable opportunities that are listed by zip code. *www.volunteermatch.org.*

• **Donate your hair.** *Locks of Love* makes wigs for kids suffering from long-term medical hair loss. *www.locksoflove.org.*

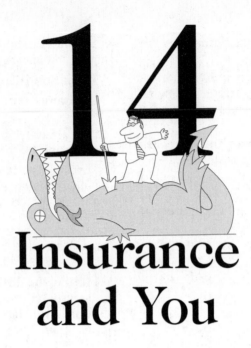

14

Insurance and You

Long-Term-Care Insurance...Essentials

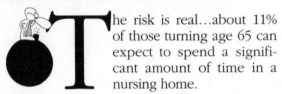

The risk is real...about 11% of those turning age 65 can expect to spend a significant amount of time in a nursing home.

The cost of nursing home care is high. The average cost for a year's stay is over $70,000 today—but in a number of areas in the country it can top $200,000.

How are you going to cover such a huge expense if the need arises? *The answer depends on your income and net worth...*

• **The "poor"**—and those who spend down their assets to become poor—can usually rely on Medicaid to cover the cost of a nursing home stay.

• **The "wealthy"** can afford to use their incomes to pay for such care without affecting their assets or the standard of living for other family members.

• **Those in the middle**—individuals with a net worth, say, of between $500,000 and $5 million—should consider buying a long-term-care policy.

There are a variety of factors to weigh in deciding whether to buy a long-term-care policy, and when. *For example...*

CAN I AFFORD IT?

Premiums for long-term-care policies aren't cheap. They can run between $2,000 and $10,000 a year for those under age 70, and as much as $15,000 or even $20,000 a year for those 70 and older. Like life insurance policies, the younger you are when you take out the policy, the lower your premiums will be.

Caution: Premiums for long-term-care policies are considered "level premiums"—that is, they don't increase as you age. *However—* the insurance company has the right to increase the premiums for a whole *class* of policies. This could happen with long-term-care policies as

Lee Slavutin, MD, CLU, chairman of Stern Slavutin-2 Inc., insurance and estate planners, 530 Fifth Ave., New York City 10036. *www.sternslavutin.com.*

insurance companies gain more experience and find they've underpriced them.

Cost of the premium depends on…

• **The person's age when the policy is first purchased.**

• **The dollar benefit per day.**

• **The period for which benefits will be paid**—three years, five years, life.

• **The "elimination period"**—the time before benefits will start.

• **Other factors,** such as a cost-of-living adjustment to the daily benefit.

Today, the people who can afford it are taking the maximum daily benefit available ($400) and are choosing lifetime policies (instead of those running for three, five or 10 years).

TYPES OF POLICIES

The type of policy you buy really depends on what you can afford.

The best policies: Lifetime coverage for the maximum benefit ($400 a day, depending on the company)…with a short elimination period.

But if you find the cost of such coverage prohibitive, consider a more modest policy, say $200 a day, for a shorter period than life, or with a longer elimination period.

In comparing policies offered by different companies, there are nuances to consider that can affect your choice.

Example: Be sure you understand how each company counts days of care for purposes of the elimination period. Say someone needs three days of care per week. Does this count as an entire week for the elimination period or will it take seven calendar days to equal one week for the elimination period?

• **Get professional help.** Use an insurance professional who can guide you through the intricacies of long-term-care insurance.

• **Experience counts.** Stick with an insurance company that has experience with long-term-care policies, such as Genworth, Travelers, John Hancock, Fortis and Unum.

Tax break: A portion of the premiums can be treated as a deductible medical expense based on your age, thereby offsetting some of the cost for those who itemize their medical expenses.

Note: States may offer tax breaks. For example, New York has a 20% tax credit for long-term care premiums.

CAN YOU AFFORD NOT TO?

If you are in the middle—not rich and not poor—you may not accumulate enough through savings to pay for nursing home care. If you are in this situation, you should consider buying a long-term-care policy.

Example: At age 60, you buy a $100 per day benefit at a cost of $519 per year—a three-year policy with a 90-day elimination period.

Then assume at age 80, you require nursing home care. You would have paid $10,380 over the 20 years of coverage.

Had you used that same $519 each year to invest for an after-tax return of 6%, you have only $20,237 after 20 years.

This would cover just 203 days in the home (at $100 a day). The policy would cover 1,095 days.

WHEN TO BUY A POLICY

Those who are 55 years old or older should start to look seriously at long-term-care policies.

Note: In recent years an increasing number of employers have offered this coverage as an employee benefit.

If you don't have employer-provided coverage, then look into individual coverage. The younger you are when you start the policy, the lower your premiums will be.

But if you buy at 55, won't you be paying premiums for 20 or 30 years before needing benefits, if ever? Does that make sense?

While your chances are better than 50% that you'll never put in a claim, should you need to do so, you're likely to come out ahead financially if you have a policy.

Suppose a 55-year-old woman buys a policy to provide $250 a day for a lifetime if needed (with a 90-day elimination period). She would pay $3,452.20 a year in premiums.

Example: If she needs long-term care after just *one year* of paying premiums, she would recover her entire outlay in just 14 days in a nursing home of average cost.

Five years of premiums would be recovered in 69 days, 10 years in 138 days. And—20 years in 276 days.

Even if this 55-year-old were not to need any benefits until age 85, her 30 years of premiums would be recovered in 414 days.

Low-Priority Insurance Policies

Slice-of-life insurance policies such as mortgage life insurance, credit life insurance (to pay off installment loans on a car, furniture, etc.) and flight insurance should be low-priority items in the family budget. More important—and more economical—are comprehensive life insurance policies that cover a family's total financial needs no matter how the major breadwinner dies. A renewable term-life insurance policy large enough to pay off the mortgage, the car loan and business debts, and to cover college costs for the children is far better than a series of special policies to cover individual situations.

J. Robert Hunter, insurance director, Consumer Federation of America, 1620 I St., NW, Suite 200, Washington, DC 20006.

How to Get Your Insurance Company to Pay Up

J. Robert Hunter, insurance director, Consumer Federation of America, 1620 I St., NW, Suite 200, Washington, DC 20006.

Don't give up if you have trouble getting a fair claims settlement from your health insurance company. There are a number of steps you can take to fight the insurer's decision to refuse your claim.

First: Resubmit another medical insurance claim form about 30 days after the refusal. Very often, a company randomly denies a claim... and just as randomly approves the same claim when it comes in again. It does no harm to try for reimbursement of a doctor's bill by submitting your insurance forms a second time.

Second: If that does not work, contact the insurer and request, in writing, a full explanation of the refusal to pay. Sometimes the denial-of-benefits statement is filled with numeric or alphabetic codes that are undecipherable by a layperson. Request a clear explanation. There should be no ambiguity as to why a health insurer will not pay the benefits that you think are called for in the contract.

Third: Once you are given the insurance company's rationale for turning you down, you have a couple of other weapons in your arsenal...

...the insurer cannot give you an alternative reason for the refusal after you refute the initial one.

...when the refusal is based on a rule against paying for experimental treatment, you can marshal evidence from your doctor and others that the treatment was, in fact, the treatment of choice—and therefore should be covered by the policy.

Fourth: If it becomes necessary to appeal, start within the company. Write directly to the president—whose name can be found in insurance directories at your local library... or call the company and ask.

Enclose copies of all relevant documents... claims forms, medical receipts, responses from the insurer, notes of telephone conversations and any backup materials.

Caution: Never send any originals, since you may need them for future action.

Fifth: If you get nowhere at the company level, write to your State Insurance Department. Every state now has a section set up to assist consumers with complaints. You can reach them by checking directory assistance for a toll-free number.

With the correct department and address, again mail copies of the relevant documents and ask for a response. The Insurance Department won't take your side in every dispute, but it can obtain an answer from your insurance company in situations where you have been stonewalled or treated unfairly.

Ultimate weapon: File a suit against the insurer in small-claims court, or in a regular court if the amount at stake is too large to be handled by the small-claims court.

If you go to regular court, you'll need a lawyer, preferably one who takes the case on a contingency basis, where the fee is a percentage of what you ultimately recover. You can handle a small-claims case yourself. Also, if the insurer's behavior is particularly abusive, you may be able to collect punitive damages from such a suit.

Real case: A man was conned into trading in his health policy for another on the basis that the second policy was substantially improved. Yet when he filed a claim, he found the new policy paid 40% less in benefits than the old one. He sued the insurance company for fraud...and wound up collecting over $1 million in punitive damages.

Bottom line: Carefully review your policy before filing claims for illness or injury.

Go to your corporate benefits manager or insurance agent with any questions about coverage and costs. By knowing exactly what you can expect from your policy, you won't be surprised when the reimbursement check arrives. And in the event that the insurer sends you the wrong amount, you will be ready to take whatever action is necessary to obtain the money you deserve.

One Insurance *Not* to Get

Private pension plans (PPPs) are just variable life insurance policies with fancy sales pitches. Brokers may highlight a PPP's big selling point—the ability to borrow from it tax free.

What your broker won't tell you: Cash value is low in the early years due to high brokers' commissions—you'll lose money if you want to cash out. If you borrow, your money is effectively committed to *cash-value*

life insurance—not always the best investment option.

Trap: If the loan lapses, you face a big tax bill—loans get added back to the cash value to determine taxable gain.

Better alternatives: Cheap, guaranteed, convertible, level-premium term insurance and no-load mutual funds, such as Vanguard's index funds (800-523-7731).

Glenn Daily, a fee-only insurance consultant in New York City.

Most Common Mistakes When Buying Life Insurance

James H. Hunt, life actuary, Consumer Federation of America in Washington, DC, and former commissioner of banking and insurance for the State of Vermont.

In addition to offering protection for your family, life insurance can also be a good investment. But life insurance policies are complicated, and without facts and comparisons it's easy to spend a lot of money for the wrong coverage.

The most common mistakes to avoid and recommendations on what you should buy...

Mistake: To buy life insurance when you have no dependents. Agents tend to create needs where none really exist in order to sell policies. If you are single, you don't need life insurance.

Mistake: To buy insurance for which you receive solicitations by mail. It's most often a bad bargain for most people.

Mistake: To buy life insurance for your children. Unless there's some extraordinary reason, there are better ways to save money.

Mistake: To put money into a cash-value life insurance policy at the expense of funding a tax-deductible IRA or 401(k) plan. (Cash-value policies are whole life, universal life, variable life or any form of life insurance that contains a savings element.) Be cautious about variable life. It has very high built-in expenses. If you want a cash-value policy, buy universal or whole life—provided you know how to choose the right policy and company and intend to keep the policy for at least 15 to 20 years. Otherwise you'd be a lot better off with term insurance.

Mistake: To buy a cash-value policy from a high-pressure salesperson. Keep in mind that agents make five to 10 times as much commission selling you a $100,000 cash-value policy as a term policy for the same amount. So you should always be alert to the hard sell for such policies.

Mistake: To buy life insurance and not disability insurance. People may automatically buy life insurance without realizing that a long-term disability can be an even worse financial event for their family than dying. If you're disabled, you not only lose your income, but you are still incurring expenses. You don't have to buy disability insurance if you're covered at work. However, only 30% of workers have such coverage. Everyone is covered by Social Security disability, but it's very restrictive, especially for white-collar workers.

Mistake: To buy riders on your policy— such as the accidental-death benefit or the additional-purchase option. These should be treated like options on a car—high-profit items that are best avoided.

Example: Double indemnity. Contrary to popular belief, you're not worth more dead in an accident than dead otherwise.

Controversial rider: The waiver of premiums in case of disability. You don't need it if you're covered for disability. If you become disabled, you'll have enough money to keep up your life insurance premium.

The safest and best insurance protection is the purchase of annual, renewable term insurance. A nonsmoking male can buy $250,000 coverage for about $300 or less a year at age 30 and $350 or less at age 40. Women pay about 15% less, smokers 50% to 100% more, depending on their age. For a family with one wage earner and group insurance at work, at least five times annual income is one rule of thumb.

Compare any cash-value or term policy you're thinking of buying with the policies sold by USAA Life* of San Antonio, Texas. Salaried representatives at its home office sell by phone. It usually has the best values on whole-life, universal-life and term insurance. *Alternative:* Ameritas,** which also offers second-to-die policies. USAA doesn't. Some policies are so complicated that it's impossible to figure out exactly what you're getting without a special computer program.

Example: If a universal-life policy says it pays 7%, that may be figured on whatever is left after a lot of expenses. You have to compare it with what you would have earned if you'd bought term and invested the difference. Assuming you hold the policy 20 years, 7% may turn out to be more like 5½%.

Reevaluate your older policies. If your old policy is a term policy, you should assume you can replace it with a lower priced policy, at least if you're a nonsmoker. If your old cash-value policy doesn't pay dividends, it probably should be replaced. If it does pay dividends, you'll be better off keeping it, especially if it has a low policy-loan interest rate.

*www.usaa.com...**www.ameritas.com

Life Insurance Test

Add up your assets—IRAs, savings, investment, etc. Subtract the amount that will be needed for estate taxes, mortgages, children's education, etc. If the balance won't generate enough income to support survivors, you need more life insurance. *Best buy:* Annual term insurance. Don't forget disability insurance. At age 50, you're more likely to be disabled than to die suddenly.

The late P. Kemp Fain, Jr., Asset Planning Corp., Knoxville, TN, quoted in *Dun's.*

What Life Insurance Companies Don't Tell You

Venita VanCaspel Harris, certified financial planner.

Buying the wrong kind of life insurance is one of the major reasons people fail to become financially independent. *The other major reasons:* Investment procrastination. Lack of financial goals. Ignorance of what to do with money to accomplish those goals. Failure to apply tax laws to advantage.

LIFE INSURANCE TRAPS TO AVOID

• **A policy that does not use a current mortality table.** Many premiums are still being paid and policies are still in force based on the American Experience Table. That's the death rate from the days of Abraham Lincoln. Another table, the 1941 Commissioner's Standard Ordinary (CSO) table, was devised before penicillin was discovered. The current 1958 table is out of date. If you have a policy based on an old table, you may be paying as much as 300% more than you need to because you are on the wrong table. (Most policies are based on the 1941 table.)

• **Cash-surrender policies.** Many consider them to be one of the greatest frauds in our country today. Insurance companies convince people that these are worthwhile because they give you a level premium on a whole-life policy and you can borrow your cash value. *Reality:* Insurance is based on a mortality table, and all the funny banking in the world won't change that. The companies are willing to give you a level premium on whole life because you are overpaying until you reach age 72. Then you can underpay when you don't need the insurance anyway. *Parallel:* Would you go to the telephone company and say, "Could I overpay my bill for each of the next 30 years for the privilege of underpaying after age 72?"

On the cash-value side, you would never go to a bank that takes away everything you deposit the first year and then charges you to deposit money in the account. Then if you want to borrow, it charges 5½% for your own money. And if you die, the insurance company can keep the money. No one would open that kind of bank account. Neither should you accept such terms from an insurance company.

Principle: People are willing to believe they can combine a living estate and a dying estate. In reality, these are incompatible. Insurance should be bought as an umbrella in case you die before building up a life estate. Don't ever consider it a method of building up your net worth (or "living" estate).

• **Dividend participating policies.** These are not really dividends. They are partial returns of an overcharge. Again, people believe that they can combine nest eggs for life and for death. A controversial Federal Trade Commission report says that if you keep a policy for an average period, you would receive 1.3% on your money. That means it takes 55.4 years for $1 to become $2.

Worse: If you hold the policy under five years, you could have a negative interest as high as 18%. Holding for 10 years could produce a negative 4%.

• **Insurance that is in your pension plan.** The incidental costs are much higher than most people are led to believe. After all, your pension plan is for living, not for dying.

BETTER METHODS OF INSURING

If you can pass a physical, you get a lower price per thousand on insurance if you switch to annual renewable term or 10-year deposit-level term.

Which to choose: If you know you are going to need insurance for the next 10 years, there is merit in the 10-year deposit-level term, since your premiums will be level for 10 years. However, realize that you are being overcharged in the beginning and undercharged at the end. But by making a deposit, you do get a discount on the rates you pay.

Best: If you believe you will soon start making enough to take care of your family out of your living estate (the money you build up out of investments over a lifetime), you will want to drop your insurance incrementally as your estate grows.

How to manage it: If you have a dependent who requires $1,000 a month if you die, then you need an estate of $200,000 (at a 6% return a year—half of that at 12%). If you have only $20,000 in your living estate, you need a $180,000 death estate (or insurance policy). As you build up your living estate, you can annually decrease your death estate. When your living estate rises to $50,000, then your death estate should go down to $150,000. Naturally, you may want to adjust this in accordance with inflation. However, your goal is to be self-insured so that benefits don't hinge on death.

Insurance should be viewed as a way to buy time before you build up your own future.

How to Choose A Life Insurance Company

Joseph M. Belth, PhD, editor of *The Insurance Forum*, Box 245, Ellettsville, IN 47429.

Most people now know that they need to purchase life insurance from a reputable insurance company.

But exactly how do you evaluate the financial condition of a company? And how do you choose among several that are established, healthy and reliable?

Here are five steps consumers can take to select the best insurer for their needs…

Step 1: **Determine how much life insurance you need.** Selecting a life insurance company is only one major decision you must make—and it's not the first one.

Before researching insurers, you'll need to determine the financial needs your family would face in the event of your death. There is no formula that will apply to everyone, because family circumstances vary widely.

But in addition to your expenses, assets, debts and short-term income needs, you will have to consider several difficult, personal questions in order to calculate your family's long-term needs.

Examples: Would your spouse work following your death? Would he or she sell your current home in order to move to a less costly one or have to move in with relatives?

Step 2: **Decide what kind of life insurance you wish to buy.** The variety of life insurance products on the market can be overwhelming to consumers. Most insurance companies can offer dozens of policies that can be further altered with riders, or optional clauses.

Helpful: The life insurance needs of almost any family can be met with one, or some of each, of just two types of policies—term and cash-value insurance.

●**Term insurance has no cash value or savings component.** It carries a relatively low premium for a large death benefit. Premiums increase with age…and as the policy is renewed.

●**Cash-value insurance**—straight life, universal life, variable life, etc.—accumulates cash value each year as premiums are paid. Premiums generally stay level for the duration of the contract.

Step 3: **Select several financially healthy insurers.** In order to do this, consumers must rely on professional rating firms, because the evalution process is complex.

Five rating firms use their specialized knowledge to publish ratings of life and health insurance companies: A.M. Best Company, Standard & Poor's Corp., Moody's Investors Service, Duff & Phelps Credit Rating Co. and Weiss Research.

Consumers should check all ratings that are available on the companies they are considering. Do not rely on what an insurer says about its own ratings.

Caution: While each firm generally does a good job evaluating insurers, they are not perfect. Each uses its own criteria, so the ratings are not uniform.

Example: An A+ is the highest rating from Weiss, the second highest from Best and the fifth highest from Standard & Poor's and Duff & Phelps.

Look for companies that have received very high ratings from at least three ratings services.

Step 4: Investigate the pricing of the policies you are considering, and rule out all that are not reasonably priced.

To determine whether a policy is reasonably priced, it is necessary to obtain a large amount of information about a policy and make comparisons with certain benchmarks. This policy information includes premiums, cash values (if any), death benefits and dividends (if any) for each year.

Pay close attention to figures that are guaranteed by an insurer, as opposed to illustrations—or those that are not guaranteed.

It is not practical to search for the cheapest policy, since there are numerous factors that affect premiums.

Step 5: Compare the provisions of the candidate policies. Life insurance policies are complex legal documents, and their provisions can vary widely. *Some examples of the provisions to examine...*

• **Does the company pay interest on the death benefit** between the date of death and the date of the settlement check?

• **Does the company reimburse the beneficiary** for any unearned portion of any premiums paid prior to death?

• **On a term policy,** what are your rights regarding renewability? How about convertibility to another type of policy?

• **What are your rights** with regard to borrowing against the policy? Cashing it in?

• **What are the provisions** of the policy's incontestability clause and suicide clause?

PERSONAL ADVANTAGE

On close comparison, one or more policies will emerge as superior.

It will be up to you to decide which provisions are most important to you and which you are willing to pay for.

A New Policy May Be Better Than An Old One

Buying a new policy may be cheaper than reinstating a lapsed one if you're considerably older now. Age is only one factor in setting premiums. Of equal or greater importance are fluctuations in the interest rate. The higher the rate, the lower the premium. Generally, higher interest rates may lower premiums more than your increasing age may raise them.

Christopher Collins, CLU, Solomon, Collins & Associates, Lincoln, NE.

Health Insurance— Choose Wisely

Bruce S. Pyenson and Jim O'Connor, principals with Milliman USA, an actuarial consulting firm. Mr. Pyenson is coauthor of *J.K. Lasser's Employee Benefits for Small Business.* John Wiley & Sons.

Most health insurance is provided through group policies available in the workplace. But there are millions of people who are self-employed or between jobs who have to find individual coverage on their own. Medicare also offers different coverage options.

While there are plenty of good policies out there, finding one that fits your needs takes some digging.

SIZE UP YOUR NEEDS

The health-care needs of families with young children are different from those of singles starting new jobs...couples without children...and empty nesters. Families with infants want a full range of preventive care that covers everything from routine vaccinations to ear infections. Healthy singles may only need bare-bones coverage for unexpected catastrophes.

In these days of managed care, there are four basic types of coverage…

HEALTH MAINTENANCE ORGANIZATIONS (HMOs)

A very prevalent type of group coverage, HMOs provide comprehensive medical care through networks of physicians. Typically, you pay $5 or $10 per in-network doctor visit and don't have to fill out forms after each appointment or worry about meeting a deductible requirement.

If you have a special health problem, you typically must first consult your primary care physician—also known as the *gatekeeper*. This physician may treat you or may refer you to a specialist. If you decide to use an out-of-network specialist or hospital, coverage—if any—is limited.

With limited choice about which doctors and hospitals to use and limited access to specialists, these plans are usually the most economical. Your out-of-pocket costs are fairly low for the wide range of coverage you get.

Best for: People with children who are new to a community—they have no relationships with physicians or hospitals. Also good for people with children whose current physician and hospital are part of the HMO network.

PREFERRED PROVIDER ORGANIZATIONS (PPOs)

These types of policies—which are more expensive than comparable HMOs—give you the ability to go outside the plan network for your medical care. Most PPO plans don't have a gatekeeper system, so you usually don't need approval to see specialists.

If you see a physician within the network, you get one level of benefits (usually 80% of a claim is covered). If you see a physician outside the network, you get another, lower level of benefits (only 60% to 70% of the claim might be covered).

Best for: People who want more choice about health-care providers…and whose doctors are part of the PPO network.

INDEMNITY POLICIES

These plans pay benefits no matter what doctor or hospital you go to. Such traditional policies appeal to people who have lived in the same community for a long time and have established ties to physicians and hospitals. While they guarantee you the most latitude in terms of choosing your health-care providers, indemnity plans are also the most expensive. Sometimes people who want the flexibility of an indemnity policy opt for high deductibles of as much as $10,000 to reduce monthly premiums.

"ANY DOCTOR" POLICIES

These hybrid plans use a PPO approach for hospitals but allow you to see any licensed physicians you wish. They are cheaper than indemnity policies but more expensive than full-fledged PPOs.

Best for: People who feel comfortable with the hospitals in the PPO network but want the flexibility of using any doctor they choose.

FINDING THE BEST PLAN

• **Research what is available in your state.** Because each state regulates insurance, choices will be limited. Not all insurance companies offer policies in all states. And a company's policies may be different in different states.

If your car and homeowner's insurance is with a company that sells through a network of agents, start by calling your agent.

If you belong to a professional or trade group or a college alumni association, find out if these organizations offer special health policies for members. Such policies often cost less than individual policies but more than group policies. If you have chronic health problems, these policies can be a good deal since you may not be able to get an affordable policy on your own.

• **Determine what different types of policies will cost you.** Call two major companies that write health insurance nationwide.

For HMOs: Aetna (800-872-3862)…United HealthCare Group (877-311-7848).

For PPOs, "Any Doctor" and indemnity: Assurant Health (800-800-1212)…Mutual of Omaha (800-775-6000).

Simplify your search by using the Internet. Two sites that provide up to 20 different premium quotes are *www.insure.com* and *www.insweb.com*.

Be sure to get the answers to some crucial questions…

• **Does the plan cover maternity, mental health and substance abuse?**

• **What are the rules concerning preexisting conditions** (health problems you had before taking out the policy)?

• **Ask the insurer about rate increases.** You want to know how often and by how much insurers boost their premiums each year. Ask what the increases have been for the past several years. Some companies charge very low initial rates but then raise premiums by a large amount. Rate increases are currently running 10% to 15% a year. If your insurer is boosting rates by 30% or more annually, it's time to shop around.

• **Find out if customers are satisfied.** Get the names of current HMO members. Ask if they've experienced delays in obtaining membership cards, problems communicating with physicians, difficulty getting pharmacies to accept their coverage, trouble getting doctor's appointments quickly or trouble getting prompt referrals to specialists.

You can also call your state insurance or health department (they usually are listed in the state government pages of your telephone directory). Some states develop statistics that indicate complaint ratios of HMOs.

If you have an established doctor, you might also call him or her for feedback on the plan you are considering, particularly for HMOs.

You Can Avoid a Physical Exam

Insurance medical exams are quietly being abandoned by insurance companies, even for $100,000 to $200,000 term insurance sales, according to a major insurance broker. The reasons are the high cost of the exams and the poor reliability of the information given by those seeking insurance. Even the best exams, say the insurers, protect them only for about

six months anyway. Now they often rely on a medical history taken by the insurance broker. They may also request an electrocardiogram and a chest X ray.

Secrets to Fast Payment from Your HMO

William M. Shernoff, senior and managing partner at the law firm Shernoff Bidart Darras (*www.sbd-law.com*), which represents policyholders who are seeking claims payments from insurance companies and HMOs, 600 S. Indian Hill Blvd., Claremont, CA 91711. He is author of *Fight Back & Win: How to Get Your HMO and Health Insurance to Pay Up*. Capital Books.

The larger the dollar amount of a claim filed with an HMO, the less likely the HMO is to pay for all—or even most—of the claim.

No matter how frustrated you become with the HMO, don't give up. Managed-care companies count on most people to accept their decisions on claims, even if the companies are wrong.

Here's how to get satisfaction on your medical claims…

• **Take an active role in the claims process.** Unlike conventional—or indemnity—insurance policies, in which you personally file your claims, HMOs handle your claims for you.

But if anything goes wrong—such as an HMO doctor's office neglecting to file the right forms or paperwork being improperly filled out—the HMO may deny the claim or delay payment for it. *Helpful…*

If your case is not routine: Ask the HMO to send you copies of all the claims that have been filed on your behalf. Review them, and promptly forward any missing information to the HMO's home office.

Don't be afraid to contact the claims examiner who is assigned to your case. Ask the examiner to explain any decision that you believe is unfair. If you're not satisfied, move up the chain of command and contact the examiner's supervisor.

With a complex medical problem that will require ongoing treatment: Establish a personal relationship with the case manager (who oversees the examiner) in charge of your paperwork.

As a participant in the HMO, you have the right to see how the case manager has written up your problem—and what the HMO has recommended to your physician. When HMO employees know that you are taking an active role in your care, they are less likely to put up roadblocks.

•**Don't take the company's first *no* as the final answer.** File an immediate appeal in writing.

Important: Carefully follow the complaint procedure outlined in your HMO handbook.

Explain why you feel your benefits were wrongfully denied...and clearly state what action you want your HMO to take.

To protect your future legal rights, include the following sentence in every letter that you write to the HMO...

"This appeal relates only to the denial of the benefits in question. It does not constitute, and shall in no way be deemed an admission, that I am limited in my right to pursue a 'bad faith' remedy in state court."

Send your complaint letter by registered mail, return receipt requested—even if you are not required to do so. It's amazing how often HMOs claim they never received communications from patients...so you should have proof to the contrary. Request a written response within 30 days.

Set up a folder for all the paperwork on the grievance, and track on a calendar each step of the complaint process and when the HMO's responses are due.

•**Go straight to arbitration if you feel you are not getting a fair hearing.** The *internal* appeals procedures set up by HMOs may not be as impartial as they seem.

Some are biased in favor of the health plan because decision makers in the appeals process are not likely to disagree with their fellow employees.

The HMO's appeals process is not your only remedy. You also have the right to arbitration, an independent process conducted by third parties who are not usually beholden to the HMO. The sooner you can get your appeal heard in this setting, the better. Your HMO handbook lists the arbitration entity.

•**Get another medical opinion from doctors outside your HMO.** If your HMO doctor is reluctant to order a costly or experimental test or procedure that you're convinced you need, get a second, or even a third, opinion—even if you must pay for it out of your own pocket.

If these outside doctors agree with you, ask them to write to the HMO on your behalf. The aim is to establish a written record that supports your case, should you later appeal.

•**Get documentation for using a non-affiliated emergency room.** Most people who seek care in an emergency room that is not affiliated with their HMO network do so when they are away from home.

If you must visit a nonaffiliated emergency room, request a letter from the facility documenting that you had a real medical emergency. The letter should also state that you could not be transferred to a facility in the HMO network without endangering your health.

•**Make as much noise as possible.** Start in your own company's human resources department with the person who is the official liaison with the HMO. Then contact local consumer hot lines and consumer affairs reporters at television stations and newspapers.

Also complain to your local, state and federal elected officials—your mayor, state representatives and US senators. It's also wise to contact your Better Business Bureau and state attorney general.

Complain to the regulators. Contact the appropriate state regulatory agency—usually the Department of Insurance or the Department of Corporations—and ask about the procedures for filing a complaint against the HMO. Many states have waiting periods, but in some emergency cases a complaint may be filed and heard within 72 hours. Be sure to let your HMO know that you are contacting the state regulator.

If you are covered by both an HMO and Medicare, you can also appeal to the MAXIMUS Federal Services, Eastgate Square, 50 Square Drive, Suite 210. Victor, NY 14564. (585) 425-5210, *www.medicareappeal.com.*

If the Center for Health Dispute Resolution rules in your favor, you can then have the HMO provide appropriate care and treatment or have the HMO pay for the care and treatment you received in the interim.

If you lose, you can then file a complaint with the Administrative Law Justice division of Medicare.

• **Seek legal redress if necessary.** If your claim is modest, file a claim in small-claims court. You don't need a lawyer, and the odds of winning are good. Your case will probably be heard within six months.

If you have a major claim, look for a lawyer who specializes in "bad faith" cases against insurance companies and HMOs. You're best off hiring an attorney who works on a contingency basis. This means the attorney gets nothing if you lose but takes at least one-third of any amount you recover from the HMO.

Short-Term Health Protection

Short-term health insurance can protect you between jobs. It may also be suitable for recent college graduates who are no longer covered by their parents' insurance...and for Medicare beneficiaries traveling abroad and not covered by other policies.

Cost depends on copays, deductibles and coverage limits. *Important:* Renewal is not automatic—you must reapply at the end of each coverage period.

Limitations: Coverage may be limited to 180 days within a year...short-term policies do not cover maternity costs—except the cost of complications associated with birth...not all states allow the sale of short-term health insurance.

Roy Diliberto, president, Financial Planning Association, Denver.

Get Medigap Insurance

Medicare patients who expect to be dropped by their HMOs—a growing trend—should apply now for traditional Medicare insurance. Also apply for Medicare gap insurance (Medigap). That may take as long as three months to take effect. *Downside:* Paying $30 to $50 a month for Medigap. *Upside:* More choice among medical practitioners...and an opportunity for better care than from a cost-cutting HMO. *Note:* Nobody can be turned down for Medicare. Medigap has limitations on renal disease and hospice care.

Frank N. Darras, a partner at the law firm Shernoff Bidart Darras (*www.sbd-law.com*), which represents policyholders who are seeking claims payments from insurance companies and HMOs, 600 S. Indian Hill Blvd., Claremont, CA 91711.

Medigap Traps...and How to Avoid Them

Robert M. Freedman, partner, Freedman, Fish and Grimaldi, LLP, elder law and elder care consultants specializing in estate planning, 521 Fifth Ave., New York City 10175.

Most Americans age 65 and older enroll in Medicare as their primary health insurer.

But Medicare was not designed to provide comprehensive coverage, and the gaps leave policyholders liable for potentially huge medical expenses.

To cover the gaps, about two-thirds of the 39 million Americans enrolled in Medicare purchase supplemental coverage, or "Medigap insurance."

Choosing a supplemental policy has become simpler since federal regulations standardized Medigap plans in 1992. Insurers may now offer 10 plans, labeled A through J plus two alternatives tied to Medicare Advantage (formerly called Medicare + Choice). Consumers can easily compare costs. But there are still many variables to consider when choosing a Medigap policy. *Here are the most important...*

• **Which plan is right for you?** The new standardized Medigap policies allow you to choose a package of benefits to suit your needs and budget.

Plan A is the most basic and least expensive.

Plans B, C or D will meet the needs of most seniors.

Plans H, I and J are the most comprehensive and the most costly.

In some cases, you may have to pay for a benefit you don't need in order to get those you do.

Example: All but the most basic plans cover foreign travel emergencies—whether you want the coverage or not.

When comparing plans, note that certain benefits are really not worth much. Be realistic about which out-of-pocket medical expenses you are willing to pay for yourself.

Examples: Many people believe they need the Part B deductible benefit offered in Plans C, F and J—but the deductible is only $100 a year. Plans D and E are identical, except that Plan D covers up to $1,600 a year in at-home recovery costs, while Plan E covers $120 a year in preventive screening. Even if you use the $120 benefit every year for 10 years, it's not worth as much as the $1,600 benefit is worth if needed just once.

• **How much does Medigap insurance cost?** Medigap plans have been standardized—but prices and levels of service have not.

Example: You may find a lower rate from a mail-order company that doesn't have to pay agents' commissions, but you might prefer to pay a slightly higher premium to buy from a local agent who will help file your claims.

Most insurers base their premiums on the buyer's age and state of residence. Rates are generally uniform for men and women. United HealthCare, under contract with AARP, charges a fixed premium per plan regardless of a policyholder's age, but adjusts premiums by state.

Insurers may also have different intervals between premium increases, different rules governing conversion and renewability or different maximum benefit limits.

Not all insurers offer all 10 plans, and not all states have adopted the standardized system.

Shop around! Annual premiums can vary enormously from one insurer to another.

• **When should I buy a Medigap policy?** If you are 65 or older, you can qualify for any Medigap policy without regard to preexisting conditions for the six months after you enroll in Medicare Part B. There may be, though, a six-month exclusionary period for coverage of these conditions.

• **What if I already have coverage?** Many people already own one of the hundreds of Medigap policies that were on the market in the past, or have insurance through an employer plan. There is no need to switch to a standard plan if you are happy with your coverage. It is now illegal to sell duplicate or unnecessary Medigap coverage to any person, so if you do decide to switch, you will have to surrender your old policy. You may have to requalify to upgrade.

If you are covered by an employer or older Medigap policy, call your benefits manager or insurer to check on the future of your coverage.

Reason: Many employers have been cutting back on retiree health benefits, including group health plans that once paid many non-Medicare-covered benefits. And many insurers are discontinuing their older Medigap plans now that the new plans are on the market.

Catch: Insurers are not required to offer coverage that is comparable to their discontinued products. Result...many retirees are suddenly faced with the need to find new Medigap coverage.

Frequent problems: A policyholder is offered an opportunity to convert an old Medigap policy to a new plan—but the insurer only offers Plans A and B, and the coverage is inferior to the old plan. Or, if the replacement policy has a new benefit, the insurer can impose a waiting period for coverage.

The policyholder decides to switch to a new insurer. If accepted by a new company, there is no waiting period for coverage of preexisting conditions...but insurers can turn down applicants with preexisting conditions.

Solution: Some providers, including AARP, usually don't consider an applicant's health except when issuing policies H, I and J.

• **Are there alternatives to Medigap policies?** Medicare Part B participants are eligible to enroll in Health Maintenance Organizations (HMOs) if they live in a plan's service area. However, if you belong to an HMO, you probably don't need Medigap insurance.

The majority of states have a new and possibly less expensive type of private Medigap insurance called Medicare Select. Participants in this plan agree to use a selected group of health-care providers. The insurer picks the group, which may include a local managed-care organization.

Medigap coverage for prescription drugs may not be as good as coverage under Medicare Part D—consider changing your Medigap policy so that you obtain prescription drug coverage separately (through Medicare Part D).

There are also Medicare Advantage Plans that eliminate the need to carry a Medigap policy.

• **What is not covered by Medicare and Medigap insurance?** When calculating your potential medical expenses, remember that Medicare/Medigap policies do not cover eye care, dental services, hearing aids, routine checkups—procedures deemed not medically necessary—and, perhaps most important, long-term nursing home or custodial care.

Traps in Company-Provided Disability Insurance

William M. Shernoff, senior and managing partner at the law firm Shernoff Bidart Darras (*www.sbd-law.com*), which represents policyholders who are seeking claims payments from insurance companies and HMOs, 600 S. Indian Hill Blvd., Claremont, CA 91711. He is author of *Fight Back & Win: How to Get Your HMO and Health Insurance to Pay Up*. Capital Books.

It's not unusual for people who receive life insurance at work to supplement their policy by buying additional coverage.

Yet relatively few bother to calculate whether the company's disability insurance will cover their financial needs if they are out of work for an extended period of time. They simply assume that the company's benefits are sufficient.

In fact, employer-sponsored disability insurance is very often woefully inadequate.

Many employers purchase the minimum amount of protection for employees, and most employees are unaware of how easy it is for insurers to wriggle out of paying them.

In most cases, a company's short-term-disability policy will pay only 70% of your salary for between 13 and 26 weeks.

Long-term-disability insurance usually begins after 26 weeks, paying only 60% of your salary —and then up to only $60,000 a year.

TRAPS

• **There may be a gap of as much as three months** between the time short-term disability ends and long-term coverage begins.

• **Disability income is taxable unless you have purchased your own coverage,** so you'd actually take home even less. The amount of additional coverage that you need depends on your monthly living expenses—and how much of your savings is available for such purposes.

Here's how to tell whether you need additional coverage, and what to look for when shopping for a supplemental insurance policy...

• **Estimate what your monthly expenses would be** if you were unable to work for 90 days or longer. Once you've arrived at this figure, determine what your take-home benefit would be. If the monthly sum is too low to meet your needs, you should buy additional coverage to make up the difference.

Buying your own policy also has two other advantages...

• **You can take an individual or supplemental policy with you if you change jobs.**

• **The younger you are when you purchase the policy,** the lower the fixed premium will be throughout the time you own it.

Before you buy—understand the plan's definition of disability. Most insurance contracts have more restrictive standards for defining disability than do most states. This is due to a loophole in the federal Employee Retirement Income Security Act (ERISA), which overrides state laws and prevents insurance companies from being sued in state courts for damages.

Although most states say you are legally disabled if you cannot perform the substantial tasks of your work with any regularity, many insurance policies define disability as the inability to perform any of your work-related tasks now or ever again.

Example: A paralyzed surgeon who is unable to operate on patients but can still read or dictate medical reports would be considered disabled by most states, but not by many insurers.

•**Beware of "offset" clauses.** These allow the insurer to deduct from your monthly benefit any income you already receive from other sources, such as workers' compensation or Social Security. These deductions can cut your monthly insurance benefit in half.

•**Not all "lifetime" policies are the same.** Many actually pay for only a certain period (usually one or two years) if you are disabled from your occupation. They will pay over a lifetime only if you can prove that you are disabled from working at any occupation.

Many high-earning professionals have lost the lifetime benefits they thought they were entitled to because the insurer proved that they could perform a low-wage job.

Example: A bedridden executive could still work in telephone sales.

•**A lifetime policy offers little protection if your job or coverage is terminated due to a disability.** According to certain state laws, it is illegal for an employer or insurer to cut off a policyholder's benefits if he or she contracts a disease or suffers an accident. But this frequently happens to policyholders, anyway, because they have little legal recourse in these matters due to the ERISA loophole.

Example: There was a recent case in which an employer was permitted to dramatically reduce an employee's AIDS benefit after the employee discovered that he had the disease.

As a result, most group coverage offered by an employer is illusory. If you lose your job due to disability, your employer can terminate your lifetime coverage after one year.

•**Look for a policy that does not tie coverage to the cause of a disability.** Many policies will pay only if you are disabled by an accident, not a sickness. Some insurers have even been known to unjustly convert accident claims to sickness claims to avoid paying out.

Example: An insurer may say that injuries from an accidental fall were really caused by dizziness due to an underlying condition such as arthritis, sunstroke or high blood pressure.

SELF-DEFENSE

•**Buy a policy that considers you disabled if you can't do the important tasks of your own job.** Until legislation closes the ERISA loophole, it is preferable to buy noncancelable, guaranteed-renewable disability insurance. You can do this on your own or through a professional or church group that offers such a policy.

•**Be prepared for disputes.** Even with individual policies, it is not uncommon for disputes to occur between policyholders' doctors and insurers' doctors over the extent of a disability.

Most insurers send disability cases to "independent" medical examiners for review. But these doctors are usually far from independent, since they receive a large volume of work from the insurer. While many review cases in good faith, they must work with the definition of disability supplied by the insurer, even if it is contrary to state law.

Solution: If your disability claim is denied, enlist the help of your physician. Also, get a truly independent second opinion and consider seeing an attorney.

•**Those who can't afford the premium for a new policy** should save some money each month to be used in case they become disabled. Be sure to save enough to cover any gap between when short-term disability ends and long-term coverage begins.

•**At work, require your company's insurance agent to sign a written statement.** *It should say:* "If you become disabled, even if your employer terminates you because of your disability, we will keep paying your claim for the period specified in the policy."

• **Don't forget to protect your home.** Mortgage insurance policies are usually sold in such a way that policyholders believe that their mortgage payments will be made for life if they become disabled.

Trap: These policies are often limited in time, say for just two years. If you have a 30-year mortgage and are permanently disabled, two years of mortgage payments won't prevent you from losing your home.

Solution: Make sure the insurance policy is for the life of the mortgage—or find a disability policy that pays a high enough benefit to meet your needs.

How to Buy Disability Insurance

You can generally get coverage up to 50% of your income. Policies cover all illnesses not specifically excluded. This includes psychiatric disabilities. Pregnancy is usually excluded, but not complications from pregnancy. *What to look for in a policy...*

• **Noncancelability.** As you get older, you're more susceptible to disabilities, and they last longer. You can get a policy that's noncancelable to age 65, with the option to renew if you keep working.

• **Cost-of-living clause.** This pays additional benefits when the cost-of-living index goes up. The annual adjustment is usually limited to 6%, although some policies pay more than this. There's also usually an upper limit, such as twice the original benefit.

• **Waiting period.** One- to six-month periods are common. Choose as long a period as you can. Why? You'll get higher coverage for the same premium. With a short waiting period, you may be paid for some illnesses you could probably ride out without help; but you'll get proportionately less in time of real need if you're hit by catastrophic long-term disability.

• **Definition of disability.** You want a policy that defines disability as inability to work at your regular occupation. Also, the policy should pay for illness that first manifests itself while the policy is in force. This protects you if you have a condition (such as heart disease or cancer) that you don't know about when you buy the policy.

• **Residual-disability benefits.** A residual-benefit clause pays partial benefits if you can work part-time or at a lower paying job. *Example:* A violinist who lost the use of his fingers from arthritis took a teaching job at a lower income. He could collect a percentage of his disability benefit equal to the percentage of his lost income.

Leonard B. Stern, president of Leonard B. Stern & Co., insurance and consulting firm, New York City.

Disability Insurance for Homemakers

Full-time homemakers can now get insurance that allows them to hire replacement help if they become disabled. About one-third of the country's largest disability insurance firms now offer such policies. Rates are based on age and coverage.

American Council of Life Insurers, Washington, DC. *www.acli.com.*

Property Insurance Trap

Traditional policies pay only the "actual cash value" of an item that's lost, stolen or destroyed. *Example:* A sofa purchased five years ago for $600 is destroyed in a fire. At today's prices a comparable replacement costs $900. But the cash value of that five-year-old sofa—if you tried to sell it secondhand—is only, say, $150. So all you could collect under a traditional policy is $150.

Replacement-cost insurance seems to be an attractive alternative. But in practice, most of these policies pay off only the smallest of either replacement cost, repair cost or four times the actual cash value.

In the example, the payout would be $600, four times the actual cash value. And the policyholder would be $300 short of the price of a new sofa. *Cost of coverage:* About 15% higher premiums on a typical homeowner's policy, 25% higher for condominium and co-op owners and 40% extra on a tenant's policy.

Covering Computer Equipment

Computer equipment, like any other household possession, is covered by home insurance policies. *Exception:* Expensive equipment may necessitate upgrading of your present policy. And if you use the computer for business, consider a separate business policy to cover damage, theft or destruction of data.

Insure Your Home-Based Business

Home-based businesses are only minimally covered by traditional homeowner's insurance. Most will not cover computer-stored information, paperwork, accounts receivable or other business elements.

Self-defense: Expand existing homeowner's policies to provide business coverage if your business is considered incidental—usually defined by insurers as generating less than $5,000 in annual gross income. *Cost:* $50 to $100/yr. For larger home-based businesses, buy a business owner's package that works with your homeowner's policy. *Cost:* $250/year and up.

Scot McCartney, independent insurance agent, Ardsley, NY.

Umbrella Policies: How to Protect Against Catastrophes

Leonard B. Stern, president of Leonard B. Stern & Co., insurance and consulting firm, New York City.

In a litigious society, if you have substantial assets you are fair game for lawsuits and heavy damage judgments simply because you do have those substantial assets.

Homeowner's insurance and automobile insurance policies offer basic liability coverage for injuries and damage caused by you or your family (even your pet) and by your car or small boat. (Larger boats and many recreational vehicles require separate policies.) These policies cover accidents that happen on your property as well. You pay higher and higher premiums as you raise the limits of your liability coverage.

However, the amount you owe when you are sued for damages is determined by the courts, not by the limits of your insurance coverage. Judgments have skyrocketed in the past decade. If you are not prepared, a judgment can be financially ruinous. The more you own—houses, jewelry, boats, cars, investments—the more you can be expected to pay.

MINIMUM LIABILITY RECOMMENDATIONS

• **Automobile bodily injury.** $100,000 per person, $300,000 per accident.

• **Automobile property damage.** $25,000 per accident.

• **Boat owner's liability.** $100,000 per occurrence.

• **Homeowner's liability.** $100,000 per occurrence.

ENTER THE UMBRELLA

If your net worth is a great deal more than these minimums, you need more protection. This is where umbrella liability insurance becomes useful. An umbrella policy provides excess coverage for all your primary liability insurance.

Example: A guest is injured at a party around your swimming pool. The courts award him $300,000 for medical costs and lost pay. Your homeowner's policy has only a $100,000 liability limit. The umbrella policy covers the $200,000 gap. And then your car goes out of control and plows into a new addition on a neighbor's house. The courts assess the damage at $40,000. Your car insurance pays a maximum of $25,000. Again, the umbrella policy picks up the $15,000 shortfall.

COST OF UMBRELLA POLICIES

Personal umbrella liability insurance is sold in increments of $1 million of coverage. Premiums generally start at around $200 a year. More than 75 companies now offer this blanket coverage for personal (rather than business) liability. *Biggest difference in policies:* Requirements for minimum-liability coverage in primary homeowners, car, boat and recreational vehicle contracts. Each personal umbrella liability policy has its own conditions, definitions and exclusions, too. In shopping around, look for a policy that includes all your family's potentially hazardous activities.

Interesting bonus: Personal umbrella policies give primary coverage for one area of liability not touched on by other general types of liability insurance—slander and libel.

Bottom line: Personal umbrella liability insurance is designed to protect individuals with substantial property, who are vulnerable to lawsuits and costly judgments. For them it is inexpensive insurance against catastrophic losses in court.

Canceled Check Is Proof That Fire Insurance Is Paid for, Right? Wrong!

Fire and casualty policies should be in hand (on file) before the full premium is paid. One firm, after finding its plant burned to the ground, didn't have the policy it had paid for. Though it produced the canceled check to the broker, its claim was disallowed. The wise course is to buy insurance as you would an automobile—give the broker a small deposit, but don't pay up until the policy is delivered.

 # Cut Your Car Insurance Costs

Jack Gillis, director of public affairs at Consumer Federation of America, 1620 I St., NW, Suite 200, Washington, DC 20036. He is author of *The Car Book*. Gillis.

Despite declining auto insurance rates, 75% of car owners haven't changed their insurance policies—or even inquired about doing so—within the last five years.

Here's how to pay less for your insurance coverage…

•**Compare policy rates on the Web.** This process takes about a half hour. First look at the sample rates charged by all insurers that do business in your state.

•*www.insure.com* provides a link to every state insurance department. At the home page, enter your state in the box labeled "insurance in your state."

Once you have a benchmark rate, visit a site that can locate policies with the lowest rates.

•Insweb (*www.insweb.com*). You type in the information about your driving history. Then this Web site sifts through the insurance companies in its database to find the ones that have the lowest prices. This service is free.

•**Shop aggressively every two years.** Different insurers target certain types of drivers at different times and then offer lower rates based on how closely you fit their preferred "top tier" profiles.

You're a candidate for a lower insurance rate whenever…

•Points are removed from your license.

•One of your vehicles is removed from your policy.

•Your kids no longer drive your car.

•Your car is no longer used for commuting.

• **Maximize your policy's discounts.** Discounts can cut your premium in half. Most insurers offer as many as 20 different discounts. Most don't tell you about all of them unless you specifically ask. *Helpful...*

- Antitheft devices
- Air bags
- Antilock brakes
- Car-pool drivers
- Low mileage
- Nonsmokers
- Graduates of driver-training courses
- Multiple policies
- No accident in three years
- Older drivers who don't drive at night

• **Ask insurance companies if they offer low-rate group policies.** More insurers now offer organizations group policies that have discounted rates for members.

Examples: Retirement organizations, alumni associations, credit unions...and some credit card issuers, too.

• **Eliminate unnecessary coverage.** Increasing your monthly deductible from $200 to $500 could reduce your collision and comprehensive premiums by as much as 30%.

Consider eliminating collision and comprehensive coverage if your car is completely paid off...more than four years old...or worth less than $4,000.

To research car values: National Automobile Dealers Association (*www.NADA.com*)...or Kelley Blue Book (*www.kbb.com*).

• **Buy a less desirable—or safer—car.** Buying a model that is a favorite with thieves or statistically in frequent accidents can send your premiums sky-high.

For cars with high theft rates: The National Insurance Crime Bureau (*www.nicb.org*).

For cars with the highest safety ratings: Insurance Institute for Highway Safety (*www.iihs.org*).

When You Are Hit By the Uninsured (Or Underinsured) Motorist

Richard P. Oatman, assistant claim counsel for Aetna Life & Casualty, Hartford, CT.

An accident with an uninsured or underinsured motorist can be financially ruinous. As part of your own policy, underinsured (in some states) and uninsured motorist's coverage is obtainable to deal with such accidents.

UNINSURED COVERAGE

Most states have statutory requirements that automobile liability insurance policies include uninsured motorist's coverage.

• **Financial-responsibility limits.** The law requires that uninsured motorist's coverage be provided in an amount mandated by the state. These financial-responsibility limits vary.

• **Getting more coverage.** Usually you can buy coverage up to your liability limits. *Example:* If you carry $300,000 in liability, you can get the same amount in uninsured coverage.

• **Proof of fault.** Under uninsured coverage, your company has to pay you only what the other party is legally liable for. So the other party must be proved to be at fault.

• **Comparative negligence provisions.** In some states, if the other driver is proved to be somewhat at fault, you can recover proportional damages from your own insurance company.

• **Making a claim.** You are placed in an adversarial position with your own insurance company. You must prove the extent of the injury, establish its value and negotiate with your own carrier to settle. If you can't reach a settlement, most claims will go to arbitration, not to court.

• **Limits.** Most mandatory uninsured motorist's protection covers only bodily injury. Property damage is covered under your collision insurance, after the deductible. (As with any collision claim, your rates may go up after filing.)

UNDERINSURED COVERAGE

This type of coverage is becoming more and more popular. Some states require that underinsured coverage be offered. In others, it is optional. *With underinsured coverage...*

● **You must first recover the maximum amount** from the other party's liability policy before you can collect on your own policy.

● **As with uninsured coverage,** you are in an adversarial position with your carrier and must prove that the value of your injury has exceeded the liability limits of the other party's policy.

Important: Uninsured motorist's coverage will not pay you if the other driver has any insurance at all, no matter how inadequate.

PEDESTRIAN ACCIDENTS

You will be covered by your uninsured motorist's coverage just as if you were in a car at the time. If you don't own a car, you might be able to get coverage under the policy of a family member in your immediate household who does own one. If neither you nor anyone in your family has coverage, you can apply to a fund that some states maintain to cover such accidents or pursue a court action directly against the responsible party.

Children Can Sue Insured Parents

A child could sue his or her parents for damages from an auto accident caused by the parents' negligence. (The doctrine of parental immunity from lawsuits is waived in negligence cases to the extent to which the parent is covered by insurance.) The court noted that the insurance company could have protected itself by adding an appropriate clause to the policy.

Ard v. Ard, 414 So. 2d 1066 (Fla.).

No-Hit Protection

Auto insurance policies are required by state law to cover hit-and-run accidents. One driver wrecked her car when another vehicle veered at her, forcing her off the road. The other car then sped off. But the insurance company refused to pay for the accident because the damaged car was not actually hit by the other one. So the car's owner sued. *Court's decision:* A hit-and-run accident is any accident caused by a person who runs away. There doesn't actually have to be a hit involved. The insurance company had to pay.

Su v. Kemper/American Motorist Insurance Cos., R.I. Sup. Ct.

Health Insurance For You...for Your Business

Alan Mittermaier, president, HealthMetrix Research, Inc., a company that assists older adults in finding the right health-care providers, Box 30041, Columbus, OH 43230. *www.HMOs4seniors.com.*

Many business owners avoid buying the type of health insurance they need because they're adequately covered under a spouse's insurance plan. Or—they simply give their own health care low priority because other business matters seem much more important.

Trap: Without adequate health insurance, you put yourself, your family and your business at unnecessary risk.

Fortunately, despite recent rises in health insurance costs, there are still ways to find affordable coverage tailored to your needs. *How to do it...*

SHOP FOR SPECIAL GROUP POLICIES

You may be eligible for various types of advantageous group coverage—even if your business is a sole proprietorship. That can be a big advantage, because groups buy cover-age in bulk and pass a large portion of the savings on to individual policy holders.

Groups that often provide health insurance to members include…

• **National and state associations of business owners.**

• **Professional associations.**

• **Chambers of commerce.**

Members can nearly always purchase health insurance at a lower cost through these organizations than by buying it directly from the insurance company. The savings can be so great—typically 10% to 30%—that it easily offsets the cost of membership.

Option: Using the same policy for yourself and your family that the company offers—or is considering offering—to its employees. Even though you may want better coverage for yourself and your family than what you can afford for your employees, the insurance company that provides the company with group coverage is likely to offer a discount on a supplemental policy for you.

HMO OR INDEMNITY POLICY?

As a general rule, HMOs are less expensive than conventional indemnity plans. But—for business owners, there are two possible disadvantages. An HMO, for example, typically does not offer policy options that you can find by shopping around at indemnity insurance carriers. *Example:* A higher cap on lifetime benefits.

Also, if you don't live in or near a metropolitan area, there may be no HMOs to choose from.

NEW WAY TO SHOP

If group coverage isn't practical, there's little alternative to buying individual coverage for you and/or your family.

Consult an agent who represents more than one health insurance carrier.

An even more efficient way to compare policies is to use the growing number of Web sites that help make comparisons. The sites let you compare premiums and coverage from hundreds of insurance carriers. There's no charge for this information.

Typical sites ask you to key in such personal data as age, weight and health condition, as well as the price you want to pay and the type of coverage you're looking for. Some give you nearly instant on-line quotes for several carriers …others have an agent contact you by phone… and still others E-mail the information to you.

My favorite: Quotesmith.com, a service that compares premiums and coverage from more than 300 carriers and replies on-line, usually within a minute or two. Check it out at *www.insure.com.*

On-line insurance quotes are especially useful because insurance agents don't always understand the needs of business owners, who require coverage that will protect them and their business during a prolonged illness. Young businesses have different needs than older ones.

In this case, on-line services can help by letting you quickly compare policies that cover specific medical conditions and different levels of benefits.

COMPARING POLICIES

Regardless of how you find potentially suitable policies, compare them for more than just premiums and general extent of coverage. Look also at deductibles, copayments, lifetime benefit caps, coverage of existing medical conditions and restrictions on consulting specialists.

Mistake: Trying to save money by buying a policy with high deductibles but relatively low caps on lifetime benefits.

Very high deductibles—$5,000, or even $10,000—may make sense if you can easily afford them. But many owners of smaller businesses would find it very difficult to cover this cost. Owners should generally look at policies that protect them and their families during catastrophic or prolonged illnesses. That includes high caps on lifetime benefits.

A cap of even $1 million might seem more than adequate, for example, but many catastrophic conditions require medical care that can quickly exceed that amount. Similarly, it usually pays to look for a policy with a single annual deductible rather than a deductible for each illness.

Reason: If you or family members suffer from multiple hospitalizations, deductibles can quickly reach a level that may be difficult to pay if you're also sustaining a business.

Before deciding on the premium level that you can afford, consult your tax adviser about what portion of premiums may be tax deductible under recent federal law.

Once you find a policy that suits your needs, take a close look at the insurance company itself—unless you already have firsthand knowledge of it. While the majority of carriers are solvent and reputable, today's health-care industry is rapidly changing. That means many new companies are starting up, and some older ones are faltering.

To check out an insurance company: Phone the insurance commission in the state where the carrier is headquartered. Ask for information on customer complaints and financial status.

Since it is normal for almost any company to have a few customer complaints, make a comparison by asking for the complaint record of several other carriers in addition to the one you're considering.

Caution: An insurance company doesn't necessarily have to be insolvent to be in poor financial condition.

Ask each company you are considering about problems with financial reserves. That's the key indicator of the health of insurance carriers, and state insurance commissions routinely report on problems. Many commissions also post such information on their Web sites.

An alternative source for insurance company ratings is TheStreet.com, *www.thestreet.com.*

15

Fighting the IRS

Solve Your Tax Problems In Advance

Many financial decisions turn on tax considerations. But what if you are not sure of the tax consequences of your decision? *For example...*

• **You're considering an exchange of property,** but only if the exchange is ruled tax free.

• **A modification of a divorce settlement is proposed.** How will it affect the status of payments?

• **You're working out an arrangement to defer compensation.** But if it doesn't meet all the tax requirements, you could find yourself being taxed on income you won't receive for years.

• **You want to know if a scholarship is tax free.**

• **A family member needs extensive physical therapy.** Can you build a swimming pool and deduct the cost as a medical expense?

You can't make a sound decision until you know how the IRS will view the transaction.

The solution: Get a private-letter ruling. Any taxpayer (or authorized representative) can get an IRS ruling on the tax effect of most proposed transactions. The IRS charges a fee for these rulings. Corporations have used this procedure most often. A ruling is equally available to an individual. And it applies to tax questions involving estates, trusts and gifts, as well as to personal income taxes.

TAX PROTECTION

If you get a favorable ruling in advance, your tax position is fully protected. Even if other taxpayers are treated differently, or if the IRS changes its mind, the ruling in your case will not be changed retroactively except in unusual circumstances. (*Note:* A private-letter ruling is binding on the particular transaction it covers. Similar situations involving other tax-

284

payers will probably be treated the same way, but not necessarily.)

The IRS gives you a chance to talk the situation over before a ruling is issued. If it appears that some aspects of the transaction may lead to adverse tax results, you can modify or amend your proposal to come up with a plan that will qualify for the ruling you want. *Caution:* There's no point in asking for a ruling if you're sure it will go against you. Study the rulings issued to other taxpayers with similar problems. These rulings are all published, and you can find them through several tax services. Also, your accountant or attorney can probably talk with IRS people and sound them out informally.

Letter rulings generally can't be appealed. You can appeal to the courts only after a return has been filed and tax assessed.

HOW TO GET A RULING

There is no prescribed form. Send a letter to the Internal Revenue Service. The IRS will generally get in touch with you within 21 working days. *Include in your letter…*

•**A complete statement of all the facts.**

•**A carefully detailed description** of the transaction.

•**Names, addresses and taxpayer identification numbers** of all persons involved.

•**Copies of all relevant documents.**

•**An explanation of the transaction's business purpose.** ("Business" includes personal and commercial financial dealings.)

•**A statement of which ruling you are asking for.**

•**Citation of authorities (regulations, decisions, etc.).**

•**Arguments supporting your position.**

•**Whether the issue, or an identical issue,** is being examined, litigated, etc.

•**A request for a conference to discuss the matter.**

•**The location of the district office that has jurisdiction.**

•**A penalty of perjury statement.**

•**Some of the confidential information** (names, addresses, etc.) is deleted before publication of IRS rulings. You should state which information you want deleted and why.

OTHER REQUIREMENTS

You must put everything in writing. If you supply any information verbally, it must be confirmed in writing within 21 days or the IRS will not consider it. If the IRS requests additional information, it must be submitted in writing. Information must be complete. If you leave out or misstate material facts, the ruling could be invalidated.

CONFERENCE

You're entitled to a conference with the IRS. Ask for it when you submit your original letter. The conference is more informal than a hearing. You'll get a chance to argue your position with IRS representatives and see what their opinion is likely to be.

This is the time to find out what objections, if any, the IRS has to your proposal and what changes are necessary to make it acceptable. You or your representative may well be able to come up with modifications to the proposed transaction that will lead to a favorable ruling.

Safe strategy: If the IRS's reaction is negative and you can't come up with an acceptable modification, withdraw your request. Having no ruling at all is better than having an unfavorable one. *Reason:* You must attach any unfavorable ruling to your tax return.

When the IRS will not rule: There are some issues the IRS will not rule on, either by law or as a matter of policy. *Examples:* Purely hypothetical questions, or certain issues involving determinations of fact. *Other major "no-ruling" issues…*

•**The prospective effect of estate taxes** on the property of a living person.

•**Issues on which there are court decisions** the IRS may be planning to appeal.

•**Issues on which no regulations have yet been issued** (unless the application of the law itself is obvious).

•**The effect of pending legislation.**

•**Whether a proposed action would subject** a taxpayer to criminal liability.

Last-Minute Filing Tips

Tom C. Klein, CPA.

Don't forget to sign. Both husband and wife must sign a joint return. Be sure to put your name and Social Security number on every form and every piece of paper attached to the return—if they get separated, they may never find their way back.

Check your arithmetic. Make sure you used the right tax table. Mistakes will delay your refund. If you owe money, you may be charged interest.

Tip: Round figures to the nearest dollar. You'll make fewer errors.

Put forms in order. The return on top (Form 1040), then Schedules A, B, C, etc., followed by numerical forms in order.

Don't forget the following forms if they apply…

• **Form 2210, if you owe more than 10% of the total tax.** Use the form to figure whether you owe a penalty or come within one of the exceptions (e.g., your current-year tax payments at least equal last year's tax).

• **Form 6251 (Alternative Minimum Tax).** If you are liable for the Alternative Minimum Tax, you must file Form 6251. It applies if you have tax-preference items, such as accelerated depreciation or intangible drilling costs, or claim certain large itemized deductions, such as state and local taxes.

• **Form 4684, for casualty and theft losses.**

• **Form 8283, if you gave more than $500 in property to charity.** This is a statement showing the nature of the property, valuation, etc.

Answer all questions or check the correct boxes…

Your occupation: You can use general terms like executive or administrator.

On Schedule B (Interest and Dividends): Questions on foreign bank accounts or trusts.

On Schedule C (Self-Employed): Questions on accounting methods and home-office use.

On Form 2441 (Child-Care Credit): Questions on employees hired to work in your home.

Attach all W-2 forms from employers. But you can file without a W-2 if you have to. Attach an explanation of why the form is missing, along with any evidence of wages paid and taxes withheld, such as a final pay stub.

Put on enough postage when you mail the return. If it comes back you could be hit with a penalty for late filing. Don't use a postage meter. The date may be unacceptable as proof. If you're worried about proving you filed on time, use certified mail. Better yet, deliver the return to the IRS personally and get your copy receipted.

Extensions: If you aren't able to file on time, you can get an automatic six-month extension by filing Form 4868.

Caution: You get an extension of the time to file, not the time to pay. Estimate the tax due and send it in with Form 4868 (if you pay by credit card on-line, no form is required). If your estimate is too low, you'll be charged interest. If you're too low by more than 10%, you may be subject to a penalty.

Unanswered Questions Cause Problems

Income tax returns with unanswered questions are considered no returns. That means the statute of limitations never expires and you can be audited no matter how many years have passed. Unanswered questions can also delay refunds, result in interest charges and call attention to your return by IRS agents (since the computer automatically spits out the return). If a question doesn't seem to apply to you—Do you have any foreign bank accounts? Do you claim a deduction for an office in your home? Just answer "no," but answer.

Dealing with the IRS

Peter A. Weitsen, CPA, partner, WithumSmith+Brown, CPAs, 1 Spring St., New Brunswick, NJ 08901. *www. withum.com.*

There are ways to make the IRS bureaucracy work for you and work efficiently. But you must know how the system operates and where to call or write to get results.

COLLECTION NOTICES

Problem: Even though you've written the IRS an answer to its collection notice, the notices keep coming. You get a second notice, and a third one and then one that says, "Past Due Final Notice (Notice of Intention to Levy)." This final notice (sometimes it's the third in a series) is the one to watch out for. *Trap:* The IRS can seize your bank account without first having an IRS employee meet with you. They can notify you by mail and then automatically take money from your account.

Self-defense: If you get such a final notice, immediately call the phone number given on the notice and explain that you've already written to them and you don't owe tax. The collection-division employee who answers the phone at that number has the authority to put a hold on collection action if given a good reason. Unfortunately, not all of them will take that step.

Loophole I: If the person who answers your call isn't receptive, excuse yourself and call back. You won't get the same person. There's a decent chance that your second call will be answered by someone who is willing to put a hold on the levy.

Loophole II: You can delay collection action on a tax deficiency you're protesting by filing a claim for a refund. The refund claim will cause the IRS to automatically put a hold on collection action. This is a smart move if you've missed the deadline for filing a Tax Court petition.

Late-Filing Excuses That Work

Any person who fails to file a federal income tax return without obtaining a filing extension faces the prospect of stiff tax penalties. But penalties can be avoided if the taxpayer acts quickly to present the IRS with an adequate late-filing excuse. *Here are some excuses that usually work...*

• **The death or serious illness** of an immediate family member.

• **Incapacitating illness** of the taxpayer himself/herself.

• **Absence of the taxpayer from home** due to circumstances beyond his control.

• **Destruction of the taxpayer's records** due to circumstances beyond his control, such as fire or flood.

• **A competent tax adviser told the taxpayer** that a tax return wasn't necessary.

• **The IRS failed to provide the taxpayer with necessary forms** after he requested them to do so in a timely fashion.

To present the excuse, the taxpayer should file the overdue return as quickly as possible, with an explanation of the delay attached. If the IRS is satisfied the taxpayer acted reasonably under the circumstances, it will abate any penalty. But the IRS is not required to accept any excuse, so expedient action by the taxpayer is a must.

Taxpayers who face penalties for misfiling returns or misreporting income will do the best they can to come up with a good explanation. Some excuses work—others don't.

EXCUSES THAT WORK

• **Reliance on bad IRS advice from an IRS employee or an IRS publication.** If the advice came from an employee, you must show that it was his or her job to advise taxpayers and that you gave him all the facts.

• **Bad advice from a tax professional can excuse a mistake** if you fully disclosed the facts to the adviser. You must also show that he was a competent professional, experienced in federal tax matters.

• **Lost or unavailable records will excuse a mistake** if the loss wasn't the taxpayer's fault and he makes a genuine attempt to recover or reconstruct the records.

• **Incapacity of a key person can be a legitimate excuse for filing late.** *Examples:* Serious illness of the taxpayer or a death in his immediate family.

EXCUSES THAT DON'T WORK

• **Pleading ignorance or misunderstanding of the law** generally does not excuse a mistake. *Exception:* Where a tax expert might have made the same mistake.

• **Someone else slipped up.** You are personally responsible for filing your tax return correctly. You can't delegate that responsibility to anyone else. If your accountant or lawyer files late, for example, you pay the penalty.

• **Personal problems don't carry much weight with the IRS.** For example, don't expect to avoid a penalty by pleading severe emotional strain brought on by a divorce.

Easy Ways to File For Extensions

Irving L. Blackman, CPA, retired founding partner, Blackman Kallick Bartelstein, LLP, 10 S. Riverside Plaza, Chicago 60606. *www.taxsecretsofthewealthy.com.*

Better late than never is not a good idea when filing your tax return. Each year more and more Americans face April 15 without the complete information they need to file a proper return. *Frequent problem:* Partnership data from tax shelters is missing. Some promoters are months late in sending out the K-1 schedules that contain individual partners' tax information. What should you do?

Fortunately, there is an easy answer—file extension Form 4868 on or before April 15. The extension automatically gives you until October 15 to file. But it does not give you extra time to pay. The form requires that you estimate the tax you still owe and send it in with your extension request.

Not filing your tax return when due is an expensive disaster. You must pay interest from the due date of the return to the date the tax is finally paid.

There are two additional penalties. The first is a penalty for failure to pay on time. It is .5% per month on the net amount of tax due, up to 25%. This penalty can be avoided if, when you file your return (having gotten a proper extension),

the balance of tax still due doesn't exceed 10% of your total tax liability and you pay the balance with your return. The failure-to-pay penalty goes up to 1% a month after you receive an IRS notice to pay tax. There is an even stiffer penalty for failure to file your return on time. This penalty is 5% per month (for each month or fraction of a month), up to 25% maximum.

Example: Joe Lately mails his return on June 4, along with a $10,000 check for the tax he owes. Since Joe had not filed an extension request, the IRS bills him for the interest plus a $1,100 penalty (5% for one full month plus 5% for a fraction of a month, or 10%, plus .5% for two months for failure to pay). If Joe had filed Form 4868, the most he would pay would be interest plus the .5% penalty for two months (1% x 10,000 or $100).

If you can't pay: Some people put off filing their returns because they owe a sizable balance that they can't pay right away. This is not a good idea. For one thing, the penalties will be much higher ultimately. And putting off filing because you can't pay is probably the most common way that people fall into the trap of not filing at all. That can be disastrous. It may even lead to criminal charges.

How to handle it: You can choose to charge the balance owed to your credit card, but you'll pay a convenience fee of almost 2.5% to the authorized company that can process the payment (Official Payments Corporation at 800-2PAY-TAX, *www.officialpayments.com,* or Link2Gov Corporation at 888-PAY-1040, *www.link2gov.com*). Or you can request an installment agreement (attach Form 9465, *Installment Agreement Request,* to your return). If the amount owed is under $10,000 and certain conditions are met, you have up to three years to complete your payment to the government.

Taxpayer Penalizes IRS For Lateness

You file your tax return in February and get a refund check in May—but no interest. Does the government owe you interest on the money?

No. The government doesn't have to pay interest if it sends your refund within 45 days of the date the return was due—April 15—not 45 days from the date you filed it. But if it doesn't get the refund out within the 45 days, it has to pay interest all the way back to April 15 even if it's only one day late.

No Penalty for Late Filers

Late tax filers may escape penalties because the IRS has *no way of checking* whether or not a person filed an extension request on time. The General Accounting Office (GAO) reports that the IRS has no procedures for tracking Form 4868 extensions and that "as a matter of policy," it generally does not assess failure to file penalties because of this lack. The GAO also reports that, in many cases, taxpayers avoid penalties by producing copies of extensions that were "purportedly" filed on time even though the IRS has no record of them.

Hidden Treasures in Your Old Tax Returns

Steven L. Severin, CPA, a tax partner with Deloitte & Touche LLP, Seattle.

It's surprising how often people pay more income tax than they have to. Overlooked deductions, alternative (money-saving) ways of computing tax liability, little-known exemptions and credits—there could be big dollars in missed tax-saving opportunities on your old returns, up to three years old in most cases.

You can still get refunds you overlooked the first time around by filing an amended return (Form 1040X). The procedure is simpler and safer than most people realize.

All the form requires is some basic identifying data, an explanation of the change that's being made, and a recomputation of the tax. You don't have to redo the entire return. And the IRS will figure out how much interest it owes you.

The IRS does not automatically audit you just because you've filed for an additional refund. But it is useful to thoroughly document the basis for amending your return. The clearer it is, the less likely it will be looked at twice.

What if there's a problem area on your return that's unrelated to the item you're amending? For example, you've just found out that you could have claimed a dependency exemption and a large medical deduction for your mother-in-law, whose nursing home bills you were paying two years ago. However, you deducted a lot of travel and entertainment business expenses that year, and you'd have a hard time pulling those records together if the IRS decided to check them.

In practice, the possibility that the IRS will even look at such an unrelated area of your return is low. But you can make things even safer by working with the statute of limitations. *How:* You wait to file until a week or so before the deadline for requesting a refund. The same deadline applies to the IRS. It can't assess additional tax unless you failed to report more than 25% of your income or committed tax fraud.

The worst that could happen, in the unlikely event that the IRS does examine other areas of your return and finds a deficiency, is to apply that deficiency against the refund you've requested. It can't bill you for additional tax due.

The deadline is three years from the original or extended due date of the original return.

Here are items to look for...

• **Medical expenses for medical dependents.** You can sometimes deduct, for tax purposes, medical expenses you've paid on behalf of someone for whom you can't claim a dependency deduction because he has too much gross income. That person must have met all the criteria for being claimed as a dependent, except that his own income was too high. You must have provided more than one half of the total support for a medical dependent.

• **Exemptions.** Occasionally, someone who's not a member of your household could have been claimed as a dependent if he is related to you, received more than half his support from you, lived in your home for the entire year and didn't have too much nonexempt income of his own.

• **Shared support.** Several people may have been contributing to support someone, with no single person contributing more than half of that person's support. With the consent of the others, one member of the group can claim a dependency exemption if the group as a whole provides more than half the support.

• **Miscellaneous possibilities.** Job-hunting expenses, noncash charity contributions or subscriptions to business investment and tax publications.

Once you've filed your return, it takes three to six months to get your refund. You are entitled to interest from the due date of the return. The IRS will figure out the various interest rates that applied back to when your original tax return was due.

Don't get impatient. One taxpayer hadn't gotten his refund from an amended return when he filed the next year's regular return. So he just subtracted the money he figured the IRS owed him. That maneuver cost him some heavy underpayment penalties. The two transactions were treated separately.

Attorneys' Fees Collectible

Attorneys' fees continue to be collectible from the government after tax reform if the government takes an unreasonable position and the taxpayer eventually wins the case. The old allowance of up to $25,000 has been replaced with a per-hour cap adjusted annually for inflation ($170 per hour for 2008) on attorneys' fees.

Tax Break on Retirement-Fund Withdrawals

The IRS has simplified the withdrawal rules for taxpayers who have more than one IRA account.

You can calculate the minimum required withdrawals from each account, but you can also add them all up and withdraw the total amount from any account or accounts that you choose. You might withdraw the entire total from one account and leave all the others untouched.

Index